Surviving against the Odds

A John Hope Franklin Center Book

Surviving

against the Odds

Village Industry in Indonesia

S. ANN DUNHAM

Edited and with a preface by
ALICE G. DEWEY *and* NANCY I. COOPER
With a foreword by Maya Soetoro-Ng
and an afterword by Robert W. Hefner

Duke University Press
Durham & London
2009

Unless otherwise specified, all photos are

provided by Bron Solyom.

We thank the University of Pennsylvania's Annenberg School

for Communication and John L. Jackson Jr., Ph.D., the Richard

Perry University Professor of Communication and Anthropology,

for their support.

DEDICATED

TO MADELYN AND ALICE,

who each gave me support in her own way,

TO BARACK AND MAYA,

who seldom complained when their mother

was in the field

CONTENTS

FOREWORD

Maya Soetoro-Ng

I HAD A MARVELOUS TIME AS A CHILD, surrounded by pictures of anvils and forges, and stories about the magic of fire. My mother taught me to differentiate between a truly fine *keris* blade with its many layers subtly interwoven, and a sloppily crafted or unrefined blade. Many hours of my childhood were spent in the homes of blacksmiths or by their furnaces. When we visited the blacksmith known as Pak Marto, I would look for the reliably present feral dogs chasing chickens outside his home. Boys knocked plastic water bottles, and papayas were often being pulled from their treetop nests.

On those trips the greetings that the village women exchanged with Mom conveyed an intimacy that made clear they had fully taken each other's measure. Their connection had been established to a sufficient degree for laughter to be easy. Mom had come to a real understanding with them, it seemed, and not just the women; she was welcomed and trusted by all. This made me proud, I remember, for many of the same reasons my pride swells at the sight of my brother, our president; Mom too moved with such ease through every world, and people opened up at the sight of her smile.

Mom took me to see potters, weavers, and tile makers too. Indeed our visits to the blacksmiths were not so much designed to teach me the intricacies of blacksmithing as the awesome power of purposeful art and the relationships between artist and community that existed in so many villages. Mom was interested in such things as the blacksmith's teaching or leadership style, and in the elaborate and often ancient rituals of determining the suitability of a keris to its owner. She was interested in the place where vision meets execution, and where the poetic and the prosaic share space. She loved the way something beautiful could speak about the spirit of both the maker and the owner; the skill and soul of the blacksmith are revealed in the keris, but so too is the desire and perspective of the buyer. She was captivated by how long smiths had been honing their craft, and was moved by the very particular details but also the universally shared properties of metal-forging communities. Blacksmithing came to represent the strength of artistic human creation more generally with its ability to transform lives and to endure over centuries in spite of bleak forecasts about its survival.

I remember clearly the day that our mother defended her dissertation; I helped her to organize her photographs and photocopy her bibliography. I squeezed her hand tightly and asked if she was nervous. She responded with a barely perceptible nod. "Really?," I asked, adding after a moment of silence, "You know you're going to be excellent in there. You've worked so hard." She explained that while she was confident about the integrity, originality, and utility of the work, she was worried that others wouldn't be as interested in the lives she wrote about as she was.

She had so much respect for the communities where she conducted her research. Always logical and rigorous, our mother's scholarship was made truly meaningful by the fact that she loved the people she wrote about and hoped that others would hear their song. She also cared a great deal about the pragmatic applications of her work and the power of scholarship to improve the lives of the subjects as well as the thinking of the reader. She wanted the art of the smiths to endure, yes, but she also wanted their families to survive, and she wanted microfinance programs to be supported so that communities could become more fully engaged and individuals more universally empowered. I am delighted that our mother's book is being published and I am grateful to Duke University Press for making this dream of hers come true. My hope is that this book will be read by those who come to love the particularities of its world and who also see the myriad potential applications of its ideas and methods to other worlds.

EDITORS' PREFACE

Alice G. Dewey

IN 1995 I RECEIVED A LETTER from my student S. Ann (Soetoro) Dunham, in which she said that she was applying for a grant which would give her time to make some alterations to her Ph.D. dissertation. The dissertation was over a thousand pages long, and the aim was to make it a more suitable length for publication. Ann planned her dissertation so that several chapters could be excerpted in their entirety and published in a separate volume that would be of interest to archaeologists, prehistorians, and students of the cultural aspects of metalworking. A good start, this would only have reduced the remaining manuscript to some 650 pages, still too long for a book. The plans for revision and publication were interrupted when Ann passed away in November 1995. Some years later her daughter, Maya, asked me if I would take on the task of getting this book manuscript into shape, knowing that as Ann's dissertation chair and longtime friend, I was the most suitable person to take on the task. I was glad to do so, since I had accompanied Ann on visits to Kajar village on Java, which is the ethnographic focus of her study, as well as other sites. And after I retired from teaching, I had the time to do the work and felt that the manuscript in its various dimensions was extremely valuable.

My first recollection of Ann is from a time when I served on the anthropology department's admissions committee that was tasked with selecting incoming graduate students. I clearly remember reading the application of the woman who had been living in Indonesia for some five years with her Javanese husband and two children and had become fascinated with a number of the crafts for which Java is famous. I immediately recognized a like-minded scholar, as my dissertation had been a study of the peasant markets which, among other things, sold handicrafts such as those made by Ann's informants. The anthropology department accepted her as a graduate student and I became her advisor and eventually a good friend. Ann was not only a dedicated and brilliant scholar but also one who championed the people she studied by developing practical measures to improve their financial position. In the years that followed I met her in Java on a number of occasions, visited her field sites, and saw how she had become like a member of the families of the craftspeople.

But Ann was not only the intellectual; she also enjoyed life and had a fine sense of humor. Once she spent a few days at my house in my absence when she was passing through Hawai'i on her way to the East Coast. Ann was already familiar with my somewhat eccentric household, which consisted on average of four students, five dogs, three cats, a large cage full of birds, and various tanks of fish. In fact she and Maya had previously lived for some months as members of that household. Because my room was the only one available during her stopover, she slept in my bed. Unfortunately, she was soon shocked to find out that my sixteen-pound cat made a habit of leaping through the window beside my bed at around 2 a.m., landing on the occupant with a resounding thud. Being a very generous person, Ann accepted my belated apology and enjoyed telling the tale of her adventure to our friends. And somehow "the Blob," as my cat was known, seemed to gain weight as the tale got repeated. I am also reminded of a time when Ann and I had been staying with my Javanese family in Yogyakarta and needed to fly to Jakarta for a couple of weeks. Maggie, our hostess, very kindly made us a large bag of the delicious Javanese snack of palm sugar, ginger, and peanuts to eat throughout our stay, making more endurable the heat and massive traffic jams of the big city. I am embarrassed to admit that by the time we landed in Jakarta less than an hour later, we had already consumed the entire bag of goodies.

As I worked to reduce the dissertation to manageable size I was reminded that Ann originally meant to cover five villages, each with a different type of handicraft—bamboo, clay, textile, leather, and blacksmithing—its own organization and problems, and its own solutions. Not only did each village represent an interesting example of the economic organization of a part of Java, but each craft had its own beauty, whether the *keris* (ceremonial dagger) of the blacksmiths or the stunning batik cloths of textile workers. One wishes that Ann had had the time to write them all up, each with its own lesson in how to help build the wealth of the village. But in fact I suspect that she would never have had the time, because she was becoming widely known as an expert in the development of microcredit programs, having worked in cultures as different as Pakistan (where craftspeople were commonly seen as of low caste or even outcaste rank) and Kenya (where one's tribal identity is still of importance).

The particular crafts chosen by Ann demonstrate the great variety of handwork in rural Java. The first encompasses the making of simple items from bamboo, including pieces used in construction such as split bamboo mats (the heaviest type) for walls. At the other end of the spectrum are birdcages, baskets, and hats made of very narrow strips in two layers, so tightly woven that they keep off the rain as well as the sun, with a pleasantly jaunty look which becomes men and women. (The bamboo crafts village of Sodo is mentioned in chapter 3 in a narrative about one of its residents.) This craft is an example of the very simplest sort of work common in Java. The material grows in everyone's backyard, and the only tools needed are various types of knives, so the objects are inexpensive.

In the villages where clay working is done, people have a more complex task. They must be near an area where they can mine clay and get a supply of the leaves, twigs, and other materials used to fire the clay objects. They also need some knives to cut the clay and a "slow wheel" to shape the objects. The traditional products include elegant water bottles, cooking utensils, and large water storage jars. These were usually made by women in the past and found in most kitchens in Java. More recently development workers introduced a new product: figures of characters from the Hindu epics, the Ramayana and the Mahabharata, which have been adapted by Javanese to become part of their own cultural perspective. A favorite is the King of the Birds, who is killed in his attempt to rescue Princess Sinta, the heroine of the Ramayana, thus demonstrating the value of self-sacrifice.

The third craft which Ann investigated was the making of the famous Javanese resist-dye batik cloth. Here again we find some motifs drawn from the Hindu epics, such as bird wings that represent Garuda, the mythical bird on which the god Vishnu rides. There are also even more ancient motifs like the *parang rusak* (broken blade), which in the days of Javanese kingdoms could only be worn by royalty as a part of their sumptuary rights. Traditionally women applied the wax by hand with a small tool (*canting*), as if writing with a pen. In fact this delicate and time-consuming detailing is called *tulis*, the root word for "writing." A very fine batik can take six months to make and sell for the equivalent of several hundred dollars. Development specialists eventually introduced a new technique using a copper stamp, manufactured separately and used mostly by men, to apply the wax in large blocks in order to turn out batik more quickly. Both these techniques take great artistry and skill, which is why batik is considered a high art. Even more recently, silk-screening and the printing of traditional batik motifs have become common, resulting in lower production costs and selling prices.

Ann also investigated the making of the hand-carved and hand-painted leather puppets used in the performance of the shadow theater, *wayang kulit*. Some of the stories performed, like *Murwakala*, are actually rituals intended to prevent a malevolent deity (*Kala*) from attacking vulnerable children and others. Most commonly the tales told derive from the Mahabharata and the puppets usually depict the characters that appear in that epic, such as kings, demons, and noble heroes. There is also a special class of characters that appear as clowns but in fact are the most ancient Javanese characters, and in some cases the most powerful. The drawing of the puppets to be carved must be done by a puppet master or artist who is so knowledgeable about wayang kulit that he knows all the characters and other symbolic shapes, and the workers who carve the puppets out of stiff leather must be very precise, as must be the people who apply the intricate painting.

Any one of these crafts would have made for an interesting dissertation, but Ann chose blacksmithing, I think, because it is the most complex manufacturing task, with the iron worked in the fire and on an anvil—a sacred place to which offerings are made. Archaeologists tell us that the craft goes back some two thousand years, and there are several instances of temple reliefs, e.g., Sukuh, with a god such as Ganesha or heroic noble such as Bima portrayed as a blacksmith. Most of the objects created by blacksmiths are everyday hammers, knives, hoes, and plowshares—items that are commonplace and unexciting, even if extremely useful. But there is another dimension to the skill, the making of the beautiful keris, done in alternating layers of blackened and shiny silver-colored iron, with intricate patterns shimmering like water flowing in a stream. Each pattern has its name and meaning, and each keris has its own nature, which must be compatible with the nature of the person possessing it, lest the person be damaged by the power of the keris. How could anyone resist such a rich story?

Once three chapters of Ann's dissertation were removed for separate treatment, my work on this book began. Chapter 1 should be read by anyone who does international development work: it covers the mistakes and accomplishments of development workers from the colonial Dutch period to the late 1900s. Chapter 2, "The Socioeconomic Organization of Metalworking Industries," is a gem of clarity in which Ann explains an extremely complex activity. Chapter 3 is on Kajar Village, in the Gunung Kidul regency (or district) of the special province of Yogyakarta. This is the blacksmithing village to which Ann returned time and again, tracing the changes which overtook the village as electricity was brought in and the steep mountain roads were improved.

Chapter 4, "Relevant Macrodata," is necessary reading if one is to follow trends such as the increase in the number of blacksmiths over the years. The chapter may be hard going for the reader, but it was also extremely hard work for the author. Ann dealt with large masses of data, which she carefully mined for useful insights. For example, a comparison of census figures from 1974–75 and 1986 suggests a decline in the number of smithies (enterprises) classified as "household industries" (using only household members as workers). Ann noted that the decline was illusory: some of the household smithies had grown in size between the two censuses and taken on hired laborers, and therefore moved up to a different category—there were more workers, not fewer, in this type of enterprise. She also noted that even a true reduction in employment might have reflected only the extension of electricity to rural areas and with it the introduction of labor-saving machinery, so that the same number of smithing enterprises could produce more tools with fewer workers. Because of her meticulous attention to detail and her familiarity with the blacksmithing occupation, Ann was able to guide the reader through a maze of data. It is not that common for anthropologists to be as comfortable sifting through a great volume of (not always reliable) statistics as they are in their personal relations with their informants, but Ann was clearly an exception.

Chapter 5, "Government Interventions," covers both successful and ineffective programs and should be of particular interest to development specialists and policymakers. The last chapter, "Conclusions and Development Implications," sums up Ann's fourteen years of enthusiastic, painstaking, and successful efforts (see the Appendix, which lays out the various jobs and activities she engaged in while she carried out her research). Ann was one of the hardest-working people I have ever known, and yet she never seemed hurried or hassled, was always cordial, helpful, and ready to listen to what the other fellow had to say, and had a genuine respect for the way people from other cultures saw the world. It seems clear to me that she has passed these traits on to her children. What is more, the people of the villages became her friends, to be visited over and over during her years in Java. At the time of her death she was as much at home in Java as in Hawai'i (New York, on the other hand, was just too cold).

Throughout her adult life Ann worked to help the marginalized people of this world. These include those who may start working when they are four or five years old and go on until old age helping to support their families and being good neighbors in their villages. She raised her children to live up to the same ideals, and we are fortunate that her son, Barack Obama, learned his lessons well; I for one will be eternally grateful for her influence on him. In going through my papers I came across a letter from Ann dated February 1984, in which she mentions that her son "Barry" was working for a firm which did consulting work regarding the social, political, and economic conditions in developing countries. She goes on to say: "He seems to be learning a lot about the realities of international finance and politics . . . and I think that information will stand him in good stead in the future." She was not to live long enough to know what a prescient statement this was. I hope that this book will continue S. Ann Dunham's work of helping craftsmen and women the world over.

Nancy I. Cooper

IN THIS BOOK S. Ann Dunham, known to me as Ann Soetoro, writes about a Javanese blacksmithing village called Kajar, located about nine kilometers away from the village where I lived while conducting research on women singers in 1989 and 1990. Both villages lie within the rural regency of Gunung Kidul (literally, southern mountains), consisting of over 46 percent of the land area and 22 percent of the population (in 1990) of the special province of Yogyakarta (Daerah Istimewa Yogyakarta). We were both doctoral students at that time, with Alice G. Dewey as our graduate advisor. We met on several occasions in the city of Yogyakarta during this period, such as when Ann's daughter, Maya, came for the summer and when we both attended an international conference held there. On a trip to Singapore from Java, Ann generously brought back computer equipment that I desperately needed and on another occasion gave me an invitation to a royal wedding reception in the palace (through her consultancy work she knew the family of the Sumatran bride who was marrying a Javanese prince). And yet at the time, neither of us saw our studies as having a great deal in common, as we used quite different approaches and topics. In short, Ann focused more on practical, material aspects of village life and I focused on expressive culture and gender relations among musicians.

Of course many aspects of culture are interrelated in what anthropologists call a holistic way, and our projects did intersect. For example, in chapter 3 Ann describes one of the annual *Bersih Desa* (village purification) celebrations in Kajar, during which a shadow play was performed, accompanied by indigenous gamelan music in which the singers of my research took part. And she compares the characteristic expression of women working in the male domain of blacksmithing to that of these singers by saying: "it seems to be a protective expression, one adopted by women in an 'exposed' position subject to possible public misinterpretation." Also, some of the blacksmiths whom she studied made gongs and other instruments played in gamelan ensembles (see the illustration on page 143). Even the name of a musical genre popularized in the 1990s in Gunung Kidul that I studied recently, *campur sari*, is a term also used to refer to the intercropping of cassava and dry rice, a practice described in Ann's work. Campur sari literally means a mixture of essences and provides a convenient metaphor for cultural connections and mixtures among the rural dwellers of Gunung Kidul.

Living in this dry, hilly landscape with limited water resources and marginal agricultural land, people had to be especially resourceful and creative in learning to "survive and thrive," to paraphrase the subtitle of Ann's original dissertation. Most villagers I knew in the area lived in houses of wood and bamboo, with earthen or concrete floors, no plumbing, and in some cases no electricity. The cost of kerosene for cooking stoves was beyond most families' means, so large stones were arranged on the floor to form a square in which branches were placed, to fuel the fire over which cooking pots were poised. The better-off families had wells, grew small crops for partial subsistence, or worked for wages, for example as teachers, civil servants, or construction workers. Singing was one occupation which, while very specialized and somewhat seasonal, brought in a relatively high income and some celebrity. Blacksmithing was another nonagricultural occupation, one linked with spiritual power, able to sustain rural families even during times of drought and famine. Thus I can say from firsthand observations that Ann's descriptions of village life, economy, and relationships are accurate and insightful, and in their clear elegance they help readers to understand a rural way of life in a faraway place. Having grown up in a rural environment myself and knowing something about surviving against the odds, I feel that Ann with her working-class background was able to grasp the ethos as well as the material realities of rural life. In our work in Gunung Kidul, both Ann and I were describing ordinary people who faced long odds because of environmental and structural realities, but who nevertheless prevailed through their individual and cooperative agency. As cultural anthropologists we were both studying the remarkable ingenuity, work ethic, and entrepreneurial spirit exhibited by rural people of few given resources. What they produced from their own bodies, minds, and spirits, whether using hands or voices, whether an exquisite keris or sung poetry that moves a listener to tears, represents the best of what it means to be human in a particular part of the world.

Ann was first a cultural anthropologist, secondly a specialist in economic anthropology (studying how people produce, distribute, and consume goods), and thirdly an applied, rather than an academic, anthropologist, one who worked as a consultant for various philanthropic and governmental institutions charged with aiding ordinary people. One of the distinguishing characteristics of anthropology as a discipline is the fine-grained, person-to-person focus on different lifestyles that all typify humanity in a broad sense. Cultural anthropology, one of the four subfields, focuses on that most characteristic of human traits, the creation and use of culture, understood by anthropologists as human beings' unique way among animals of surviving and thriving in the world. While there are numerous ways of defining it, culture is a concept that encompasses the shared practices, attitudes, and configurations of knowledge developed and used by human groups. Most of these components of culture in a particular society interact in a constantly changing dynamic arising from daily interactions among individuals as they live their lives. Even though cultural elements are constantly in flux, patterns do emerge for a period, much as a moving stream of water develops eddies and pools. Ann analyzed these patterns of change to see what had worked or not worked and noted some of the causes and consequences. She did this so perceptively that readers can take away something of value, whether or not they are interested in economy, the craft and art of blacksmithing, or rural lifestyles, and whether or not they are familiar with this part of the world.

We can get a glimpse into Indonesian history before the period of the fieldwork in chapter 3 when Ann, in true ethnographic style, highlights a series of disasters and events recounted to her by villagers in interviews. These are some of the milestones in the lives of their ancestors and themselves, and they remain in their collective memory. Among these events are the ash falls of several volcanic eruptions, known locally as "rains of ashes" (*hujan abu*), first Tambora on Sumbawa Island to the east in 1815, then Krakatau to the west of Java in 1883, and then a "third rain of ashes" from an unnamed eruption in 1912. The villagers called the long period of Dutch economic dominance and colonial rule "Dutch times" and the Japanese occupation during the Second World War *jaman Japang*. I am reminded of the occupation every time I travel the road from the city of Yogyakarta to the town of Wonosari in Gunung Kidul, passing an old landing strip, now grown over with weeds and upon which goats graze, that was built by villagers as forced laborers for the Japanese forces. As unpleasant and frightful as this period was for residents, Ann with characteristic fairness points out some of the unexpected benefits that it also brought. Nationalism had been developing, so as jaman Japang ended Indonesian leaders seized the moment by having Sukarno proclaim independence on 17 August 1945 on behalf of the people of Indonesia. The Dutch would not relinquish their rule without a fight, however, and the revolutionary war ensued. From 1946 until the Netherlands admitted defeat late in 1949, Yogyakarta was the capital of Indonesia, interrupted only by the "time of the first clash" in villagers' terms, referring to the taking of Yogyakarta by Dutch forces in 1948. This important event has been mythologized in the area, as related in one of my interviews with the famous singer Nyi Tjondroloekito. She said that when Dutch commandos entered the Yogyakarta palace and confronted Sultan Hamengku Buwono IX, he said, "My life and death is one and the same with the common people." The "time of the second clash" was the taking back of Yogyakarta by Indonesian forces in 1949. The "time of famine" (jaman *gaber*) in 1962–63 was followed by the "fourth rain of ashes," caused by the eruption of Gunung Agung on Bali Island, just east of Java. In 1965 Sukarno's Old Order regime ended disastrously, precipitated by an attempted coup followed by massacres of ordinary people suspected of being communists, including killings in Gunung Kidul. Kajar residents called this the "time of Gestapu." This memory remains traumatic in the psyches of many to this day and is seldom discussed openly. The New Order regime of President Suharto emerged out of this national nightmare and continued beyond Ann's lifetime, ending only in 1998 after a collapsing economy brought on by the Asian economic crisis was followed by rioting and calls for reform.

Yogyakarta thus earned its relative autonomy and special designation in modern Indonesia from its role in the struggle for independence. Much of the credit goes to the sultan at that time, Hamengku Buwono IX (he who cradles the world in his lap), who with the help of prince Pakualam VIII had already instituted reforms making Yogyakarta's "village administration . . . probably the most enlightened in Indonesia," according to M. C. Ricklefs in *A History of Modern Indonesia* (1981, 208). This modern foresight is remarkable in that the lineage of the sultans of Yogyakarta is steeped in tradition going back to ancient times. This sultan went on to become vice-president of independent Indonesia, an office from which he later resigned, and governor of the new province of Yogyakarta. His son, Hamengku Buwono X, the current sultan, is also known as a fair and just governor, and a charismatic figure symbolizing for many in the province their rich cultural heritage. In the late 1990s he marched with students and residents in the streets of Yogyakarta in favor of democratic reform and organized a mass prayer in his palace with Buddhists, Hindus, Catholics, Protestants, and Muslims; the province has remained a safe center of calm until the present. It is therefore no mystery why residents of Yogyakarta, including those in Gunung Kidul, identified strongly with the sultanate in Ann's day and continue to do so, even though the central Javanese courts no longer wield the traditional powers they once had.

One of my favorite passages in Ann's narrative is about a dream that the head of the Kajar blacksmithing cooperative, Pak Sastro, had the night before a surprise visit by Sultan Hamengku Buwono IX, and the consequences of direct contact with this figure, considered to embody great spiritual power. It is an intimate story that only a trusted interviewer who has sufficient rapport with a subject would be able to elicit. Delightful to read, this story reveals the close identification that many rural people had with the ruling élite despite their unequal positions in the traditional hierarchy, an inequality that was amplified by colonialism and transformed into modern forms of social stratification in the postcolonial era. Across boundaries of rank and class there was a similar attitude toward family, work, spirituality, music and the performing arts, and the power of forging and working with metal. One could say that the lives of the blacksmiths and musicians of Gunung Kidul are different threads in a cloth of human meanings and practices, a cloth that connects people of quite different talents, aspirations, and abilities to a worldview of their and their ancestors' own making. That cultural textile, with its patterns, colors, and textures, like that of any society, is one that thrives on human aspiration, agency, creativity, and courage. Ann very ably and faithfully represents this rural worldview to a later and larger global community through this book, and it is hoped that the lives she illuminates here will speak to similar lives and hearts the world over.

I would like to add a short narrative of how I came to be an editor with Alice G. Dewey of *Surviving against the Odds*. After graduating and working in Singapore and California for a number of years, I returned in 2005 to teach at the University of Hawai'i, where I was in almost daily contact with Alice. Just as Maya had approached her earlier, Alice came to me one day, asking if I knew how to convert a whole stack of floppy disks into something more usable for editing a large manuscript. She was planning to edit Ann's dissertation and publish it as one or more books, and the only digital copy of the manuscript was on the old disks that Maya had given her. I quickly realized how motivated and determined Alice was to proceed with the project when she next came to me with a compact disk that someone else had converted for her and wanted to sit down with me to start the editing process. Already pressed with teaching too many classes plus an administrative job, I nevertheless agreed, not knowing how I would find the time. We sat down one day and started cutting the huge document according to Ann's own instructions to herself for revising the dissertation as a book. Little by little, whenever I found time I would enter corrections made by Alice on a hard copy that I had printed out and began to participate more fully in all aspects of editing. Thus the project began very modestly and sporadically, with no funding at first, by a retired professor and an adjunct who worked on it as a labor of love in honor of their former student and colleague. We had little inkling in the early stages that Ann's son would become president of the United States. We simply thought that Ann's work deserved to be published, that Maya with a family and career was not in a position to bring about publication herself, and that Alice, who had chosen not to adopt computer technology, would need technical help. We were fortunate to obtain a grant from the CIBER division of the Shidler College of Business at the University of Hawai'i to cover costs during the intensive editing stage and began thinking about a publisher.

Also around that time, after a well-attended colloquium held by the Women's Studies Department, at which Alice, Bron Solyom, and I had spoken about Ann, I decided to organize a panel for the American Anthropological Association (AAA) in her honor. I asked our department chair, Geoff White, to put me in touch with someone in the AAA who might help me to get the panel invited. On Alice's eightieth birthday, when a few of us were eating cake just outside my office, my phone rang: it was the co–program chair for the 2009 AAA conference, Deborah Thomas. She helped me to eventually qualify the panel as an executive session and then put me in touch with Ken Wissoker, editorial director of Duke University Press. After several reviews and a great deal of work by many enthusiastic participants at Duke, this book gradually came into being.

Since the time when Ann's dissertation was filed in 1992 it has become increasingly common for anthropologists to include in their written work accounts of their personal experiences in the field, in the name of reflexivity. Partly because of the conventions of her time and partly because her specialty was economic anthropology, and her topic one that involved more quantification than most, Ann did not recount her personal experiences directly, although one does get a sense of her presence throughout. To provide a glimpse of her work we have reproduced here a few excerpts from her field notebooks, in her own handwriting, along with an early letter that she wrote to Alice from Yogyakarta. Also included is a recent photograph of Ann's personal Javanese keris. Crafting a keris is the highest form of blacksmithing to which a master smith can aspire. It requires spiritual potency, appropriate rituals, and the passage of one year. In fact the common name of the village, Kajar, is derived from the name of a sacred spring that has a naturally occurring image of a keris visible on a submerged stone at its base. Ann writes that "villagers consider this image of a keris as proof that the men of Kajar are fated to be smiths." Ann's keris (see the last of the color illustrations), its forged iron with a black patina juxtaposed with an ethereal nickelous lamination pattern (*pamor*), reveals the strength and beauty possessed by Ann herself. She had a strong outer presence that was at once confident yet unassuming, with an inner softness and vulnerability that few saw. Professionally she managed to convey her keen intellect and pragmatism with sincerity and relative ease across cultures by simply being herself. One of the last images I recall of her in excellent health was at the 14th annual conference of the Indo-Pacific Prehistory Association (IPPA), held in Yogyakarta in August and September of 1990. I remember how intently engaged Ann was in each speaker's presentation, how knowledgeable she was on a wide range of topics, and how well she interacted with scholars from around the world. Had she lived longer, there is little doubt among those who knew her well that she would have made an even greater mark in anthropology, development studies, and microcredit than her legacy already accords her. This book should be one step in helping to bring her legacy to light for many people who were not privileged, as we were, to know her as the *orang besar*, or "great person," that she had become in Indonesia.

EDITORS' ACKNOWLEDGMENTS

WE APPRECIATE THE MANY PEOPLE who supported us in this project and regret that only a few who made direct contributions will be noted here. We would like to begin by thanking the Women's Studies Department at the University of Hawai'i, particularly Aya Kimura and Meda Chesney-Lind, for organizing and holding a colloquium in honor of S. Ann Dunham. Meda also put us in touch with Shirley Daniels, director of the University of Hawai'i Center for International Business Education and Research (CIBER), which funded the intensive editing period. We greatly appreciate this funding, which made it possible for us to accomplish the work in record time. In the early stages Jan Rensel and the late Nina Etkin were helpful with general advice about the editing process and approaching and selecting a publisher. Unfortunately Nina will never see the final product. We are also grateful for the facilities, office space, and occasional clerical assistance provided by the Department of Anthropology at the University of Hawai'i. Geoff White, as chair of the department, has been supportive from the beginning and was instrumental in putting officials in the American Anthropological Association (AAA) together with us so that we could arrange the panel at the annual conference in Philadelphia at which the book will be launched. Elaine Nakahashi, as usual in her job as secretary and virtual manager of the department, creates a work environment that is both friendly and conducive to productivity. We will never forget how she stayed after work one day to keep the copy room open while we printed out the very first copy of the new manuscript. Marti Kerton, administrative and fiscal support specialist, became a confidant and troubleshooter for us in spite of her heavy workload. Our student workers Christen Ige and Eliza Udani cheerfully aided with scanning, faxing, and a number of other tasks that eased our load. Deborah Thomas, executive co-chair of the AAA 2009 conference with John L. Jackson Jr. (both University of Pennsylvania anthropologists), was calm, personable, and generous in all her communications, even though we have yet to meet her as of this writing. And we can never thank her enough for suggesting Duke University Press as a potential publisher and putting us in touch with Duke's editorial director, Ken Wissoker. We thank him and the many people at Duke who enthusiastically worked on this project and regret that only a few key people will be named. Fred Kameny, the managing editor at Duke, took on the role of copy editor for this project and worked with such speed that we had little rest between the time we submitted a version of the manuscript to him and the time when we received it back with his suggestions. His excellent work eased our job considerably. Remarkable for an academic book, there was little to disagree about, so our relationship with all the folks at Duke was great, making the work that much easier and more enjoyable. We know that for every person we might communicate with there are many more working diligently behind the scenes, and we want them to know that their work is valued as well. We thank the anonymous reviewers of the manuscript for useful suggestions and guidance as to what both scholars and general readers might require. Our fellow anthropologist and scholar of Indonesia Robert W. Hefner became an enthusiastic supporter of this project early on by agreeing to read the manuscript and eventually to write an afterword. In spite of his many responsibilities and incredibly full schedule, we have felt free to turn to him with any question or problem, knowing that he would give rea-soned, sensitive, and timely advice. We thank Bron Solyom for her ar-chival expertise, for helping us to sort through photographs and field notes, for making the photographs in her possession available, and for general advice and support. Garrett Solyom, an expert on Java-nese keris, was kind enough to take an original photograph of Ann's personal keris at our request and make it available for publication. We are grateful that the John Hope Franklin Center at Duke University, in keeping with its interdisciplinary and international mission, has honored Ann's book by adopting it. Maya Soetoro-Ng entrusted us with her mother's work and good name and, although she is one of the busiest people we know, made sure that she was available when we needed her. Her confidence in us gave us additional motivation to make this project a top priority. We can only hope that all these friends and colleagues will be as happy with the product as we are, and that they know how much we appreciate their roles in the process of making it happen. Our deepest thanks must go to our dear departed friend and colleague, S. Ann Dunham, without whose consummate work none of this would have taken place.

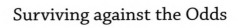

Surviving against the Odds

ACKNOWLEDGMENTS

The following people were of great assistance in helping me to complete this book:

—IR. DJAKA WALUJA AND DRA. SUMARNI, a husband-and-wife team who worked as my original field assistants in Kajar village and who explained many matters pertaining to Javanese rural life; Djaka also assisted with drawings and maps;

—ALICE DEWEY, my committee chairperson, who was generous with her insights on Javanese culture and accompanied me on several field trips in the Yogyakarta area, including a field trip to Kajar village in 1991;

—I MADE SUARJANA, a journalist based in Yogyakarta who helped me to collect additional data from Kajar and Batur villages and provided many insights on Balinese thought and culture;

—GARRETT AND BRONWEN SOLYOM, who provided comments on the Glossary, as well as stimulating discussion on matters pertaining to the *keris* and other artifacts of Javanese and Balinese culture; Garrett kindly lent me an unpublished student paper which proved useful.

A special debt of gratitude is owed to the Department of Industry of the Republic of Indonesia. Any criticisms of the department contained in this book are offered in a constructive spirit by one who considers herself more an insider than an outsider. BIPIK, the department's special unit for the training and guidance of small industries, was the Indonesian sponsor for my original field research in the Yogyakarta area between 1977 and 1978. The department's office in Semarang provided me with a home between 1979 and 1980 while I was working on the Provincial Development Project. Eight district offices of the department cooperated in 1988 on a survey of nonagricultural enterprises which I carried out for Bank Rakyat Indonesia.

Over the years numerous officers from all levels of the department's hierarchy have made themselves available to discuss technical and development matters, and have provided the benefit of their knowledge and experience. Without their generous help, it is doubtful that I would even have been able to locate many of the villages discussed in this book. There are too many of these officers to mention all of them, but special thanks are owed to:

—IR. FELIK LENGKONG, head of the department's Subdirectorate for Metal in 1991, who made time in his busy schedule for a lengthy interview and provided me with a useful unpublished survey carried out by the subdirectorate;

—IR. RIANTO, BIPIK field worker for Kajar village in 1978–79, now working in the provincial office in Yogyakarta;

—I MADE JAYAWARDANA, field officer from Gianyar district on Bali, who arranged and accompanied me on several tours of industrial villages on the island between 1988 and 1991.

The East-West Center provided me with a grant in 1977–78 to carry out fieldwork, for which I am grateful. Mendl Djunaidy, program officer in the center's Resource Institute, was also helpful in arranging support services during the final writeup phase.

Acknowledgements are also due to the following copyright holders who allowed me to use illustrations from their publications: Cornell University Southeast Asia Program, Yale University Press, the Board of Trustees of the National Gallery of Art, the Asia Society Galleries, Harcourt Brace Jovanovich Australia, Random House, and Oxford University Press. Haryono Guritno was also kind enough to allow me to use an illustration from a privately published book.

Finally, all anthropologists must acknowledge a debt of gratitude to their informants. Villagers in Indonesia are invariably friendly, pleasant, and willing to patiently answer many questions concerning their enterprises and personal finances, even when dozens of neighbors and village children are crowded in the doorway or looking in the windows. I do not recall ever being treated rudely by an Indonesian villager, or ever having had an unpleasant fieldwork experience while in Indonesia.

I have a special affection for Kajar, the principal research village for this book. It is a wonderful and mysterious place. Among the many residents of Kajar who provided information over the years, I should acknowledge the special help of Pak Paeran, the village headman; Pak Sastrosuyono, the leading entrepreneur and former head of the blacksmithing cooperative; Pak Hartoutomo, the head of social welfare; and Pak Atmosumarto, head of the largest hamlet in Kajar village. Each has endured numerous questions over the years and contributed a great deal to my understanding of the economic history of their village. The homes of Pak Sastro and Pak Atmo often served as cool refuges during a hard day of fieldwork. Bu Sastro's wonderful store, selling every item imaginable, served the same purpose. Any criticisms of the economic role that these residents play in village life should not be construed as criticisms of them as individuals.

S. ANN DUNHAM

buyers come to pick up the ganging
livestock mainly from kecamatan Tepus,
12 KM from Wonosari near Baron beach;
only a little from Kajar

lurah says still getting transmigration
orders every year
Coop meets once ~~of~~ every 3 mo. now;
official head is Tarjono
the Dept. of Industry Induk (service
center) is still operating; operators are 4
persons, all from Dinas Per, none from
Kajar
Induk moved in 1979, he says, from its
original inconvenient location in Redoksari
- wages now, acc. to lurah, are:

    empu 2000 - 5000 Rp
    panjak 1500 - 3000
    tul kikir done borongan because
           have used electr. last 2
           years
male ag. workers 2000
female ag workers ~~ ~~ 1250

blower now costs 60,000 Rp
are 2 types of gurinda, rotary + hand-
    held which moves over face of
    the blade

Undated field notes taken on a visit to Kajar.

TOOLS MADE IN KAJAK
* most common

KERET (utk. JANGIR = CARI RUMPUT dan MENGGEMBURKAN TANAH : for weeding).–
Pesanan : Tanjungkarang. (Sumatra).–

CANGKUL IRIAN JAYA.– (HOE).

UNTUK WEEDING
Pesanan dari Bogor.

TATAH (utk. buat lobang di kayu).–
Ada ± 10 macam yg. hampir sama.–
WOOD ~~CRAFTN~~ CARVING TOOLS.–

∗

CATUT = KAKATUA utk. mencabut paku.–
TO REMOVE NAILS. OR CUT WIRE.–

Tools commonly made in Kajar.

20

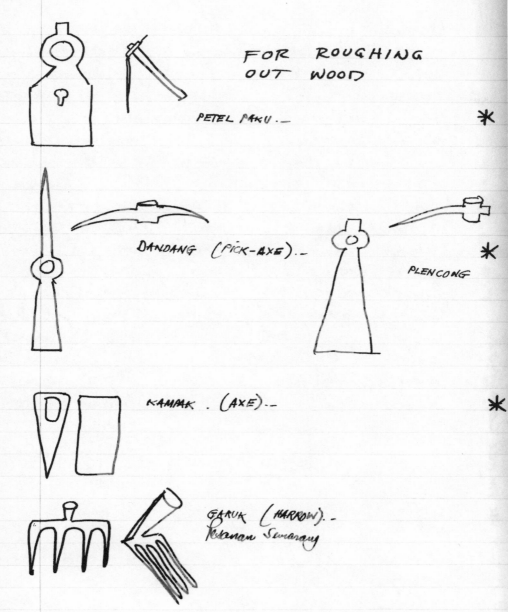

FOR ROUGHING
OUT WOOD

PETEL PAKU.— $*$

DANDANG (PICK-AXE).—

PLENCONG $*$

KAMPAK . (AXE).— $*$

GARUK (HARROW).—
Resanan Semarang

(w/J) interview with Pak Pujosastono, 6 July '7
– initial observations: large house
with stone block floors, glass windo
on inside front room with individu
pink curtains, 3 perapens to the rt
of the house with room furthest
rt. used as a ~~workshop~~ storeroom
for iron & finished tools; 3 paper &
foil signs in front room
which say welcome "Sugeng Rawuh"
wife with lots of gold jewelry; [+ gold tooth] some
store bought & some home made
furniture; most of walls of teak,
some painted; raised roof of J.K.
style in front room, with 8 posts,
carved & painted crosspieces with
words "Hidup Berdikari"; back
side walls of gedek; cardboard & woode

Berdikari =
Berdiri
atas Kaki
sendiri =
independent

butterflys as wall decorations; picture
of Suharto & ex V-P Hamenkubuwono
– character of Pak Pujo can be described
as young, 45, modest, responsible
open to new ideas, not well-educated
friendly, not apparently very
influential in the politics of the

Field notes taken during a visit on 6 July 1978 to the blacksmithing village of Kajar.

KAJAR

July 30, 1984
w/ Maya

visited Kajar; talked 1st w/ Bapak &
Ibu Sastro (Satrosuyono)
says Pak Rianto, former BIPIK
field worker, now lives in Jogja;
Joko has also visited recently
w/ a group of students
are now 130 perapens (compared
        in 1977), & 760 smiths
says industry has grown because,
since 1981-82 have been making
tools for govn. transmigration program
why they sell thru a dealer in Jogja;
says they haven't felt the effects of
competition from factory-made
goods
nor are they having any trouble
getting supplies of iron or charcoal
— still not casting but have
learned to finish edges w/ process
called "dikrom"
went out & saw new row of four
perapens near Pak Sastro's house;
using diesel-powered polishing
tool (wh/, hand-held, moves over
surface of the tool with rotary
motion

Field notes dated 30 July 1984 on a trip to Kajar with Maya.

KAJAR 1991

visit to Kajar in Aug, 1991, w/ Alice, her friend Joan, BRI unit + ~~cabang~~ cabang people

(2) met ~~[2nd]~~ with Lurah (Pak Pairan, nephew of Sastro)

YOUNGER BR

are 1200 HH. in desa w/ total pop. of 6250 and total area of exactly 5 KM square (= 5,000,000 meters SQ = 500 hectares)

so pop is now 1250 per KM SQ — if so, is a great increase

lurah says ~~[that]~~ ketela (cassava) is still grown, tho people have switched to a rice diet (rice purchased)

cassava sold wet after peeling; sold on the open market to tengkulak

are stores in Wonosari (toko pengumpul) which act as collecting points

they take the cassava to Cilacap + from there it is shipped to Japan

lurah says it is made into animal feed

set up 1984 in Kajar III

gamping factory of Pak Sastrowijojo (different Sastro) still operating, 30 — 50 workers

demand exceeds what they can supply;

Field notes dated August 1991 with people from the local government offices, an official from the People's Bank of Indonesia, Alice G. Dewey, and a friend.

Jan. 9, 1976

Dear Alice,

Very sorry to have missed you on your recent trip here! Actually I missed you by only three hours! I was in Jogja during the last 5 or so days of your stay, but was tied up getting settled in, buying a desk and lemari, getting visits to old relatives out of the way, etc, so had not made contact with the G. M. people. When Lolo got back to Jakarta and found your letter, he phoned my sister-in-law (two houses down from IRRI) inter-local saying you were in Jogja, but by the time she sent a message over to my house and I got out to Bulok Sumur, you had just left. It is really too bad because I had lots of things of interest to talk over with you, not to mention I would have enjoyed catching up on departmental news. Nonetheless, I hope you found a place to stay in Jakarta and had a good trip back.

As for myself, I am very happy to be staying now in Jogja. What an enjoyable city it is, especially as compared with Jakarta! I am getting a little tired of people saying "Hello, Mister" to me everywhere I go, but otherwise love it. Actually I had hoped to move to Jogja at midyear, but was unable to win a contract release from my old school in Jakarta (they sponsored me via an Asia Foundation grant for my first two years in Hawaii).

As it turns out, however, I had plenty to do to keep me busy in W. Java, and was able to carry out reasonably complete surveys of 3 village areas within radius of Jakarta ie Tjikarang (red brick industry), Plered (ceramics) and Parung (pandanus floor mats). Due to the delay in moving to Jogja however, I am requesting a leave of absence from EWC for the next year and will continue on my own funds. As I have banked most of my Center checks, it should not be a problem. Am now in the process of clearing permits and documents.

What are your plans for this coming year? As I recall you are going on sabbatical in June? Are you still planning to come to Java? Have you settled on a research topic yet? Sartono mentioned that you might be working on an independent research project, but said he didn't know anything definite about it. Having gone over with Sartono the current projects at IRRS, nothing seems very related to my work on cottage industry. Perhaps the project mentioned in your letter will relate in a general way, if they are collecting data on non-agriculture income sources. The original project which Koekman Soetisno invited me to work on (a project on small handicraft factories to be financed by the Dutch government) has apparently fallen through. At present I have been "adopted" as a guest at Masri's Institute

and they have be , very kind abo t making[3] available their facilities, as well as giving me some
valuable help on measures of underemployment,
a problem which has been bedeviling me
kebral of the Institute's projects scheduled
for this year relate in a dilect way to what I
am doing, and I hope to get involved. Masri
has also asked me to give a couple of staff
seminars. Haven't settled on a topic yet, but
presumably will relate to my research.

    Do let me know if you will be coming over
in June. Also if you would be interested in a
house-sharing arrangement, as I will be
needing to change houses about that time. At
present I am staying with my mother-in-law
on the corner of Taman dari inside the Benteng,
but according to old law foreigners are not
allowed to live inside the Benteng. I had to
get a special dispensation from the kraton on
the grounds that I am "djaga-ing" my mother-
in-law (she is 76 and strong as a horse
but manages to look nice and frail). In
June I am having Barry come over for the
summer, however, and will probably need to
find another place, since I don't think I can
stretch an excuse and say we are both
needed to djaga my mother-in-law.

    Drop me a note when you get time and let

me know what is going on in th department. 4

Is Bill still in Irian? Have you heard whether he turned up anything interesting? Are the Kellers back yet? How is Florence getting along? Sent a load of stuff for her back with Barry last August, but haven't heard whether she received it. My mother seemed to have some trouble in locating her. How are the Solyoms? Will they be coming over in July as planned? How about Carol Burch? Did she ever decide what part of Indonesia she wanted to work in? Did anything come through for Iris?

Will close for now. Best regards to everyone in the department, Benjy, et al. My current mailing address is:

Dj. Polowidjan 3
Jogjakarta

Take care and hope to see you before the year is out.

Regards,
Ann

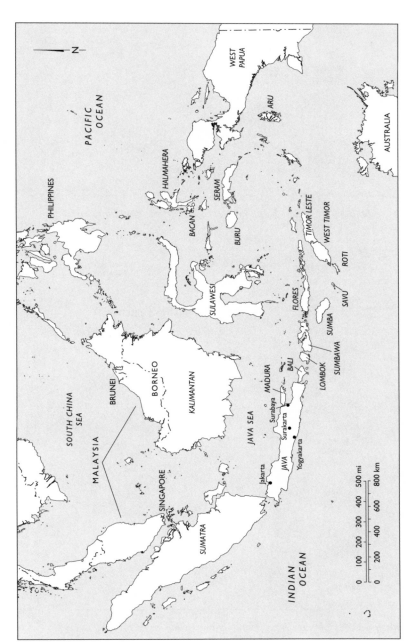

MAP 1. *Indonesia (Adapted from King and Wilder 2003, xxvii)*

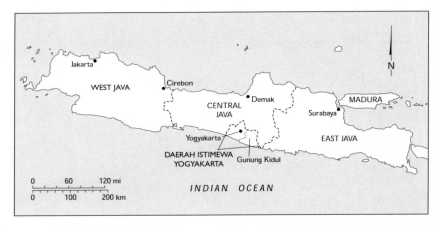

MAP 2. *Island of Java and its four provinces (Adapted from Koentjaraningrat 1985, 23)*

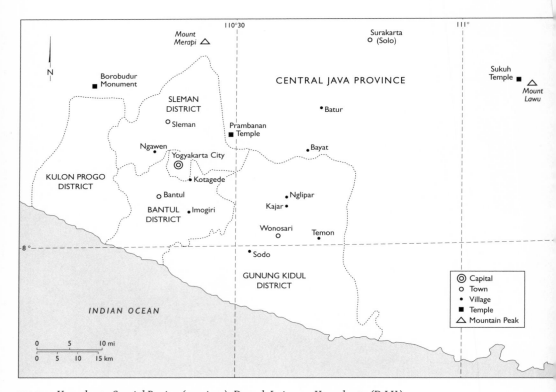

MAP 3. *Yogyakarta Special Region (province), Daerah Istimewa Yogyakarta (D.I.Y.)*

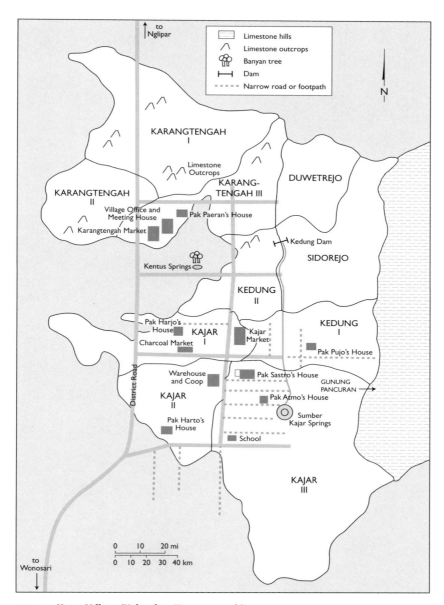

MAP 4. *Kajar Village (Kelurahan Karangtengah)*

Ann with a group of villagers on Lombok Island, where she had a development program under way. (below) Ann with Indonesian government officials and visiting development workers in a mountain village of Sulawesi Island.

Ann with one of the women of a rural village on the island of Lombok.

Ann in Bali (Tanah Lot temple in background).

Ann admiring the ducklings and chicks raised by farmers on Bali.

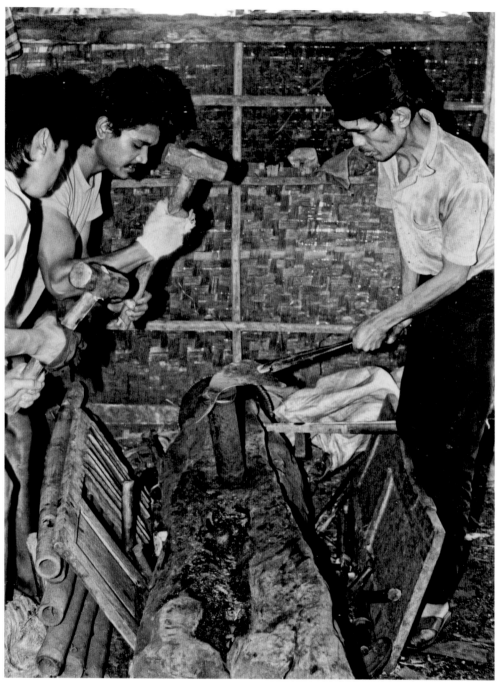

An empu (right) with two panjak, Kajar village.

A perapen in West Java. (below) An empu (right) with three panjek making a sickle, Kajar village. Note the nail-shaped anvil.

(opposite) An empu making pick-axes, Kamasan village, Bali; note that there are two quenching troughs in the foreground, a bamboo trough filled with used motor oil and a stone trough filled with water.

A young boy working the bellows, Kajar village.

(opposite) An empu quenching the white-hot tip of
a pick-axe in a large stone trough, Kajar village.

A small pande (blacksmith's) temple in Sukawati village, Bali.
(below) A husband-and-wife team using a large bamboo tool to unload the kiln, Ngawen village.

(opposite) The only Islamic official in Kajar village,
making offerings and burning incense at
the Bersih Desa festival.

An old ceramic furnace used for brass casting in Batur village. (below) An old Chinese box bellows in Batur village; it is built into the right side of the kiln.

(opposite) Making a repoussé silver bowl in Kamasan village, Bali; the tool used by the smith is tipped with bell metal, a type of bronze.

Pouring molten iron into earth molds, Batur village.

*(opposite) The wife of one of the empu in Batur village
flattening disks of silver into sheet.*

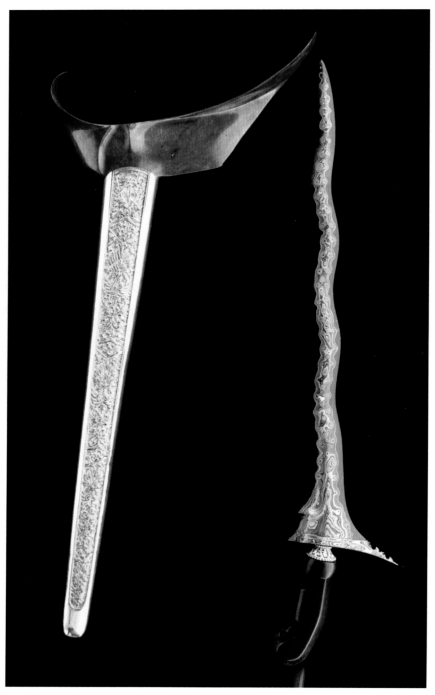

*Ann Dunham's keris. Blade made by Empu Djeno Harumbraja
(1929–2006), Gatak, Ngayogyakarta. Private collection.*

CHAPTER 1

Introduction

THIS BOOK CONCERNS several types of nonagricultural activities in rural Indonesia, namely blacksmithing and other small metalworking industries. A study of these industries is needed because in recent decades there has been a shift of labor out of agriculture and into nonagricultural sectors of the peasant economy in Indonesia, and in some other densely populated countries with a predominantly peasant population. Accordingly, third world governments and international aid agencies are devoting more of their attention and resources to programs for nonagricultural activities.

Social scientists working in Indonesia, on the other hand, have been very pessimistic about the development potential of nonagricultural activities. They have assumed that agriculture, particularly wet-rice agriculture, always generates more income per labor-hour than nonagricultural activities. It follows from this assumption that peasants do not willingly leave the agricultural sector. Instead, they are forced out by growing inequities in the distribution of irrigable land and the loss of traditional rights to earn rice income by working for shares. Models of rural change developed by social scientists working in Indonesia have been based almost entirely on fieldwork carried out in lowland wet-rice villages on Java. While lowland wet-rice villages constitute a majority of all villages, there are many other types of villages in Indonesia which do not grow wet rice, or where wet-rice cultivation is less important than other economic activities. These include villages which specialize in small industries, fishing or aquaculture, market trade, long-distance circuit trading, livestock production, building and construction, small-holder cultivation of cash crops, and the collection of salable materials in government forests.

Very few studies have been done of villages which specialize in activities other than wet-rice cultivation. The rural industrial sector has been particularly neglected by social scientists, although national statistics show that small industries are the primary occupation of 8 percent of the employed rural population. In a country as large as Indonesia, 8 percent of the employed rural population translates to between three and four million villagers.[1] Studies of villages which specialize in activities other than wet-rice cultivation would probably force a rethinking of present socioeconomic models. Patterns of resource allocation in these villages may be very different than in wet-rice villages. It seems an obvious point—but one which has usually been overlooked—that villages tend to specialize in the activity which they perceive as most profitable. That activity, which is determined by a combination of ecological, demographic, and historical factors, is not always wet-rice cultivation. There is a need to move beyond models which perceive wet-rice cultivation as the only important activity in rural Indonesia and toward models which perceive specialization in wet-rice cultivation as only one of many options available to rural Indonesians.

It is unfortunately not possible to cover in detail all types of peasant industries in a single study. I have therefore chosen to focus on a single subsector: metalworking industries. This subsector includes iron forging (more commonly known as blacksmithing), iron casting (limited to two villages in Central Java), the casting of copper and its alloys bronze and brass, silver- and goldsmithing, new industries based on the welding of factory-made tubing and sheet metal (usually aluminum or zinc), and repair industries, including the work of cutlers who sharpen tools and tinkers who mend metal items.

The word "smith" can properly be used to include all types of producers who make items from metal. Using this broad definition, we can estimate that there are about 200,000 smiths working in Indonesia today. This estimate is based on industrial surveys carried out by the Indonesian Central Bureau of Statistics (BPS). According to these surveys the number of cottage and small-scale enterprises in code 38, the international industrial code for metalworking, increased from 18,389 to 39,421 in the eleven- or twelve-year period between 1974–75 and 1986 (see table 1). During the same period the number of workers employed in these industries increased from 77,886 to 118,211. About 40 percent of all workers were traditional blacksmiths making agricultural and workman's tools. Industrial code 38 includes several industries not discussed in this book, such as more sophisticated machine and electronic industries. Most of the enterprises making these products are large, so their inclusion in code 38 does not appreciably affect the figures for cottage and small-scale enterprises.

A Note on Terminology

The choice of the term "peasant" in this book is deliberate, and is intended to affirm my ties to the subspecialty of economic anthropology and to the large literature on peasants in that subspecialty. I am willing to accept any one of several well-known definitions of peasants, as long as that definition acknowledges that peasants are not merely agriculturalists but engage in other economic activities as well. The recognition that peasants are not merely agriculturalists is usually attributed to Raymond Firth in his study of Malay fishermen (Firth 1966 [1946], 5–7). Other well-known definitions of peasants are as follows:

> Peasants . . . constitute part societies with part cultures. [They are] definitely rural—yet live in relation to market towns; they form a class segment of a larger population which usually also contains urban centers . . . . They lack the isolation, the political autonomy and the self-sufficiency of tribal populations; but their local units retain much of their old identity, integration and attachment to soil and cults. (Kroeber 1948, 284)

> [The peasant society is] a half society . . . a part of a larger social unit [usually a nation] which is vertically and horizontally structured. The peasant component of this larger unit bears a symbiotic spatial-temporal relationship to the more complex component, which is formed by the upper classes of the pre-industrial urban center. (Foster 1953, 163; Foster 1967, 5)

> [In speaking of peasants the author is] not discussing simple communities of small-scale subsistence producers, wherever they may be found, but communities that represent the rural expression of large, class-structured, economically complex pre-industrial civilizations, in which trade and commerce and craft specialization are well developed, in which money is com-

Table 1: Number of Establishments and Persons Engaged in Metalworking Industries and All Industries, 1974–1975, 1979, and 1986

Industry Division	Year	NUMBER OF ESTABLISHMENTS			
		Large or Medium >19 Workers	Small 5–19 Workers	Household 0–4 Workers	Total
Metalworking	1974–75	500	2,957	15,432	18,889
industries	1979	796	6,814	32,009	39,619
(Code 38)	1986	1,272	5,018	34,403	40,693
All industries	1974–75	7,091	48,186	1,234,511	1,289,788
	1979	7,960	113,024	1,417,802	1,538,786
	1986	12,765	94,534	1,416,636	1,523,935

NOTE: Code 38 excludes metalworking industries making jewelry, decorative items, souvenirs, and musical instruments.

SOURCE: Central Bureau of Statistics, *Statistical Yearbook of Indonesia*, 1989, 300–301.

monly used, and in which market disposition is the goal for a part of the producer's efforts. The city is the principal source of innovation, and the prestige motivation brings novelty to the country. (Foster 1960–61, 175; Foster 1967, 5).

Other authors who have contributed to the by-now fairly standard-ized definition of peasantry include Sjoberg with his concept of the "preindustrial city" and Redfield with his concept of the "folk-urban continuum."

Thus a definition of a peasant community must contain at a mini-mum the notion of a structural relationship with urban centers and urban markets. In classic peasant societies the urban center is a pre-industrial one. The court centers (*kraton*) and harbor principalities of Indonesia before the twentieth century fit this image well. Some au-thors have suggested that a new term is needed to describe peasan-tries which interact with partly or entirely industrialized urban cen-ters. Foster has suggested the term "postpeasants," and Geertz uses the term "post-traditional" to describe twentieth-century lowland Javanese villages. Geertz's term is not value-free, for he describes the "post-traditional" village as follows: "Unable either to stabilize the equilibrated wet-rice system it had autochthonously achieved before

Industry Division	Year	PERSONS ENGAGED			
		Large or Medium >19 Workers	Small 5–19 Workers	Household 0–4 Workers	Total
Metalworking	1974–75	55,867	22,113	55,773	133,753
industries	1979	105,686	49,527	79,447	234,660
(Code 38)	1986	181,641	39,577	78,634	299,852
All industries	1974–75	661,704	343,240	3,899,856	4,904,800
	1979	870,019	827,035	2,794,833	4,491,887
	1986	1,691,435	770,144	2,714,264	5,175,843

1830, or yet to achieve a modern form on, say, the Japanese model, the twentieth-century lowland Javanese village—a great, sprawling community of desperately marginal agriculturalists, petty traders, and day laborers—can perhaps only be referred to, rather lamely, as 'posttraditional'" (Geertz 1963, 90). I prefer to avoid these negative connotations and will therefore use the term "peasant" without a qualifier. It should be understood, however, that Indonesian cities and even Indonesian villages are partly industrialized. The industrial transformation is most apparent in the transport sector, but it is beginning to make itself felt in the productive sector as well.

Blacksmithing occurs in the context not only of peasant society in Indonesia but also tribal society. The number of tribal smiths is very small in comparison with the number of peasant smiths. Moreover, tribal smiths often obtain their raw material supplies and market a portion of their products in cities on the coast. Thus they do interact with urban centers, although the residents of those centers usually belong to different ethnic groups.

Outside the field of anthropology the term "peasant" is little used. To economists and policymakers it has a quaint ring. Probably for this reason I have tended to use three other terms in the body of the book: village industry, rural industry, and small industry. "Village industry" and "rural industry" are self-explanatory and are perhaps the most satisfactory terms in that they connote nothing other than location. "Small industry" is used in a general way to mean production units with few workers, wherever located and however organized. In chapter 4, on relevant macrodata, the term has a different meaning. The Indonesian Bureau of Statistics (BPS) divides industries into four groups: cottage and household, small, medium, and large. Cottage and household industries are defined as those with 1–4 workers including the owner, and small industries are defined as those with 5–19 workers including the owner. Thus when BPS or the government speaks of "small" industries, it is usually referring to workshops. Blacksmithing really straddles these two categories, the size of units varying from two to eight.

I prefer to avoid the terms "cottage industry" and "household industry." These terms imply that the home is used as a workplace and that the labor force consists of unpaid family workers. Some rural industries fit this description, but many others do not. Blacksmithing, for example, is usually carried out in a separate building, some distance away from the house in the corner of the yard or in a field. In most blacksmithing villages a high proportion of the labor is hired. Many other rural industries build separate workshops or roofed-over work sheds and make use of hired labor.

The Marxist term "petty commodity production" is sometimes used by social scientists, mainly in Britain, to refer to village industries. Joel Kahn and his students use this term, as does Gillian Hart. Yet for many readers the term is confusing, because "commodity" has the more general meaning of agricultural cash crop. Furthermore, as Marx used the term it properly refers to enterprises where the producer is the sole owner of the means of production. It does not, therefore, include enterprises which use hired labor. Since many village enterprises in Indonesia do use hired labor, the term has been avoided in this book.

In development literature, village industries are usually lumped together with petty trade, service, and livestock operations under the cover term "nonfarm enterprises." Terms with a similar connotation are "off-farm enterprises" and "nonagricultural enterprises." Consultants who work with village industries are usually considered "nonfarm" or "small enterprise" specialists. Employment, likewise, is "nonfarm," "off-farm," or "nonagricultural." The term "nonagricultural" is acceptable in the Indonesian context, but the terms "nonfarm" and "off-farm" are meaningless and should be avoided. Indonesians have villages and fields, but they do not have farms in the western sense.

Dutch Colonial Views on Peasant Industries and Their "Inevitable Demise"

Peasant small industries are an ancient and very stable form of economic organization in Indonesia. The earliest stone and copper plate inscriptions in the old Javanese language reveal that peasant industries not unlike those of today were in existence by A.D. 800. Furthermore, they were already embedded in a recognizable social matrix which included marketplaces in a ring, each associated with one of the five named market days (Wisseman 1977, 199–201, 211).

Despite the apparent stability of peasant small industries in Indonesia over a period of at least twelve hundred years, Dutch colonial authorities began predicting their demise as early as the nineteenth century. To some extent this may have been wishful thinking. Until the advent of the "Ethical Course" in colonial policy in the 1890s, the Dutch, like colonial authorities elsewhere, enthusiastically followed a policy of trying to substitute European imports for the products of local industry. In this way, it was thought, they could create a magnet which would attract the wealth of the Indies toward Holland. Given that ideas about "stages" of economic development and social evolution were very much in the air in the latter decades of the nineteenth century, it is somewhat unsurprising that the demise of small industries should have been considered inevitable and even desirable. After all, how could the micro-enterprises of the Indonesian countryside possibly compete with the mighty factories of Europe?

Even the well-meaning architects of the Ethical Course did not have much faith in the survival ability of peasant small industries. It was still assumed during this period that direct, unbuffered contact between the economic forms of the East and those of the West would inevitably lead to the collapse of the former. It was only hoped that a breathing space could be provided by protectionist measures, during which time native industries would have a chance to evolve toward firms and factories resembling western models. There was never any doubt that this was the eventual goal, or that failure to achieve this goal would lead to the total collapse of native industries.

There was some disagreement among the Dutch as to the cause of the gap between native industries and those established along western lines. Colonial policymakers during the Ethical Course believed that lack of capital in the native sector was the main cause, and they blamed their predecessors for deliberately creating a capital drain. A second cause that they identified was lack of information and suitable technologies. To remedy these shortcomings they created the first credit programs and extension services in the Indies, what we would today call "development programs." Between 1901 and 1905 they organized a state pawnshop monopoly and a popular credit service, passed an industrial plan for developing cottage and small-scale industries, established departments of industry and agriculture, and organized extension services in these two sectors (Boeke 1953, 110–11). A system of protective tariffs and quotas was put in place. An official commission set up in 1902, the Commission for the Investigation into the Declining Living Standards of the Indonesian Population, employed nearly six hundred researchers to carry out studies of all aspects of village life on Java and Madura, including cottage industries. Between 1905 and 1920 this commission published thirty-five volumes of reports. In 1925 the Central Bureau of Statistics was set up and took over the task of accumulating quantitative data on social conditions in rural Indonesia (Koentjaraningrat 1975, 56–57).

During the early years of the Ethical Course it was hoped that Indonesian peasants would take an active part in improving their own welfare, through cooperatives and similar entities. But as time went on, the policy became increasingly paternalistic in its implementation. Development became something done to and for the natives, for their own good, whether they wanted it or not.[2] This tradition of government meddling in the economic affairs of the peasants was firmly established during the Ethical Course and passed on to the extension services of the post-revolutionary Indonesian government.

Reaction to the Ethical Course came from several fronts. Dutch business interests were impatient with protectionist measures, which were interfering with their ability to make profits in the Indies, and they lobbied the government in the Netherlands to get them reversed. They longed for a return to the economic "liberalism," free enterprise, and free trade policies of an earlier era. A growing class of better-educated Indonesians also wished to escape Dutch paternalism and take over the management of their own affairs. This wish expressed itself first in the formation of various types of native organizations based on religion, ethnic background, social class or caste, and occupation, and eventually in the formation of Indonesian political parties.

Economic Dualism and Boeke's Views on Peasant Industries

Another, somewhat quirky, reaction came from J. H. Boeke, a Dutch economist who wrote a thesis at Leiden University in 1910 on "The Problem of Tropical Colonial Economy." At the time he had never been to the Indies, yet his ideas did not change fundamentally over the next forty-five years, during which time he served in the Indies' government, held a chair in eastern economics at Leiden, and published three very influential books. Boeke's views can be summarized as follows: The economy of the Indies is "dualistic," consisting of a western capitalistic system imposed on an eastern precapitalistic system. Interaction between these two systems destroys native handicraft and trade, because it offers new products—the mass products of European industry—but does not provide any new work opportunities. The gap between the eastern and western systems probably cannot be bridged by development or welfare programs. For one thing, the gap is already too large as a result of several centuries of colonial experience which severely damaged or destroyed native industries and trade. For another, the gap is caused by basic cultural differences between East and West, not just by differential access to the factors of production. Because of these cultural differences, it is unlikely that Indonesian natives will ever be able to adopt factory or firm types of organization. They have limited economic wants and needs, and will stop working as soon as they achieve those needs. (Thus western economics cannot be applied to their situation, because it assumes unlimited needs.) Native Indonesians place a greater value on social rather than economic needs. They are not interested in capital accumulation and will only engage in wage labor until they have earned enough to meet their tax or other money obligations. Although unwilling to work hard to accumulate capital, they are interested in speculation and gambling because these offer the possibility of gain without any expenditure of labor. They lack organizational ability and work discipline, and will abandon other enterprises in order to run off to their rice fields during the planting and harvesting periods. They place no value on their own time and are incapable of rationally calculating profits.[3]

Boeke not only described the character of the Indonesian native but also the social structure of the Indonesian village. In doing so he made use of Tonnies's contrast between Gemeinschaft and Gesellschaft. An Indonesian village is a Gemeinschaft, i.e. an organic body bound together by personal ties of family, neighborhood, and religion rather than impersonal ties of contract. Villages are "communal" and "homogeneous" because competition and wealth accumulation are considered antisocial acts. Poverty is general and shared, and the economic differences between households are small.

Boeke went on to describe native enterprises. The Indonesian village is based on subsistence agriculture and this determines its basic character. Attempts to introduce cash cropping are probably futile. Since subsistence agriculture produces no surpluses, or at any rate just small lots, it follows that there is little to sell. Trade and markets, introduced from abroad by Malay and other foreign traders, are alien to the village community. The number of visitors to native markets may be large, but buying power is slight and the total value of what is traded is extremely small. There are no professional traders in the marketplace, just producers who engage in trade occasionally. The market value of the goods traded is too small to permit expenditures on transport, which necessitates a pattern of decentralized and alternating marketplaces. The prices in the marketplaces are fixed and known to everyone, and there is no competition. Trade is wholly in the hands of women.[4]

Village industry is not alien but merely supplementary to subsistence agriculture. This fact makes it variable in output and very unremunerative. A good harvest results in less industrial activity. Industry is reserved for off-seasons, leisure hours, and times of need. It is discontinuous and occasional. It is done mainly by women, and men will only take it up if the need is very pressing. This is because the sums earned are so minute, and because labor remuneration forms only a small fraction of the price of the final product. Because of the small returns, and because the means of production lie repeatedly idle for considerable periods, producers are reluctant to make any capital investments. Thus the industries remain small, primitive in technique, and traditional. Similarly, there is little money with which to purchase raw materials, and insofar as these must be obtained by exchange, a perpetual indebtedness results, which affects prices negatively. Somewhat contradictorily, prices for small industry products are not determined by market forces but by tradition. This results in prices which are low but stable. Youngsters learn village industry techniques from relatives and neighbors, rather than from technical schools as in the West. This results in a pattern of local specialization for which there is no economic rationale. Producers who make similar items cluster and cooperate, rather than spread out and compete as they would if they were behaving in a rational economic manner. Their enterprises are small, with little or no internal division of labor. They do not respond to changes in market demand or price, and will continue producing as long as the price is even slightly above the cost of raw materials. They have little interest in finish, accuracy, or standardization, which makes it impossible to export their products (Boeke 1953, 44–45, 48–49, 100–102, 184–88).

Boeke admitted that some villagers spend the greater part of their time on industrial pursuits. He asserted, however, that those who did so were family members comparatively little occupied with agriculture, or members of landless families. He criticized the colonial government for conflating industry as a main occupation with industry as a secondary occupation, and believed that failure to observe the distinction had been the cause of many costly disappointments in efforts to promote industrial development (Boeke 1953, 48–49).

Boeke emphasized the relationship between the village industry and agricultural sectors. Because their lack of finish, accuracy, and standardization makes the products of village industries unsuitable for export, the products depend on a domestic market which consists mainly of subsistence farmers. Subsistence farmers produce very few surpluses for sale, and thus their buying power is low. Even if agriculture increased its output through technical improvements, this would do little to help village industries. The reason is that people's need for food is limited and hence the demand for food products is highly inelastic. Any increase in food production will only lead to a decline in food prices. Hence there is always a strict balance between the number of people in the agricultural and the nonagricultural populations (Boeke 1953, 187).

Boeke developed a scheme of eight successive stages through which industrial production passes:

1. Household industry: production to supply the worker's own needs, unconnected with trade or the social division of labor;

2. Handicraft: production for local trade, in which there is immediate contact between producer and consumer without the intermediary of the professional trader; often production to order; no stockpiling;

3. Cottage industry: production for the market, for an unknown destination, sold to a wholesaler who accumulates a stock;

4. Manufacture: production in a common workshop, under the supervision of a manager, with technical division of labor but no mechanical aids of any importance; wage labor; as a rule, stockpiling;

5. Factory: technical, mechanized business for mass production of a single article;

6. Complex business of the nature of a factory: production of several marketable articles having in common a part of the productive process or manufactured from the same raw material;

7. Compound business functioning as a single enterprise: several businesses that are entirely separate technologically, such as the raw material industry, the fuel and other auxiliary material–producing industry, production of the finished article, transportation, and distribution, all combined in a single company with joint commercial and financial management;

8. Complex enterprise: an organization combining a number of entirely or partially independent enterprises, whether more or less similar in nature, in a single financial whole. (Boeke 1953, 100–101)

According to Boeke the first four stages are precapitalistic or early capitalistic, and native industry never rises above the fourth stage. He admitted that there were some nonwestern factories in Indonesia that made cassava flour, batik cloth, and native cigarettes, but maintained that these were either undercapitalized or owned by nonindigenous Asians such as the Chinese. Native Indonesians, at any rate, feel most at home in cottage industry, where the sale of commodities is left to intermediaries.

Having said that there is such an enormous gap between western and native sectors of the economy, Boeke does not really offer any solutions or a way out. The best that he can suggest is that the native sector be left alone to gradually evolve in its own way. In making this suggestion he appears to have been influenced by Gandhian ideas on village self-reliance.[5] This suggestion was naturally not very satisfying to the colonial authorities, who were charged with doing something positive to improve native welfare. Furthermore, there was the danger that Boeke's ideas would be used as an apologia for cutting the Indies development budget.

Boeke had his critics in Dutch academic circles from the very beginning.[6] Two points were especially singled out for criticism. First, most critics felt that he had exaggerated the differences between the economies of Europe and the Orient. Second, most disagreed on the need for a special theory to deal with the economic systems of colonial countries such as Indonesia. Despite these quite valid criticisms, Boeke had a tremendous influence on two or three generations of Indonesianists. Until 1965 virtually every scholar who wrote about the Indonesian economy felt the need to come out in favor of Boeke or to denounce him.

Here we can note a special irony: the Netherlands was one of the last European countries to industrialize. Until about 1870 the Netherlands economy was based on shipbuilding, sea trade, farming, and unmechanized handicraft workshops that made goods such as hand-loomed woolens, lace, and porcelain. It was very similar to the Indonesian economy before the Dutch and other European powers began to blockade Indonesian seaports in the sixteenth and seventeenth centuries. When Boeke wrote his thesis in 1910, he seems to have been comparing Indonesia with England, where the Industrial Revolution had begun in the late 1700s, not with the Netherlands.

Rather tragically, many Indonesian academics and officials also came to accept Boeke's negative characterization of their society. His ideas so worked their way through the colonial government apparatus that they still appear in "trickle-down" form in development planning documents of the present-day Indonesian government. In the late 1970s I worked with the Indonesian Department of Industry in Central Java. One of my tasks was the annual review of development project proposals submitted from the district or regency (*kabupaten*) offices. Nearly every proposal began with a background statement criticizing Indonesian village industries in terms which could have been taken straight from Boeke. Needless to say, most of the authors of these documents were lower- to middle-level government officials who had never heard of a colonial officer named Boeke. They were just passing on ideas from their superiors and predecessors which had long since become part of the department's tradition.

In the debates between Boeke and his critics, British and American anthropologists can recognize many of the same issues that were argued by the substantivist and formalist schools of economic anthropology in the 1960s. The resemblance appears to be largely a case of parallel development. As mentioned above, ideas about stages of economic development and social evolution were in the air from the latter part of the nineteenth century on, influencing the work of such major and diverse writers as Durkheim, Lévy-Bruhl, Maine, Tonnies, Marx, and Weber. Within the emerging field of anthropology these ideas can also be found in the work of Morgan, Tyler, and Lowie. British and American anthropologists were more directly influenced by these early authors than by Boeke, whose work did not begin to appear in English translation until 1947. Yet it is interesting to note that both Karl Polanyi, leader of the substantivist school, and Raymond Firth, leader of the formalist school, were familiar with Boeke's writings and cite him in their later works. The position of Polanyi, who argued that formal economic theory could only be applied to western market economies, is analogous to that of Boeke, while the position of Firth is analogous to that of Boeke's Dutch critics.

Coping with Economic and Political Chaos, 1930–1970

The Depression of the 1930s, and the attendant collapse of the international commodities market, had a devastating impact on peasant welfare in Indonesia. Some rural areas were forced to revert temporarily to a barter economy because the peasants had become dependent on cash cropping and wage labor on plantations to supply their need for cash (van der Kolff 1936). The colonial government had no choice during the Depression but to restrict the most important types of commercial agriculture and shift exports to the mining sector, the labor requirements of which were comparatively small. Dutch administrators felt overwhelmed by the twin problems of poverty and rapid population growth, particularly on Java. Attempts in all directions to raise the income of the people became imperative.

In these efforts the promotion of small and medium-sized industries was assigned an important place. Priority was given to those industries which manufactured essential commodities at prices which the Indonesian people could afford. Tariffs protecting native industries from cheaper imports, particularly imports from other Asian countries which were more industrialized, were left in place. Import quotas were lifted and import duties lowered or eliminated on certain types of machinery, tools, and raw materials needed by Indonesian producers. Home industries were given a 10 percent preference when bidding on government purchases. In some industries, for example hand-loomed textiles and clove cigarettes, an attempt was made to limit production or limit the number of enterprises to raise prices. In a probably misguided effort, a system of central boards was set up to help the small industry sector. The idea behind these boards was that small industries would manufacture only unfinished products, which would then be purchased by the boards and finished in centralized finishing plants. The boards would supervise quality control and maintain buffer stocks to protect the industries from market fluctuations. They would also act as joint purchasing offices for raw materials, tools, and equipment, and as sales offices for the finished products. Although the boards were regional, small industries making similar products were organized in cooperative societies under the boards. Credit was also channeled through these boards. A special Fund for Small Industry was set up which made loans under government guarantee in conjunction with the General Popular Credit Bank. A similar Fund for the Financing of Medium-Sized Industries was set up as a separate organization to assist workshop enterprises. Industrial planning, one aim of which was to prevent the establishment or expansion of capital-intensive industries which competed directly with cottage industries and workshops, was begun in 1937. In the development vocabulary of the time, competing capital-intensive industries were labeled "socially undesirable." By contrast, cottage industries and workshops were labeled "socially useful" because they provided income and employment for the Indonesian population.

The results of all these efforts were mixed: the volume of small industry production showed some increase during the 1930s, but prices for small industry products remained depressed. Boeke describes these interventions and discusses the "indispensableness of government interference in the struggle between western and eastern industries." But such interventions are the very antithesis of village self-reliance and of leaving the native sector alone to evolve in its own way (Boeke 1953, 285–94).

The period between 1940 and 1970 was difficult for Indonesia. The Depression was followed in rapid succession by the Second World War, the Japanese occupation, the Revolutionary War, the campaign to wrest Irian from the Dutch, the "Crush Malaysia" campaign, the economic neglect that characterized the late Sukarno years, and the political convulsions of 1965–66. There was little enough time during these years for economic planning, and plans that were drawn up were often aborted. All forms of peasant economic activity suffered, including agriculture, trade, and industries. At one time or another agriculture was affected by cutoffs in the supply of imported fertilizer, the departure of many males from rural villages to take up arms, military confiscations of the rice harvest to feed troops, and confiscations of agricultural tools to be made into weapons. Trade and industry were also hurt by the decreased buying power of the agricultural population, which had formed the bulk of their market. Added to this was the disruption in supply and marketing networks caused by warfare. Textile industries particularly suffered because they had come to depend on imported inputs such as yarn, cloth, and dyes.

American Social Scientists and the Modjokuto Project

Until the 1950s most research in Indonesia was done by Dutch and European explorers, missionaries, and administrators. In 1952, however, a team of American social scientists arrived and took up residence in or near a small town in East Java, to which they gave the pseudonym "Modjokuto." This team consisted of six graduate students from Harvard University, led by a Yale linguist. Their work was sponsored by the MIT Center for International Studies, whose director for research projects on Indonesia was the economist Benjamin Higgins. The team worked according to a broad plan of division of labor and gradually, between 1960 and 1971, produced a number of published volumes on various aspects of Javanese village and small-town life. These included Hildred Geertz's *The Javanese Family* (1961), Alice G. Dewey's *Peasant Marketing in Java* (1962), Robert Jay's *Religion and Politics in Rural Central Java* (1963) and *Javanese Villagers* (1969), and Clifford Geertz's *The Development of the Javanese Economy* (1956), *The Religion of Java* (1960), and *Agricultural Involution* (1963). The Geertzes made a subsequent field trip to Bali, and Clifford Geertz wrote a comparative study of social development and economic change called *Peddlers and Princes* (1963), which contained some case material on cottage and small industries. Jay wrote another manuscript on agricultural systems which unfortunately was never published but circulated privately. For non-Dutch speakers these works, as well as several journal articles published by the same authors, formed a baseline study of Javanese and Indonesian life, seen as it was during the economically and politically difficult years of the early 1950s.[7] Of these works Dewey's market study and the economic works of Clifford Geertz relate most directly to the concerns of this book.

Dewey's study of a peasant market should have lain to rest a number of misconceptions. Having studied with Raymond Firth in London, she stands firmly in the formalist camp. She convincingly demonstrates that Indonesian peasants are shrewd maximizers, keenly aware of profits and the value of their own time. Although cash was scarce on Java in the 1950s, peasants were eager to acquire it so that they could purchase consumer goods and additional food items. Nearly all transactions in the marketplace were monetized. Prices were set by bargaining and responsive to fluctuations in supply and demand. Dewey provides details on the social and credit relationships between different classes of traders. She demonstrates that cooperation between traders is compatible with rational maximizing. The ethnic Chinese role in market trade was more prominent in 1953 than it is today. Dewey compares Javanese and Chinese traders and concludes that although the Chinese had the advantage of a stronger extended family and other in-group ties, the Javanese were learning to compete in the arena of larger-scale wholesale cash crop trade.

In two appendices Dewey presents historical data on Indonesian commerce and critiques Boeke on some of the same grounds we have discussed, namely his failure to recognize the usefulness of formal economic theory in studying nonwestern economies, and his highly stylized picture of what the "genuine eastern village" ought to be. Dewey's data on Indonesian commerce are taken from studies by van Leur and Schrieke, both published for the first time in English in 1955. These studies reproduce a number of European travelers' accounts from the sixteenth and seventeenth centuries. Dewey uses these data to refute the notion that trade is a recent introduction to

Javanese society from outside. As she points out, "trade was so well established that it took the Europeans over two hundred years of warfare and fierce competition to suppress the local merchants and take over the international trade for themselves" (Dewey 1962, 190). The sixteenth- and seventeenth-century accounts mention not only trade but also internal marketplace (*pasar*) trade, in the hands of both Javanese and Chinese merchants. This trade was largely monetized, using small coins imported from China and other types of coins as well. In some places, where the supply of money was insufficient for trading, certain forms of quasi-money were used such as jewelry, pepper, and cloth. Turning to the eighteenth and nineteenth centuries, Dewey points out that the Dutch did not introduce a western capitalist system into the Indies but instead a "pseudofeudal" system of forced deliveries and forced labor that resembled corvée. Peasant entrepreneurship survived outside of, and in spite of, the sectors of western interference. Peasant industries survived whenever they could match the price or desirability of western imported goods, which was often (Dewey 1962, 198, 202–3).

Boeke Reincarnated: Geertz's Views on Peasant Industries, Involution, and Takeoff

It has been the fate of Clifford Geertz to become the Boeke of his generation, and for many of the same reasons. Much of Geertz's *Agricultural Involution* (1963), the book which gained a great deal of fame for him, consists of secondary analysis. The book is a curious amalgam of ecology, colonial history, and notions about economic "takeoff." The ecological section contrasts the sawah systems of densely populated "Inner Indonesia" (Java and Bali) with the swidden systems of more sparsely populated "Outer Indonesia," and notes the capacity of sawah systems to respond to additional inputs of labor without deteriorating. In the section on colonial history Geertz describes the economy of Inner Indonesia in terms of economic dualism. He faults the colonial authorities for introducing measures which led to rapid population increase. He describes the "Culture System" (1830–70), under which the Javanese were forced to convert a portion of their land to the production of cane and other cash crops, thus reducing the area available for food crop production.[8] He repeats the colonial error of assuming that irrigated rice and cane were ecologically compatible.[9] Toward the middle of the book he introduces the term "involution," borrowed from the American anthropologist Alexander Goldenwiser. Goldenwiser used it to describe ornate art forms made up of a repetition of a limited number of pattern units. As Geertz uses the term, agricultural involution apparently differs from agricultural intensification in having a cultural component. In other words, as the Javanese population increased during the colonial period and rice agriculture of necessity became more intensive, the culture also became more complex, intricate, and effete.

The section on colonial history in *Agricultural Involution* owes much to Boeke. In addition to the concept of economic dualism and the emphasis on the disastrous consequences of rapid population growth, there are many more specific parallels — for example, the frequently repeated assertions that Javanese villages are homogeneous and that Javanese villagers engage in poverty sharing (Geertz 1963a, 97, 100, 116, 123, 146). Despite these obvious parallels Geertz scarcely mentions Boeke by name, and when he does it is to put him at some distance: "The difference in 'economic mentality' between Dutch and Javanese which Boeke took to be the cause of dualism was in fact in great part its result. The Javanese did not become impoverished because they were 'static'; they became 'static' because they were impoverished" (Geertz 1963a, 142).

The fact is that both Geertz and Boeke specifically deny blaming Indonesian culture for poverty, but both describe Indonesian culture in such negative terms that their denials ring hollow. Boeke came dangerously close to perpetuating what Syed Hussein Alatas has called "the myth of the lazy native" (Evers 1980, 3; citing Alatas 1977). Geertz associates involution with the *abangan* worldview — the view of the 85 percent or so of Javanese villagers who do not consider themselves "fanatic" Muslims, and whose religious beliefs and ceremonial cycle incorporate many pre-Islamic elements (Geertz 1963a, 101–2). Some particularly mordant phrases used to describe Javanese culture in *Agricultural Involution* are "advance toward vagueness," "flaccid indeterminateness," and "a richness of social surfaces and a monotonous poverty of social substance." Javanese villages are described as "large, dense, vague, dispirited communities" and the Inner Indonesian heartland as a "largely homogeneous post-traditional rural slum" (Geertz 1963a, 102–3, 116, 129).

In the last part of *Agricultural Involution* Geertz introduces the concept of economic "takeoff." This concept is taken from Walter Rostow's popular book *The Stages of Economic Growth*, published in 1960. The essence of the concept of takeoff is that development is not a smooth process of evolutionary change but a discontinuous process, and that to take off a society must reach a critical mass of savings, investment, and other economic measures at the proper moment in history. If it fails to reach that critical mass, takeoff will misfire and the society will lapse into stagnation. Having missed the moment, the society may not be able to recover it. Population will continue to grow but labor productivity will remain the same or decline; there may be no second chances for development. Geertz compares Japan and Java during the critical period between 1830 and 1870. During this period, which coincides with the Culture System on Java, Japan achieved the preconditions necessary for takeoff but Java did not. A key difference was that Japan invested in the urban industrial sector while the Dutch on Java invested in the rural plantation sector. Thus "the Japanese peasant had to go to town and become a full-time reasonably disciplined member of a manufacturing system," while the "Javanese peasant did not, literally, even have to move from his rice terrace" (Geertz 1963a, 142).

Like Boeke, Geertz is very pessimistic about the future of Java. Java is "an anthology of missed opportunities, a conservatory of squandered possibilities." "The world has moved on, both in and outside Java, and the alternatives which face her today are not those which faced Japan a century ago" (Geertz 1963a, 130, 139). Geertz leaves open a small window of hope by noting that Java still had one trump card to play: fertilizer. In this observation, at least, Geertz was prescient.

Given the similarities between Geertz and Boeke, we are forced to ask why Geertz was so reluctant to acknowledge Boeke. After all, what is "involution" but a description of the native sector in a dualistic system? We can only guess that Geertz's ambivalence was due to criticisms of Boeke by Geertz's colleagues. Dewey's critique, published the previous year, has already been mentioned. In addition, Benjamin Higgins, the Indonesia research director at the MIT center, had published an important article on Boeke in 1955. This was one of the first reviews of Boeke in English, and the forerunner of a spate of other articles.[10] As Indonesia research director, Higgins contributed the foreword to *Agricultural Involution*, in which he explains that take-off was the "common thesis" of all the scholars working on Indonesia at the center (Geertz 1963, ix).

Again we note the curious tendency for western stereotypes about Indonesia to become part of the way Indonesians think about themselves. *Agricultural Involution* was translated into Indonesian in 1976. It is probably the most widely read work of social science in Indonesia and has frequently been used as a textbook in Indonesian universities. This is so despite published criticisms by such prominent Indonesian social scientists as Koentjaraningrat (1975, 202–4), Sajogyo (1976, xxi–xxxi), and Mubyarto (1978). "Involution," together with the linked concept of "shared poverty," has become part of the everyday discourse of Indonesian policymakers and intellectuals (White 1983, 18).

Geertz again uses the concept of takeoff in *Peddlers and Princes*. Now his time frame shifts forward by about ninety years, and he states that Indonesia is currently (i.e. in 1963) in the middle of a pretakeoff period that began about 1920. The chief characteristic of such a period is that "traditional equilibrium has been irrevocably lost but the more dynamic equilibrium of an industrial society has not yet been attained" (Geertz 1963b, 3–4). Takeoff is still possible in Indonesia, but care must be taken to see that it does not misfire. Geertz criticizes economists for focusing on the economic component of development to the exclusion of the social and cultural components. He notes that what seems to be a discontinuous and revolutionary process from an economic point of view is probably a continuous and evolutionary process from the social and cultural points of view. He goes on to compare two "pretake-off towns," Modjokuto and the old Balinese court town of Tabanan, describing the trade and small industry sectors in these towns. Whereas the entrepreneurs in Modjokuto come mainly from the pious Islamic trader group (*santri*), they come mainly from the ruling family in Tabanan. Geertz concludes that there is no single path to development but rather a number of possible paths. "A modern economic system may be compatible with a wider range of non-economic cultural patterns and social structures than has often been thought" (Geertz 1963b, 144). He urges social scientists to break out of the unilinear Gemeinschaft and Gesellschaft way of thinking and develop a workable "middle range" sociological theory of economic growth (Geertz 1963b, 147).

Peddlers and Princes is a more hopeful book than *Agricultural Involution* and, in its overall concept and conclusions, a better book. Yet we must note that many of Boeke's generalizations about trade and small industry are repeated. Pasar (marketplace) trade is again described as something alien, introduced from abroad. It therefore occupies an "interstitial" position within Javanese society. This is because pasar trade "is, for the most part, not a local growth but was introduced from outside at a point when Java had already achieved very high levels of social, political and religious development." Geertz identifies the fourteenth century and the Hindu kingdom of Majapahit in East Java as the time and place at which the pasar pattern took its characteristic historical form. The Javanese see the trader as an outsider, with values very different from the rest of the population. The status of the trader is "ambiguous at best, pariah-like at worst" (Geertz 1963b, 42–44).

In *Peddlers and Princes* Geertz surprisingly states that handicrafts and village-based industries have "almost entirely disappeared" on Java, and are "now of only marginal importance" (Geertz 1963b, 21, 89). He then goes on to describe these industries as similar in essence to traditional agriculture:

> They are highly labor intensive, subject to wide seasonal fluctuations in activity, essentially loose and undynamic in their organization, and, because of the dwarf scale on which they operate, very difficult to capitalize effectively. In the village context, such industries are in fact usually treated as an adjunct to farming: when things are slow in the fields, activity picks up in brick-making, coconut oil manufacturing, or basket-weaving; and vice versa. Such household industries are viewed as additional cash crops, ones whose "growing seasons" can be inserted in between those of the ordinary crops to give a better balance to the yearly round. The result is an approach to manufacturing which is interested less in steadily increasing efficiency or in continually rising wages and profits than it is in a reliable, riskless source of supplemental income, in return for the irregular application of otherwise idle, unskilled labor. (Geertz 1963b, 70)

Despite these generalizations Geertz continues by describing how several small food-processing industries of this type had developed in the urban setting into small factories. One brown-sugar factory had even mechanized and was employing forty workers in shifts. Indeed, when he can avoid overgeneralizing and derogatory language in *Peddlers and Princes*, Geertz provides a good deal of informative case material on small construction, garment, food-processing, and other enterprises.

Unlike Java, according to Geertz, Bali has maintained a strong tradition of rural handicraft, marked by village and kin-group craft specialization: "In one hamlet almost everyone makes tiles, in the next nearly everyone manufactures musical instruments, or works silver, or manufactures salt, or weaves, or makes pots, or produces coconut oil. All the carpenters in a locality hail from one place, all the tailors from another, all the palm-wine makers from a third, and so on" (Geertz 1963b, 89). Some of this production is contributed to the temple or to the palace, but most of it is disposed of commercially. According to Geertz, Balinese village society is best seen as a set of overlapping and intersecting corporate groups called *seka*. A seka is a small group formed on the basis of a single criterion, such as residence in the same hamlet or membership in the same kin group, temple congregation, or irrigation society. At the time when Geertz was staying in Tabanan, some of these seka were setting up more modern enterprises, such as retailing cooperatives and brick or tile factories. Some aristocrats were also exploiting vertical politico-religious loyalties to raise capital. They did this by levying contributions or selling shares to villagers, groups of villagers, or hamlets in the district. This capital was then used to set up trading corporations and manufacturing enterprises. Some of these enterprises had become quite large, with hundreds of stockholders.

In comparing Modjokuto and Tabanan, Geertz notes that the aristocratic entrepreneurs of Tabanan had an advantage in raising capital but were subject to social pressures to redistribute their profits. Modjokuto's merchant entrepreneurs, on the other hand, were free to "rationalize" their enterprises but had difficulty raising capital owing to the individualistic pattern of pasar trade. They also had a bigger "Chinese problem," facing more competition from Chinese merchants. After making this comparison Geertz raises the interesting question of whether a large-scale industrial structure could possibly arise out of small enterprises such as those found in Modjokuto and Tabanan. Given the massive capital investments needed for large-scale industrialization, he concludes that these enterprises may be quaintly irrelevant. "There arises," he says, "the uneasy feeling that it is not the English but the Russian industrialization experience which is proto-typical for our age" (Geertz 1963b, 79).

Modernization Theory and Its Impact on Public Policy

Although Geertz is a cultural anthropologist in the Parsonian tradi-tion, one senses in many of his works that he was writing for a differ-ent audience: an audience of development theorists from the Ameri-can "modernization" school. The 1950s and 1960s saw the emergence of a new occupation, development consultancy. Many of the newly independent governments of the third world sought help in rebuild-ing and restructuring their economies. They began hiring economists out of western universities and to a lesser extent other types of so-cial scientists. These economists needed a plan of action, something positive and goal-oriented which they could take to their new bureau-cratic bosses. They opted for "modernization theory," borrowed from the fields of sociology and political science. Critics have questioned whether "modernization theory" can really be called a theory at all, since it does not posit a relationship between any variables. Rather, it is a kind of conceptual clothesline on which development programs can be hung. This clothesline is strung between nonwestern (usually rural peasant) and western society, and asks how the former can be transformed into the latter. Various intermediate stages are usually identified, so that the transformation does not have to take place all at once, and progress can be incremental. The transformation takes place through "contact-diffusion," i.e. by exposing the peasants to new ideas and new organizational models. This can be done through rela-tively inexpensive means, such as extension programs and technical training courses, and these may be buttressed by some reapportion-ment of the factors of production, such as through credit programs. But there is no need for land reform, nationalization of private enter-prises, or other radical restructuring of society. This is because devel-opment is seen as a problem of culture change. It is not the culture of the governing élite which needs changing, of course, but just tra-ditional peasant attitudes and values. It is these attitudes and values which are standing in the way of progress. One appeal of modernization theory to third world governments, therefore, is that it does not threaten entrenched power blocs and is not socially disruptive.

Modernization theory is also appealing because it is basically optimistic. Like dualistic theory, it starts from the premise that there is a wide gap between the capital-intensive western type of economy and the labor-intensive peasant economy. But dualistic theory is pessimistic about the possibility of bridging that gap, while modernization theory says that governments which have the political will can bridge the gap with patience, correct planning, and the judicious application of resources.

The concept of economic takeoff is a variant of modernization theory. It differs from modernization theory in seeing development as a discontinuous process, and presumably in being quantifiable. Takeoff is still considered a useful concept in the field of economics, but attempts to quantify it have not proved very successful.

Another variant of modernization theory is entrepreneurship theory. A considerable body of literature from the 1960s, with authors from a number of fields, principally sociology and psychology, tries to analyze the personality structure of successful entrepreneurs. Some studies focus on economically successful subgroups and minorities, in an effort to determine the reasons for their success. *Peddlers and Princes* fits comfortably within the definition of entrepreneurship literature, since it compares entrepreneurs from three very different backgrounds: ethnic Chinese, pious Muslim businessmen, and aristocratic Balinese. Behind entrepreneurship literature, of course, is the concern that peasant culture will not be able to supply the entrepreneurship needed for national development. Going back to Boeke, this is because peasants presumably engage in "poverty sharing," value social over economic needs, and do not respond to economic incentives.

The simplistic unilinear version of modernization theory seems particularly apt when discussing the Indonesian industrial sector. More than in any other sector, it seems possible to delineate a clear series of stages of economic growth—from cottage industries to small workshops to small factories to large factories. Mechanization usually occurs at the small factory stage, or at least it did until electricity became widely available in rural areas in the 1980s. Put-out operations do not fall too neatly within this four-stage scheme; there is also the sticky question of what to do with some of the really large factories (with hundreds of workers) that are still not mechanized, such as some of those producing textiles and hand-rolled clove cigarettes. But most industrial enterprises in Indonesia can be fitted into this scheme. Development then becomes a question of assisting or motivating the owners of cottage industry and small workshop enterprises to move up to the next stage. One way of doing this is by teaching them to become better entrepreneurs.

The Central Bureau of Statistics has used a three- or fourfold scheme for all industrial surveys conducted since 1964. But there is a difference between using a scheme for classificatory purposes and using it for development purposes. In and of itself, a classificatory scheme makes no value judgments on the relative worth of different organizational forms, and has no policy implications.

Modernization theory, together with its variants, has been criticized in the literature on the grounds that it is simplistic, linear, and ethnocentric. Moreover, modernization theory is subject to many of the same criticisms as dualistic theory: that it exaggerates the differences between East and West, blames the poor for their poverty by focusing on cultural differences, and ignores different factor proportions in the allocation of productive resources. Little of this criticism has reached Indonesia. Most of it originates with dependency and world-systems theorists such as Andre Gunder Frank, who have focused their attention primarily on Latin America.[11] Evers notes that the term "modernization" is often used in a general way by Southeast Asian scholars, without necessarily indicating allegiance to the modernization theories of American sociologists (Evers 1980, 6, citing Evers ed. 1973).

The regime of the late President Sukarno became a marketplace for western ideas about development. Modernization theory and its variants were promoted by such visiting American scholars as Higgins and Hoselitz. Rostow also visited Indonesia in the late 1950s, and the idea of takeoff was popularized by both President Sukarno and his foreign minister, Subandrio, who linked it to the populist nationalism of the period (Chalmers 1989, 22). A new Indonesian translation of the term "takeoff," *tinggal landas*, was coined. At the same time, leftist elements in the country were calling for a more radical restructuring of society, in particular land reform. A land reform bill was passed in 1960 but never effectively implemented, and agitation by those seeking to have it implemented created much of the tension between land-owning and landless peasants that exploded in violence a few years later.

The leftist elements in Indonesia were brutally eliminated in 1965–66, and land reform became a taboo subject. For a while the idea of takeoff, associated with President Sukarno, also lost favor. It had apparently been absorbed by state planners, however, and gradually crept back into official usage under the New Order regime of President Suharto. Chalmers points out that what had originally been a policy objective became ideology. Since the 1970s economic takeoff has been enshrined in successive five-year development plans as the ultimate objective of Indonesia's development program (Chalmers 1989, 22).

The Green Revolution and Social Equity Problems

Long-term planning and agricultural intensification programs were both tried during the Sukarno years, but largely failed because of chaotic political and economic conditions.[12] By 1969 the monetary situation was stable enough that the New Order government could launch its first five-year development plan (Repelita I). This plan emphasized the goal of self-sufficiency in rice production and the rehabilitation of infrastructure. Self-sufficiency in rice production was to be accomplished by the large-scale adoption of new rice inputs. These inputs included chemical fertilizer, pesticides, and new high-yielding rice varieties. They were provided to farmers through a package program of credit and extension called BIMAS, which after 1973 was heavily subsidized by oil revenues. To the surprise of many observers, the goal of self-sufficiency has largely been accomplished, despite a major setback in 1972–73 owing to a devastating attack of *wereng* rice pest. As Ben White recently observed:

> One of Indonesia's major and, to many observers, surprising achievements during the life of the "New Order" regime has been her transition from the world's largest importer of rice (at times during the 1970s importing one-third of all the rice available on the world market) to a situation in which national rice self-sufficiency can now be expected in normal years. To many it has been particularly surprising that this success has been achieved as much on the tiny farms of Java as on other islands. Despite acute popula-

tion pressure and the pessimism voiced by agronomists and others during the 1970s, who considered that Javanese agriculture was already driven to the limits of intensification and "involution" and therefore incapable of further sustained growth, paddy production in Java since the early 1970s has been comfortably outstripping population growth for the first time in a century. (White 1989, 66)

The increases achieved in rice production have been truly spectacular, amounting to a Green Revolution. Between 1954 and 1968 yields on Java averaged between 1.63 and 1.83 tons per hectare. After the start of the Green Revolution they jumped to 2.56 tons per hectare. They have continued to climb during every subsequent five-year planning period, and by Repelita IV (1984–88) yields were averaging 4.66 tons per hectare, or nearly three times previous levels (White 1989, 73).

Increases in rice production have not been achieved without considerable cost. One major cost was environmental pollution from pesticides, which affected the entire food chain. The government is now trying to deal with this problem through an integrated pest management program. A second major cost, perhaps avoidable, was an increase in intravillage stratification. Critics of the program say that a disproportionate share of the new inputs was channeled to the large landowning group, and that the position of this group was strengthened vis-à-vis other groups in the village. There is no doubt that this group, which the government also relies upon for political stability and for disseminating its messages about development, now constitutes a powerful rural élite. Furthermore, members of this group have invested some of their profits from rice production in mechanized equipment, which has given them an advantage in other sectors of the rural economy. Examples would be rice mills, trucks and minivans, diesel engines, outboard motors, and embroidery and weaving machines. They have also used some of their profits in a more purely "capitalistic" fashion—to acquire use rights to land through rental or pawning arrangements, or by extending credit to the other villagers at high effective interest rates. Apparently the issue of whether peasants make good entrepreneurs has been resolved in the affirmative! Some of them clearly do. What is less clear is whether the standard of living of the other 90 percent or so of villagers has improved or declined, not relative to the village élite but in absolute terms. In other words, has the subsistence floor for landless and smallholder families moved up or down?

The increase in stratification in the rice sector has been accompanied by an increase in stratification in other sectors, including the small industry sector. Although very small firms which rely on unpaid family labor still account for about 60 percent of all rural enterprises, other patterns have emerged, including the presence of put-out enterprises which rely on hired piece-rate workers and small workshops which rely on daily wage workers. Even when no hired labor is used, large and small enterprises may be linked by credit relationships. Credit may be in the form of raw material supplies or, less commonly, cash advances for working capital. The extension of credit usually implies the right to market the finished product. Most small industry villages are now stratified into two, three, four, or even more groups. At the top there is typically a single entrepreneur or a small group of entrepreneurs who act as raw material and credit suppliers, and market the products of many other households. Below this there may be a group of small to medium enterprise owners who are still trying to function independently by buying their raw materials on the open market for cash, and marketing their own products. Below this is a group of small enterprise owners who are not independent, who are tied to large enterprise owners through credit relationships. Below this there may be a class of put-out or hired workers. Many variations on these basic patterns are possible.

If we ask why increased stratification in rice agriculture has been accompanied by increased stratification in other sectors, one answer seems to be investment linkages: large landowning households invest the additional income from the sale of rice surpluses in unrelated enterprises. Sometimes, though, the largest entrepreneur in a village-based industry owns no rice land, and is proud of having succeeded despite being from a landless family. Investment linkages can also go in the other direction. Profits earned in enterprises unrelated to rice can be used to buy up or rent rice land.

It is perhaps a mistake to think of stratification as new, because it also emerged at various times during the colonial period. It seems to be associated with periods of increased prosperity and increased amounts of capital circulating in rural areas. Periods of impoverishment and decapitalization, by contrast, seem to be associated with a decrease in stratification. Perhaps this is due to greater social pressures on wealthy villagers to redistribute part of their wealth during times of hardship, what Boeke and Geertz refer to as "shared poverty," and what some anthropologists refer to as leveling mechanisms. Another explanation is that the engine of class differentiation is credit, and a lack of capital in rural areas inhibits this process. This raises what is probably the key development question in Indonesia and the world today: Are growth and equity compatible goals? From a policy point of view, this question can be rephrased as follows: Is it possible to channel new inputs and structure incentives in such a way that growth is accompanied by a reasonable degree of equity?

An awareness of serious equity problems dawned in the 1970s, and Repelita II and III (1974–83) both emphasized employment and distributional equity (*pemerataan*) alongside economic growth. Equity, of course, is not just an economic problem, but a sensitive social and political problem as well. Perhaps for this reason "equity" (like "development" and "takeoff") was transformed into an ideological buzzword, constantly referred to in government speeches and publications. Nonetheless, many critics of the government feel that these references are just window dressing, and that equity issues have not been seriously addressed.

Industrial Policy under the New Order Government of President Suharto

Some large-scale economic surveys were carried out by the Central Bureau of Statistics in the 1970s, providing a much improved database for national planning. These included the Agricultural Survey of 1973, the Industrial Census of 1974–75, and the National Social-Economic Survey (SUSENAS) of 1976. These surveys pointed to two disturbing trends: a failure of the large-scale industrial sector to expand, as hoped, and absorb any significant amount of labor; and a massive shift of labor out of the agricultural sector into other non-agricultural sectors of the rural economy, primarily petty trade, services, and small industry.

The failure of the large-scale industrial sector to absorb any significant amount of labor led to a rethinking of the unilinear industrial policy of the early Suharto years. By the time of Repelita III (1979–

84) the goal of promoting cottage and small industries had been de-coupled from the goal of developing the large-scale industrial sector. Continued support of the large-scale industrial sector was seen as important because the high value added in that sector contributes to national growth. At the same time, there was a renewed enthusiasm for supporting the cottage and small-scale industrial sector for the sake of employment. Quoting from a 1979 World Bank report:

> The present industrial structure shows two distinct characteristics. On the one hand there exists a fairly modern, large scale, capital intensive, re-source based industry sector being highly dependent upon foreign capital and technology. This modern sector has limited impact on industrial em-ployment and few linkages with the general manufacturing sector which in itself remains dependent upon imported capital goods, spare parts and raw materials. On the other hand there exists the traditional indigenous small scale industry which employs more than four million persons and artisans but has been relatively unaffected by developments in the modern sector.
>
> On the eve of the Third Five Year Plan . . . government planners and policy makers are reassessing the past performance and future role of the manufacturing sector. They seem to be concerned, as the Bank staff are, with the relatively . . . small (10 percent) share of manufacturing in total employment and slow growth in industrial employment;
>
> It is being increasingly recognized that while large scale projects in a re-source rich country are required at some stage of development, they must form part of the overall efforts and must be accompanied by developments of other industries that contribute to employment of a large part of the population. (World Bank 1979, V. II, 7–8)

Although enthusiasm for supporting cottage and small-scale indus-tries revived, the programs for achieving that goal were carryovers from earlier development plans, and in some cases from the era of the Ethical Course. These programs will be described and evaluated in greater detail in a subsequent chapter. Briefly, they include:

—designating villages with large clusters of industries as "Centers" (*Sentra*);

— stationing technical extension workers at these centers;

— organizing enterprise owners in small industry cooperatives;

— providing inputs (bulk supplies of raw materials, equipment, credit) through these cooperatives;

— conducting technical training and small enterprise management courses for groups of enterprise owners;

— conducting study tours to other production sites for groups of enterprise owners;

— setting up demonstration technology projects at or near the centers;

— constructing Common Service Facilities at or near the centers;

— establishing linkages between large and small firms through a "Foster Father" (*Bapak Angkat*) program;

— establishing mini-industrial estates, usually on the edge of urban areas where power is available in adequate supply;

— sponsoring and taking part in urban sales emporia, industrial shows, and craft fairs.

Social Science in the 1970s: Reaction to Geertz and the Green Revolution; Growth in Nonagricultural Sectors and the Push-Pull Debate

The sectoral shift in labor allocation seen in surveys from the 1970s has been interpreted negatively as a loss of employment opportunity and income in the agricultural sector (the "push" hypothesis) and positively as a growth of opportunity in other sectors (the "pull" hypothesis). Those who favor the push hypothesis point to a few micro-studies which show that income from certain nonagricultural activities is less than income from rice agriculture, but the number and scope of these studies are inadequate to generate any confidence in the hypothesis. Those who favor the pull hypothesis say that the market for nonagricultural products is largely rural, and has benefited from generally increased levels of prosperity resulting from the Green Revolution (demand linkages). Again, more data are needed to confirm or refute the hypothesis. This book describes a small industry subsector in which labor productivity (earnings per hour of labor) and total earnings tend to be at least as high as those of agriculture, thus tending to support the demand element. It does appear, though, that this effect varies from industry to industry.

In the 1970s a new generation of English-speaking social scientists (British, American, and Australian) came to Indonesia and undertook village-based studies. This group included Benjamin White, Ann Stoler, Gillian Hart, Jennifer and Paul Alexander, William Collier, and several others. Initially the members of this group were interested in the social and economic effects of the Green Revolution in lowland wet-rice villages. Later some of them branched out into studies of other types of villages. Collier and Hart, for example, looked at fishing villages on the north coast of Java, Collier at transmigration villages in both Sumatra and Kalimantan, and Stoler at villages on or near plantations in Sumatra. None of the group chose to study a small industry village, although White and Hart made comments about small industries based on incidental data collected in wet-rice villages.

The quality of the studies carried out by these scholars is superb. Furthermore, the studies gained in depth over the years as historical data on agricultural systems during the colonial period came to be included. Much of the data had to be translated from Dutch sources and was not previously well known to English-speaking academics. The work of these scholars was unfortunately marginalized to some extent, and ignored by Indonesian policymakers.

Most of the authors from the group wrote one or more criticisms of Geertz's *Agricultural Involution*.[13] Indeed, this small book has supported an entire cottage industry of criticism over the years. Most of the criticisms are familiar, and center on the derogatory language that Geertz used in describing Javanese society and culture, his pessimistic (and, now it seems, unwarranted) view of Java's future, his characterization of Javanese villages as homogeneous, and his overemphasis on poverty-sharing mechanisms. In addition, there are criticisms of the way Geertz interpreted colonial events, for example population growth during the period of the Culture System. The fallacy that irrigated rice and sugar are ecologically compatible has already been mentioned. The irritation that the scholars of the 1970s felt toward Geertz is understandable if one remembers that they were primarily interested in the intravillage stratification and class differentiation which resulted from the Green Revolution. One should contrast his work on this point with that of Robert Jay, also a member of the Modjokuto team.[14]

In 1976 White introduced the useful concept of "occupational multiplicity." He borrowed the concept from a study of rural Jamaica by Comitas (1973). As used by White and others, occupational multiplicity refers to how individuals and households commonly allocate resources between different enterprises. As a strategy, occupational multiplicity has the advantage of reducing risk, and allowing individuals and households to make the best possible use of their time and other resources. To take but one example, many village industries are primarily dry-season activities because they involve the collection and drying of raw materials and organic fuels, or because sundrying is one stage in the production process. Examples include clay product, food-processing, and many basketry and matting industries. Production in these industries either stops during the rainy season or is reduced by half or more. Traditionally, therefore, these industries have alternated seasonally with agriculture, which is primarily a rainy-season activity. The expansion of irrigation systems and multicropping has obscured this pattern somewhat on Java and Bali, but population growth has increased the labor supply so that most dryseason industries can continue production even if the enterprise owners are engaged in rice farming. The point here is that occupational multiplicity should be seen as a positive strategy for maximization. Authors such as Boeke who criticize villagers for abandoning other enterprises to "run off" to their rice fields at harvest and planting time miss the true economic meaning of what is going on. According to rural banking surveys that I carried out in 1989–91, the average rural household has three to four income sources, and the number of income sources is positively correlated with total household income. In other words, better-off households tend not only to enlarge the size of existing enterprises by using hired labor but also to branch out into new enterprises (Sutoro 1990, 5).

In her dissertation (1978) Hart introduced the related concept of "asset classes." By this she means that all major productive assets owned by a household, not just rice fields, should be considered when determining the class position of a household. In Hart's research village, for example, fish ponds are also important. We can add that in a small industry village the ownership of four-wheeled transport vehicles, diesel engines, work sheds, and storerooms may be at least as important as the ownership of rice fields or other cropland. White, Stoler, and Hart all carried out rural labor allocation studies, but Hart probably did the most work in this area. Her dissertation includes a limited discussion of decision making as it applies to interclass differences in labor allocation strategies. But in general, the large body of anthropological decision theory, developed principally with reference to Latin America, has not been applied by scholars working in Indonesia.

Most of the scholars who were active in Indonesia in the 1970s favor the "push hypothesis." In their view the Green Revolution, and related developments such as the introduction of milling in place of the hand pounding of rice, led to the loss of agricultural jobs and income, particularly for rural women. They also assert that according to the balance of evidence, incomes in alternative nonfarm activities are lower. An exception is William Collier, who reversed his opinion on this issue and became an advocate of the pull hypothesis in the early 1980s (Collier 1981b; Collier et al. 1988). As levels of prosperity have continued to increase in recent years, the pull hypothesis has gained more adherents.

Pressure to Deregulate and Its Possible Impact on Peasant Industries

Most of the protectionist legislation from the years of the Ethical Course was carried over into the Sukarno era. This protectionist legislation not only included import quotas and tariffs but also licensing restrictions on the establishment of large foreign or domestically owned enterprises, which competed with certain types of cottage and small-scale enterprises. The Sukarno regime maintained and added to this legislation, because it thoroughly distrusted the private sector and preferred industrial development by the public sector. Protectionist attitudes continued during the early years of the Suharto era. There is ample evidence that the first generation of trained Indonesian economists, men like Mohammed Hatta and Sumitro Djojohadikusumo, regarded free competition as undesirable and unfair. This view particularly applied to free competition between large enterprises (foreign or domestic Chinese) and small domestic enterprises (especially indigenous *pribumi*).

In the late twentieth century the government came under heavy pressure from foreign donor nations and agencies to adopt free-market policies as a condition of receiving aid. The aim of these policies was to free up the economy and eliminate "tollgate" opportunities for corruption and monopolies. By 1985–86 the majority of Indonesian economists and policymakers had come around to this view, and deregulation was under way. But there was still some reluctance in the government to expose village industries to direct competition from imported and factory-made products, for fear of causing their "in-evitable demise" and a consequent increase in unemployment. Some protectionist legislation remained in place. For example, until 1989 the government used a "positive list" for licensing large industries. Large-scale private investment was only allowed in those industries on the list and forbidden in all others. In 1989, as part of the process of deregulation, the government adopted a shorter "negative list" of industries in which large-scale private investment was restricted in some way, with the assumption that investment was unrestricted in all industries not on the list. The new negative list included the principal village industries, including those making traditional food products, certain types of thread and textiles (including hand-spun silk thread, *ikat*, batik, and hand-woven textiles), slaked lime, unglazed terra-cotta pottery, nearly all hand tools made from metal, traditional musical instruments, soft-fiber products (basketry and matting), and products made of leather, horn, and shell. Conspicuously absent were the brick and roof-tile industries. A similar list was issued for import quotas, tariffs, and taxes.

In planning for development the Suharto government initially relied on a group of foreign-trained academic economists from the University of Indonesia's faculty of economics, some of whom later took up cabinet posts. Over the years the government also came to rely on a very large group of foreign consultants, based in nearly every government ministry and at all levels of the government, both in Jakarta and in the provinces. Some of these consultants were ideologically neutral, indifferent, or confused. The remainder fell into two broad groups. The first included consultants who viewed equity issues as being of primary importance. They generally stopped short of recommending radical restructuring because of the enormous social and political risks involved. Instead they argued that a careful structuring of the programs for channeling inputs would result in greater equity. Consultants from this group who worked with small industries generally favored continuing some level of protection. The second group of consultants argued that whatever the government's ideological commitment to equity, growth should take precedence because it would eventually lead to a higher standard of living for all social groups. When applied to the village industry sector, this usually translated into benign neglect for very small enterprises, and financial incentives to encourage larger enterprises to "rationalize" and thus increase labor productivity.

Peasant Prosperity in the 1980s and 1990s

As Indonesia entered the 1990s, rural areas appeared to be undergoing a period of unprecedented prosperity, particularly on Java and Bali. Geographical pockets of poverty remained, and there were some poor households in every village. The landless, the elderly, and persons living in female-headed households were still vulnerable. Nonetheless, even skeptics were willing to admit that a majority of rural households were now living well above the poverty line. This contrasts with the early 1970s, when a majority of rural households were living below the poverty line. Some concrete indications of increased prosperity are discussed below.

In the early 1970s most village houses were still one- or two-room affairs made with split bamboo walls, thatch roofs, dirt floors, and no glass windows. Now many villagers were able to build larger and sturdier houses with brick and plaster walls, tile roofs, cement floors, and glass windowpanes. Most village children had been kept out of school in order to work full-time. Now parents tried to keep their children in school until they completed the sixth grade. Children still worked, but usually their work was limited to 2–3 hours a day after school. More children (though still a minority) went on to junior and senior high school. Household expenditures on school fees and school-related items such as books and uniforms went up dramatically (Sutoro 1990, 11). In the past many poor households and villages could not afford to eat rice all the time. People from these households and villages had to substitute cheaper and (by Indonesian standards) less desirable starchy staples such as corn and cassava. Now nearly all households could eat rice at least twice a day.

In the early 1970s motorized vehicles were rare in village areas, and people either walked or rode bicycles. Twenty years later ownership of four-wheeled vehicles was still limited to the village élite, but many other households owned motorcycles and scooters. Public transportation also improved in the 1970s owing to the so-called colt (minibus) revolution. Fleets of privately owned minibuses now went up and down the larger roads in rural areas, transporting passengers and goods for a small fee. Electricity was formerly limited to the wealthy few (very few) villagers who owned a diesel engine. But electric power lines were extended to most rural areas in the 1980s, and a majority of households were able to afford the installation fees. Kerosene lamps all but disappeared in rural areas, replaced by electric lights. Generally the wattage was not enough to operate large machinery, so diesels remained an important capital asset, but most households did have enough wattage to operate small machines.

Villagers began to use banks, not only for credit but also for savings. In the early 1970s there had probably been little capacity for saving in rural areas (although that capacity may have been underestimated). Now rural bank savings exceeded rural bank lending in many areas. Two government banks, Bank Rakyat Indonesia and Bank Dagang Negara, set up village banks at the *kecamatan* (subdistrict) and *desa* (village) levels, so that villagers no longer had to travel long distances to use banking services. The focus of rural credit programs had generally shifted away from wet-rice production to nonagricultural enterprises. The reasons for this are complex, but include the generally lower default rate on loans to nonagricultural enterprises. Other prosperity indicators could be identified in the areas of clothing, household furnishings, health care, and entertainment.

The prosperity now seen in rural Indonesia was fragile, in the sense that much of it could be lost if there were another widespread failure of rice harvests which lasted several seasons, as occurred once in the early 1960s and again in the early 1970s. Declining prices for Indonesia's oil on the world markets, such as occurred in 1983 and 1986, also affected the government's ability to fund development programs and subsidize rice inputs. Nonetheless, confidence in the economy was high enough that "takeoff" once again became a topic of discussion.[15] People wondered whether takeoff was occurring already, or would occur in the near future. Government planners predicted that takeoff would occur during the sixth Five-Year Development Plan (1995–99). At the same time, other government officials said that they would prefer to talk about sustained growth rather than takeoff.

Indonesia's policy was to continue with a two-pronged industrial strategy: supporting small industries for the sake of equity and employment, and large industries for the sake of growth and GNP. This strategy assumed, like all strategies before it, that village industries were not competitive. This book differs from most studies of small industries in emphasizing their long-term stability and competitive advantages within the context of the rural market.

Information Sources

The information in this book was collected between 1977 and 1991. Various research methods were used, including informal visits and interviews, structured interviews using question lists and question-naires, and photographic documentation. The persons interviewed included village officials, village industry producers, suppliers of raw materials, buyers of village industry products, and Department of Industry officials at several levels and from several directorates and subdirectorates. The primary data were supplemented with second-ary data of various types, including reports from the Central Bureau of Statistics in Jakarta and from development and funding agencies such as the World Bank and ILO, reports and conference papers from fellow consultants working in the areas of nonagricultural employ-ment and small enterprise development, and published social science journal articles and books.

During most of the fourteen years during which information was collected, I was employed in Indonesia as a development consultant, university instructor, and program officer for funding agencies. Part of the data was collected in the course of carrying out these other tasks. Several research phases are identified in the Appendix. The principal research village for this book is Kajar, the first blacksmithing village that I ever visited. I was fortunate to have had a fourteen-year relationship with the people of this village, to have visited it many times during that period, and to have witnessed both the changes that it underwent and the remarkable strength and tenacity of its traditions.

CHAPTER 2

The Socioeconomic Organization of Metalworking Industries

Location and Distribution of Enterprises

IT IS A RULE OF THUMB in rural Indonesia that productive enterprises are clustered while repair and service enterprises are dispersed. The same holds true for blacksmithing. Enterprises which make new tools are clustered. The size of the cluster varies, from about five smithies (*perapen*) to two or three hundred, with thirty being both average and typical. Larger clusters may extend over hamlet or even village boundaries. The village of Kajar described in chapter 3 contains one of the largest clusters, with approximately 1,300 smiths divided among 222 perapen. This cluster occupies most of the male labor in four contiguous hamlets. Smiths who make new tools usually do this work more or less full-time, leaving agriculture to other members of the family or other households.

In contrast, smiths who repair tools are generally scattered, one or two to a village. They seldom get enough work to do this full-time, except perhaps for a few weeks before the planting and harvesting periods. Most repair smiths are village-based. Some are based in the marketplace, which enables them to draw on a pool of customers from a wider area. In this case they may be able to make a full-time occupation out of repair work. This is particularly true of cutlers (*tukang asah/tukang gerinda*), who sharpen tools but do not make major tool repairs. Major tool repairs require a complete setup that includes a fire hearth and a bellows, and these items require more space than is available in a market stall. Locating a perapen in the marketplace might create an unacceptable fire hazard as well. Tinkers — smiths who repair pots and pans by patching and welding (*tukang pateri*) — may also be in the marketplace. Sometimes cutlers and tinkers are itinerant, going door to door and announcing their services with a familiar cry or the rattle of a metal clacker. The itinerant cutler will bring his edge grinder or grind stone (*gerinda/batu asah*), the tinker a small portable arrangement called an *ubub pateri*, consisting of a miniature rotary bellows attached to a small brazier that holds a handful of charcoal.[1] Although the rest of this chapter concerns smiths who make new tools, it should not be forgotten that many repair smiths may go uncounted in industrial censuses.

Boeke denounced the clustered pattern of production industries as having no economic justification. He believed that it contradicted the economic law of competition between enterprises making similar types of goods. He attributed this pattern to the villagers' habit of learning their craft from family and neighbors, rather than going to vocational schools. While it is true that boys learn the craft of smithing from male relatives and neighbors, the cluster pattern of production does have an important economic function, because it facilitates supply and marketing. Also, blacksmiths often receive their raw materials from supply intermediaries who deliver to each perapen. Because enterprises are clustered, a single supplier can easily serve many households and the unit cost of transport for those supplies is less than if smiths were dispersed over many villages. Similarly, buyers often want to purchase large lots of tools. Because enterprises are clustered, they can obtain a large lot by visiting a single village. If enterprises were dispersed, buyers would have to visit many villages to obtain a large lot, and the unit transport cost would be higher.

Of course both supply and marketing can be carried out through the integrative mechanism of a marketplace. This is often true where the number of perapen is so small that it does not pay intermediaries to visit the village regularly. The raw materials used in smithing (scrap iron and charcoal) are both bulky and heavy, and the smith who lives in a village with more perapen benefits greatly by direct delivery. Here we can note that cheap motorized transport, in the form of minivans and minibuses available for hire, is relatively new, even on Java. Until the 1970s iron and charcoal purchased in the marketplace had to be carried home by shoulder pole or bicycle sidecart.

Buyers also prefer to deal directly with blacksmithing villages rather than going through the marketplace because they can place advance orders for certain types of tools. For example, farmers on Java where the soils are light use a two-kilogram tool called a *pacul* which resembles a spade but is used like a hoe. Farmers in parts of the outer islands where the soils are heavy use a three-kilogram pacul. A buyer who was selling to the outer islands might therefore wish to place a special order for three-kilogram pacul. Scrap iron and steel come in different qualities and grades. Sometimes buyers like to specify the grade used in making up their order, or even supply the metal themselves.

Since the main product of blacksmiths is agricultural tools, we would expect the density of villages with a cluster of blacksmithing enterprises to vary with the density of the agricultural population. This is generally true, and there are more blacksmithing villages on Java and Bali than on the outer islands. Still, the number on the outer islands is not insignificant, and sometimes the villages there have large numbers of smiths and serve a wide area. Examples would be the village of Massepe in South Sulawesi, with 869 smiths in 1990, and the village of Sungai Puar in Minangkabau (West Sumatra), with 433 smiths in the early 1970s.

If we take thirty perapen as average and typical for a blacksmithing village, we can estimate from industrial census statistics that the national density of blacksmithing villages is about nineteen per province (*provinsi*) and two per district (kabupaten).[2] This accords well with on-the-ground surveys, if we adjust for the higher density on Java and Bali. On these islands there are generally about four blacksmithing villages per district. This density refers only to traditional blacksmithing industries making hand tools and does not include other types of metalworking villages.

Structure of the Labor Force

The perapen is the basic organizational unit of the blacksmithing industry. Thus the word "perapen" not only means "fire hearth" and "workplace" but also "enterprise" and "work group."

There is an ancient division of labor used in all perapen which recognizes four jobs or roles based on task. The terms used for these jobs or roles vary from tribe to tribe and village to village. The rather poetic Javanese terms from Kajar village are used below; other terms can be found in the Glossary.

The head of the perapen work group is the *empu*, or master smith. He orchestrates the production of every tool made in the perapen, in much the same way that a *dhalang*, or puppeteer, orchestrates a puppet performance or a ceremonial specialist orchestrates an offering. During production the empu takes up a squatting position between the fire hearth and the anvil. He first inserts the tool blank in the bed of hot charcoal in the fire hearth, using a pair of short-handled tongs. When he determines that the blank has reached the proper temperature for forging, a determination based on the color and intensity of red achieved, he removes it from the fire hearth and lays it across the anvil. While the blank is being hammered into shape by the hammer swingers, the empu turns it this way and that, determining the surface and angle of each blow. A traditional Javanese empu taps out coded instructions for the hammer swingers on the side of his anvil with a small mallet. This sets up a light counterpoint to the hammer swingers' heavier rhythm. The blank will begin to lose heat after about a minute of hammering, and must be reheated several times before it takes on its final shape. If chisels and wedges are needed to further shape the tool, the empu holds them in place while they are being hammered into the hot metal. Later in the day, after all the tools have been forged, the empu will heat each one again, and plunge it in the quenching bath.

Ideally an empu is an older man, one who has a great deal of skill and experience but perhaps is no longer strong enough to swing the hammer. It is not uncommon to see an empu who is in his sixties or even seventies. The empu's role overlaps with that of the magician, ritual specialist, puppet master, poet, priest, and even musician. Less magic adheres to the other three roles in the perapen (but still some). If any offerings are made in the perapen, for example offerings to the anvil, it is usually the empu who makes these offerings. On Bali it may be the empu's wife. If any ceremonies are conducted in the village which involve blacksmithing or metal, it is usually the empu who participates in these ceremonies.

The ideal image of an empu as a wise older man is not always adhered to in practice. Many empu are in their forties, thirties, or even late twenties. Nonetheless, a man would not undertake the role of empu unless he had had at least ten years' experience performing other roles in the perapen. In practice, there are two types of empu, hired and self-employed. Hired empu work in a perapen owned by another villager. Empu wages are very high by village standards, and perapen owners naturally look for the most experienced man they can find. For this reason hired empu are usually older men. Self-employed empu own their own perapen and act as their own empu. They do this to avoid paying wages to a hired empu. They are often younger men. In large and highly stratified blacksmithing villages, a high proportion of the empu are hired. In smaller villages with just a few perapen, all the empu may be self-employed.

The second role is that of the *panjak*, or hammer swinger. There are between one and three panjak to a perapen, depending on the size and weight of tools being made. For small and lightweight tools such as kitchen knives and harvesting sickles, one panjak is usually enough. For large and heavy tools such as spades and pickaxes, two or three panjak are needed.

During the course of production the panjak takes up a position behind the anvil, facing the empu. When the empu lays the red-hot tool blank across the anvil, the panjak swings his hammer overhead, bringing it down in a heavy blow which changes the shape of the metal blank and simultaneously increases the metal density. The hammer used by the panjak resembles a western sledgehammer but has a smaller head and is somewhat lighter in weight.[3] If two or three panjak are used, they hit the blank alternately, setting up a one-two or one-two-three rhythm which sounds like music. The word "panjak" in Javanese can also mean musician or performer, and the association is probably due to this rhythmic sound. When one enters a large blacksmithing village, this sound can be heard coming from all corners of the village.

The job of panjak is the most physically demanding of the four jobs in the perapen and must be carried out by men in their prime. Indonesians are generally of small stature, and hard work makes them wiry rather than brawny. Nonetheless, panjak are more heavily muscled than other village men. A boy is not usually big or strong enough to become a panjak until he is about sixteen. Men seldom work as panjak past the age of fifty or fifty-five. While the job of panjak does not require as much skill as that of empu, it does take some experience to learn to work in a coordinated rhythm with the other panjak and aim the hammer blow at the correct spot on the tool blank.

The third role or job is that of the *tukang ubub*, or bellows worker. The tukang ubub sits on the bellows platform and works the bellows, alternately raising and lowering the bellows plungers in a one-two rhythm of his own. He does this while the metal blank is being heated in the fire hearth, and takes a rest while the panjak are hammering the tool. If a small bellows is used without a bellows platform, as sometimes occurs on the outer islands, the bellows worker stands behind the bellows. The job of tukang ubub is the easiest to learn and the least demanding physically. A few hours of practice, and the task is mastered. It is usually performed by a young boy who is just starting out in the perapen. Occasionally it is performed by a blind man or even a woman (see below).

The fourth job is that of *tukang kikir*, or filer. The tukang kikir files or grinds the edges of the tools to make them sharp. He may perform other finishing tasks as well, such as polishing the surface of the tools with files, or dipping the edges in a protective coating of rustproofing. The tukang kikir sits apart from the other workers, in a corner of the perapen or in a shady place under the eaves just outside the perapen. While working he sits sometimes cross-legged and sometimes with one foot extended, holding in place a small rack on which the tool rests. This rack is made either from two notched buffalo horns or from wood carved to resemble two horns. To carry out his task the tukang kikir uses a variety of files. The steel in these files must be harder than the steel in the tools being filed. For this reason expensive imported files are usually used. Sometimes the tukang kikir also uses a gerinda or rotary edge grinder. Filing is tiring work, but it requires endurance more than strength or skill. It can be carried out by almost any adult man. If an older man performs this task he just takes the work a little more slowly, and stops more often for sips of smoky sweet tea.

The first three tasks correspond to stages in the smith's life cycle. A young boy usually starts off in the perapen as a tukang ubub. After he performs this task for several years, during which time he grows in size and strength, he graduates to the task of panjak. He performs this task for many years and then graduates again to become an empu. He may become an empu in his thirties or forties when he builds his own perapen or inherits one from his father. Or, if he spends his life as a hired worker, he becomes an empu when he can convince a pera-pen owner that he has the requisite experience and skill. There is an advantage in becoming an empu as soon as possible, because the work is less demanding physically and empu wages are higher than panjak wages. But the number of positions for an empu is limited, and a man may not be able to get such a position until his strength and health as a panjak begin to fail him.

The number of workers in a perapen varies from two to seven. A full-sized perapen which makes heavy agricultural and workmen's tools has six or seven workers, consisting of one empu, three panjak, one tukang ubub, and one or two tukang kikir. In a full-sized perapen the tukang kikir perform their task full-time and do not do any other type of work.

A medium-sized perapen has four or five workers, consisting of one empu, two or three panjak, and one tukang ubub. There are no full-time tukang kikir. Instead the other workers quit forging about 3:00 p.m. and spend the two or three hours in the early evening filing the tools they have forged during the day.

A small perapen has three workers, consisting of one empu, one panjak, and one tukang ubub. A small perapen is limited to the pro-duction of small and lightweight tools such as kitchen knives and sickles. A perapen can even get by with two workers by having the panjak double as a tukang ubub. He does this by jumping up to the bellows platform and pumping up the fire when the tool blank is being heated, and then jumping down to swing the hammer when the blank is red-hot again. If a panjak doubles as a tukang ubub he gets full pan-jak wages.

Some of the largest perapen in Kajar village have eight or even nine workers. In these perapen the empu only forges the tools but does not quench them. The work of quenching the tools is done by a fifth type of worker called a *tukang sepoh* (quencher), who performs this task full-time. Kajar is unusual in this respect, and in most blacksmithing villages there are only four types of workers.

Perapen with outside owners—those which rely on hired empu—tend to be larger than those owned by self-employed empu. Self-employed empu rely as much as possible on unpaid family labor, usually their own sons, younger brothers, or live-in nephews. They only use hired labor when there is not enough unpaid family labor to go around. Happy indeed is the blacksmithing family which has a number of grown-up sons who are not yet married and still living at home! Wages are high in blacksmithing villages, at least as high as the highest wages paid to male agricultural workers. Every pera-pen owner, whether self-employed or not, must therefore balance the added productivity achieved by the use of hired labor against the outlay for wages. Many blacksmithing villages have a shortage of skilled smiths available for hire, which may also force a perapen to get by with fewer workers.

When hired labor is used it is usually drawn from neighboring households which do not own perapen. Thus the hired workers are old friends and neighbors, or the sons of old friends and neighbors. Most blacksmithing villages avoid hiring workers from outside the village, even when there is a labor shortage. This may be based on the fear that outside workers would go back to their own villages and set up perapen which would compete for the same market. Thus the village tends to act in concert to protect its production secrets and market position by excluding outsiders. When asked directly why they do not hire outsiders, however, blacksmiths generally give a different reply. They say that only men from their village have the natural "talent" (bakat) to become smiths, and that one must inherit this talent. Workers from non-smithing villages would not be able to learn the requisite skills because they are not descended from smiths.

It is not possible to trace the origin of the industry in every blacksmithing village. In some villages where the industry is ancient, even the oldest informants will not be able to say anything about its origin. They will just say that the industry is turun temurun, passed down from generation to generation. In other villages older informants can pinpoint the start of the industry. A review of case histories from this second group of villages indicates that the industry spreads by out-marriage, not by hiring outside workers. In other words, if a smith marries a woman from another village and goes to live in her village, he may set up a perapen there.[4] He may bring one or more friends or brothers from his home village to help out, and in this way the industry gets a toehold in the new village. Eventually he and his friends or brothers from the home village will have sons and grandsons who start perapen of their own. All of them will be descended from blacksmiths, which seems to be the critical point. This pattern of expansion by way of outmarriage is not limited to the blacksmithing industry but holds true for other village industries as well.

Labor Conditions and Wages

Labor conditions in the blacksmithing industry are tolerable by rural Indonesian standards. Perapen are usually built in a shady area of the houseyard or under a grove of trees near the bank of a stream. The half-walls used in construction let in enough light so that one can see, but allow for good air circulation and dissipation of heat from the fire hearth. If the peaked roof of the perapen is covered with thatch or clay tiles, there will be little additional heat buildup from the sun. Sometimes perapen on the outer islands are roofed with sheet zinc, which is much less comfortable.

There is little available information on the health conditions of smiths. We might expect to see some lung damage from the inhalation of smoke and soot over a period of years. There is less smoke from a charcoal-burning fire than a wood-burning fire, but still a considerable amount. There are also larger particles of charcoal soot circulating in the air in a perapen, as witnessed by the fact that a smith's body is completely covered by soot at the end of a workday. Added to this is that most smiths smoke clove cigarettes while they work. The Department of Industry has periodically tried to distribute goggles to smiths to protect their eyes from flying sparks and bits of metal. These are seldom if ever worn, because they are hot and impair vision. Sweat runs down the smith's face and builds up inside the goggles, causing them to fog over. It is my impression that eye injuries are relatively rare, and are prevented by the angle of the panjak's blow to the metal blank, which causes sparks to fly out horizontally away from the smiths rather than up in their faces. It is sometimes said that smiths develop cataracts from staring at the fire or at red-hot tools too long.

Elderly empu sometimes suffer from atrophied calf muscles from working in a squatting position near the heat. This can cause lameness. The Department of Industry has tried to persuade smiths to dig work pits in their perapen for the empu and panjak to work in. Here they have had more success, and about one-fourth of all perapen now use work pits. But the use of a work pit reduces the length of the panjak's downward blow, and has unknown effects upon the spinal column. Elderly empu may also suffer from a crippled right hand, unable to fully uncurl or extend their fingers, the result of gripping the hot tool blank with tongs for hours at a time, pulling it out of the fire, and plunging it back in again.

In most perapen work begins around 8:00 a.m. and ends around 5:00 p.m., with a break for lunch. This is not a hard and fast rule. If the perapen owner has fields which he farms himself, he may prefer to go to the fields at sun-up, work for a couple of hours, and begin work in the perapen a bit later. Or he may prefer to do his farming in the late afternoon, in which case he will stop work in the perapen a bit earlier. Full-time smiths tend to spend about eight hours a day working in the perapen, while farmer-smiths tend to spend about six hours. If a perapen receives a large order, all workers are expected to put in overtime in the evening hours until the order is filled. Formerly work was done in the evening by the light of a gas lamp. Now many perapen are equipped with an electric light bulb.

The pace of work in a perapen can be described as relaxed but steady. Unlike many village industries in which workers are paid by the piece, smiths usually receive daily wages, but they are expected to fulfill certain targets which are well known to everyone in the village. For example, if they are producing spades, they may be expected to finish twenty-five per day before they quit working. If they are producing sickles, they may be expected to finish sixty per day. Naturally targets are more important in perapen which use hired labor than in those which use all-family labor. If a perapen which uses hired labor does not fulfill its daily target, there will be no profit left for the perapen owner after paying wages. Targets also protect the wage worker from exploitation. If the accepted target is twenty-five per day, it would not be reasonable for the perapen owner to expect his workers to produce thirty-five or forty.

Villages differ in how they handle the problem of work stoppages due to cash flow problems. In some villages hired workers receive a guaranteed daily wage, even if they have no raw materials to work on. In this case the perapen owner may have the right to ask them to do other kinds of work during slow periods, for example repair his house or work in his fields. In other villages the risk of work stoppages is shared by the workers. They receive no wages if there are no materials to work on, but they have the right to look for temporary jobs elsewhere, including jobs in other perapen.

I have uncovered evidence that wage systems are relatively new in the blacksmithing industry. Formerly a share system was used. After a batch of tools was sold, the price of the raw materials used was deducted. The remainder was divided up among the perapen owner and the workers according to a system of fixed shares. If the perapen owner was also the empu, the typical system allotted two shares to the empu, one share to each panjak and tukang kikir, and one half-share to the tukang ubub. More complex systems were sometimes used, but the ratio between the highest share (for the perapen owner or empu) and the lowest share (for the tukang ubub) was never more than four or five to one. Some elderly Javanese blacksmiths interviewed in the 1970s could still remember when share systems were used on Java. In addition, share systems are still found in some blacksmithing villages on the outer islands.

Share systems are not limited to blacksmithing, and they may once have been more widespread in the rural economy. Sharecropping is still common in rice agriculture, of course, but in rice agriculture the share is divided between two persons only, the landowner and the sharecropper. Sharecropping ratios of one to one, two to one, and five to three are common, depending on which party pays for such inputs as seed, fertilizer, pesticide, and hired labor. Two-person share systems are also used in raising livestock, and they define the relationship between the owner of the livestock and the person who cares for it. Recently paddy tractors have become common in some parts of Indonesia, and the relationship between the owner of the tractor and the hired driver is usually defined in terms of a two-person share system (Sutoro 1988, 22–25).

More directly comparable to blacksmithing is the share-catch system used on fishing boats off the north coast of Java. Stratification in the fishing industry is very similar to that in blacksmithing. There are wealthy boat owners who do not go to sea, called *juragan darat* (land captains). They may own more than one boat, and they play a role which is comparable to that of the *empu pedagang* in blacksmithing villages. Next there are *juragan laut* (sea captains), who each own one boat and go to sea with their boat crew. Their role is similar to that of *empu pekerja*. Then there are *jurumudi* (also sometimes called juragan laut), who do not own their own boats, but are hired by juragan darat to work as boat captains. Their role is comparable to that of a hired empu. Under the jurumudi are the boat crew. Collectively the crew are known as *pendega*, in much the same way that smiths are known collectively as *pandai*. The pendega are divided into a number of roles or jobs, including oarsmen, netmen, fish catchers, and boat boys. Traditionally the catch was divided up between the boat owner, captain, and crew according to a complex share system similar to that described for blacksmithing. Share systems are still used on some small boats, but larger boats use wage systems.[5]

Other economic activities which sometimes use share systems are fish ponding, building construction, coastal salt production, and stone quarrying. Share systems are designed to provide workers with fair compensation according to their relative contributions of labor-time, skill, and capital. Share agreements always include the owner of the key capital asset (perapen, boat, rice field, fish pond, salt flat, head of cattle, tractor), and they act to keep the share of that person within socially acceptable bounds. Share systems also benefit the owner by spreading the risk among the workers, for example the risk of crop failure on a rice field or the risk of a low catch on a fishing boat. They also ensure that the workers do not slack off or grow careless, as they have a stake in the outcome.

Table 2 reproduces wage data from my earlier monograph (Sutoro 1982). The data were collected from three blacksmithing villages in Yogyakarta and Central Java between 1978 and 1980. The table shows that wage systems in blacksmithing still approximate the older share systems. Panjak, tukang kikir, and panjak who double as tukang ubub all receive the same wage. This wage is roughly half the wage paid to the empu, and roughly double the wage paid to the tukang ubub. The table also shows that wage systems are more subtle than share systems. They provide a range of possible wages for any given role. Thus a very skilled and experienced empu can be paid more than a relatively new and less experienced empu. Overtime wages are not listed on the table, but they are usually higher than regular wages (Sutoro 1982, 47).

Share systems are called *bagi hasil* in Indonesian, and wage systems are called *upah*. An upah can be calculated daily, in which case it is called *upah harian*, or weekly or monthly (*upah minguan* or *upah bulanan*). Blacksmithing wages are calculated daily but are not paid until the new batch of tools is sold. This means that most blacksmiths receive their wages every five or seven days.

In addition to *bagi hasil* and *upah*, there is a third system of paying hired workers in rural Indonesia. This is *borongan*, a piece-rate sys-

Table 2: Selected Data from Three Blacksmithing Villages

	Kajar	Hadipolo	Kuniran
Number of *perapen* in the village	98	87	23
Number and percent of *perapen* which use female *tukang ubub*	approx. 17 (17.3%)	10 (11.5%)	0 (0%)
Daily wages for *empu*	Rp 600–900	Rp 1000–1500	Rp 650–750
Daily wages for *panjak*	Rp 300–400	Rp 800	Rp 350–500
Daily wages for *tukang ubub* who double as *panjak*	Rp 300–400	Rp 800	Rp 350–500
Daily wages for *tukang ubub* who do not double as *panjak*	Rp 200	Rp 400	—
Daily wages for *tukang kikir*	Rp 300–400	filing done by everyone	filing done by everyone

SOURCE: Sutoro 1982, 47.

tem that is very common in many rural industries. Hand-loom cloth weavers are paid by the meter, for example, and seamstresses by the garment. Brickmakers are paid by the thousand bricks made, and tile-makers by the thousand tiles. Other examples could be given. Many industries combine part-time female and child borongan labor with full-time male upah harian labor. A common arrangement is to use large amounts of female and child borongan labor to produce semifinished products and smaller amounts of male upah harian labor for finishing tasks. Often the women and children work under a put-out arrangement in their own homes, while the men are provided a workspace in the owner's home or workshop. The disadvantage of borongan, from the workers' point of view, is that it is very vulnerable to layoffs in slow seasons or when the owner has cash flow problems. Owners feel some responsibility to guarantee a steady living to their upah harian workers, and they feel no such responsibility toward their borongan workers. The advantage of borongan from the workers' point of view is that it allows them to earn money at their own pace, working part-time if they desire, and often in their own homes. Although the proportion of part-time female and child labor is higher among borongan workers, some full-time male occupations also use the borongan system of payment. Notable among these are the building and construction trades.

The borongan system is seldom if ever used in blacksmithing. Perhaps this is because the labor force is predominantly male and full-time. Also, the making of a single tool requires the cooperation of the whole work group, which often includes the owner. The smiths who make vessels from cut-out sheet copper are sometimes paid borongan, however, as are the polishers in copper, copper alloy, and silver industries.

In addition to wages perapen workers often get food, drinks, and cigarettes from the owner. Here again there is variation from village to village. In some villages the workers are entitled to receive a full midday meal, plus snacks with their tea. If they work overtime they are also entitled to receive a full evening meal. In other villages workers go home for their meals and receive only snacks in the perapen (usually small cakes from rice flour or sticky rice). In some villages the perapen owner is expected to supply clove cigarettes, whereas workers must buy their own cigarettes in other villages. The total value of these items is not negligible and must be included in any calculation of real wages. If a full meal plus snacks and cigarettes are provided, their value may amount to as much as tukang ubub wages, or half the wages for a panjak or tukang kikir.

Use of Female and Child Labor

There is a traditional division in Indonesia between village industries which are all-male, those which are all-female, and those which use a mixed male and female labor force. Blacksmithing and other metalworking industries are considered all-male. Other industries falling in the male group are stone- and woodcarving, house building, puppet making, and rattan furniture making. Female industries include all the various textile, matting, and garment industries. Notable among the mixed industries are those making clay products (pottery, bricks, and roof tiles) and bamboo basketry. Food-processing industries are either all-female or mixed. As a rule wages and earnings are highest in all-male industries and lowest in all-female industries. In mixed industries wages and earnings for male workers are higher than wages and earnings for female workers (Sutoro 1982).

Despite this traditional division, Indonesians are seldom rigid about anything and are usually willing to make exceptions if circumstances warrant. There are therefore a few women employed in metalworking industries. In some blacksmithing villages, including Kajar, women are occasionally used as tukang ubub. The use of women as tukang ubub is generally a sign of a shortage of male labor. When male labor becomes available the women are usually replaced. Many blacksmithing villages that I visited have never used female labor, and the smiths there expressed mild shock or amusement at the suggestion. Others use female labor when necessary but are somewhat defensive when asked about it, going out of their way to explain that the woman is just there temporarily, that nothing improper goes on in the perapen, and that permission has been obtained from the woman's husband or father to hire her. If the woman is a relative of the empu or one of the other men working in the perapen, as she often is, there is less anxiety.[6]

When women work as tukang ubub they remain on the bellows platform, do not jump down, and do not participate in general conversation. They sit rather stiffly and adopt a peculiar masklike facial expression, from which all emotion and animation has been erased. In an earlier monograph I compared this expression to that of a classical Javanese dancer, a *pesinden* singer with a gamelan orchestra, or a bride on display at a traditional wedding. It seems to be a protective expression, one adopted by women in an "exposed" position subject to possible public misinterpretation. Women who work in blacksmithing may feel vulnerable to criticism because they have entered a male realm where traditionally they do not belong (Sutoro 1982, 58, 152).

Although there is a taboo on women working in the perapen, and particularly on women coming in contact with the fire hearth or anvil, there is no taboo on women performing metalworking tasks outside the perapen. Thus women from blacksmithing villages may start small metalworking industries of their own which involve the cold-working of metal. They carry out these industries in their home rather than in the perapen. An example would be the production of cheap aluminum flatware, cut out of sheet metal with shears.

Women also provide a support function by preparing the meals, drinks, and snacks consumed by the perapen workers. If the workers receive a full midday meal, the shopping, preparation, serving, and cleanup connected with this meal may occupy several hours of a woman's time. In this case we must consider the woman an additional "hidden" worker. Usually this work falls to the wife of the empu. If the wife of the empu is busy she may ask her daughter to do the work, or hire a woman from a neighboring household. If the perapen workers only receive snacks, these may be purchased from a nearby *warung* (small store or roadside stand), rather than made at home.

Many perapen suffer work stoppages because of seasonal cash flow problems and profit squeezes (see below). It helps in such a situation if the empu's wife has an enterprise of her own, for example a warung, which generates a continuous flow of income year-round. Even if the total income earned by that enterprise is small in comparison with the income earned from blacksmithing, it can be important in meeting daily living expenses during periods when the perapen is closed or operating part-time.

Women from blacksmithing households which own cropland often perform many of the agricultural tasks traditionally considered male, for example land preparation. This is because most of the male labor is fully absorbed in the perapens. In Kajar the agricultural sector is largely managed by women, who supplement their own labor by hiring wage agricultural workers from outside the village (Sutoro 1982, 60–61).

The taboo on women in the perapen also holds for foundries making items of copper, brass, or bronze. These industries do sometimes use women and children as polishers. Piece rates for polishers are very low in comparison with wages paid to casting smiths. Polishing is often done in the yard outside the perapen. In the copperworking village of Jolotundo in Central Java, women and children are given the task of going door to door to collect kitchen charcoal—the accidental residue of wood-burning cooking fires. The men of the village use this low-grade charcoal for welding.

The situation is very similar in gold- and silverworking industries. If these industries make large items, such as tea sets or trays, they need a full fire hearth and bellows arrangement to melt down metal beads or scrap in a crucible, preparatory to producing sheet. In these operations women are used for polishing or pounding out metal sheet, but not for jobs which involve contact with the fire hearth. But workshops that make small jewelry items from purchased sheet and wire may get by without a fire hearth or anvil, and use small hand-held blowtorches instead. In this sort of operation there is variation from village to village in the attitude toward using female labor. The large silverworking village of Kota Gede near Yogyakarta uses predominantly male labor, while the village of Celuk on Bali, which makes a very similar range of jewelry items for the tourist trade, uses approximately equal amounts of male and female labor.

The use of child labor in village industries appears to have gone down dramatically toward the end of the twentieth century, as school attendance rates went up. This is particularly true of hired children between the ages of five and twelve. In the 1970s it was still common to see very small children putting in ten- to twelve-hour workdays under sweatshop conditions, earning pitifully small sums of money. In textile industries children as young as five were employed full-time as bobbin and spool winders. Mercifully, this situation is now less common, and most children in the rural industrial sector are employed in family-owned enterprises, where they spend two or three hours a day working after school.[7]

Blacksmithing is atypical among village industries in that it has never used the labor of small children. This is because younger boys simply do not have the physical strength to work in the perapen. Occasionally one will see a boy aged ten or eleven pumping the bellows, but twelve to fourteen is the usual age to begin working full-time. Nowadays many boys from smithing families complete grade school before they begin working. In the copper, copper alloy, and silver industries children are still used as polishers. In the silverworking villages of Kota Gede and Celuk, children as young as ten may begin making jewelry items. But again, it seems that children are working fewer hours per day.

Stratification

It is another rule of thumb in village industries in Indonesia that large clusters of industries are highly stratified, while small clusters are relatively unstratified. In large clusters it is common to see four or even more strata, whereas there may be only one or two strata in a small cluster. This rule of thumb applies not only to blacksmithing and metalworking but to all other types of industries as well. It also holds true for many agricultural occupations, for example fish pond-ing and poultry raising. In a large and well-stratified blacksmithing village such as Kajar, there will usually be four strata.

The first stratum consists of raw material and tool traders, the wealthiest men in a blacksmithing village, who do not work in the perapen. On Java these men are sometimes called empu pedagang (trading empu) to distinguish them from empu pekerja (working empu). If there is only one empu pedagang in a village, he will wield a tremendous amount of power over the industry there. Alternatively, there may be several empu pedagang who compete with each other, but there are rarely more than five to a village. Some empu pedagang only sell raw material supplies such as scrap iron and charcoal. Some only deal in tools, buying up tools from a number of perapen and transporting them to distant marketplaces and cities to sell. More commonly, the empu pedagang do both supplying and buying. In this way they can tighten their grip over the weaker perapen owners.

The arrangement between empu pedagang and perapen owners works as follows. Weaker perapen owners who have cash flow prob-lems and cannot afford to buy their raw materials on the open market receive their raw materials as a form of short-term credit from the empu pedagang. When they have converted the scrap iron to tools, they are then obliged to return the tools to the empu pedagang for marketing. The empu pedagang pays them a predetermined price for the tools, after first deducting the cost of the raw materials. The empu pedagang potentially benefits from this arrangement in two ways. First, he has cornered the market for a large number of tools, and of course takes a profit from each one. To do this he pays the perapen owner a price per tool, which is 5 or 10 percent below the outside market price. Thus we can say that there is a hidden interest payment of 5 or 10 percent. Second, the empu pedagang determines the valua-tion of the raw materials supplied—the amount that will be deducted from the price paid for the tools. Sometimes he deducts the true mar-ket price of the raw materials, content to make his profit just from selling, but often he overvalues the raw materials he supplies. With iron and steel he can do this by charging a higher than market price for the usual grade used, or he can charge the usual price but supply an inferior grade. Either way there is again a hidden interest payment.

Of course this hidden interest payment does not represent pure profit for the empu pedagang, because he must bear any transport costs, for example gasoline and a driver's salary.

Usually the empu pedagang buys his scrap iron from urban scrap yards (toko besi). On Java the biggest scrap yards are in the northern coast cities of Semarang and Surabaya. Sometimes an empu pedagang is able to reap big profits by obtaining the rights to salvage iron from a building, bridge, or other structure that is being demolished. He is thus able to obtain the iron at a low price per kilogram while charging the perapen owners the usual market price, though he may have to hire some salvage labor.

Although empu pedagang do not work in the perapen, they often own one or more perapen. When they do, all the labor in their perapen is hired. There are several reasons why an empu pedagang would want to own his own perapen. First, it gives him a steady additional source of tools. Second, after the prices of raw materials and wages are deducted, the empu pedagang gets some profit from his perapen. Interestingly, the profit to the empu pedagang is usually less than the wages paid to his hired empu, and less than a perapen owner would earn if he worked as his own empu, but if the empu pedagang owns several perapen, the total amount he receives will be greater. Third, many empu pedagang build a special perapen with a diesel engine and one or more pieces of electrically powered finishing equipment, such as mechanical edge grinders (*gerinda listrik*). An empu pedgang who has such a perapen may demand that perapen owners who receive credit from him deliver semifinished rather than finished tools. Of course, the price paid per tool is then lower. In a few villages empu pedagang have purchased other types of mechanized equipment such as metal drills and metal-bending machines.

The primary prerequisite for becoming an empu pedagang is capital, in the form of both cash and equipment. An empu pedagang must have enough capital to buy up large lots of raw materials and tools. His cash flow position must be strong, because he may have to wait a month or more to be paid for his work from the time he buys raw materials in a distant city, transports them back to the village, distributes them to the perapen owners, waits until the perapen owners have converted the raw materials into tools, pays the perapen owners for the tools they have made, transports the tools to one or more markets, and sells them to tool buyers there. He may also be forced to give credit to the tool buyers, perhaps delivering the tools in return for a down payment (often 50 percent). Powerful empu pedagang also own certain types of capital equipment. Chief among these are warehouses for storing raw material supplies and tools, pickup and flatbed trucks for transport, diesel engines, and mechanical edge grinders.

It is an irony that most development projects carried out in black-smithing villages work through the most powerful empu pedagang in the village and act to strengthen his position. If a government-sponsored cooperative is set up in the village, for example, the empu pedagang is usually elected to head the cooperative. If raw materials or cash credits are channeled through the cooperative, he is usually the person asked to distribute the credits, and the government credits simply take the place of his own capital without altering the structure of dependency relationships within the village.

Finally, the empu padagang's stratum includes members of his household. They share his socioeconomic status and may help with the management of his business, particularly when he is away on buying and marketing trips.

The second of the four strata consists of independent perapen owners. In a highly stratified village there is usually a group of working empu who own their own perapen and try to remain independent and avoid forming a dependency relationship with an empu pedagang. Partly this is a matter of not wanting to pay hidden interest charges, which cut into their profit per tool, and partly it is a matter of pride and status within the community. To remain independent a perapen owner must have enough capital to buy his own raw material supplies on the open market. He must also develop and maintain his own marketing links.

Transport is usually a problem for independent perapen owners. Unlike the empu pedagang, they generally do not own any type of four-wheeled vehicle. They must therefore use a rented truck or mini-van, which means that their unit cost of transport is high. If an independent perapen owner wants to market the tools he has made every week or two, which is the usual practice, there may be a problem of excess capacity: there may not be enough tools to fill up the rented vehicle. Sometimes perapen owners get around this problem by renting a vehicle jointly.

Another way of handling the transport problem is by dealing with small traders and intermediaries. Charcoal is often bought from outsiders who deliver it to the village. Some outsiders are charcoal makers themselves — people who live in areas where there are still abundant forests and who make charcoal for a living. Others are small traders who travel back and forth between charcoal-making villages and blacksmithing villages. Iron is less commonly delivered to the village, but it may be available from a scrap yard in a nearby town.

An independent perapen owner generally markets his tools locally, rather than trying to sell to distant markets where prices may be higher. Again, this is to avoid the high costs of transport, and the work time which would be lost by making long marketing trips. Various methods of marketing are used, including direct sales to consumers in a local marketplace, sales to small traders who work out of the marketplace, sales to stores and roadside stands in the area, and sales to petty traders who come to the perapen. Included in this second stratum are members of the independent perapen owner's household, because they share his socioeconomic status. The male members of the household usually help in the perapen as unpaid family workers who share in profits.

The third stratum consists of dependent perapen owners. Many working perapen owners in a highly stratified village have succumbed to what seems like the inevitable, by forming a dependency relationship with an empu pedagang. Although the dependent perapen owner loses a portion of his profits in this way, there are considerable advantages. First, he does not have to worry about working capital for raw materials or transport. This means that his perapen can operate full-time year-round, and no time is lost to the work stoppages that characterize perapen with cash flow problems. His only capital outlay is for wages, and wages are usually paid on the day that the perapen owner delivers his tools to the warehouse of the empu pedagang. On Java, where there is a five-day market week, this is usually once every fifth day. The warehouse is always conveniently located within the village, usually near the empu pedagang's home. The perapen owner receives payment for his tools at the time of delivery, and simultaneously picks up a new load of raw materials to work on. He takes these back to his perapen, where he immediately divides up part of the payment among his workers in the form of wages. He then sets something aside for incidental expenses, such as food and drinks for his workers and, nowadays, electricity. The rest represents his profit.

Another advantage from the point of view of the dependent perapen owner is that he loses no time in purchasing raw materials or marketing tools. It is common for independent perapen owners to shut down their perapen one day a week and spend that day on purchasing and marketing. Some independent perapen owners spend the whole day in the local marketplace, retailing tools to consumers. The dependent perapen owner, on the other hand, is freed from any such necessity. He and his workers can spend 100 percent of their time on production-related tasks. Thus the output of the perapen usually goes up if the owner enters into a dependency relationship.

Yet a third advantage is the avoidance of risk. This is somewhat less of a problem in blacksmithing than in, for example, food-processing industries. Iron and steel tools do not really deteriorate over time. If they become rusty, they can always be polished up again. Nonetheless, there is the risk of having one's capital tied up in unsold tools during a period of slow market demand. In such circumstances the independent perapen owner might not be able to pay wages to his workers, or purchase a new load of raw materials to work on. The result, again, is work stoppages which cut into profits.

My calculations indicate that dependent perapen owners usually earn at least as much as independent perapen owners. Although they pay hidden interest to their empu pedagang, this is usually compensated for by less worktime lost and higher output. That is, they earn less per tool made, but as much or more overall. This pattern cannot be assumed but must be determined empirically for each smithing village; the critical variable will be the percentage of hidden interest taken by the empu pedagang. The members of the dependent perapen owner's household are also included in this stratum. As in independent households, the male members usually help in the perapen as unpaid family workers.

The fourth stratum consists of hired workers who receive wages but do not share in profits. These workers come from households which do not own perapen and their status may therefore be somewhat lower. Hired workers may perform any of the four jobs in a perapen, including that of empu.

The line of distinction between unpaid family and hired workers has become somewhat blurred in recent years. Many perapen owners have begun paying money wages to their older sons or brothers, to avoid possible hard feelings. This is particularly true in perapen which use a mixed labor force—where family members work alongside hired workers. Younger sons may be given pocket money rather than wages, on the grounds that they are already having their room, board, clothing, and educational expenses paid for by their parents. The tendency to pay wages to family members is not limited to blacksmithing but is becoming common throughout the village industry sector. In the silverworking village of Celuk on Bali, for example, family members in their late teens and early twenties are given wages. They are then expected to pay for their clothing, transport, and school expenses out of their wages.

It should be noted that empu pedagang do not force perapen owners into dependency relationships. The initial contact is almost always made by the perapen owner, who clearly perceives the advantages and disadvantages of a dependency relationship. When the perapen owner finally approaches an empu pedagang, it is usually after considerable thought and consideration of his cash flow. The pros and cons of depending on an empu pedagang are the subject of constant conversations between men in coffee shops, and endless calculations scribbled with pencil stubs on the backs of envelopes. Boeke's notion that villagers are not profit-oriented, or do not attempt to rationally maximize profits, seems absurd to anyone who has ever spent the evening hours in a village coffee shop.

The empu pedagang walks a narrow plank when determining the amount of hidden interest that he will take: the grade and quantity of raw materials he will supply, the price he will charge for materials, and the price he will pay for finished tools. He naturally wants to charge as much interest as possible to maximize his own profits. But if he charges too much, more perapen owners will try to operate independently, and he will lose control over his tool supply. Moreover, unless he has a monopoly position in the village, another empu pedagang may compete by offering perapen owners better terms.

That perapen owners enter voluntarily into dependency relationships does not eliminate their feelings of resentment toward the empu pedagang. In a highly stratified village there is always considerable grumbling about the power wielded by those at the top. The village may exert social pressure on the empu pedagang to redistribute some of their wealth by sponsoring village ceremonies or festivals, building a new village meeting house or mosque, loaning out their vehicles for weddings and other nonbusiness purposes, or making personal cash loans to villagers who may or may not repay. Although the empu pedagang gains prestige by redistributing some of his wealth, he feels resentment as well. Interviews with several empu pedagang indicate that they view themselves as hardworking businessmen and entrepreneurs who are constantly besieged by unreasonable requests.

Not all blacksmithing villages are so stratified. In a blacksmithing village with a small number of perapen, there may be only one or two strata. If all the workers are unpaid family workers who are close relatives of the perapen owner, then we can speak about a one-stratum or unstratified system. If some of the workers are hired and come from other households, then it can be called a two-stratum system.

In the copperworking industry stratification may be even more complex than in blacksmithing. This is because the production of copperware involves two separate processes, the production of copper sheet from scrap and the production of copper vessels from sheet. The production of copper sheet is usually handled by one or a few large entrepreneurs who own large melting furnaces and employ hired male laborers for daily wages (harian) or piece rates (borongan). The large entrepreneurs buy up scrap copper in bulk, which is melted in the furnaces, poured into disk-shaped molds, and then pounded into sheets. These sheets are then sold or (more commonly) distributed on credit to many small enterprise owners. The small enterprise owners, working in their own homes, make copper vessels (rice steamers, rice pots, tea kettles) by cutting the sheet with metal shears, shaping, and soldering it. In the copperworking village of Jolotundo in Central Java, the men who melt copper and produce sheet are called *tukang gembleng*, while the men who produce vessels from sheet are called *sayang*. Sayang may be either independent or dependent, and they may employ their own hired workers. Women and children from sayang families handle polishing chores and collect kitchen charcoal for fuel.

Silver- and goldworking villages can also be very stratified. The upper stratum consists of a group of large entrepreneurs who have the capital to buy silver and gold in bulk from government trading corporations. They distribute this silver and gold to small producer households, who convert it into jewelry and other items, using family or hired labor. Usually the large entrepreneurs own jewelry stores or "showrooms" where they retail the products made by the small producer households. There is often a workroom attached to the showroom where hired workers make additional items for sale. As in blacksmithing, there may also be an intermediary class of producer households who try to remain independent by buying their own silver and gold in smaller quantities.

It should be clear by now that capital is the engine of stratification. Capital can be used in two ways, as wages and as credit. Capital used as wages results in a two-stratum system, divided between those who pay wages and those who receive them. Such systems are typical of small clusters of village enterprises. Capital used as credit adds two more strata to the system: those who give credit and those who receive it. This results in a four-stratum system, typical of larger clusters.

Entrepreneurs and Entrepreneurship

In every large blacksmithing village there are a few perapen owners who harbor the secret hope of competing with an empu pedagang, and one day becoming empu pedagang in their own right. Life histories collected from several empu pedagang indicate that this is unlikely. Empu pedagang nearly always begin their careers as traders, not as smiths. Often they have never worked in a perapen and have no smithing skills. If they have worked in a perapen, it was just for a brief period in their youth, before taking up trading.

To launch his career the empu pedagang must acquire enough trading capital to buy up a large lot of scrap iron and charcoal, enough to distribute to several perapen owners. He may begin by selling these supplies outright, but he must eventually start distributing supplies on credit to gain control over the marketing of tools made. At the beginning of his career, an empu pedagang may rely on rented transportation, but eventually he must buy a four-wheeled vehicle of his own, usually a used truck of some type. This enables him to increase his profit margin by reducing the unit cost that he pays for transport. Eventually the successful empu pedagang begins to invest in other types of capital equipment such as diesel engines, production machinery, warehouses, and specialized perapen used for tool finishing. His capital position will be strengthened along the way if he can get himself chosen as the head of a government-sponsored cooperative, or if he can qualify for cheap loans from a government or private bank.

Obviously the empu pedagang needs capital in large blocks, not small increments. Petty traders who work out of the local marketplace, or who go door to door in a smithing village selling charcoal or buying up small lots of tools, seldom if ever become empu pedagang. An empu pedagang needs a large block of capital when he launches his career by buying his first large lot of supplies to distribute, and an even larger block when he purchases a vehicle. Vehicles are very expensive in Indonesia, about double the price in the United States. Even a used and somewhat battered truck will cost between U.S. $5,000 and $7,500 (Rp 10–15 million), depending on size and capacity.

There are very few ways for a villager to acquire a large block of capital, and most are related to land. If a villager owns a large amount of rice fields or other cropland, he will receive a considerable block of capital after a successful harvest. Alternatively, he can use a smaller piece of land to acquire capital by pawning it, renting it out, selling it, or (nowadays) using it to guarantee a bank loan. There are a number of rural credit schemes in Indonesia which make guarantee-free loans, but the amount available is never more than about U.S. $250 (Rp 500,000). Larger bank loans always require land documents as guarantees, although they accept types of land other than rice fields, for example house plots. There are a few other ways that a villager can acquire a large block of capital. He can sell some other type of capital asset, for example a house or a team of bullocks. He can borrow the money from a relatively well-off relative, usually a parent or parent-in-law; loans from relatives are usually interest-free. Better-off rural families sometimes give a child a "nest egg" of working capital, usually at the time of marriage. The purpose of this nest egg is to help the child start his or her own enterprise. Here again, it is usually land-owning parents who are able to help out with loans or marriage gifts of cash.

Given that most wealth in rural areas is land-based, we would expect all empu pedagang to come from families with large holdings of rice fields, in keeping with the hypothesis of strong investment linkages between the agricultural and industrial sectors. Career profiles of individual empu pedagang do not provide a clear-cut answer to this proposition. At least some empu pedagang come from smallholder or landless families. The two most common sources of start-up capital for empu pedagang are sale of a piece of inherited land and an open-ended loan from a parent or parent-in-law. The sale of inherited land may mean that the empu pedagang becomes a landless person. Of six empu pedagang interviewed, four claimed to be landless except for their houseplot and the land on which their warehouses and pera-pen were located. The other two owned considerable amounts of land, but they had purchased it in recent years, after becoming wealthy as traders. One of these two (the empu pedagang from Kajar) was from a smallholder family but married a woman from a prominent large-holder family. His wife kept her fields in her own name, and he has since purchased additional fields in his name. It is probable that some or all of his start-up capital came from his wife during the early days of their marriage. Based on this admittedly small sample, it might be better to think of village industry as an alternative avenue to wealth and prestige for ambitious members of smallholder families.

Despite individual differences and idiosyncrasies, it is possible to construct a very general personality profile for empu pedagang. First, they usually consider themselves businessmen, entrepreneurs (*pengusaha*), or traders rather than smiths. In their view trading is more prestigious than smithing, probably because it does not involve manual labor. Here we can draw a parallel with the large landowner who uses hired and sharecrop labor to farm his fields, and never per-forms any manual labor himself. Second, empu pedagang tend to be more secular than smiths and less involved in traditional ritual and magic practices. Whereas smiths tend to define prestige in terms of magical power, and reserve their highest respect for elderly working empu whose skill is seen as a mark of that power, empu pedagang tend to define prestige in terms of economic power. Based on the lit-erature of entrepreneurship, we might expect empu pedagang to turn to more orthodox religious practices, yet I have not seen instances of this in blacksmithing villages. Third, empu pedagang are relatively uninterested in political power, except as it can be used to advance their business interests. Thus they may strive to become head of a government-sponsored industry cooperative, but seldom run for *lu-rah* or other political office. Generally they are content to leave the governing of the village to others, as long as village officials facilitate or at least do not interfere with their business. Of course they obvi-ously prefer to have good relations with village officials, and some-times there is a convergence of élites, as when the son of an empu pedagang marries the daughter of a lurah. In general, however, empu pedagang are less interested in village politics than the large farmer group. Fourth, empu pedagang have traveled more widely in the course of their trading activities than the average villager. As a result, they usually speak *bahasa* Indonesia well, and have a more sophisticated understanding of life outside the village. This understanding includes matters pertaining to their business, such as regional market forces and price variations, but also unrelated matters such as the cultural differences between tribes, or between city people and village people. Fifth, empu pedagang are interested in new technologies per se, and try to acquire these technologies whenever possible. When I first began visiting Kajar, for example, I brought a camera with which to make field photos. The main empu pedagang there showed a great deal of interest in this camera, and it was not long before he had acquired one and learned how to use it. He was also the first in the village to acquire a four-wheeled vehicle, a diesel engine, and a television set. The interest in new technologies is just an expression of a more general interest in anything "new" or "modern." Sixth, empu pedagang feel no special obligation to help villagers who are less well off. It is not that they are socially irresponsible. Rather, they feel they have worked hard to build up their enterprise, and that anyone else could do the same just by making the effort. It follows that empu pedagang feel some resentment at the constant social pressures to share their wealth. They nonetheless succumb to these pressures in many instances, fearing, perhaps correctly, the unpleasant consequences of ignoring public opinion.

Supply, Marketing, and Transport

Some information on supply, marketing, and transport has already been given. In general, empu pedagang travel longer distances than independent perapen owners in search of supplies. They buy their supplies as close to the source as possible, eliminating one or more layers of middlemen. On Java this may mean traveling to Surabaya or Semarang, cities on the north coast where ships are dismantled and scrap and bar iron from abroad often enter the country. There are large scrap yards in Surabaya and Semarang, which sell high-grade scrap for a relatively low unit price. High-grade scrap means large bars or rods which can conveniently be cut into tool blanks. Ship plate, railroad rails, and building reinforcement rods (*plat*, *rel*, and *besi baton*) are considered high grade. Automobile shock absorbers made of spring steel (*per mobil*) are also popular for some purposes. For their supply of charcoal, empu pedagang take their trucks directly to the charcoal-producing villages, again eliminating one or more layers of middlemen.

By contrast, independent perapen owners buy their supplies from middlemen. They buy either from scrap yards and stores in a nearby town or marketplace, or from small traders who visit the village. Either way they pay a higher unit price than empu pedagang do for supplies. Some independent perapen owners also use high-grade scrap, but if they have cash flow problems they may be forced to use lower grades. Lower grades consist of thinner, smaller pieces of metal, often with a considerable amount of rust. They include such things as old knives, old fry pans, packing-case bands, bedsprings, and bicycle spokes. Lower grades are suitable mainly for producing knives and very small tools such as woodcarving chisels. In general there is a positive correlation between the size of a tool and profits. Thus perapen who make large tools from high-grade scrap earn more total profit than perapen who make small tools from low-grade scrap.

Empu pedagang also travel farther in search of marketing outlets. They have a better understanding of regional variations in supply, demand, and price, and are able to take advantage of those variations to increase their profits. For example, the rice-growing season does not begin at the same time in every district. By traveling a circuit to different districts, the empu pedagang may be able to hit the peak season for agricultural tools in each district.

Some industries work strictly by the job order while others engage in stock accumulation. Blacksmithing combines the two. If a buyer contacts a perapen owner and places an order, the perapen owner will stop producing other types of tools and give priority to that order. If there are no orders the perapen owner will continue to accumulate stock, selecting the types of tools to be made based on his market experience and any information obtained from tool traders. Although villages and districts differ in this regard, a ratio of one to two or one to three is typical. In other words, two or three times as many tools are made under the stock accumulation model as under the job order model. Each system has its risks. If tools are made by the job order, there is the risk that the tools will not be picked up. This risk is reduced if the buyer is well known to the perapen owner, supplies some of the scrap iron used, or gives an advance payment. The risk of stock accumulation is that production levels will outstrip market demand during slow periods, creating a cash flow crisis for the perapen owner. Perapen owners try to develop trade partners who will place standing orders or at least frequent orders. The Indonesian word for trade partner is *langganan*, which implies an open-ended or continuous relationship. In the blacksmithing trade the best langganan are the owners of hardware stores or wholesale tool traders in the marketplace, who can be counted on to place fairly large regular orders. If a perapen owner has two or three dependable langganan who take most of his production, the task of marketing is greatly facilitated. The perapen owner makes a delivery to his langganan once a week or once a month, according to their agreement, and receives instructions at the same time for the next order. Langganan relationships are highly prized and carefully nurtured. They often extend over a period of many years, and may even be passed down from father to son. It is considered discourteous to interfere with the langganan relationship of another perapen owner from one's own village, but the langganan of a perapen owner from another blacksmithing village is fair game.

The langganan relationship is characterized by a curious type of credit arrangement. When the relationship is first established and the perapen owner delivers his first load of tools, his langganan gives him 50 percent of the payment, with the promise that he will receive the remaining 50 percent when he makes his second delivery. At his second delivery he receives the remaining 50 percent for his first load, plus 50 percent of the payment for his second load. At his third delivery he similarly receives the remaining 50 percent for his second load, plus 50 percent for his third load, and so on. Thus except for the first delivery, he always receives 100 percent, but the langganan always owes him money. The purpose of this arrangement is to symbolize the continuity of the relationship. If the credit is ever fully paid off, it is a sign that the relationship has been severed. Credit within the framework of a langganan relationship does not entail hidden interest. In fact, langganan often demand and receive preferential price treatment.

The usual direction of credit in rural Indonesia is from raw material supplier to village industry producer to product buyer. This sometimes creates the appearance that smaller and weaker parties are giving credit to larger and stronger ones. For example, there are armies of rural poor women in Bantul district south of Yogyakarta who make hand-waxed batik cloth for large stores in the south of the city. The women give credit to the stores, in the sense that they receive only 50 percent of their piece-rate payment at the time they turn over (*setor*) the waxed cloth to the stores. It must be remembered, though, that much of the credit extended is within the framework of established langganan relationships which operate as described above. Thus the batik waxers view the store owners as their langganan, and except for the first time they setor, they actually receive 100 percent payment every time they come in.

The situation is similar in the blacksmithing industry. Petty charcoal traders who visit the village often extend partial credit to the perapen owners, whom they view as their langganan. Local scrap yards may also give credit to the perapen owners on purchases of iron. The perapen owners in turn extend credit to the hardware stores and wholesale market traders who buy their tools. Occasionally the direction of credit is reversed. For example, a buyer who comes to the village and places a large order may give an advance payment to help cover the cost of raw materials. When a buyer comes to the village to place a large order, he usually prefers to work through a single perapen owner. If the order is too large for the perapen owner to handle on his own within the buyer's deadline, he splits it with other perapen owners, giving priority to close relatives and friends. In effect the other perapen owners become his temporary subcontractors. The first perapen owner coordinates delivery and payment, and has the right to take a small commission (*komisi*) off the top as a finder's fee. The splitting of orders between two, three, or even more perapen is very common.

Any perapen owner can coordinate an order that is split between a small number of perapen. Yet without a four-wheeled vehicle or warehouse, an ordinary perapen owner cannot handle a really large order. Such an order is nearly always turned over to the empu pedagang, in his capacity as either a private businessman or the head of the cooperative. The empu pedagang divides up the order among all the perapen owners who have formed a dependency relationship with him. This is yet another reason for perapen owners to enter a dependency relationship. Otherwise they will be left out when a large order is divided up.

Large buyers prefer to do business with the empu pedagang. The alternative, running all over the village trying to deal with many individual perapen owners, is usually unacceptable. Buyers sense that the empu pedagang is an important, capable person whom they can trust to look after their order. In exchange for a slightly higher price per tool, the empu pedagang coordinates all aspects of production, from purchasing to delivery, guarantees that production deadlines will be met, and also guarantees some measure of quality control and standardization.

Sometimes the large buyer is an agent of the government, or a government subcontractor. The metal casting hamlet of Batur, for example, was dependent for many years on government contracts to produce spare parts for sugar-refining machinery and locomotives. Similarly, the main empu pedagang from Kajar had a standing order for many years to produce agricultural tools for the government's transmigration program. The government did not purchase these items directly from Kajar, but through an ethnic Chinese subcontractor who lived in the city of Semarang.

Seasonality and Labor Continuity

Many village industries are affected by seasonality. One cause of seasonality is a change in the availability or price of a key raw material. Makers of tapioca chips (*krupuk*), for example, can get tapioca flour cheaply after the cassava harvest, but the supply goes down and the price goes up a few months later. This may cause a profit squeeze. If profits are eliminated by such a squeeze, the industry stops producing temporarily.

A change in the supply or price of renewable fuels also affects many industries. Clay product industries use a variety of renewable fuels, including wood, rice straw, cane straw, and bamboo leaves, to fire their products. Petty traders who sell these materials may stop collecting in the rainiest months. The price of those fuels which are still available goes up, again causing a profit squeeze. For many industries sun-drying is a key stage in the production process. This is true of clay product industries, since the products must be sun-dried for several days before they are fired, and of matting and soft-fiber industries, since the fibers must be sun-dried before they are woven. It is also true of many food-processing industries, such as those producing salt fish, dried banana chips, and cassava chips. Again, the difficulty in sun-drying may cause production levels to drop by 50 percent or more during the rainy season.

Seasonality in small industries can also be caused by a change in the availability or price of labor, either unpaid family or hired labor. This is particularly true during the rice planting and harvesting seasons, when workers can earn a relatively large amount of income, in the form of cash or harvested rice, in a short time. Even when workers earn more total income from small industry activities, they often try to get away during the planting and harvesting seasons. Some enterprise owners just accept this, while others try to retain their workers by threatening to fire them or by offering them bonuses to stay.

Seasonality can also be caused by a change in market demand. In the Yogyakarta area and in Bali, demand for all types of handicrafts is strongly affected by the ebb and flow of tourists. The big months for tourists are June to August, when schools let out in Europe and America, and December to January, when Australian tourists visit during their Christmas holidays. There are smaller peaks for domestic tourism during the Indonesian school holidays and the major Islamic holiday of Lebaran (Ramadan). Garment and shoe industries are particularly affected by seasonal changes in market demand. Most Indonesians try to buy a new outfit for themselves and their children for the Lebaran holidays, creating a sharp peak of demand for about six weeks before these holidays. Garment industries that produce clothing for the tourist market are affected by the tourist seasons. Industries making school uniforms or school sports outfits experience a sharp peak during the two months before school starts, after which demand drops off to nearly zero.

If seasonality is caused by a change in the supply or the price of key raw materials, an entrepreneur with a large amount of capital can take advantage of the situation by stockpiling. He (or she) can buy up raw materials in bulk when they are cheap, store them in a warehouse, and then make a profit by distributing them to small producers when the price goes up. If an entrepreneur has his own production enterprise, stockpiling gives him the advantage of using cheap raw materials year-round while smaller producers are suffering seasonal profit squeezes. In villages which make cassava chips, large entrepreneurs try to buy up as much tapioca flour as possible after the cassava harvest, when it is cheap. They do this by driving their trucks directly to the flour factories in cassava-growing districts. They use part of the flour for their own production enterprises and distribute the rest to small producers when the price goes up. If seasonality is caused by a change in market demand, an entrepreneur can also take advantage by stockpiling. He does this by buying up finished products in the slow seasons when producers are short of cash and willing to sell cheaply. He stores these finished products in a warehouse until the price goes up, at which point he markets them. If the entrepreneur has his own retail outlet, this gives him a bigger profit margin in the peak seasons than retailers who do not stockpile. If he does not have his own outlet, he can distribute the goods at a profit to small retailers. In Bali, for example, woodcarvers are often forced to sell their statues cheaply to large traders in the slow tourist seasons. They do this because they need money to live on, to pay their workers, and to buy new supplies of wood. Some of the large traders own art galleries and retail the statues directly to tourists. Others are intermediaries, who sell the statues to art galleries. Some entrepreneurs in the statue industry stockpile at both the supply and marketing ends, stockpiling both the wood used in carving and the finished statues. Stockpiling at the marketing end is also common in the painting industry in Bali.

Blacksmithing and other metalworking industries are also affected by some of these types of seasonality. The supply of iron is steady year-round, but the supply of charcoal is not. It is difficult to make charcoal from wood that is wet, so the supply goes down and the price goes up in the rainy season. Deliveries from charcoal makers become erratic in the rainy season, and perapen owners are forced either to stop producing or to go to town to look for charcoal supplies. If they find charcoal supplies the price is likely to be high. It is not uncommon in the rainy season for perapen owners to spend more on charcoal than on scrap iron. Not surprisingly, empu pedagang nearly always buy up large amounts of charcoal in the dry season when it is cheap, and stockpile it in their warehouses for distribution during the rainy season. This gives them a considerable advantage over independent perapen owners, who generally do not own warehouses and do not have the capital to stockpile.

There is also seasonality in the demand for tools. Certain agricultural tools are needed at certain times during the rice-growing cycle. Spades, hoes, harrows, and plow tips are needed during the planting season, weeding tools during the growing season, and harvest knives (*ani-ani*) or sickles during the harvest season. Traditionally villagers bought new agricultural tools and repaired their old tools just before the start of the rainy season, creating a single sharp peak of demand. That pattern still prevails in areas where a single rainy-season crop of rice is grown, for example in drier districts and in parts of the outer islands where irrigation systems are not well developed. In areas where multicropping has been introduced, the single sharp peak has been transformed into a series of smaller peaks. The demand for carpentry tools, on the other hand, still peaks sharply in the two or three months after the rainy-season harvest. This is because villagers have plenty of cash in their pockets for housebuilding and house repairs, and the weather has dried out sufficiently to permit construction. There may be other peaks based on local activities. Stone quarrying, for example, tends to be a dry-season activity because the pits fill up with water during the rainy season. Thus in districts where stone quarrying is important, demand for crowbars, pickaxes, and sledgehammers goes up at the beginning of the dry season. Although the demand for many types of tools is seasonal, there are a few products that show continuous demand, for example kitchen knives.

Because demand for many types of tools is seasonal, most perapen vary the products that they make from month to month and week to week. Every blacksmithing village knows the local pattern of demand, and perapen owners adjust their production to fit this pattern, deviating only when they receive special orders. Tool traders also provide additional information on demand. By varying the products that they make, most perapen are able to stay open year-round. But obviously a perapen owner who has enough capital to stockpile tools for a few weeks until demand goes up, and continue buying supplies and paying wages even when there are no sales, is in a better position than the perapen owner who does not have enough capital to stockpile.

Cash flow problems during periods of slow market demand, combined with profit squeezes due to seasonal increases in charcoal prices, act to drive the weaker perapen owners into the arms of empu pedagang. This is particularly so if the perapen owner's household has no source of income other than blacksmithing with which to meet daily living expenses. As mentioned above, it helps if the female members of the household, who are not usually busy in the perapen, have enterprises of their own which generate a continuous flow of income year-round.

Technical Change and Labor Productivity

Technical change has begun to affect perapen in recent years. Formerly only persons who could afford to buy large diesel engines had access to electric power. Such persons were few, seldom more than one or two per village. In the 1980s the government extended electric power lines to most densely populated rural areas, enabling ordinary perapen owners to use small pieces of low-wattage machinery. The two most popular types of machines used are the *blower* (an electrically powered rotary bellows) and the gerinda listrik (an electrically powered edge grinder). Some perapen owners make their own blower and gerinda listrik, using small motors cannibalized from old sewing machines and motorcycles. But urban machine shops are now producing these items cheaply, and most perapen owners are buying them ready-made. It is estimated that one-quarter to one-half of all perapen now use at least one piece of electrically powered machinery. The price for the smallest model of blower is about the same as for an electric fan, about U.S. $15 (Rp 30,000). Larger and more powerful models may cost up to ten times that much, but are still within the range of many perapen owners. Gerinda listrik come in many sizes and types, varying in price from about U.S. $50 to $750 (Rp 100,000 to 1,500,000). The larger and more powerful models are usually owned by empu pedagang, who continue to power them with diesels. Ordinary perapen owners use the cheaper and smaller models.

Table 1 (pages 4–5) shows that the number of household and small enterprises in code 38 increased from 18,389 in 1974–75 to 39,421 in 1986. During the same period the number of workers increased from 77,886 to 118,211. If we divide the number of workers by the number of enterprises, we see that the average size of enterprise declined from 4.24 workers to 3.00 workers. This is probably the result of the small-scale mechanization described above.

The two blacksmithing jobs that have been most affected by mechanization are those of tukang ubub and tukang kikir. With the help of a blower, usually positioned near the fire hearth, it is often possible to dispense with a full-time tukang ubub. Power outages are still frequent in Indonesia, so that perapen keep their ubub setup intact and use it when the electricity is down. Otherwise they would lose several hours of work time per week. During power outages it is usually possible to call a wife or child from the house to work the ubub temporarily. Otherwise one of the panjak works the ubub.

A perapen that previously hired a tukang ubub can increase profits by using a blower instead. This is because the cost of electricity needed to power the blower is much less than the wages and meals given to a tukang ubub. It makes perfect economic sense, yet one cannot help regretting the loss of the ubub, an ancient, beautiful, and symbolically important piece of equipment. As electricity becomes more reliable, we can expect more and more ubub to be consigned to dusty and cobwebby corners, thus changing forever the aspect of the perapen.

Electrically powered gerinda are used for grinding and sharpening the edges of tools. Inside the gerinda is a grindstone which must be frequently replaced, just as files are frequently replaced. While operating the gerinda, someone must hold the tool in place. Thus it is not possible to dispense entirely with tukang kikir. Moreover, some surface filing and polishing of the tools is still needed, which is done with hand files. A large perapen that formerly used two tukang kikir may be able to get by with one if the owner has purchased a gerinda. If a small perapen formerly used one tukang kikir, the owner may decide to dispense with him and ask the other workers to help with filing in the evening hours.

Thus far mechanization has been used in the blacksmithing industry to increase profits for the owner by reducing labor costs. The average labor productivity per worker for the remaining workers has gone up, because fewer workers are being used, but the total productivity of the perapen has remained the same: production targets have not been increased. This is probably because the main task, forging, has not yet been mechanized. If a forging machine were developed or introduced, it would be possible to increase targets and the total productivity of the perapen would go up. This assumes that the market for tools continued to expand so that production increases were absorbed.

There are two ways that village industries can mechanize. First, they can continue to make the same types of products but adopt labor-saving technologies which increase profits to the owner by reducing labor costs. This is the pattern seen thus far in Indonesian perapen. A second way to mechanize is to adopt technologies which allow producers to expand their range of product types. An example can be taken from the Pakistani Punjab. Formerly Punjabi smiths made a range of agricultural and hand tools similar to those made by Indonesian smiths. In the 1980s some Punjabi smiths bought small, motorized metal-bending machines and drills, which they used to produce tractor tines. They were able to market these tines successfully through agricultural supply stores. Tractor tines come in sets and are attached to the tractor by ordinary bolts. When the tines wear out they can easily be replaced by the farmer. By expanding into a new product type, Punjabi smiths were able to greatly increase their profits with no displacement of labor.[8]

It is hoped that Indonesian smiths will begin to adopt this second pattern of mechanization in the future, which would bring them into direct competition for the first time with larger, urban-based machine shops and factories.

Some Special Technical Problems

There was a long-term trend throughout the twentieth century for the price of charcoal to go up. This trend, unrelated to seasonality, was caused by deforestation and the steady retreat of forest boundaries, a pattern particularly evident on Java, where most of the remaining forests are on the slopes of volcanos. Early in the century charcoal was so cheap and plentiful that villagers used it for cooking instead of wood.[9] Nowadays villagers use wood and kerosene for most cooking purposes, because charcoal is too expensive. Sellers of street food who make saté (barbecued meat sticks) still use charcoal to impart a smoky flavor to their product, and it is used for a few other specialty food items. Otherwise the use of charcoal is limited mainly to metalworking industries.

Saté sellers are able to use a cheap grade of charcoal, usually made from the twigs and branches of the *pete cina* (*lamtoro*) tree. Unfortunately this type of charcoal burns too fast and does not produce the intense but steady heat needed for blacksmithing. Blacksmiths require charcoal made from the somewhat larger branches, trunks, and stumps of hardwood species. On Java blacksmiths overwhelmingly prefer charcoal made from *jati* (teakwood). But the teak forests on Java are all protected by the Forestry Department: every tree is numbered, and it is illegal to log teak trees for the purpose of making charcoal. Some illicit charcoal production from newly felled trees undoubtedly goes on, but it is certainly more difficult and more dangerous for charcoal makers to do this than it was a century ago. The Forestry Department is now the only agency which can legally fell teak trees in government-controlled forests. They sell the wood at auction to traders, who resell it to furniture makers and woodcarvers for a very high price per cubic meter. Forestry Department agents sometimes lie in wait along the side of roads leading into blacksmithing villages, and confiscate any teak charcoal going into the village. The Forestry Department does sell tickets which allow villagers to enter government forests and collect jati leaves, twigs, and branches. The leaves are sold as vegetable wrappers, while the twigs and branches are either sold directly as fuelwood or made into charcoal. Some legal jati charcoal also comes on the market after road-widening projects.

Owing to deforestation, the price of charcoal has steadily risen relative to the price of other inputs such as iron and wages. This is the most serious problem facing smiths on Java, and there is a need to adopt an alternative fuel. The most reasonable candidates are coal, coke, and coconut-shell charcoal. Coal is available from Sumatra now that the coal mines have been reopened by the government, but most of the product is exported and little reaches the local market. At any rate, smiths report that the heat produced by coal is too great for their purposes. According to Kahn, Minangkabau smiths sometimes use surface coal collected outside old coal mines that have fallen into disuse, but it must first be converted into coke by pre-burning (Kahn 1980, 83). As for coke, most of what is available in Indonesia is the byproduct of a now-extinct technology, the coal-burning locomotive. Villages which use coke are usually exploiting waste heaps near old railway terminals which are now almost exhausted. Coconut shell, on the other hand, is available in abundance everywhere in Indonesia. It is occasionally used to make long-handled food dippers and ladles, or as a fuel for clay product industries, but much of it is discarded. Smiths in Aceh and Bali frequently make their own coconut-shell charcoal on a small scale, and it seems to be suitable for forging. What is lacking, therefore, is commercial production and distribution on a larger scale.[10]

A second problem faced by smiths is the high cost of files. Files must be made of metal harder than the iron or steel being worked on. Formerly all files were imported, usually from China, Canada, or Germany, and the price was very high by rural Indonesian standards. Nowadays some Indonesian-made files are on the market, which are cheaper but do not last as long. The average perapen uses up about two imported or four local files each month, and this cuts heavily into profits. It is possible to refurbish files, but again, the refurbished files do not last very long. If a rotary edge grinder is used, the small grindstone inside the grinder must also be frequently replaced. On Java smiths usually accumulate their iron filings and sell them by the kilogram to petty traders who go from perapen to perapen. The price received for filings is low, but it adds something to profits. On Bali and the outer islands filings are usually discarded.

Profitability

It is relatively easy to calculate the profits of perapen owners. Since there are three types of perapen owners, three formulas are needed. The simplest formula is for the perapen owner who is not independent: profit for the perapen owner and his family equals gross income from the sale of tools to the empu pedagang, after his deductions for the price of any raw materials (iron and charcoal) received, plus income from the sale of filings, if any, minus expenditure for real wages (cash plus the value of food, drinks, cigarettes, holiday gifts or bonuses, etc.) if hired workers are used, minus expenditure for electricity if used, minus expenditure for replacement of files and grindstones, minus expenditure for any incidentals used (varnish, rustproofing, wood for knife handles).

A slightly more complex formula is needed for the independent perapen owner: profit for the perapen owner and his family equals gross income from the sale of tools on the open market, plus income from the sale of filings if any, minus expenditure for iron and charcoal, minus expenditure for transporting iron, charcoal (if not delivered), and finished tools by hired vehicles or public transport, minus expenditure for real wages if hired workers are used, minus expenditure for electricity if used, minus expenditure for replacement of files and grindstones, minus expenditure for any incidentals used.

If the perapen owner acts as his own empu, his profit will be considerably higher than if he uses a hired empu. As explained above, some empu pedagang own more than one perapen and thus earn less profit per perapen because they use hired empu, but more total profit.

The business operations of empu pedagang are considerably more complex and variable. Often they consist of several "subunits" which handle trade, production, and finishing. A rough formula would apply to most empu pedagang: profit for the empu pedagang and his family equals gross income from wholesaling tools to traders, hardware stores, etc., plus income from the sale of filings and cuttings if any, plus hidden interest received from dependent perapen owners on raw materials (i.e. the difference between the actual cost of iron and charcoal distributed and the set price as deducted from payments made to dependent perapen owners), minus expenditure (actual) for iron and charcoal, minus expenditure for transport (usually gasoline and maintenance for a vehicle already owned), minus additional payments given to dependent perapen owners for tools made (after the set price of iron and charcoal given out is deducted), minus expenditure for real wages for hired labor used, including hired smiths, warehouse workers, and vehicle drivers, minus expenditure for electricity and diesel fuel, minus expenditure for replacement of files and grindstones, minus expenditure for any incidentals used.

Two expenditure items left out of these formulas are depreciation and interest payments. With the exception of files and grindstones, most of the furnishings of the perapen and the perapen itself last for many years, even generations, so that depreciation is a very minor item. With mechanization, depreciation may become more of an issue in the future. Because files and grindstones last such a short time, they have been included in the formula above as working capital rather than capital expenditures.

Nowadays many perapen owners augment their working capital or obtain capital for equipment purchases by taking out bank loans. Empu pedagang tend to take out larger loans from urban banks, while ordinary perapen owners tend to take out smaller loans from village banks. The annual interest rate on these loans usually amounts to 22–33 percent, and any interest paid to banks should be deducted from the formula given above as an expenditure. Buying trucks or minivans on credit from vehicle dealers has also become common in recent years, and the interest rates are similar to those charged by banks.

The usual turnover period for perapen owners is five or seven days, corresponding to the five-day Javanese market week or the standard seven-day week. It is convenient to calculate profit per turnover period, and then convert this if needed to monthly or yearly profit.

A somewhat more sophisticated analysis of yearly profit would take into account seasonal changes in charcoal supply and prices, seasonal changes in tool demand, infusions of loan capital, interest payments on loans, and depreciation. Given an adequate amount of information, it is possible to construct an income forecast for an individual enterprise which will predict profit levels if any variable is changed and warn of possible profit squeezes, work stoppages due to cash flow, and other problems. To be complete, it must also factor in income flows to and from other household enterprises.[11]

An analysis of the profits of blacksmithing enterprises in a number of villages leads to three conclusions:

1. Total profits for independent and dependent perapen owners are nearly the same. Independent perapen owners earn more per tool made, but they must spend a portion of their time on tasks related to purchasing supplies and marketing, so they have less time for production and their output is lower. Their enterprises are also more likely to be plagued by cash flow problems and work stoppages.

2. Profits for independent and dependent perapen owners are not very much higher than those for hired empu, particularly older and more experienced empu. In August 1991, for example, daily empu wages in Kajar varied between Rp 2,500 and 5,000 and averaged about Rp 3,500. Profits for perapen owners during the same month averaged about Rp 5,000 on a daily investment capital of Rp 50,000 to 60,000.[12]

3. Profits for empu pedagang are difficult to determine because purchasing and marketing take place far away from the village. Empu pedagang normally try to hide the actual prices they pay for iron and charcoal, and the actual price they receive from selling tools. It is safe to assume, however, that profits earned by empu pedagang are many times higher than those earned by anyone else in the industry. Furthermore, even if the empu pedagang owns several perapen, the profits that he earns from production are minor and incidental in comparison with those that he earns from trading.

CHAPTER 3

Kajar, a Blacksmithing Village in Yogyakarta

This chapter will present a relatively detailed description of a single metal-working village. The village chosen is Kajar, a large and well-stratified blacksmithing village in Yogyakarta Special Region (Daerah Istimewa Yogyakarta). While of course no village is absolutely typical, Kajar comes close, and it is atypical in only one important way: it is located in a dry agricultural zone where cassava rather than rice is the principal crop.

Data in this chapter were collected intermittently between 1977 and 1991, a period that saw a number of important changes in Kajar. The two most important reference periods are 1977–78, when four months were spent surveying in the village, and 1990–91, when the two most recent follow-up visits were made.

Location and Access

THE VILLAGE OF KAJAR is an hour's drive to the southeast of Yogyakarta in the district of Gunung Kidul. A two-lane highway leads from Yogyakarta to Wonosari, a large, bustling market town which is the capital of Gunung Kidul. Before reaching Wonosari the road begins to climb and wind through a series of low mountains. Looking back from the highest point on this road, one is rewarded with a view of the central Java plains far below.

From Wonosari a smaller road leads seven kilometers northeast to

Kajar village. It passes through the west side of the village and continues on to the small town of Nglipar. In 1977 this road was paved for only five kilometers. Public transportation in the form of buses and minibuses turned around at the five-kilometer point and returned to Wonosari, and Kajar villagers had to get off and walk the remaining two kilometers into the village. Today the road is paved the entire way, and villagers can get off at any point nearest their homes.

The village itself is crisscrossed with a network of small roads and paths. Until 1966 these roads and paths were all of dirt, which turned into sticky mud during the rainy season. In 1967 the military (ABRI) helped to pave a portion of the village roads with gravel. This made it possible for four-wheeled vehicles to enter the village, even during the rainy season. In 1978 the villagers, frustrated at promises of further government assistance which did not materialize, organized to repair the roads, using their own labor and materials. By 1990 the road situation had improved considerably. The main village road and a portion of the side roads had been paved, providing easy access to most of the perapen in the village.

Geography

Much of Gunung Kidul consists of barren karst limestone hills, where crops can only be cultivated in small pockets of soil and there are droughts so severe that the government has to truck in drinking water at the end of the dry season. Kajar is located in a transitional ecological zone. There are several round limestone hills on the east side of the village, one of which has been used as the main village graveyard for many years. Limestone also underlies most of the village at a depth of about two meters. On top of the limestone is a thick layer of soil. On the east side of the village this soil is dark brown and quite fertile. On the west side it is reddish brown and somewhat less fertile. Originally the soil of Kajar was mixed with limestone rocks, two or three parts of soil to one part of rock. Most of the rocks have long since been removed by hand and used to build terraced retaining walls called *galengan*. Limestone is white when first quarried but quickly molds and darkens, so the stone walls are dark. Limestone also occurs in outcrops in several places, mainly in the northern (nonblacksmithing) section of the village. It is mined in blocks for use as a building and foundation material. It is also mined as a raw material for the slaked lime industry.

Although there is not enough water in Kajar for irrigation even in the rainy season, the village is never entirely without water. In addition to rainfall there are three other sources of water in the village—household wells, ground springs, and two streams. The water table under the village is close enough to the surface that wells can be drilled, and about half the households obtain water for domestic purposes from wells. On the east side of the village these wells are about ten meters deep, but they go down as far as thirty meters on the west side. Making a well is not an easy task, since after the first two meters of topsoil the well must be drilled through solid limestone rock. But these wells last for generations. Although the water level in the wells drops during dry years, they never go entirely dry.

Three natural ground springs (*mata air*) bubble forth water in most years, enabling villagers who do not have wells to obtain water for domestic purposes. The largest spring, Sumber Kajar ("the Source of Kajar"), is on the east side of the village. The surplus water from this spring issues forth as a small stream which flows through the village from south to north. It has been dammed up by residents living on the north side of the village and forms a pool there. Another, larger stream called Anak Sungai Oya ("Child of the River Oya") forms the eastern boundary of the village. This stream is a minor tributary of the Oya River, which flows through the northern part of Gunung Kidul district on its way to the Southern Ocean. In drought years Anak Sungai Oya disappears, leaving a dry streambed for several months at the end of the dry season.

The land which borders the banks of the two streams is the most desirable in the village, because crops grown on this land can be easily watered. This is done with a contraption made of two ten-gallon metal containers hung on the ends of a shoulder pole. The farmer first fills the containers with water at the stream bank. Then he walks back and forth through his field, tipping the containers forward so that they act as watering cans. A similar contraption is used by households which lack wells to pick up water at any of the three springs and carry it home to use for domestic purposes.

The three ground springs are considered sacred places (*tempat kra-*

mat) by Kajar villagers. Sumber Kajar has been converted by the addition of cement walls and floors into a public bathing place and laundry area. The style in which it was built resembles the ancient bathing places of Java and Bali, but in fact the walls are of relatively recent origin. One of the other springs (Mata Air Kentus) is shaded by a large and sacred banyan tree, with a few graves nearby. This spring is lined with old stone slabs which form two cisterns. Some Javanese believe that ghosts and spirits dwell in banyan trees, and Kajar villagers avoid passing too close to this spring at night.

One reason why the springs of Kajar are considered sacred is their peculiar behavior. Once every few years they dry up and produce no water for a year or more. Then, about two weeks before the water returns to the springs, its arrival is heralded by a series of loud underground booming noises which sound like explosions. The villagers describe these booms as "magic noises" or "magic voices" (*suara ajaib*). The reason for these underground booms is not clear, but villagers say they have regularly occurred, usually at intervals of about five to seven years, for as long as anyone living in the village can remember. One can only speculate that a series of limestone caves act as water catchments underlying the village, and that the booms are caused by water reentering these caves after a long period of drought. It should be noted, however, that the cycles of the springs do not correspond closely with the cycles of weather. Sometimes the springs continue to flow in very dry years, and sometimes they dry up in wet years.

Sumber Kajar is considered sacred for another reason. At the base of the spring is a wide, flat stone, worn smooth from water action. When the water level is low, one can look down and make out the clear shape of a keris in the stone. The keris is not carved into the stone but seems to be the result of a natural color variation in the stone itself. Villagers consider this image of a keris as proof that the men of Kajar are fated to be smiths, and that men from neighboring villages do not share this fate. For this reason, the perapen of Kajar never hire outside labor, even when they are suffering a labor shortage which forces them to turn down orders. They firmly believe that the men from other villages would not be able to learn blacksmithing skills, even if they were trained by Kajar smiths.[1]

Physical Structures

On entering Kajar by the main village road, one comes first to the large house and spacious yard of Pak Sastrosuyono, the largest *empu pedagang* in the village. In front of the house of Pak Sastro (as he is commonly called) is a general store owned and run by his wife, Bu Sastro.[2] Across the road from this store is Pak Sastro's warehouse. Usually his vehicles are parked in front of this warehouse, and his workers may be busy unloading charcoal or iron from these vehicles, or loading them with tools. The village industry cooperative has its office in the same building as Pak Sastro's warehouse. A sign in front of the office announces the name of the cooperative, Koperasi Kerajinan Pande Besi Gotong Royong (roughly, Mutual Assistance Blacksmithing Handicraft Cooperative). On the north side of Pak Sastro's house is a row of perapen, some of which are equipped with diesel-operated finishing machinery. On the east side of the house is an area where two elderly gongsmiths make gamelan gongs, mainly for sale to village schools.

Continuing north from Pak Sastro's house one passes Pasar Kajar. This is a small marketplace where a lively morning market springs to life on Legi, the first day of the five-day Javanese week. In the early morning hours on Legi this market presents a wonderful spectacle, as petty traders from all over the area pour into the market with their wares. The most common items bought and sold in this market are rice, vegetables, fruits, spices, cloth, and grass for use as animal fodder.

There is another small market in the village which specializes in the sale of charcoal, on a side road just west of Pak Sastro's house. Every day petty traders can be seen at this market, squatting alongside gunny sacks full of charcoal which they have brought into the village to sell to perapen owners. The houses of Kajar are large and spacious, in a style peculiar to Gunung Kidul, with peaked roofs. Usually there is a large room in front, where visitors are received, and several smaller rooms in the back for sleeping and storage. In the center of the large room are four or eight carved wooden pillars, arranged in a square, which support the highest part of the roof. The interior space marked off by these posts forms a *pendopo* (interior pavilion), which is a simplified version of the pendopo at the Yogyakarta palace. Most of these houses are ancestral homes, passed down through several generations in the same families. They have endured because they are made partly or entirely of large planks of solid teak, attesting to the one-time presence of teak forests near Kajar.[3] In 1977 most of the houses in the village still had floors of tamped-down earth. By 1990 most families had added floors of polished stone or tile.[4]

In addition to Bu Sastro's store, fifteen to twenty other warung in the southern part of the village sell a variety of dry food items, snacks, kerosene, cigarettes, and pots and pans. Most of these warung get their supplies on credit from Bu Sastro. A few women and girls also set up wooden tables along the side of the road coming into the village, where they sell snacks and cooked food items.

In lowland Java houseyards (pekarangan) are intensively used for a variety of crops, including fruit trees, vegetables, root starch crops, spices, and medicinal plants. But in Kajar little is grown in the houseyards except tree crops. The most common of these are teak trees, coconut palms, stands of banana and bamboo, and various types of fruit trees (jackfruit, citrus, guava, sawo, *kedongdong*). Yards consist of tamped-down earth which is well kept and regularly swept clean of leaves and other fallen plant material. Although yards are not intensively used, they are large in comparison with yards in the more densely populated lowlands, one to two thousand square meters being a common size. Some families whose houseyards border their fields make no distinction between yard and field: they continue planting cassava all the way up to the house.

One item found in most houseyards is the lesung, or large stone mortar with a wooden pestle. In Kajar lesung are carved from large horizontal blocks of limestone, dug out to form a trough. In 1977 these lesung were still being used to pound most of the cassava and dry rice (padi gogo) grown in the village. By 1990 the lesung were being used only occasionally, for reasons that will be explained below.

Most houseyards also have an animal pen, which houses one or two head of cattle (*lembu*) and a few goats. These pens are in back or to the side of the house and are made of woven split bamboo (*gedek*). The cattle of Kajar are the beautiful pure-white brahmas of India. They are used for working the fields and are also valued for their manure, which before the BIMAS program of the 1970s was the only type of fertilizer used in Kajar. Cattle are also a store of wealth and a form of insurance, because they can be sold off to buy food in drought years.

They are seldom if ever slaughtered for meat, and in fact Kajar villagers rarely eat red meat at all. On festival occasions a few chickens are cooked for offerings, but otherwise the diet is basically vegetarian. The cattle and goats are fed grass collected from the roadsides, and the leaves of leguminous plants grown in the fields. Additional grass can be purchased from small traders at Pasar Kajar. Goats are sometimes set to graze on the limestone hills behind the village.

By 8:00 in the morning the sounds of forging can be heard coming from every corner of the village. Most Kajar perapen make large agricultural tools requiring three panjak, so that the dominant sound is the heavy "one-two-three" of metal hitting metal. When coming close to a perapen one also hears the light counterpoint of the empu tapping instructions on the anvil, the muffled plops of the bellows, and the scraping sounds of the tukang kikir at work filing tools. Some perapen in Kajar are built adjacent to the house, so the outside wall of the house forms one of the walls of the perapen. Where space permits, the perapen is usually built at some distance from the house, in a corner of the yard. Not all households own perapen, of course, because the men from many households work as hired laborers. In the southern section of the village, where the blacksmithing industry is concentrated, about one in every three households has a perapen. These perapen usually have half-walls of split bamboo and clay tile roofs. In their basic layout and furnishings they are identical to perapen found in blacksmithing villages throughout Indonesia. The Kajar bellows is fairly large and is made of two hollowed-out tree trunks, usually trunks of the sawo tree, which has soft, light-colored wood. This bellows is always used with a bamboo or wooden bellows platform. The Kajar quenching trough is rectangular and carved from a dark tuft stone which is not found in Gunung Kidul and must be brought from the lowlands. In the older perapen these quenching troughs have been passed down through several generations.

Village Administration

Kajar is not, in fact, the name of a village. Rather it is the name of a cluster of three hamlets (dukuh/dusun) within the village (desa/kelurahan) of Karangtengah. The official names of these hamlets are Kajar I, Kajar II, and Kajar III. Originally there was another hamlet in the village called Kajar IV, but this was merged with Kajar III when the hamlet head died and there was no one to replace him. To the north of the Kajar section of the village are two other hamlets, Kedung I and II, which are also involved in blacksmithing. Still further north are five more hamlets, making a total of ten. The five northern hamlets are not involved in blacksmithing at all. The men from three of these hamlets earn their living principally from the limestone industry. The men from the remaining two hamlets, who are circular migrants, sell noodle soup (*bakmi* and *bakso*) in the streets of Yogyakarta. Thus, as the headman of Karangtengah once explained, every hamlet in the village has its own economic specialization.

Of the ten hamlets in Karangtengah village, the most prosperous are the five southern hamlets where the blacksmithing industry is located. These are also the most densely populated hamlets, containing two-thirds of the village population. The three Kajar hamlets dominate the social and political life of the village, and most of the village leaders come from the Kajar section. The three Kajar hamlets tend to act as a faction in opposition to the two Kedung hamlets.

There are two types of village headmen in rural Indonesia, lurah and *kepala desa*. Lurah are traditional headmen who are elected by the villagers and paid by being given the usufruct rights (tanah bengkok) to farm specific fields (mostly *sawah*) which are owned by the village and used instead of a cash salary for village officials. Kepala desa, on the other hand, are appointed by the government. They are often outsiders, such as retired military men, and are paid a government salary. Karangtengah still has a traditional lurah, a man named Pak Paeran, who is the younger brother of Pak Sastro. In administering the village Pak Paeran is assisted by several other officials, including a treasurer, a scribe, a security officer, and a social welfare officer. These village officials are collectively known as pamong desa, and they are also paid with the use of village-owned land. The very powerful social welfare officer, Pak Hartoutomo, is Bu Sastro's brother. Each of the ten hamlets also has a hamlet head (*dukuh/kepala dukuh*) who reports to the lurah. Another brother of Bu Sastro is the dukuh of Kajar I, and the dukuh of Kajar III is simultaneously her first cousin and the brother of her sister-in-law.[5]

Indonesia is divided into an administrative hierarchy of provinces (provinsi), districts (kabupaten), subdistricts (kecamatan), villages (desa/kelurahan), and hamlets (dukuh/dusun). These are headed respectively by a governor (*gubernur*), district head (*bupati*), subdistrict head (*camat*), village headman (lurah or kepala desa), and hamlet head (dukuh/kepala dukuh/*kepala dusun*). Kajar can be placed within this administrative hierarchy as follows:

—provinsi: Daerah Istimewa Yogyakarta (Yogyakarta Special Region)
—kabupaten: Gunung Kidul
—kecamatan: Wonosari
—desa/kelurahan: Karangtengah
—dukuh/dusun: Kajar I, II, and III; Kedung I and II; the five northern dukuh[6]

Although Kajar is not the official name of the village, it is the name used in daily conversation, both by villagers themselves and by outsiders who are interested in the blacksmithing industry. It is also the name used in this book.

Demographics

The dukuh of Kedung I is an elderly man who was born in another village and came to Kajar about 1939. He settled in Kedung I hamlet and has remained there ever since. According to his story the land in the Kedung section of the village (i.e. Kedung I and II) was divided among forty families when he first arrived. In 1991 it was divided among two hundred families. This gives some idea of the rapid growth in the village's population during the last half-century. This growth has been caused both by natural increase and by immigration to the village, which seems to have exceeded outmigration.

According to the lurah the land area of desa Karangtengah is exactly five square kilometers. In 1978 this area was divided among 1,011 households with a total population of 5,254 (see table 3, page 130), for a density of 1,051 persons per square kilometer. The average holding per household was 4,946 square meters, or just under half a hectare. By 1991 there were 1,200 families with a total of 6,250 persons and a density of 1,250 persons per square kilometer. The average holding per household had dropped by nearly 16 percent, to 4,167 square meters.

Although average land holdings are declining in Kajar, they are still much larger than in the densely populated wet-rice lowlands of Java. This is generally true for dry-zone villages, because the productivity of the land is so much lower. Half a hectare is the typical holding in Kajar, but the typical holding in the lowlands is about 2,000 square meters. Although holdings are relatively large in Kajar, most families estimate that they produce only about a third of their requirements for starchy staples, and that they must buy the remaining two-thirds. Most of the income to buy additional starchy staples comes from the sale of peanuts and soybeans, which are grown as cash crops, and from nonagricultural occupations such as blacksmithing.

The distribution of land among households in Kajar is relatively equitable, and far less skewed than in the lowlands. Again, this is typical of dry-zone villages. About half the families in the lowlands own no agricultural fields, but it is unusual for a Kajar family to own no fields. The holdings of the pamong desa and a few élite families are larger than average, and can go up to five or ten hectares. These large holdings include land which is owned in Kajar, tanah bengkok in Kajar, and land which is rented yearly (sewah tahunan) in neighboring villages. Outside of this élite group the majority of families own something less than half a hectare, which includes both their house plot and their dry fields.

In the lowlands there are three types of fields: sawah, or irrigable fields; ladang, which are dry fields; and pekarangan, which are house plots. A family is considered landless if it owns no sawah or ladang, even if it owns pekarangan.[7] In Kajar the distinction between landed and landless is somewhat more difficult to make. This is because pekarangan plots are large and some families plant cassava on their pekarangan. Generally this is done by poorer families or families living near the margins of the village. Another factor which creates confusion is the difference between official land classification and actual use. The land registry books kept by the village scribe in Kajar date from the Dutch colonial land registration of 1936 and have been little updated. Owing to population growth in the years since, there has been a considerable conversion of ladang to pekarangan which has gone unrecorded in the registry. A survey carried out in the three Kajar hamlets in 1978 indicated that 29.4 percent of families owned pekarangan but no ladang, while another 19.3 percent owned ladang but no pekarangan. The remaining 51.3 percent owned some of each. Disregarding the type of land, all but ten families (3.6 percent) owned five hundred square meters of land or more, enough to grow some cassava. Of these ten families only two owned no land at all.

Obtaining accurate information on land holdings in Kajar proved difficult. Not only are the land registry books unreliable because they record very few of the changes that have taken place since 1936, but land sold several decades ago may still be in the name of the original owner. Land inherited and divided up by several siblings may still be in the name of a deceased parent. The reason why changes go unrecorded is that a tax must be paid to reregister a piece of land in the name of a new owner. Villagers see no reason to pay this tax unless they need an up-to-date land document for some purpose, for example to guarantee a bank loan.[8] In individual interviews most Kajar villagers are forthcoming about the amount of land they own and the amount they farm. Members of the village élite, however, try to hide the amounts, and give estimates of their holdings that are lower than the true figures. It is particularly difficult to obtain information on land rented outside the village, although this is said to be a common way for members of the élite to invest their profits.

The Agricultural Sector

Although Kajar does not receive enough rainfall for irrigation, it does receive enough to successfully grow dry crops in most years. The traditional agricultural system involved rotating dry staples with cash crops for nine months of the year. During the remaining three months, at the end of the dry season, the fields were left "bald" (gundul), i.e. left to fallow. These three months are known as the paceklik (famine) months. Elsewhere in Gunung Kidul and some other parts of Java, these months are marked by male outmigration from the village in search of wage labor. This does not happen in the blacksmithing sections of Kajar and Kedung owing to the availability of wage labor year-round in the perapen.

The principal dry crop grown in Kajar is tree cassava (ketela pohon), and this crop provided the bulk of the calories in the villagers' diets until recent years. Substantial amounts of corn and unirrigated dry rice (padi gogo) are also grown. In the Javanese lowlands the rainy season usually begins in October, but it does not arrive in Gunung Kidul until a month later. Dry staples are therefore planted in November, as soon as the soil is soft enough to till. Tree cassava and dry rice are planted in separate beds, while corn can either be grown around the edge of a field or intercropped with cassava in a system called *campur sari* ("mixing the essences"). Dry rice is a five-month crop, and after the rice is harvested at the end of March the field is replanted with leguminous crops. Peanuts and soybeans are the most important legumes grown, along with smaller amounts of other varieties such as long beans and Chinese pea pods. Legumes are also planted in the cassava fields at the end of March, by which time the cassava is tall enough to provide some shade. Wherever possible—in fields bordering the streams or near a spring—leguminous crops are watered by means of the shoulder pole contraption described earlier. Every household keeps a few kilograms of these crops for domestic consumption, and they are important for the protein and nutrients that they contribute to the diet of the villagers, but the bulk of the legumes raised are sold to traders for cash. Planting legumes may have the additional benefit of improving soil fertility. Since nearly all the secondary crops which villagers choose to plant are legumes, it is probable that the soils of Kajar are nitrogen-deficient.

Rainfall in Kajar is both unreliable and predictable. It is unreliable because one of every four or five years is likely to be a dry year when the crops fail. It is predictable because the villagers know that this failure will occur and have devised traditional methods of dealing with it. One method has already been mentioned: raising livestock which can be sold in dry years to buy food. Another method involves food storage and preservation.

After the cassava is harvested in July it can either be sold "wet" or sun-dried. Sun-dried cassava is called gaplek. To prepare it one must first peel the cassava with a knife, then sun-dry it on mats in the houseyards. Afterwards it can be stored in one of the back rooms of the house for a year or more. When the gaplek is prepared for eating it is first pounded in the lesung until it breaks up into small grains resembling rice. These grains are then cooked like rice in a pot with water to make a food called *tiwul*. Sometimes a handful of rice or corn is added to the tiwul in the pot. In 1977–78 tiwul was the principal food of Kajar villagers, and blacksmiths claimed that they were not strong enough to work unless they had tiwul to eat. Tiwul stays in the stomach longer than rice, they said, and provides more stamina.

The other two starchy staples grown in Kajar, dry rice and corn, can also be kept for considerable periods of time. Rice is sun-dried on mats like cassava, while corn is dried by being hung in bunches from the interior rafters of the house.

Traditional methods deal fairly well with a single dry year. If two dry years occur in a row, the result in much of Gunung Kidul is likely to be famine. Famines are often exacerbated by sharp increases in the market price of gaplek as supplies dwindle. The worst famine in recent memory occurred in 1962–63. According to villagers, all plants, most livestock, and many people died during this famine. Villagers call this famine *jaman gaber*, or "the time of *gaber*." Gaber is the leftover residue from grated cassava from which the cream has been squeezed. This cream is then evaporated to make cassava starch (*kanji*), and the residue is usually thrown out. The implication is that people were driven to eat gaber because they were desperate for food. Jaman gaber in Kajar coincided with a sudden increase in the number of perapen and the number of villagers employed in blacksmithing.[9] Another famine, not as serious, occurred in 1975–76, and 1991 proved to be a bad year as well. During the famine of 1975–76 the government provided rice to a hundred Kajar families.

Drought is not the only cause of crop failure in Kajar. Crop failure can also be caused by pests, or by rat infestation. Jaman gaber was exacerbated by a plague of rats which arrived in 1963. There is a traditional belief that rats come from the ocean and are sent by Nyai Loro Kidul, goddess of the South Seas.[10] According to Kajar villagers, the rats came ashore in 1963 at Tegal on the north coast of Java. They traveled east toward Semarang, eating a swath of crops as they went, and then turned south toward Magelang, Yogyakarta, and Wonosari. Finally they left by swimming back into the sea near Baron Beach on the south shore of Gunung Kidul. There was another, smaller plague of rats in 1970.

Dry crop farming is not as labor-intensive as irrigated farming. There are many days, even during the nine-month period when crops are grown, when it is not necessary to go to the fields. Most of the labor inputs are associated with planting and harvesting. Cassava has the special feature that it can be left in the ground for a considerable time after it is mature without rotting. This means that it can be harvested and converted to gaplek over a period of days or weeks, so that the very sharp labor peak associated with wet-rice harvesting does not appear. The highest inputs of labor are made by farmers with fields near a spring or stream, who may spend a good deal of time watering during the three months when legumes are grown. In wetter years they dispense with this watering. During the three-month fallow period no labor is needed in agriculture, although stone terraces and equipment may be repaired toward the end of this period in anticipation of the coming rainy season.

Because wages are higher in blacksmithing than in agriculture, men from the Kajar and Kedung sections of the village are reluctant to perform agricultural labor, not only as wage laborers but to some extent even in their own fields. This unwillingness has given rise to an unusual situation in which the agricultural sector in these sections is largely managed by the women, who supplement their own labor with hired male and female labor from other villages. Interviews with a number of married couples indicated that husbands and wives discuss agricultural decisions in the morning. Occasionally the husband will stop by the fields to have a look before he starts work in the perapen. Otherwise all management tasks are left to the wives. Every morning there is an informal labor market along the main road that passes by Kajar, where laborers from other villages congregate. They carry their agricultural tools with them, as a sign that they are looking for work. Women from Kajar come to the main road and negotiate informal labor contracts with as many workers as they need. They then supervise the workers in the fields and dole out wages at the end of the day.

Wives of perapen owners rely more heavily on wage labor than wives of men who work as hired smiths. Partly this is because households which own perapen are likely to be better off and to have more land to cultivate. Another reason is the responsibility that the perapen owner's wife bears for preparing the meals, snacks, and drinks given to the workers. Women from households which do not own perapen perform much of their own agricultural labor. Although there is a traditional division of labor in the agricultural sector in Java, which divides tasks according to gender, this is largely ignored in Kajar. Kajar women routinely perform many agricultural tasks which are elsewhere considered men's work, including soil preparation. When women till the soil they use the pacul rather than the plow. Women from households which do not own perapen may also hire out as wage agricultural laborers to women from households which do own perapen.

Labor arrangements in the agricultural sector in Kajar are not as complex as in the wet-rice lowlands. Villagers say that they formerly used a *gotong royong* system of labor exchange between households, but this has been almost entirely replaced by wage labor.[11] Households which own large cassava fields may sharecrop some of them out to poorer households under a system called bagi hasil. The share ratio is always fifty-fifty. Sharecroppers may in turn hire wage labor to help them in the fields. There is no land pawning (*gadai*) in the area, although the system of renting out fields yearly, sewah tahunan, resembles pawning.

If Kajar villagers are asked to name the principal occupation (pokok) of the village, they always reply "smithing." Although agriculture is important it is definitely the secondary occupation (samben). This is not only because smithing provides more income, but also because it is a more dependable source of income. The risk of failure in the agricultural sector in Kajar is very high because of problems with drought and pests; the risk of failure in the blacksmithing industry is minimal.

Most of the tools made in Kajar are ultimately marketed to consumers in the lowlands. This means that the blacksmithing industry interacts not only with the agricultural sector in Kajar but also with the agricultural sector in the lowlands. Villages in the lowlands are less subject to drought and crop failure than villages in Gunung Kidul. Even if there is crop failure because of drought or rice pest in one part of the lowlands, it is usually possible to look for markets in another part of the lowlands. Thus the market for tools made in Kajar is relatively stable from year to year.

The agricultural cycle in the lowlands affects the demand for tools more than the local agricultural cycle does. This can be seen from the tendency of demand to peak in August and September, when farmers in the lowlands begin preparations for the start of the rainy season in October, and traders begin stockpiling in anticipation of increased demand.

The 1980s saw a dramatic change in the food habits of Kajar villagers, namely a change from cassava to lowland rice as their principal staple. Cassava is still eaten from time to time as a snack, but in much smaller quantities. The underlying impetuses for this change were increased prosperity, embarrassment over the low esteem in which cassava is held on Java, and a desire to imitate the food habits of lowland

Javanese. The more immediate impetus was the decision by a Japanese trading company based in the south coast port of Cilacap to contract through intermediaries to buy as much cassava as the villagers were willing to sell. The cassava was purchased "wet," which means that the villagers avoided the labor of peeling and drying it. Trucks picked up the cassava in Kajar and took it to Cilacap. From Cilacap it was shipped to Japan and used to make animal feed and gasohol. The price per kilo paid by the Japanese for cassava was considerably lower than the price per kilo of the lowland rice which the villagers were now required to buy in large quantity. Nonetheless, all but the poorest households made this transition. Smiths who formerly said that they could only work if their stomachs were full of tiwul now laughed and admitted that they could work very well on rice.

Government interventions in the agricultural sector in Kajar did not prove very successful. Formerly the villagers of Kajar planted a number of traditional dry rice varieties, including two types of sticky rice (ketan). These traditional varieties were low in productivity but resistant to drought and disease. Planting several varieties reduced the risk thst pests would spread across a wide area. Eventually the BIMAS rice intensification program was expanded to include upland and dry-zone villages like Kajar. One requirement of the program was that villagers must stop planting traditional varieties. None of the new varieties distributed in Kajar were successful, and the result was a loss of traditional seed stock and a drastic decline in dry-rice production. In 1991 only five hectares of land in the village were planted in dry rice, or 1 percent of the total land area of the village. BIMAS did have one lasting result in Kajar: it introduced the villagers to the use of purchased inputs of fertilizer and insecticide.

Antiquities

A few years ago, while looking through Van Heekeren's classic work *The Bronze-Iron Age of Indonesia*, I came across this reference to Kajar:

> At one time (a few centuries A.D.) there was a lively megalithic culture in full swing in the most eastern part of Java . . .
>
> The stone-cist graves found in Wonosari in the Southern Mountains are probably of the same period. They were reported by J. L. Moens in 1934

and were examined that same year by A. N. J. van der Hoop. The stone-cist graves are found north and west of Wonosari, just below the surface of the ground. At Kadjar was a specimen lying in north-south direction. The flooring consisted of a large flat slab, the longer side walls of two vertical slabs. Small stone pillars served as additional supports of the cist. The length of the grave was 1.90 metres, the width 63 cm. and the depth 80 cm. It appeared that inside, no less than 35 human skeletons were crammed together, and it is not surprising that all skeletons except the top one had fallen apart. The top skeleton was lying on its back, the hands resting on the pelvis; others had their arms stretched along their sides. The skeletons near the top lay head southwards, whereas the bottom ones lay with their heads toward the north. A host of gifts accompanied the dead: numerous iron tools such as axes and sickle-shaped knives, small bronze rings (found in fragments) and many hundreds of *mutisalah's*, of glass (in blue, sea-green, yellow, blue with white lines), and three only of carnelian with a hexagonal cross-section. A small earthenware bowl in the shape of half a coconut was found. A few pieces of coarse fabric were attached to some of the iron objects. One skeleton had a broken iron sword in its left hand (131 × 30 × 10 mm.). In the neighborhood of this grave were other stone-cist graves, which were damaged, and also a few menhir-statuettes and some twenty menhirs. (van Heekeren 1958, 51)

This reference was a surprise, since I had heard nothing about these remains in numerous visits to the village. It became something of an obsession, therefore, to track down more information about Kajar's prehistoric past.

In the illustration that accompanies van der Hoop 1935 (reproduced in Bellwood 1985), most of the items are from the mass grave at Kajar. It can be seen that the items represent a typical Early Metal Age assembly, with one exception: all the iron tools are tanged rather than socketed, calling into question van Heekeren's date of a few centuries A.D. On the other hand, there is a notable absence of any Chinese ceramics. It seems likely that the assemblage dates from late in the first millennium or early in the second millennium A.D. It is even possible that the mountains of Gunung Kidul remained a cultural backwater where Early Metal Age culture persisted long after Indian influence had appeared in the lowlands. One of the beads (item 21) appears to be an "eye-spot" bead of the type known in Indonesia as Majapahit beads. According to Peter Francis, these were made on Java between the tenth and fourteenth centuries (Francis 1991a). The shapes of the iron tools illustrated do not closely resemble the shapes of the tools made in Kajar today. One item is identified by van der Hoop and Bellwood as a keris. It does indeed resemble a keris in being tanged and somewhat asymmetrical at the base. The slightly backward-bending curve of the blade is atypical of keris, but not unknown. Its length is 22–23 cm (about 9 inches), which would put it in the category of a keris or dagger rather than a sword. Bellwood adds the following comments on the Gunung Kidul finds: "In Java and Bali many sites have produced Early Metal phase assemblages in association with slab graves . . . In the listing of the Javanese material given by Heekeren . . . it is apparent that knowledge of these sites is extremely vague, although Hoop (1935) did present a clear report of some slab graves excavated around Gunung Kidul near Wonosari in Central Java. Well-preserved examples of these at Kajar and Bleberan . . . produced evidence for extended burials with a lot of iron tools (mainly tanged knives, a dagger, axes and chisels), bronze rings, and glass and faceted carnelian beads . . . many of these graves may overlap in date with the Javanese historical civilizations, as Hoop thought possible for the Gunung Kidul sites" (Bellwood 1985, 295, 297).

In August 1991 I revisited Kajar, accompanied by Alice G. Dewey of the University of Hawaii anthropology department. One aim of this visit was to enquire about van der Hoop's slab grave. We talked with Pak Karyodiwongso, the last keris maker in Kajar, who was present during the excavations and was able to confirm most of the details of van der Hoop's account. His version of the events of 1934 is as follows: The slab grave was located in the middle of an agricultural field. It was covered over with earth and not visible at all on the surface. Villagers first became aware that there was something buried in the ground when a team of bullocks plowing the field refused to walk over the spot. Every time the owner tried to plow that piece of ground, the bullocks walked up to the edge of the invisible grave and turned either left or right. This mysterious event was reported by the villagers to the palace in Yogyakarta. The sultan reigning at that time was Hamengku Buwono VIII. The palace sent an official to Kajar to confirm the villagers' account. The palace must also have made a report to the colonial authorities, because it sent out some Dutchmen to investigate the site. One of the Dutchmen (van der Hoop) stayed in the village with his wife and children, and spent two months excavating the slab grave. He made sure that every spoonful of earth was sifted very carefully. When the grave was opened it was found to contain the skeletons of thirty-five persons. Many iron tools were found in the graves, stacked up alongside the skeletons. The tools were different in shape from the ones made in Kajar today. They included a sword (*pedang*). Many of the skeletons wore jewelry made of beads. The Dutchmen took away all the tools, beads, and other items found in the grave, but the villagers do not know where they took these items. The Dutchmen also took two of the skeletons, but they left the remaining skeletons in the grave. The grave was then closed again. The Dutchmen paid the owner of the field for the things they took away. They also offered to buy similar beads and items that other villagers may have found. Many villagers sold things to the Dutchmen at that time.

After relating these events, Pak Karyo showed us an assortment of unremarkable keris blades, plus three tools of "old iron" (*besi kuno*) which he inherited from his father. He said that these three tools were not taken from the mass grave but were found by his father "in a forest." The shapes of the three tools again differed from those made in Kajar today. One was a heart-shaped spade or hoe resembling those found in Early Metal Age sites in Bali. All three tools were heavily encrusted with rust and appeared to have come from the same site. Pak Karyo, who is now very elderly and in poor health, is teaching his son to make *pamor keris* blades. Before he dies he plans to give the three tools to his son for use in making a keris. A keris made of such old iron will obviously be very powerful.

One of Pak Karyo's relatives then took us to the site of the mass grave, still located in the middle of a terraced cassava field. Little can be seen because the villagers have altered the site to conform to the current Kajar burial style by adding a new gravestone and a small roofed-over structure.

In September 1991 I contacted Wahyono M. of the Central Museum in Jakarta, who kindly went to the trouble of locating the Kajar finds. Van der Hoop had brought them back to the museum in 1934, where they now form part of the prehistoric collection. The museum has recently added new display rooms for the prehistoric collection, and the mutisalahs and carnelian beads from Kajar, which are very beautiful, have been put on display. The iron implements are all kept in a single drawer in a storage room behind the display rooms. I was allowed to inspect and photograph the entire collection, as well as the catalogue in which Van der Hoop recorded his finds. The iron tools are unexpectedly small and fine, and they have suffered rust damage because the high ceilings in the Museum make air conditioning impracticable. Many of the tools are *petel*—chisels used for woodworking.

In the same drawer with the iron tools from Kajar are four iron rocks. Although not recorded in Van der Hoop's catalogue, they were collected from the same mass grave as the tools. They are irregular in shape and size, and resemble Harrisson's and O'Connor's type f "slag." The largest has a maximum dimension of about 8 centimeters (3 1/8 inches). They all appear to have a solid metallic core, but this is covered by a thick layer of brown rust encrustation. I was unable to determine whether these rocks are natural iron nodules, lumps of smelted iron, or slag. In color and texture they so resemble the Kajar tools that it is hard to escape the impression that they represent the raw materials from which the tools were made. Their inclusion in the grave may indicate that the people buried there were not merely users of tools but makers of tools as well. These iron rocks do not resemble the local rocks, which are of limestone. The Central Museum divides the period between 500 B.C. and A.D. 1000 into the Bronze-Iron Age (500 B.C.–A.D. 0), the Protohistoric Period (A.D. 0–A.D. 500), and the Early Historic Period (A.D. 500–A.D. 1000). The finds from Kajar have been classified as Protohistoric, but Wahyono feels that they are probably later. He gave a rough date of A.D. 700, but admitted that they could be later still.

A perusal of the left panel of the forge relief from Candi Sukuh reveals that some of the tools are identical to the ones from the Kajar grave (see for example the two petel in the lower portion of the panel, near the foot of the "Bima" figure). Kajar is just 70 kilometers (43 miles) southwest of Gunung Lawu. Although Candi Sukuh dates from the East Javanese period (fifteenth century) and thus may be somewhat later than the mass grave at Kajar, it seems likely that the people buried at Kajar had ties with the Mount Lawu area.

Van Heekeren's account indicates that other stone-cist graves were found in the area, as well as menhirs and menhir-statuettes. Most or all of the menhirs and menhir-statuettes from Kajar may have been taken away by J. L. Moens, the Dutch official who first reported the Kajar finds (see van Heekeren's account above). Moens was a long-term resident of Yogyakarta who collected a number of antiquities. In 1980, at the time of the Indo-Pacific Prehistory Association conference in Yogyakarta, I had an unexpected opportunity to see some of these menhirs and menhir statuettes. I was asked by Ardiyanto, a well-known batik designer living in Yogyakarta, to visit his home and look at a collection which he had purchased of more than two hundred of these stones. The following story was told by Ardiyanto: Moens had collected the stones in the pre-war years from two areas, Gunung Kidul and the Pasemah Plateau in Sumatra. When the Dutch were forced to leave Indonesia in the 1950s by President Sukarno, Moens entrusted his collection to his Chinese assistant for safekeeping. The assistant's wife was nervous about having all the old stones around, feeling that they might be inhabited by spirits. She persuaded her husband to give them away to another Chinese living in Yogyakarta, who used them to fill in the double walls of a kiln he was building. To make the walls even more solid, he poured a soft-matrix cement mixture over the statues. The statues remained inside the kiln until the 1970s, when the kiln was dismantled, at which time the owner offered them for sale as a lot to Ardiyanto. Still a student at the time, Ardiyanto thought that the stones might be important and scraped together enough money to buy the entire collection. The cement was cleaned off the stones, and Ardiyanto arranged for students from the anthropology department at Gajah Mada University to photograph and catalogue them. From the Java Archives he was able to determine that Moens collected the stones in Gunung Kidul and Pasemah. Furthermore, he found out that the stones which Moens collected from Gunung Kidul were originally located in the middle of agricultural fields.

With several other participants from the IPPA conference, I had the opportunity to look over the stones. They are mostly small, averaging about 40 centimeters (16 inches) in height. Most are badly worn, as one would expect from statues which had been left in the middle of fields. They seem to fall into three stylistic categories: statues in the Pasemah style, with the original shape of the stone unchanged and human and animal figures carved into the surface of the stone; statues in the rather stiff "ancestor figure" style, which shows no Indian influence; statues in the style of the Indianized period, including statues of Ganesha and other Indian deities. There is of course no way to date the stones at this point, and it is certainly a pity that Moens was so thorough in his collecting.[12]

One other antiquity in Kajar bears mentioning. Near the top of the small hill which is used as a graveyard is a curious black stone, several feet in length. The upper surface of this stone is carved in curious convoluted shapes which are toothlike or hornlike. These shapes resemble those on the clay gable ornaments used in some parts of Java, and they also resemble the flamelike flanges on Balinese gates. The style of this stone in fact has more in common with the style of stonecarving in East Java or Bali than that of Central Java. Villagers say that the stone was already there when the village was founded, and before there were any graves on the hill.

The information on antiquities can be summarized by saying that ancient Kajar seems to have had stronger cultural ties with the Mount Lawu area and districts to the east than with the Yogyakarta area to the west. The mass grave from Kajar could be as early as A.D. 700 or as late as A.D. 1500. Although some Indian influence is evident in the tanged tools and glass beads, the general impression is of a cultural backwater that retained many features of the Early Metal Age.

Traditional Social Classes

The view that Javanese villages are homogeneous ignores the existence of traditional named social classes since at least the nineteenth century. The number of classes and the exact terms used vary from village to village. One system described by Koentjaraningrat divides the village into five classes:

1. the probot dusun, or village officials, including the lurah (referred to in Kajar as the pamong desa) — These officials have the right of usufruct over large tracts of village-owned land (tanah bengkok/siti bengkok), and they usually own large amounts of inherited land as well;

2. the tiyang baku, or descendants of the often legendary founders of the village — These villagers usually own large amounts of inherited land, although, according to Koentjaraningrat, they are still respected by the other villagers if they lose their land and become poor. Their relationship with the venerated village ancestors (cakal bakal) is often supported by their possession of an ancient house or heirlooms, or by their attachment to the sacred grave of the ancestor;

3. the kuli, or common landowning group of villagers who own both pekarangan house plots and smaller amounts of cropland — Historically

the land owned by this group may have been part of the king's domain, and they may have had corvee services to perform in compensation;

4. the *lindung* who only own *pekarangan* plots but no cropland;

5. the *pondok* or *glongsor* who are completely landless, often consisting of immigrants and newcomers. (Koentjaraningrat 1985, 187–93)[13]

It can be questioned whether the probot dusun form a class separate from the tiyang baku, since they are almost always drawn from the ranks of the tiyang baku. The reasons why the numerically greater group of smallholders and landless do not cooperate to elect one of their own are complex; they include respect for the tiyang baku which is reinforced through ceremony, the tendency for probot dusun positions (especially that of lurah) to be passed down from father to son, ties of economic dependency which prevent ordinary villagers from voting freely, and the high cost of campaigning.

In most villages the cakal bakal are regarded as the first farmers who cleared the forest and settled in that area. Some villages claim that their founding ancestor was a member of ancient royalty who left the court and wandered around as a knight or hermit, finally settling in the village. Still other villages, particularly along the north coast, claim that their founder was an Islamic saint or other religious figure.

The graves of the cakal bakal are venerated by the entire village. In certain ceremonies offerings are made to the graves, and the tiyang baku play an important role in carrying out these ceremonies. Sacred graves are called *pepunden* by the Javanese. Sometimes the graves of persons other than the cakal bakal come to be venerated as pepunden. Koentjaraningrat points out that the graves of famous deceased village leaders, famous *wayang* puppeteers or gamelan players, village healers (*dukun*), or religious leaders (*kyai*) may become pepunden and objects of veneration. There are even notorious criminals and greatly loved dancing girls and prostitutes whose graves have become pepunden (Koentjaraningrat 1985, 331). Kajar is curious in that it has two élite groups, an agricultural one whose members belong to the tiyang baku and a separate blacksmithing élite descended from the founding blacksmiths of the village. The tiyang baku all live in the three Kajar hamlets, so it appears that this section of the village was settled first while the other sections to the north were settled by later migrants. The dukuh from the three Kajar hamlets are all members of the tiyang baku, and Bu Sastro comes from one of the most powerful tiyang baku families. The tiyang baku families consider agriculture their main occupation, although some have begun trading in raw materials and tools in recent years.

The second élite group is descended from two blacksmiths, Gunokaryo and Kasan Ikhsan, who are said to have founded the blacksmithing industry in the 1920s. All the blacksmiths in the village, and particularly the empu and working perapen owners, claim to be descended from these two smiths.

It may be that there is some connection between the ancient people of Kajar, who buried their dead with an assortment of iron tools and iron rocks, and the modern blacksmiths of Kajar. If so that connection has been lost in time. The oral history of the village traces the origins of the industry to the arrival of two migrant blacksmiths in the village. The first to arrive was a man named Gunokaryo, from the village of Bayat in Klaten district. Bayat is about seventeen kilometers (ten and a half miles) northeast of Kajar, just over the border in Central Java. Although Gunokaryo had been a smith in Bayat, he worked as an agricultural laborer for nine years in Kajar before deciding to set up a perapen. That decision was precipitated by the arrival of another migrant smith, a man named Kasan Ikhsan from the village of Temon. Temon is about fourteen kilometers (eight and a half miles) southeast of Kajar, near the town of Ponjang. Whereas Gunokaryo was a common smith who made agricultural tools, Kasan Ikhsan could do pamor work and make keris as well. Together they decided to set up a perapen, and Gunokaryo went back to Bayat to get the tools and equipment they needed. The perapen was built in Gunokaryo's houseyard in Kajar I, and he was considered the owner, while Kasan Ikhsan worked as his assistant. At first the perapen only made agricultural tools. Several years later Kasan Ikhsan began taking orders for keris.

Both Gunokaryo and Kasan Ikhsan married local Kajar girls. Gunokaryo had four sons and one daughter. All the sons became blacksmiths and eventually started perapen of their own. The daughter married and had three sons, Sastrosuyono, Gitongadi, and Paeran. Sastrosuyono (Pak Sastro) came to prominence as a raw material and tool trader in the early 1960s and is now the largest empu pedagang in the village. Paeran became a pamong desa at a young age, married the daughter of the lurah, and then successfully ran for lurah himself in 1978, after his father-in-law died. He held that position into the 1990s.

Gitongadi, less successful than his brothers, owns a large *warung* on the north side of the village. Thus both the lurah of Karangtengah and the largest empu pedagang are grandsons of the first blacksmith in the village, though neither has ever worked as a smith.

Kasan Ikhsan, whose grave lies near that of Gunokaryo and is just as venerated, had two daughters. They married two men from Kajar, Martodinomo and Karyodiwongso, whom Kasan Ikhsan took as apprentices. He taught them the difficult art of pamor work, and these two men carried on the keris-making tradition in the village after Kasan Ikhsan died. Since Martodinomo and Karyodiwongso were the sons-in-law, not the sons, of Kasan Ikhsan, they do not really have the blood of blacksmiths in their veins, but this fact is conveniently overlooked by the villagers. Martodinomo, who was interviewed several times in 1978, died in 1988 at an advanced age. Karyodiwongso, whose story of the excavation of 1934 is related above, was still alive in the early 1990s but in poor health. As mentioned, he was trying to pass on his smithing skills to one of his sons. His son is of course related to Kasan Ikhsan by blood through his mother.

Gunung Pancuran, one of the limestone hills behind the village, is used as the main village burial ground. The older and more sacred graves, including the graves of the cakal bakal, are nearer the top of the hill. The graves of the cakal bakal have come to be eclipsed in importance by the graves of Gunokaryo and Kasan Ikhsan. These graves have become true pepunden and are the focus of a local cult. Whenever villagers have a problem such as illness or sterility, or when they are looking to improve their luck, they bring offerings of rice and flowers to these graves. When I contracted an eye infection while surveying in the village and the infection hung on a bit longer than normal, for about two weeks, villagers began making suggestions about how to heal it. At first they suggested that I rinse my eyes in the waters of Sumber Kajar. When this had no apparent effect, they suggested a pilgrimage to the top of Gunung Pancuran, with offerings to the graves of Gunokaryo and Kasan Ikhsan.

Ceremonies and Rituals

Every year on the first day of the first Javanese month of Suro a very important ceremony is carried out in Kajar called a Selamatan Empu.[14]

This differs from the usual Javanese selamatan in that it is limited to the empu of the village. Both empu who own their perapen and those empu who are hired participate, but the other workers in the perapen do not. Raw material and tool traders are also excluded. On the day of the ceremony all the empu in the village don formal dress and assemble in one part of the village. Formal dress for a Javanese male consists of a sarong made of batik cloth, a dark-colored jacket with long sleeves and a high neck, and a small turban made of an elaborately folded piece of batik cloth. If possible, a keris is also worn. Every empu brings a bamboo tray to the ceremony, with food offerings prepared by his household. All the empu then solemnly circumnavigate the village, walking in single file, and ending up at the base of Gunung Pancuran. They climb the hill and place the offerings at the graves of Gunokaryo and Kasan Ikhsan. They stay beside the graves, meditating or praying for some time, before descending the hill. To my knowledge this ceremony is unique to Kajar village, although it includes elements that recall other, more common ceremonies such as selamatan (a ceremonial communal meal) and nyekar (the veneration of graves).

Sometimes another ceremony is held at the end of Sapar, the second month of the Javanese lunar year, called a Selamatan Pandai Besi (Selamatan for Blacksmiths). All smiths participate in this ceremony, which is more festive and includes a wayang performance and other entertainments. This ceremony is not as important and is not held every year.

In addition to the Selamatan Empu and the Selamatan Pandai Besi, the villagers of Kajar also carry out an elaborate version of the Bersih Desa ceremony. This ceremony, which assumes the proportions of a daylong festival in Kajar, takes place during the eleventh month of the Javanese lunar year. I attended the Bersih Desa festival on 30 June 1978, which was particularly grand because it came just after the peanut and soybean harvest so that villagers had plenty of money to spend. Some excerpts from field notes taken on that day are as follows:

> There has been little activity in the perapens for the past week because people have been busy preparing for the *Bersih Desa* festival and harvesting the peanut and soybean crops. Bersih Desa means to clean the village of bad spirits. The money for the festival [has come] from selling the harvest . . . Most of the Kajar people living outside the village have come home

for the festival, arriving by bus or *colt* [minibus], wearing brightly-colored clothes to impress their family and friends . . .

This morning about 7:00 we attended a *selamatan* at the house of Pak Atmo [dukuh of Kajar III]. Excepting yours truly, only men attended and households with no adult males [were] represented by little boys or a neighbor. Every man who attended brought food, both rice and *lauk* [side dishes], and these were collected in the middle of the room. After Islamic prayers from Pak Kaum [an Islamic official], there were Javanese prayers by the oldest resident of the *dukoh*. These were followed by a speech from Pak Atmo during which Joko [my field assistant] and I were introduced and the purpose of our research explained. Then, a little bit of the food was eaten. The rest was redivided and taken home.

Selamatans [were] held separately by each dukuh in the morning; in the afternoon a joint selamatan was held in the pendopo of Pak Sastro's house. During the selamatan Pak Kaum sat in the back doorway of the pendopo, burning incense and reciting prayers over the smoke from the incense. There were three *gunungan* [mountain-shaped cones of rice, used as offerings]. Pak Lurah made a speech, and then there was a financial report from Pak Atmo. He was in charge of collecting festival contributions from all three dukuh. Lastly, a speech was made by Pak Sosial [Hartoutomo].

In the [late] afternoon there was *reyog* performance in the street and yard in front of Pak Sastro's house. This began with a group of masked dancers which included a monster, clowns, etc. They were followed by *kuda lumping* dancers [trance dancers who ride a flat, two-dimensional representation of a horse made out of bamboo]. Finally there was a group of men dressed like *perajurit kraton* [guards at the palace in Yogyakarta]. The reyog was attended by about 2,000 people, including people from other villages. At one point during the reyog a miniature house was brought out on shoulder poles with *padi* [sheaves of rice] piled on the roof. The villagers fought over this rice, while the carriers pretended to protest. There is a belief that whoever can steal a bit of this padi will get a better rice harvest during the coming year. After the performances the reyog dancers formed a procession and visited each dukuh in turn to bring back the food offerings. All day long toys, balloons, oranges and trinkets were sold [by vendors] in the yard and street around Pak Sastro's house. Pak Sastro sat alone in his wife's store most of the day and didn't participate in the festival. In the evening there was an expensive *wayang kulit* and *gamelan* performance in Pak Sastro's pendopo. A famous *dhalang* from Yogyakarta was hired to give the performance.

The cost of the whole festival was estimated at Rp 140,000, of which Rp 90,000 was spent on the wayang performance alone. Pak Atmo collected about Rp 500 from each household to cover the cost. It is said that the relative lavishness of the Bersih Desa festival at Kajar is a sign that the residents are more prosperous than those of the neighboring villages.

In most Javanese villages the graves of the cakal bakal founders are visited on the same day as the Bersih Desa ceremony (Koentjaraningrat 1985, 375–76), but in Kajar this is not done.

In dry years a special ceremony is held at Sumber Kajar, the purpose of which is to pray for rain. This ceremony seems to have a more Islamic flavor and involves berdikir, or the repeated chanting of a ritual formula.[15] The ceremony is carried out by the village heads—the lurah and dukuh—on behalf of the whole village. The village heads meet in the evening and are accompanied to Sumber Kajar by Pak Kaum, the Islamic religious official. Chanting begins and continues without a break until the next morning. Participants sway the body from side to side, slowly at first and then more rapidly and violently as the night wears on. The berdikir ceremony is carried out at Sumber Kajar rather than another location in the village, partly because of the association of rain with water. There may be another reason: a water plant which grows in abundance near Sumber Kajar shakes back and forth violently in the wind. The name of this plant is kajar, after the Javanese word kekajar, which means to shake back and forth. The village was originally named after this plant.

Still other rituals are carried out by individual smiths. Every Legi, the first day of the Javanese week, perapen owners make a small offering to the anvil. Such offerings in Javanese are called sajen. When a new perapen is built the owner must give a selamatan to which the other smiths in his dukuh are invited. Without such a selamatan it is feared that accidents and misfortune might befall the workers.

When Martodinomo and Karyodiwongso were still making keris they performed a number of rituals which were taught to them by their father-in-law, Kasan Ikhsan. According to Martodinomo, Kasan Ikhsan was an expert in ilmu kebatinan, a type of Javanese mysticism. Ilmu kebatinan literally means "science of the inner self," and it consists of a set of practices, mainly Hindu-Buddhistic in origin, aimed at gaining increased spiritual power and insight into the meaning of life. In urban areas practitioners of ilmu kebatinan are usually members of formal groups called *aliran kebatinan* (*kebatinan* means "streams"). These formal groups meet regularly to discuss religious philosophy and meditate. Often they are headed by a teacher or leader (*guru, panuntun*) who provides spiritual guidance. In rural areas there is little in the way of formal organization, and it is difficult to discern the dividing line between ilmu kebatinan and more widespread *abangan* beliefs and practices. By saying that Kasan Ikhsan was an expert in ilmu kebatinan, Martodinomo wanted to express the idea that he was not an ordinary villager but one who had a spiritual power and insight making him different from other men. Most of the rituals which Kasan Ikhsan taught his sons-in-law to perform took place during the month of Suro. He taught that every keris should be started at the beginning of Suro, and then finished at the beginning of Suro the following year. Thus a customer had to wait at least a year after commissioning a piece before he received it. Since the first of Suro is the date of the Selamatan Empu, keris making probably began after this important ceremony. In their prime Martodinomo and Karyodiwongso each received eight or ten keris commissions a year. Before starting to work on these keris they fasted for three days. A small selamatan was then performed, accompanied by sajen offerings of chicken cooked over a charcoal fire, rice, and coconut rice. The purpose of this selamatan was to protect the keris from harm during the process of forging. Holding a selamatan for the keris indicated that they were seen as animate beings. Like children about to be born, they had to be protected from possible harm. Following the selamatan for the keris, another small ceremony was held called *brokohan* or *mong-mong* (from the word *among-among*, meaning "to protect oneself"). This ceremony was a kind of personal selamatan which protected the keris smith from bad spirits. Kasan Ikhsan taught that the entire month of Suro was holy for keris smiths. During that month they must refrain from killing any animals. After the initial three-day fast they must continue to fast every Monday and Thursday during the rest of the month. During the month they must make themselves closer to God (*berbakti* or *bertaqua*). They must also get acquainted with the spirit (*roh*) which exists within the iron to be used. If a smith does not get acquainted with this spirit, he can have an accident while working, be blinded, become paralyzed, fall very ill, go insane, or even die suddenly. Some preliminary forging was done on each keris during the month of Suro, during which time the smith decided on the ultimate form of the keris. He also prayed during this preliminary forging so that the power or pamor would come out in the iron.

After the ceremonies of Suro, work proceeded intermittently on the keris throughout the rest of the year. The keris smiths of Kajar never made keris exclusively but always combined this activity with the production of ordinary agricultural tools, and the number of hours actually spent on keris production was relatively small. During the following Suro, a year later, another group of ceremonies were held, associated with finishing and consecrating the keris. First the keris were all soaked in sulfur (*larutan belerang*) for three days, then in lime juice (*air jeruk*) for another three days, which turned them white all over. Finally they were given an arsenic (*warangan*) bath, which turned the background iron black but allowed the nickelous iron to remain white. This was a dramatic moment, because the pamor patterns became visible to the naked eye for the first time. According to Pak Martodinomo, however, the keris maker could sense the patterns long before this time by using ilmu kebatinan. The arsenic bath was accompanied by a ceremony to which the people who had commissioned keris blades were invited. Other villagers often attended as informal onlookers. This ceremony was conducted by the keris smith, who softly intoned prayers as he bathed the keris, and was followed by another small selamatan for the safety of the keris. Later in the day the keris was fitted with the handle and sheath which had been purchased for it.

History of the Blacksmithing Industry in the Twentieth Century

Javanese villagers keep track of their history by a system of landmark events and periods. Thus villagers may not know the year in which they were born, but they will know whether they were born before or after jaman Japang, the Japanese occupation. Kajar villagers use the following events and periods:

— *hujan abu pertama* (the first rain of ashes): the ashfall resulting from the eruption in 1815 of Tambora volcano on Sumbawa island, east of Bali and Lombok, the largest natural explosion ever recorded;

—*hujan abu kedua* (the second rain of ashes): the ashfall resulting from the eruption in 1883 of Krakatau volcano, west of Java;

—*hujan abu ketiga* (the third rain of ashes): another major ashfall which occurred in 1912;

—*jaman londo* (Dutch times): the period before 1942;

—*jaman Japang* (Japanese times): the Japanese occupation between 1942 and 1945;

—*jaman orde lama* (time of the old order): the regime of the late President Sukarno, from 1945 to 1965;

—*jaman "clash" pertama* (time of the first clash): the taking of Yogyakarta by the Dutch in 1948;

—*jaman "clash" kedua* (time of the second clash): the reoccupation of Yogyakarta by Indonesian troops in 1949;

—*jaman gaber* (time of *gaber*): the famine of 1962–63;

—*hujan abu keempat* (fourth rain of ashes): the ashfall resulting from the eruption in 1963 of Gunung Agung on Bali;

—*jaman Gestok* (time of the Gestapu): the political convulsions of 1965–66, when many villagers were killed;

—*jaman orde baru* (time of the new order): the regime of President Suharto, from 1967 and continuing in 1992.

By village reckoning Gunokaryo set up his perapen during the Dutch times, after the third Rain of Ashes. He built his perapen in Kajar I hamlet, and the industry gradually expanded to the other Kajar hamlets. By 1935 there were several perapen, fewer than ten, but enough to form an association. The association was intended to provide protection against corrupt police officers who waited along the road outside Kajar to confiscate loads of raw materials coming into the village. The confiscation was always done after the tools had already been delivered to the perapen owner and paid for, so that the losses fell on the perapen owner and not the trader. Sometimes the police officers resold the confiscated raw materials in Yogyakarta. More often they returned them to the perapen owner after demanding a large bribe which they called a *restitusi* (from the English word). If perapen owners brought their raw materials into the village separately, the burden of restitusi payments was too great. But by combining loads they could reduce this burden. They were still forced to pay restitusi, but the association could negotiate a lower unit price which would cut less heavily into the members' profits. It would be nice to say that this problem of restitusi was a thing of the past, but unfortunately it is still going on today.

In 1942 disaster befell Kajar in the form of the occupying Japanese army. On discovering that there were blacksmiths in Kajar, the soldiers demanded that the smiths produce weapons for them. They brought loads of confiscated agricultural tools and other scrap metal to the village to use as raw materials, and provided examples of bayonets and other weapons to copy. The smiths were very frightened, so they obeyed. The Japanese also demanded that more perapen be built, and ordered Gunokaryo and Kasan Ikhsan to train men to work in these perapen. Thus there was a forced expansion of the industry to about seventeen perapen.

Later in the occupation the Japanese reversed their policy and became somewhat more humane in their treatment of Kajar villagers. Food production had declined so drastically in Indonesia that the Japanese were having trouble feeding their own troops. One cause of the decline in food production was a lack of agricultural tools in rural areas. The Japanese therefore ordered the smiths of Kajar to begin producing agricultural tools again, and brought them loads of broken weaponry to use as raw material. The smiths were also provided with training and incentives. If the Japanese brought a new type of tool to copy, for example, the smith who made the best copy was given a prize. The smiths were organized in a cooperative called PERPARI and were paid a fixed rate for every tool they made. The tools were dropped off to areas with many farmers.

The smiths of Kajar benefited in certain ways from the Japanese occupation, as frightening as the experience was. The number of perapen and the number of smiths increased, and did not decline again after the occupation. The smiths developed and expanded their range of skills by being forced to copy new items. Even today Kajar smiths attribute much of their success to this ability to copy anything that a buyer might want to order. Most importantly, they learned that tools could be made more economically from scrap than from imported European bar iron. This stood them in good stead in the postwar years when a lot of inexpensive scrap was available, generated by the war itself, such as plate from damaged ships and rails from abandoned railway projects. Imports of European bar iron, halted during the war, never resumed afterward.

The Japanese occupation may have had a negative impact on the supply and price of teak charcoal. In many parts of Java the Japanese built railways into the teak forests and began cutting down the teak trees. Gunung Kidul was one of the areas most severely affected. The teak was used for construction projects in Indonesia, such as enlarging harbors, and some of it was exported to Japan.[16] Under the Old Order government of President Sukarno, the blacksmithing industry in Kajar continued to slowly expand. As the sons of smiths grew up and married, they began to open their own perapen. Problems with restitusi continued to plague the village, involving both police and military men. Sometime during this period Pak Sastro, who was still quite a young man, began trading in raw materials. It is probable that his rapid rise to power in the village owed as much to his ability to negotiate with corrupt officials as it did to his ability to trade.

The restitusi problem led to the formation of a blacksmithing co-operative in 1962. To understand the restitusi problem it is necessary to understand that the government has a monopoly on the sale of both railroad rails and teak. Because Kajar smiths make large agricultural implements, they prefer railroad rails as a raw material. The rails that they use do not come from tracks currently in use but from railway projects begun during the colonial era or the Japanese occupation and never finished. Sometimes they also come from the small railways (lori/leri) used to transport cane from the fields to the sugar factories during the Dutch era, many of which have fallen into disuse. Legally these rails must be obtained through a government-owned company called Perusahaan Jawatan Kereta Api (Office of Railways Company), or PJKA, which supplies the buyer with a document of sale. But to buy rails from PJKA one must have a permit. For years individual smiths from Kajar applied for a permit but were always turned down. Apparently the company was only interested in selling large lots. Unable to get permits to buy rails legally, the smiths were forced to buy illegal rails sold by traders on the open market, which were probably stolen from unused tracks. The officers who preyed on the Kajar smiths for so many years were aware of this problem, and used the lack of a PJKA document of sale as a pretext for confiscation.

A similar situation prevailed with regard to charcoal. Kajar smiths occasionally use charcoal made from other woods, but greatly prefer teak charcoal. Since the teak forests are all government-owned, only the forestry department has the right to log teak trees and sell them at auction. It does this through a government-owned company called Perusahaan Hutan Negara Indonesia (Indonesian State Forests Company), or PERHUTANI. The auction price of teak is very high because it is usually sold to woodcarvers and furniture makers. Charcoal makers could not possibly afford to pay this auction price because of the low value of their product. Some teak charcoal is legal because it is made from smaller branches and stumps collected by charcoal makers from government forests after purchase of a ticket at the entrance to the forest. Nonetheless, corrupt officials of the Forestry Department have taken the position that all teak charcoal is suspect and subject to confiscation. Once again, the officials who confiscate the charcoal are not really interested in keeping it. It is almost always returned to the perapen owner after payment of a restitusi.

In 1962 the smiths received some indication from the government that they would be given a permit to buy rails legally if they formed a cooperative and registered with the Department of Cooperatives. This was done, and three men were elected to head the cooperative, Pak Sastro, Pak Paeran, and Pak Hartoutomo. The leadership of the cooperative has continued to rotate among these three men until recently, with Sastro preferring the position of cooperative treasurer (*bendahara*) to cooperative head. Since neither Paeran nor Hartoutomo is involved in raw material or tool trading, however, it is safe to say that Pak Sastro has always been the de facto head. In 1969 the cooperative was incorporated as a legal body, with the name Koperasi Kerajinan Pande Besi Gotong Royong (Mutual Assistance Blacksmithing Handicraft Cooperative). Since that time the government has channeled all assistance to the blacksmiths of Kajar through the cooperative.

It is difficult and perhaps impossible to separate cooperative business from Pak Sastro's personal business. The main activity of the cooperative is buying raw materials in bulk quantities and distributing them on credit to perapen owners. Perapen owners who accept this credit are then obligated to turn over their tools to the cooperative for marketing. Of course this is exactly the way that Pak Sastro's own business as a trader operates. All perapen owners are officially members of the cooperative and pay in monthly dues, but these dues constitute just a fraction of the working capital used to buy raw materials. Some additional capital has come from government donations to the cooperative, usually in the form of scrap iron. This has occurred just a few times in the thirty-year life of the cooperative, so it appears that most of the trading capital used by the cooperative is "borrowed" from Pak Sastro. Similarly, Pak Sastro's vehicles are "rented" to the cooperative for purchasing raw materials and distributing tools. His warehouse is also "borrowed" as a place to store raw materials purchased by the cooperative, and tools turned over to the cooperative for marketing. When the cooperative was founded Pak Sastro's house served as its headquarters. Later one of the rooms in his warehouse was converted to use as a cooperative office.

Since all purchasing and marketing done in the name of the cooperative takes place away from the village and is controlled by Pak Sastro and the drivers he employs, it is impossible for cooperative members to know what prices are paid. They suspect that Pak Sastro charges hidden interest on all iron and charcoal that he purchases and distributes, whether in his own name or in the name of the cooperative, but they have no way of proving this. Cooperative members know that Pak Sastro takes a personal profit on the tools he sells in his own name, of course, which is his right as a trader. But they suspect that he also takes some personal profit off the top of profits earned by selling tools belonging to the cooperative: in other words, that the profits posted in the name of the cooperative are not the full profits. Again, there is no way to prove (or disprove) this.

Talking to Pak Sastro about cooperative finances produces a defensive reaction, and he insists that he keeps cooperative trading strictly separated from his personal trading. This may in fact be true. As treasurer, Pak Sastro keeps a separate set of books for the cooperative, which he presents whenever the members meet. No one ever openly questions the figures in these books. In private conversations, though, the perapen owners express a good deal of cynicism about the cooperative and its finances. Since this cynicism is colored by jealousy of Pak Sastro's position, it was impossible for me to determine how much of it is justified.

The formation of the cooperative was followed shortly by the drought of 1962–63 and the rat plague of 1963, which led to severe famine (jaman gaber) in the late months of 1963. This collapse of the agricultural sector in turn resulted in a rapid expansion of the number of perapen to about fifty, as people were forced to look for income from nonagricultural sources with which they could buy food.[17]

Disaster again befell the Gunung Kidul area in 1965–66, during the period known in Kajar as "Gestapu times." Gunung Kidul was and

still is a strongly abangan cultural area, where Islam never fully penetrated and where pre-Islamic beliefs and rituals prevail. There is no
village mosque in Kajar, and Islamic ceremonies and holidays are not
accorded the same importance as the abangan ceremonies and holidays described earlier. The village administration includes an Islamic
official (Pak Kaum), but his influence appears limited. In the collabo-
ration in 1966 between the army and Islamic youth organizations to
eliminate communists in rural areas, the entire Gunung Kidul area
came under suspicion, including Kajar. According to Pak Harto, Kajar
was repeatedly visited by a certain army sergeant, accompanied by
members of the youth wing of Nahdlatul Ulama (a traditionalist
Islamic organization), who demanded that victims be turned over for
execution. Pak Harto steadfastly denied that there were any communists in the village, and there was relatively little loss of life. According
to Pak Harto, the villagers are grateful that he protected them during
this difficult period, and that is why from that time they elected him
as head of social welfare.

Jaman Gestapu was followed by a period of rampant inflation before
the New Order government of President Suharto was able to establish
economic stability. Inflation combined with currency devaluations
had a negative impact on fledgling cooperatives throughout Indonesia, because they rendered nearly worthless the funds which they
had collected in the form of dues and savings. This was certainly true
of the Kajar cooperative, and it is probable that it would have become
moribund if Pak Sastro had not kept it alive with infusions of his personal trading capital.

The blacksmithing industry began to expand again around 1972.
Whereas the expansion of the early 1960s is attributed by villagers
to problems in the agricultural sector, they attribute the expansion
of the 1970s to an improved market. The Green Revolution had begun
in the lowlands, creating an increased demand for agricultural tools
and increased incomes with which farmers could buy those tools. At
the same time, improvements in transportation made it possible for
tool traders working out of Kajar and the Wonosari marketplace to
distribute their tools over a wider geographical area. Thus both "push"
and "pull" factors appear to have led to the expansion, but at different
times.

The Indonesian government has long had a program of sponsoring
villagers from overcrowded and impoverished areas of Java and Bali

to "transmigrate" to less densely populated areas of the Outer Islands. Their usual destinations are the southern and western parts of Sumatra, the southern and eastern parts of Kalimantan (Borneo), and the southeastern and southwestern arms of Sulawesi. More recently West Irian (New Guinea) has been added to the list of transmigration sites. Every transmigrant family is supplied with some basic items needed to reestablish itself in its new environment, including a new set of agricultural tools. In the early 1970s Pak Sastro succeeded in establishing langganan trade relationships with two or three tool dealers in the city of Semarang in Central Java. One of these dealers, an Indonesian of Chinese descent, had a large contract to supply agricultural tools continuously for the transmigration program. He channeled a considerable portion of this business to Pak Sastro, who divided it up among perapen owners who had dependency relationships with him. This contract gave a tremendous boost to Pak Sastro's business, and to the industry in Kajar as a whole.

In 1976 Pak Sastro received a great shock. His Chinese langganan came to Kajar on a buying trip and stayed at Pak Sastro's house for three nights on the pretext of wanting to relax. Every evening he took a stroll alone around the village. After the langganan returned to Semarang, Pak Sastro learned that he had been busy during his evening strolls, hiring away many of the younger smiths in the village. He offered them jobs as workers in a new finishing factory that he was setting up in Semarang, with wages nearly double what most of them were earning in Kajar. Estimates of the number of workers that left for Semarang in 1976 vary widely, from thirty to a hundred. Whatever their previous jobs in the perapen, they were employed in Semarang principally as finishers. The majority were single men, although some had families which they left behind. Very few if any came back, instead becoming permanent outmigrants from the village. Their new boss apparently treated them well and paid high wages. Twice a year he rented a bus to bring them home to Kajar so that they could visit their families for a few days.

Before setting up his own factory the Chinese langganan purchased only finished tools from Pak Sastro, but afterward he demanded semifinished tools for a lower price. He stamped his own trademark on these tools before selling them. His trademark, Telaga Mas (Lake of Gold), is now one of the best-known in Indonesia. It is probable that

Kajar is not the only blacksmithing village which supplies him with tools. Although Pak Sastro felt very betrayed by his Chinese langganan, he did not sever their business relationship. The Chinese continues to be one of his biggest customers, although the profit earned by Pak Sastro per tool is undoubtedly less on semifinished than on finished tools. Pak Sastro complains bitterly about the purchasing office of the Transmigration Department because it buys its tools through urban dealers, mainly Chinese, rather than directly from village smiths. He has asked the Department of Industry to intervene on behalf of the Kajar cooperative with the Transmigration Department, but to no avail.

Both the rice intensification program made possible by the Green Revolution and the transmigration program are government-sponsored development efforts. Since these have largely been responsible for creating the "pull" effect noticeable in Kajar by stimulating market demand, it is accurate to say that Kajar has benefited from government development efforts, albeit indirectly. Direct interventions carried out by various government agencies in Kajar have been less successful. Those agencies which have been most active in Kajar are the Wonosari branch offices of the Departments of Industry and Cooperatives. Local officers of these agencies are apt to take credit for the expansion of industry in Kajar, but there is little evidence to support this claim. At best the interventions carried out in Kajar have had a modestly positive effect. At worst they have exacerbated the process of class formation within the village.

The problem of restitusi no longer exists with regard to railroad rails because of the emergence of a new class of intermediaries who could handle the problem. These are the owners of large urban scrap yards who supply metal to village smiths. Some of these intermediaries are ethnic Chinese, while others are pribumi (ethnic Malay). These intermediaries have permits from PJKA to buy rails, and they supply village smiths with the documentation they need to prevent confiscation. But the problem with regard to teak charcoal has continued unabated. When I first visited Kajar in 1978, Pak Sastro and the Cooperative had just lost a load of charcoal worth Rp 350,000. At a meeting with about fifteen perapen owners at Pak Sastro's house in 1991, they admitted on questioning that they were still being forced to make restitusi payments for charcoal.

The Ruling Clique

Seven persons dominated social, political, and economic life in Kajar for the last third of the twentieth century. Six of these persons lived in the Kajar section of the village and were close relatives: Pak Sastro, Bu Sastro, Pak Paeran, Pak Harto (Hartoutomo), Pak Atmo (Atmosumarto), and Pak Harjo (Harjopawiro). Personal status in Kajar largely depends on one's social distance from the members of this ruling clique. The seventh person, unrelated to these six, was Pak Pujo (Pujosartono), the largest perapen owner in the Kedung section of the village.

Pak Sastro is an ordinary-looking Javanese man of average stature and build. He dresses simply in a shirt and short trousers, and there is nothing to distinguish him in outward appearance or demeanor from the other villagers of Kajar. He prefers to keep a low profile in public meetings, and allows others to do most of the talking. Although one hears many stories about Pak Sastro from other villagers, some of them bordering on the fantastic, he seldom talks about himself or his accomplishments. When he does, he tends to downplay those accomplishments. If asked to discuss the extent of his property, or his wealth, his financial contributions to village ceremonies or improvement projects, he always gives underestimates. In part this can be attributed to Javanese culture, which places a high value on personal modesty and abhors bragging. But it is also probably due to a realistic assessment of his situation in the village. He is both highly respected and resented to a considerable degree.

Pak Sastro's mother was Iman Tani, the only daughter of Gunokaryo. His father was a farmer and not a smith. Neither Pak Sastro nor his brother, Paeran, has ever worked as a smith. When it came time for Pak Sastro to marry, he took the daughter of one of the most prominent cakal bakal families in the village as his wife. His wife, Bu Sastro, brought a considerable amount of inherited property to the marriage, including the large houseyard and house where they have lived for many years. Kajar villagers practice matrilocal residence, and Pak Sastro moved from Kajar I to Kajar III after his marriage. Bu Sastro's yard and house have played a key role in the success of Pak Sastro, since all manner of visitors to the village (buyers, suppliers, government officials, representatives of development agencies) stop first at Pak Sastro's and explain their business. He is therefore often in a position to seize new opportunities before other villagers come to hear of them.

Pak Sastro and his brother, Paeran, came to prominence around 1960 when they were both still in their early twenties. This is the year that Paeran first became a pamong desa, and Pak Sastro began trading raw materials and tools about the same time. From the beginning Sastro traded on a relatively large scale, and it is probable that much of the start-up capital he used for trading came from his wife.

Pak Sastro does not use the word "trader" (pedagang) in referring to himself. Instead he uses pengusaha, a modern Indonesian word which can best be translated as "entrepreneur." His conversation is sprinkled with business terms, many of them derived from English, which he has picked up in government-sponsored training courses and in conversation with Department of Industry officials and other outsiders. Like many Javanese, Pak Sastro is fairly self-contained and prone to understatement. There is one topic that causes him to speak with greater animation and enthusiasm, and that is new technologies. Pak Sastro was the first person in Kajar to own a diesel-powered electric generator, an electrically powered edge-grinding machine, an electrically powered bellows (blower), a four-wheeled vehicle, a television set, electric lights, and a camera. Partly this was because he had the money with which to purchase these items, and partly it was because of his enthusiasm for new technologies and anything which he perceives as modern.

One scene of Pak Sastro and his wife stands out in my memory and expresses the poignancy of his relations with the other villagers. While returning from household interviews one evening in 1978, I passed by Pak Sastro's house. He had just purchased the first television set in the village, and was able to pick up programs broadcast from Yogyakarta. Since the village electrification program had not yet begun, the first sets used in rural areas were battery-operated. Pak Sastro and Bu Sastro tried to watch the set in their own home, but hundreds of other villagers crowded uninvited into their house to get a glimpse of this strange new device. Finally, in exasperation, Pak Sastro was forced to place the set in the window of his house, facing outward toward the houseyard. As a sign of their superior status, and their ownership of the the the set, Pak Sastro and Bu Sastro were allowed to sit on two chairs placed in the yard in front of the set. The rest of the village stood up to watch, crowded behind them in the yard.

The second member of the ruling clique is Bu Sastro, a pretty woman from a prominent landowning family in the village. Like her husband, Bu Sastro is a trader, one who specializes in the type of foodstuffs and dry commodities which one finds in a small country store in Indonesia: rice, sugar, salt, flour, kerosene, cooking oil, cigarettes, matches, tinned biscuits, hard candy, dried chips, plastic and aluminum pails, brooms, and many other items. She owns the largest store (warung/*toko*) in the village, which she opened in 1965; it runs along the north side of her house and is attached to it. Bu Sastro sells directly to customers, as well as to the many other warung scattered about the Kajar and Kedung sections of the village. Six of these warung are relatively large, including one on the north side of the village owned by Gitongadi, another brother of Pak Sastro. The remaining fifteen or so are very small. Bu Sastro uses Pak Sastro's vehicles and drivers to make regular purchasing trips to Wonosari and Yogyakarta. Access to these vehicles has given her an advantage in her trade and allowed her to become a wholesaler as well as a retailer. Of course the other warung owners could make their own shopping trips to Yogyakarta and Wonosari, but they would have to use rented transportation which would cost at least as much as the hidden interest charged by Bu Sastro. Bu Sastro gives credit on request to both wholesale and retail customers, and it is commonly said that everyone in the village has a running debt to Bu Sastro's store. When she gives credit to retail customers, there is a 5 to 10 percent increase in the price of the items purchased.

Like the other women from Kajar, Bu Sastro takes primary responsibility for managing the agricultural fields that she and Pak Sastro own. She does not do any agricultural work herself, of course, but hires and supervises a large number of agricultural workers. This is a considerable task when one considers that Pak Sastro and Bu Sastro own many different plots which are scattered about the village. According to the village registry, Pak Sastro owns four pekarangan plots totaling 1.47 hectares and nine separate ladang plots totaling 3.51 hectares. Bu Sastro owns other plots in her own name and the names of her parents. In addition, Pak Sastro and Bu Sastro rent some fields yearly, which are not listed in the registry. Some fields, particularly those rented in neighboring villages, are probably sharecropped out, in which case Bu Sastro would not have the task of managing them. But she does manage a number of plots, and thus must divide her time between this task and running her store.

Pak Sastro and Bu Sastro were unable to have children of their own. This tragedy was overcome somewhat when Pak Harto allowed them to adopt one of his children, a very beautiful little girl named Sulastini. That little girl is now grown and has a husband and daughter of her own. She helps Bu Sastro in running the store and supervising the agricultural work. In addition, Bu Sastro took in several other children over the years, who helped her mind the store and run errands. These were also the children of relatives, but they did not have quite the same status as Sulastini. Some of the boys were employed by Pak Sastro as drivers and tool finishers when they grew up.[18]

Another member of the clique is Pak Paeran, whose trim figure and upright bearing give him the illusion of perpetual youth. From 1942 to 1976 the lurah of Karengtengah was a man named Mangunharjo. Paeran formed an alliance with Mangunharjo by marrying his daughter, and was appointed head of village prosperity (Kepala Bagian Makmuran). He served in this pamong desa position until his father-in-law died, at which time he successfully ran for lurah. He held the position from 1978 into the 1990s and seemed likely to hold the position for life. Like Pak Sastro, he is a reserved man, careful in everything he says and does, who wants to project a more "modern" image. Thus, although Pak Paeran is an elected lurah, his manner of running the village is more new than old. Just as Pak Sastro does not involve himself directly in village politics, Pak Paeran does not involve himself directly in raw material and tool trading. Still, he is one of the three founders of the cooperative and has always held one of the leadership positions in it. In addition, he plays the important gatekeeper function of guiding outsiders to the cooperative and, probably, away from rival perapen owners. It is the custom in Indonesia that outsiders entering a village for the first time stop at the lurah's office or house first, state their business, and ask permission to conduct that business in the village. This custom does not apply to petty traders or farmers from neighboring villages. It does apply to outsiders of a certain rank, such as large buyers, government officials, university students doing research, persons working for development agencies, and all foreigners. If an outsider did not stop at the lurah's office it would be considered impolite, and villagers would be reluctant to talk to him. Before discussion progressed too far, someone would gently suggest that a visit be paid to the lurah. If this was not done, the lurah would be sent for. Thus Pak Paeran, in his gatekeeper role, largely controls interactions between important outsiders and Kajar villagers.

According to Pak Paeran, his major source of income is farming. As the lurah he has use rights to the largest share of village-owned land (tanah bengkok), which is provided to him in lieu of a salary. In addition, he and his wife probably own some inherited and purchased fields.[19] Although unacknowledged, it is probable that both Pak Paeran and Pak Harto, as co-founders and officials of the cooperative, have some profit-sharing arrangement with Sastro which enhances their incomes. Thus although they are not involved directly in raw material or tool trading, they probably obtain considerable income from this activity.

Pak Hartoutomo is somewhat older than the other members of the clique and often acts as an informal advisor to them. As the brother of Bu Sastro, he comes from the same powerful cakal bakal family. From 1961 to 1965 he was the head of village security (Kepala Bagian Keamanan). In 1966 he was elected head of social welfare (Kepala Bagian Sosial). According to his version of events, he protected the village during the Gestapu period. From the time Mangunharjo died in 1976 until Paeran was installed as the new lurah in 1978, Pak Harto also served as acting lurah.

In his personality Pak Harto is somewhat more old-fashioned than Pak Sastro or Pak Paeran. More than most Kajar villagers, he feels strong ties to the Yogyakarta palace, and particularly to Sultan Hamengku Buwono IX, who died in 1988 after forty-eight years on the throne. Pak Harto frequently mentions the sultan in personal conversation, and speculates on such matters as why the sultan stepped down from the vice-presidency. A peculiar story frequently told by Kajar villagers links Pak Harto with Sultan Hamengku Buwono IX. I heard and wrote down this story three times. The most complete version is as follows:

> In 1962 Sultan Hamengku Buwono IX was touring Gunung Kidul. He wanted to take a rest, and asked to stop at Kajar. This happened on a *Selasa Legi* [a Tuesday that fell on Legi, the first day of the five-day Javanese week].

The night before [the arrival of the Sultan], Pak Sastro had a dream. In his dream he heard a magical voice [*suara gaib*] which told him that an important guest was coming the next day. The voice also said that if Sastro wanted to become a wealthy man, he must offer this guest a snack. Whatever was left over from the snack after the guest left, Pak Sastro should save.

When the Sultan came the next day he stopped at Pak Sastro's house. He was seated in a certain chair and given one piece of *lemper* [sticky rice cooked in a wrapping of banana leaf] and one boiled banana. The Sultan took one bite of each. After he went home Pak Sastro saved the leftover lemper and banana in a cupboard in a special room, and he locked the cupboard. He also put the chair on which the Sultan had sat in that room and forbade anyone to enter. He did not tell anyone about his dream, but he gave the key to the cupboard to Bu Sastro to keep.

Thirty-five days [one *selapan*] later Pak Harto had a dream. He also heard a magical voice in his dream which told him that if he wanted to become a wealthy man, he should eat the food that Pak Sastro was saving in his cupboard. The next morning Pak Harto went to Pak Sastro's house, but Pak Sastro was gone. He asked Bu Sastro [Harto's younger sister] for the key to the cupboard and said he wanted the things saved there. Bu Sastro gave him the key. Pak Harto opened the cupboard, saw the moldy food, and swallowed it. Neither he nor Bu Sastro knew that the food was from the Sultan.

Because of this Pak Sastro to this day cannot make any decision without consulting Pak Harto. Pak Sastro is the one who became wealthy, but he never makes decisions or signs papers without consulting with Pak Harto first.

This story resembles certain traditional tales from the Gunung Kidul area. For example, there is a similar tale about two ancestors of the later Mataram dynasty named Kyai Ageng Giring III and Ki Ageng Pemanahan. In that story it is the water of a special coconut that is drunk by mistake. A magical voice had promised that the descendants of whoever drank the water from the coconut would become important kings of Java.

The sacred grave (pepunden) of Kyai Ageng Giring III is in another village in Gunung Kidul named Sodo. As it happens, I also did survey work in Sodo, about ten kilometers southwest of Wonosari, where there is a large bamboo basketry and birdcage industry. The industry in Sodo is dominated by a man named Arjopancuran (Pak Arjo), who plays an economic role analogous to that played by Pak Sastro in Kajar. In Sodo they tell a similar tale about Pak Arjo. They say that Sultan Hamengku Buwono IX came to Sodo to visit the grave of Kyai Ageng Giring III, who is his ancestor seven times removed. Before going home he stopped to rest at the home of Pak Arjo. The sultan was given a chair to sit on in a shady place. He was also given coconut water to drink, because there was not enough time to boil water for tea. After drinking the coconut water the sultan gave his servant a Rp 50 coin to give to Pak Arjo. Pak Arjo said that he did not want the money and would rather have a blessing from the sultan. The sultan sent back the message that Pak Arjo should not judge the coin by its face value but should save the coin carefully. After that Pak Arjo became the richest man in Sodo, and all his children became rich too.

A villager from Sodo recounted a more complete version of the story of Kyai Ageng Giring III:

> Kyai Ageng Giring III stayed in the village of Giring, which is the home of our ancestors. He had land, however, in the area where Sodo now exists. One day Kyai Ageng Giring III got a revelation [*wahyu*] from God ordering him to plant a coconut tree in his ladang field in Sodo. The coconut tree grew very tall and it was called Kelapa Gagak Emprit (the Gagak Emprit Coconut Tree). This name means that if a *gagak* [a large bird] looked down on a man from that tree, the man would look as small as a tiny *emprit* [a very small bird]. Kelapa Gagak Emprit had only one fruit, which was called Buah Kelapa Gagak Emprit [fruit of Gagak Emprit].
>
> Then Kyai Ageng Giring III was told [by God] to drink the water of Buah Kelapa Gagak Emprit, because whoever drank it would have a child who would reign over Java. Kyai Ageng Giring III picked the coconut, but since it was still morning and he wasn't thirsty yet, he trimmed the coconut to make it ready for drinking and saved it on a rack in his kitchen. Then he went to the fields and told his wife not to let anyone drink the water from the coconut.
>
> While Kyai Ageng Giring III was working in his fields, his cousin, Ki Ageng Pemanahan, came to his house. Ki Ageng Pemanahan saw the coconut and drank the water without permission. [This symbolizes how the wife of Kyai Ageng Giring became pregnant by Ki Ageng Pemanahan.] Because of this, the son of Ki Ageng Pemanahan became the king of Java. Kyai Ageng Giring III asked to be buried where the coconut was planted.

Although the story of Pak Sastro and Pak Harto resembles other tales from the area, it serves in the minds of Kajar villagers to explain many things. First, it explains why Pak Sastro, starting about 1962, became wealthier than anyone else in the village. Indeed, his rise to economic power must seem magical to the other villagers. Second, the story explains the collaborative relationship between Pak Sastro and Pak Harto, according to which Pak Harto is not overtly involved in iron and tool trading but undoubtedly plays an important role behind the scenes. One villager likened Pak Harto's role to that of a dhalang, or puppet-master, the implication being that Pak Sastro was just a puppet in the larger drama of the village. Third, that Pak Harto came to Pak Sastro's house, and ate the snacks without permission, may symbolize Pak Harto's having allowed Bu Sastro to adopt one of his children. Fourth, the story reaffirms the ties of the village to the Sultanate of Yogyakarta, and shows the great respect and affection that the villagers have for the sultan. Every act of the sultan—touring the realm, stopping to rest, eating a snack, sitting in a certain chair—is charged with symbolic importance and is thought to determine the prosperity and welfare of villagers living in the realm.

A cynic might say that the story also helps villagers to accept emerging class differences without too much anger or stress, and thus serves to protect Pak Sastro. While it may serve this function, there is no evidence that the story originated with Pak Sastro. Indeed, judging from his attempt to present himself as a modern businessman, it seems unlikely that he would tell such a tale. The story probably originates from the simple historical fact, well known to all the villagers, that the sultan stopped to rest at Pak Sastro's house one day in 1962.

Pak Atmosakimin, the fifth member of the ruling clique, is the head of Kajar III, the largest dukuh in Karangtengah. It is also the psychological "center" of village life, because Sumber Kajar and Pak Sastro's house are both located there.

Pak Atmo is a small, shrewd, comical man, fond of a good joke. In style he more closely resembles the old-fashioned type of headman. He is the brother-in-law of Pak Harto, and his mother is the aunt of Pak Harto and Bu Sastro. Not only does he run Kajar III, but Pak Atmo can always be called on to help out with villagewide activities, for example collecting contributions for the Bersih Desa festival. Pak Paeran and Pak Harto use Pak Atmo as their second-in-command. Like the other dukuh in the village, Pak Atmo derives his income mainly from farming tanah bengkok lands.

Pak Harjopawiro, the sixth member of the clique, is the dukuh of Kajar I. Among blacksmiths Kajar I holds a special place of honor because Gunokaryo built the first perapen there. Both Martodinomo and Karyodiwongso, the keris makers, came from Kajar I.

Less imposing in personality than the other members of the clique, Pak Harjo is a member mainly by virtue of being the brother of Pak Harto and Bu Sastro. Thus he comes from the same powerful cakal bakal family. His wife is the daughter of Martodinomo and thus comes from a smithing family. Again, we see the alliance of the two village élite groups through marriage. Like Pak Atmo, Pak Harjo makes himself available to help out with villagewide activities. His income derives mainly from tanah bengkok, but he has imitated his more powerful brother-in-law, Pak Sastro, by doing some small-scale raw material and tool trading on his own. He has also opened a perapen near his house, which makes the usual type of agricultural tools.

Economic Changes between 1977–78 and 1990–91

The period between 1977–78 and 1990–91 witnessed a number of important economic changes in Kajar.

First, pressure on the agricultural resource base continued to increase. As can be seen from table 3 (page 130), the population of Karangtengah (Kajar) village rose from 5,254 to 6,250, and population density per square kilometer rose from 1,051 to 1,250. Although landless rates remained low in comparison with the lowlands, the average size of holdings declined. As a consequence, nonagricultural occupations became even more important than before.

There was also a major change in the agricultural strategy of households. Formerly households combined the subsistence production of staple crops (cassava, corn, and dry rice) with the cash crop production of legumes (peanuts and soybeans). Traditional methods of food preservation, largely by drying, were applied to the staples. By 1991 villagers had largely given up subsistence agriculture. The amount of land under dry rice cultivation had been reduced, partly in response to government pressures to grow varieties not suited to the environment, and the amount of land under cassava cultivation had been increased. Most of the cassava was being sold "wet" to the Japanese for export. Since peeling and drying cassava is a tedious process, this change in agricultural strategy freed up a good deal of labor for other economic activities. The cash cropping of legumes continued to be important in 1991.

The change in agricultural strategy was linked to a change in the main dietary staple, from cassava to rice. By 1991 Kajar villagers ate cassava only as a snack and in small quantities, while most of their calories were obtained from purchased rice grown in the lowlands. The money with which to purchase rice was obtained partly from the sale of cassava and legumes, and partly from nonagricultural activities such as blacksmithing and the production of slaked lime. The shift to a diet of purchased rice had at least two important advantages from the villagers' point of view. First, it freed them from the risk of famine due to frequent droughts in the area. Second, it raised their social status, since eating cassava is associated with poverty in the Indonesian mind.

The blacksmithing industry continued to expand. Table 3 shows that the number of perapen increased from 90 in 1977 to 140 in 1991. The number of smiths also increased, but less rapidly, from 760 to 800. The average size of the perapen labor force declined from eight to six workers, largely because of the adoption of new labor-saving technologies.

When deflated and expressed in U.S. dollars, real wages for hired workers in the perapen increased. For example, panjak and tukang kikir formerly received Rp 300–400 per day, plus Rp 200 worth of food and drinks. This amounted to between $1.07 and $1.28 per day. By 1991 they were receiving Rp 2,000–2,500 per day, plus Rp 750–1,000 worth of food and drinks. This amounted to between $1.40 and $1.78 per day. Since the real price of purchased lowland rice remained approximately stable, this meant that the buying power of workers increased.

Average working capital needs per perapen per day, also deflated and expressed in U.S. dollars, increased from about $17 to about $28. This increase seems to have been due largely to an increase in the real price of scrap iron. The real price of rails rose from $0.24 per kilogram in 1977 to $0.35 per kilogram in 1991. The real price of lower-grade scrap rose from $0.07 per kilogram to $0.20. Real labor costs also rose, as described above.

Despite increases in working capital expenditures, nearly all pera-

Table 3: Economic Data on the Blacksmithing Industry in
Kajar Village, 1977–1978 and 1990–1991

	1977–1978	1990–1991
Number of households	1,011	1,200
Number of persons	5,254	6,250
Persons per square kilometer	1,051	1,250
Number of perapen	90–98	130–140
Number of workers	760	800
Exchange rate ($1 =)	Rp 414–519	Rp 1963
Iron prices, per kilo	Rp 30 (scrap)	Rp 400 (scrap)
	Rp 100 (rails)	Rp 700 (rails and reinforcement rods)
Charcoal prices, per kilo	Rp 40 (cheaper woods)	
	Rp 60 (teak)	Rp 150 (teak)
Empu wages, per day	Rp 600–900, depending on skill	Rp 2,500–5,000, depending on skill (ave. 3,500)
Panjak wages, per day	Rp 300–400, depending on strength	Rp 2,000–2,500, depending on strength
Tukang kikir wages, per day	Rp 300–400	Rp 2000–2500, or piece rates
Tukang ubub wages, per day	Rp 200	Rp 600–1500
Value of extra food and drinks given to workers	Rp 200	Rp 750–1000
Number of women in perapen	17	10
Agricultural wages for men, per day	Rp 200–300	Rp 2,000
Agricultural wages for women, per day	Rp 150	Rp 1,250

(*Table 3: Continued*)

	1977–1978	1990–1991
Price per imported file	Rp 1,500	—
Working capital per day per perapen	Rp 6,000–10,000	Rp 50,000–60,000
Number of 4-wheeled vehicles in village	2–3 (Pak Sastro)	+ 30, of which 15 belong to Pak Sastro
Cost of rice, per kilo	Rp 125–130 (high-yielding)	Rp 250–300 (1984)
	Rp 180 (local varieties)	Rp 500–555 (1991)
Cost of gaplek (dried cassava), per kilo	Rp 85	Rp 50 (1984; in 1991 no longer making gaplek—selling cassava "wet")

pen owners interviewed reported increased profit levels. These increased profits were due to an expanded market, allowing perapen owners to increase their volume of production and raise their prices. Price increases were justified by improvements that had been made in the appearance and quality of tools produced. These improvements were mainly in the area of finishing, and included machine polishing, rustproofing, and chrome plating.

Electricity was installed in the village in 1988, rather later than in the lowlands. Most households now own a single unit (450 watts), enough to power electric lights in their home or perapen, and enough to power low-wattage equipment such as a small blower. Kerosene-burning lamps have become a thing of the past.

Many of the perapen have purchased labor-saving machinery. Nine of the larger and better-capitalized perapen have imitated Pak Sastro in buying large gerinda and blower which they power either with diesel engines or additional purchased units of electricity. They use these machines for their own production, and also earn extra income by doing finishing for smaller perapen as piecework. Three of these nine perapen are becoming large enough to challenge the position of Pak Sastro. Smaller and less well-capitalized perapen have also purchased new technologies within their price range, particularly blower. Some new types of rotary handheld polishers (*mesin slep*) have recently become popular and are available in both large and small models.

Despite the adoption of labor-saving machinery, perapen owners complain about a shortage of labor in relation to market demand.

Boys from the village are staying in school longer. With the purchase of blowers, the labor of young boys as tukang ubub is no longer so important. Because they are staying in school longer, some boys are developing new aspirations which will inevitably take them away from the village world. Yet earnings in blacksmithing generally exceed those available in the urban informal sector in nearby cities such as Wonosari and Yogyakarta, so there has been relatively little outmigration from the five southern dukuh thus far.

Kajar is not as dependent as before on the Chinese tool dealer from Semarang. New trade relationships have been opened with dealers in Surabaya and Yogyakarta. Nonetheless, the basic marketing problem remains the same: urban tool dealers prefer to buy semifinished tools, which they finish in their own workshops using hired labor, because they can then stamp them with their own trademark, and they can obtain semifinished tools for a lower price and capture a larger share of the value added. As of 1991 about half the tools made in Kajar were sold semifinished.

To use a trademark in Indonesia it is necessary to have a type of permit called an S.I.I. (Standard Industri Indonesia). The Kajar cooperative has approached the government to obtain such a permit, but thus far to no avail. At present the finished tools produced in the village continue to be stamped with the counterfeit trademarks of brands imported or smuggled in from Taiwan, Germany, and China. Such tools sell better, they say, than tools which have no trademark.

Except for a few tentative experiments, there has been no significant expansion into new product types. At a group meeting in 1991 Pak Sastro and several other industry leaders said they were familiar with casting technology but were afraid they could not compete with "Ceper" (the hamlet in Tegal district).

Previously, Pak Sastro was the only villager who owned a four-wheeled vehicle. He owned two or three trucks and minivans, which gave him a great advantage over other enterprise owners. By 1991 the number of four-wheeled vehicles in the village had increased to about thirty. Pak Sastro owned fifteen of these vehicles and had started a new transport enterprise. The remaining fifteen were owned by other villagers, some of them independent perapen owners. In addition to four-wheeled vehicles, many more villagers owned motorcycles than before. Village roads had been upgraded to asphalt in the Kajar section, but not yet in the Kedung or northern sections.

Stratification began to affect the slaked lime industry after 1977. Formerly the industry was organized in small production units and limited to the northern part of the village. In 1984 a cousin of Pak Sastro's set up "Pabrik Topo Gamping," a slaked lime factory in Kajar III. The factory now employs seventy-five hired workers. Some of the limestone processed in the factory comes from the village, but much of it is brought in from Tepus subdistrict, some nineteen kilometers away on the south coast of Java near Baron Beach.

The exterior and (below) the interior of a perapen in Kajar village.

An empu making a sickle, Kajar village.

An empu at work, Kajar village.

A young boy sitting on a bellows platform and working the upright double piston bellows, Kajar village.

A woman working a large bellows, Kajar village.

A tukang kikir at work filing tools, Kajar village; note how he uses his left foot to hold the tool.
(below) A buffalo-horn tool used by the tukang kikir when filing, Kajar village.

Pak Sastro in a quiet moment, Kajar village.

Pak Sastro's warehouse, Kajar village; the bags on the left are filled with charcoal.
(below) The interior of Bu Sastro's store; her daughter, Sulastini, is standing on the left.

Making gamelan gongs called bonang *behind Pak Sastro's house.*

A tool seller, Wonosari marketplace.

Offerings made to the anvil on Legi, the first day of the Javanese five-day market week, Kajar village.

A tool seller, Wonosari marketplace.

A tool seller, Wonosari marketplace; the market can be seen in the background.

The top of Gunung Pancuran, the burial hill behind Kajar village where the graves of the first empu are located.

(opposite) Pak Martodinomo, one of the last keris makers in Kajar.

A pair of beautiful steel ceremonial knives used for sacrificing animals and making offerings in Bali, made by Mangkuwija, a smith from Klungkung. They are inlaid with silver and further ornamented with brass. The image of Merdah, one of the Balinese sacred "clowns," is engraved on the back of the knife at left.

An elderly Javanese meranggi carving keris sheaths, Girirejo village.

A furnace used for making brass bells by the lost-wax method, Ngawen village; the furnace is loaded and pieces of old roof tiles have been placed over the top for better heat containment.

Making large soldered copper pots, Jolotundo village.

Selling copper rice steamers, Wonosari marketplace.

A tungkik used for iron casting in Batur village; it is a smaller version of a Dutch cupola, but has been mounted on a swivel so that it can be tipped forward.

CHAPTER 4

Relevant Macrodata

In this chapter consideration turns toward the future of metalworking industries in Indonesia. The emphasis is on the future as envisioned by government development planners and aid agencies. It should be remembered, however, that villagers are not passive participants in development. They accept or reject development schemes on their own terms and according to their own criteria. If they perceive that a scheme will have immediate positive benefits which outweigh any possible costs of participation, they will eagerly participate. If the costs seem to outweigh the benefits, polite excuses can usually be found for nonparticipation.

This chapter reviews the macrodata available to government development planners. Some general trends are sketched at the beginning of the chapter, but the emphasis is on macrodata which relate to small and very small metalworking enterprises, i.e. those employing fewer than twenty workers. Deficiencies in the data are discussed, and the main conclusions which can be drawn from the data are summarized.

Some General Economic Trends

SOME OF THE TRENDS which affected the Indonesian agricultural sector in the 1970s and 1980s were touched on in chapter 1. These include a further decline in the ratio of land to population in rural areas as population growth has exceeded permanent rural-to-urban migration; a sharp increase in the productivity of *sawah* owing to the technological innovations of the Green Revolution; an increased consolidation of sawah holdings in the hands of a relatively small

Table 4: Percentage of the Employed Population by
Economic Sector, 1971–1985

Economic Sector	Population Census 1971	Sakernas 1976	Sakernas 1977	Sakernas 1978
1. Agriculture, forestry, hunting, fishery	66.3	61.6	61.5	60.9
2. Manufacturing industry	6.8	8.4	8.6	7.4
3. Transportation, storage, communication	2.4	2.7	2.9	2.5
4. Wholesale and retail trade, restaurant	10.8	14.4	14.0	14.9
5. Services	10.3	10.7	10.5	12.3
6. Others (including mining and quarrying, utilities, construction, and finance)	3.4	2.2	2.0	5.3
7. Total	100.0	100.0	100.0	100.0

SOURCES: Figures in first six columns are taken from Analisa Pendahuluan Hasil Sensus Ekonomi 1986 [Preliminary Analysis of the Results of the 1986 Economic Census], 28. Sakernas is the National Labor Force Survey, Susenas the National Socioeconomic Survey. Figures for 1985 are calculated from table 3.8 in the Statistical Year Book of Indonesia (1989). Both are publications of the BPS (Central Bureau of Statistics).

rural élite through rental, pawning, and outright sale; a somewhat increased rate of landlessness in terms of sawah holdings (although rates were already high before the period in question); and a shift of labor and resources from the agricultural sector to other sectors of the rural economy, especially petty trade, services, and small industries. Tables 4 and 5 document the last of these trends. Although the absolute numbers of employed persons increased in every sector because of population growth, table 4 shows that the proportion of the labor force in agriculture declined by 11.6 percent between 1971 and 1985. During that same period, the proportion in trade increased by 4.2 percent, in services by 3.0 percent, and in industries by 2.5 percent.[1] The shift of labor out of agriculture is part of a longer-term trend that began in the 1960s.[2]

Table 5 points to some gender differences in this trend. It shows that proportionately more women than men left the agricultural sec-

Economic Sector	Population Census 1980	Susenas 1982	Population Intercensal Survey 1985	Percentage Change, 1971–1985
1. Agriculture, forestry, hunting, fishery	55.9	55.5	54.7	–11.6
2. Manufacturing industry	9.1	10.4	9.3	+2.5
3. Transportation, storage, communication	2.8	3.0	3.1	+0.7
4. Wholesale and retail trade, restaurant	13.0	14.8	15.0	+4.2
5. Services	13.9	11.7	13.3	+3.0
6. Others (including mining and quarrying, utilities, construction, and finance)	4.3	4.5	4.5	+1.1
7. Total	100.0	100.0	100.0	

tor between 1971 and 1980. Of those who left the agricultural sector, women went primarily into petty trade and service occupations, while men were absorbed more evenly across the various sectors of the economy.

Although less frequently discussed in the literature, there seem to have been a number of parallel trends in the rural industrial sector:

— improved cash flow in rural areas, leading to a reduction in time lost to work stoppages and more continuous production throughout the year;
— a decrease in the importance of seasonality in rural areas because of the declining role of agriculture in household incomes: this again has led to more continuous industrial production throughout the year;
— an increase in the proportion of full-time to part-time labor used in small and household industries;
— an increase in the proportion of hired to unpaid labor in small and house-

Table 5: Percentage of the Rural Employed Population
by Economic Sector and Sex, 1971 and 1980

Economic Sector	1971			1980			PERCENTAGE CHANGE, 1971–1980		
	Male	Female	Total	Male	Female	Total	Male	Female	Total
1. Agriculture, forestry, hunting, fishery	75.9	72.3	74.6	68.9	63.7	67.2	-7.0	-8.6	-7.4
2. Mining and quarrying	0.2	–	0.1	0.9	0.3	0.7	+0.7	+0.3	+0.6
3. Manufacturing industry	5.2	11.3	7.3	6.1	11.7	8.0	+0.9	+0.4	+0.7
4. Transportation, storage, communication, and utilities	1.9	0.1	1.3	2.7	0.1	1.8	+0.8	–	+0.5
5. Construction	2.2	–	1.4	3.9	0.2	2.7	+1.7	+0.2	+1.3
6. Wholesale and retail trade, restaurant	6.9	11.7	8.6	7.4	15.9	10.3	+0.5	+4.2	+1.7
7. Services	7.8	4.6	6.6	10.0	8.1	9.4	+2.2	+3.5	+2.8
8. Total	100.0	100.0	100.0	100.0	100.0	100.0			

SOURCE: Calculated from table 3.13 in Poot, Kuyvenhoven, and Jansen 1990, 66.

hold industries: this is obscured somewhat by the relatively new custom in rural areas of paying wages to family members who are young adults;

—an increase in the proportion of male to female labor in rural industries;

—a sharp increase in real value added for all sizes of enterprises, not just large and medium: this increase gives some support to proponents of the "pull" theory discussed in chapter 1;

—a rapid increase in employment in large, medium, and small enterprises, with a possible decrease in employment in very small (household) enterprises.

Table 6 documents the fifth of these trends, the change in the relative proportion of male to female labor. It shows that the proportion of men in the rural industrial labor force increased from 45.8 percent in 1971 to 50.5 percent in 1980. Again, the absolute number of persons employed increased for both men and women, but the rate of increase was faster for men, 4.6 percent compared to 2.4 percent for women. Information relevant to some of the other trends in the industrial sector will be provided below.

Available Data Sets

In Indonesia the job of collecting and publishing statistical data on economic and welfare-related subjects is carried out by BPS (Biro Pusat Statistik, or Central Bureau of Statistics). BPS is a nondepartmental body directly under the president, a setup intended to guarantee its independence from other government agencies. The quality of the work produced by BPS steadily improved in the post-Independence years, and it is now equal or superior to that of parallel agencies in other developing or developed nations. This improvement has generated its own difficulties. Because of the constant rewriting of definitions, guidelines, and survey forms in an effort to make them better, there are serious problems of comparability between earlier and later surveys.

In its surveys BPS divides industries into four size segments— large, medium, small, and cottage or household. New and very different definitions of these segments were adopted at the time of the census of 1974–75 (see table 7). For this reason it is difficult to

Table 6: Number and Percentage of Persons Employed in Urban and Rural
Manufacturing Industries by Sex, 1971 and 1980

	1971			1980			AVERAGE ANNUAL RATE OF CHANGE		
	Male	Female	Total	Male	Female	Total	Male	Female	Total
1. Urban manufacturing industries	467,000 (67.7%)	223,000 (32.3%)	690,000 (100.0%)	913,000 (66.5%)	460,000 (33.5%)	1,374,000 (100.0%)	+7.7%	+8.4%	+8.0%
2. Rural manufacturing industries	1,125,000 (45.8%)	1,333,000 (54.2%)	2,458,000 (100.0%)	1,685,000 (50.5%)	1,652,000 (49.5%)	3,337,000 (100.0%)	+4.6%	+2.4%	+3.5%
3. Total, urban and rural	1,592,000 (50.6%)	1,556,000 (49.4%)	3,148,000 (100.0%)	2,598,000 (55.1%)	2,112,000 (44.8%)	4,711,000 (100.0%)	+5.6%	+3.5%	+4.6%

SOURCE: Table 3.13 in Poot, Kuyvenhoven and Jansen 1990, 66; based on data from Population Census, 1971 and 1980.

Table 7: Old and New Definitions of Industrial Enterprises

Segment	Old Definition Used in Industrial Census of 1964–65	New Definitions Used in Industrial Census of 1974–75 and Economic Census of 1986 (Susenas)
Large Industry (LI)	100 or more employees without power equipment or 50 or more employees with power equipment	100 or more persons engaged
Medium Industry (MI)	10–99 employees without power equipment or 5–49 employees with power equipment	20–99 persons engaged
Small Industry (SI)	1–9 employees without power equipment or 1–4 employees with power equipment	5–19 persons engaged (including working owner, paid workers, and unpaid family labor)
Cottage/ Household Industries (CI)	Establishments without paid workers (i.e. which rely entirely on unpaid family labor)	4 or fewer persons engaged (including working owner, paid workers, and unpaid family labor)

compare the data collected in the 1964 census with those collected in 1974–75 or subsequent years. In addition, political and social disruption is thought to have affected the quality of the data collected in 1964. For these reasons the 1964 data are seldom used and will not be considered here.[3]

In an earlier part of this book it was shown that the number of participants in rural metalworking enterprises generally varies between two and seven, including the working owner, unpaid family workers, and hired workers. Thus these industries tend to straddle the BPS definitions of "household" and "small," with roughly four-fifths falling in the household category and one-fifth in the small category. Nearly all the blacksmithing industries which produce knives and small tools from low-grade scrap are household industries by the currently used

BPS definitions, while those which produce larger agricultural and workman's tools from scrap of better quality may be either household or small industries. With the exception of a few of the largest casting enterprises at Batur village, none of the industries considered in this book falls in the medium or large category.

This situation may not be unique to metalworking industries. Table 8 is taken from the most recent edition of the BPS *Statistical Yearbook of Indonesia* and is a more complete version of table 1 in chapter 1. It shows that the average size of household enterprises varied between two and four workers for all industrial subsectors between 1974–75 and 1986, while the average size of small enterprises varied between six and ten workers. The average size of medium and large enterprises, on the other hand, varied between 55 and 563 workers. Thus there still seems to be a "dualistic" gap in the industrial sector in Indonesia.

I see the so-called household industries as not qualitatively different enough from the small industries to warrant their statistical separation. Many household industries now supplement family labor with hired labor and use low-wattage electrical equipment, while many small industries are carried out in the home or houseyard. Moreover, household and small industries are generally clustered in the same villages or urban neighborhoods, and use the same supply and marketing channels.

The statistical separation of household and small industries would not be a problem if BPS used the same survey forms. Unfortunately different forms with very different types of questions are used, and there is only partial overlap. Thus there may be problems of comparability within the same census. Even when the same data are collected, there is a tendency to publish the small industry data in more complete form.

Definitions of labor force participation have also varied. In the section on household and cottage industry in the Industrial Census of 1974–75, a person was considered a "participant" if "any time was devoted at all in the activity, however small the time, or how infrequent the participation was." In other words, a person joining the activity for about half an hour a month would have been counted as a "participant" in the activity. In the section on household and cottage industry in the Economic Census of 1986, working owners and unpaid family workers were not counted if they put in "less than one-third of the usual working hours," or about thirteen hours a week with the usual workweek reckoned as forty hours (Central Bureau of Statistics 1987b, 90–91). This difference in the definition of labor force participation may account for some or all of the supposed decline in household industry employment. Table 8 indicates that household industry employment declined from 3.9 million to 2.7 million between 1974–75 and 1986. A number of observers have made much of this apparent decline, taking it as further evidence of the inevitable and imminent demise of household industries. But it may be largely a statistical artifact.[4] Since more women than men work part-time as unpaid family workers, they would have been more likely than men to have been omitted under the new definition of the labor force that took effect in 1986, and therefore the decline in female labor may have been artificially heightened. Another, less important factor in the apparent decline may be the transformation of some household industries into small industries through growth and the addition of hired workers.

There are some other problems of comparability. The rural areas of seven low-density provinces were excluded from the census of 1974–75 for reasons of accessibility and cost. These areas, containing something less than 5 percent of the national population, were included in the census of 1986, as was a new province, Timor Timur.

Because of the very large number of household industries, complete coverage has been considered impractical and a sampling method has been used instead. In 1974–75, for example, 8 percent of the population census blocks were sampled and the published national figures were an estimate based on this sample. To avoid the effects of seasonality, one-twelfth of the blocks were interviewed each month between August 1974 and July 1975. A very different method was used for the small industry section. A total enumeration of all the small industry enterprises nationwide was carried out from June to August 1975, with no correction for seasonality (World Bank 1979, vol.2, 21).

Although government agencies such as the Department of Industry rely heavily on BPS to supply them with planning statistics, they are permitted to collect statistics and conduct surveys on their own, with funding approval from the National or Regional Planning Boards (BAPPENAS, BAPPEDA). Often fieldworkers are asked to collect statistics as part of their routine administrative duties. Sometimes, however, a special-purpose survey is conducted. These surveys are seldom published and are used for internal planning purposes. In 1987 the

Table 8: Number of Establishments and Persons Engaged by Industrial Subsector
and Size of Establishment, 1974–1975, 1979, and 1986

			NUMBER OF ESTABLISHMENTS			
Industry Code	Type of Industrial Products	Year	Large/ Medium >19 Workers	Small 5–19 Workers	Household 1–4 Workers	Total
31	Food, beverages, and tobacco	1974–75	2,367	24,275	434,284	460,926
		1979	2,420	57,280	617,668	677,368
		1986	3,875	38,925	443,595	486,595
32	Textiles, wearing apparel, and leather goods	1974–75	2,066	5,792	139,680	147,538
		1979	2,147	9,692	177,246	189,085
		1986	2,852	15,068	149,124	167,044
33	Wood and wood products, including furniture	1974–75	407	5,456	534,862	540,725
		1979	633	15,144	434,376	450,153
		1986	1,160	14,393	467,071	482,624
34	Paper and paper products, printing and publishing	1974–75	289	867	2,628	3,784
		1979	358	1,263	—	1,621
		1986	602	2,348	7,130	10, 080
35	Chemicals and chemical, petroleum, coal, rubber, and plastic products	1974–75	899	1,382	5,317	7,598
		1979	823	1,786	—	2,609
		1986	1,591	2,596	7,530	11,717
36	Non-metallic mineral products (glass, cement, lime, clay)	1974–75	480	6,749	80,599	87,828
		1979	675	19,814	104,997	125,486
		1986	1,208	13,582	105,789	120,576
37	Basic metal industries, including smelting	1974–75	18	—	—	18
		1979	22	—	—	22
		1986	30	—	—	30
38	Fabricated metal products, machinery, and equipment	1974–75	500	2,957	15,432	18,889
		1979	796	6,814	32,009	39,619
		1986	1,272	5,018	34,403	40,693
39	Other manufacturing industries	1974–75	65	708	21,709	22,482
		1979	86	1,231	51,506	52,823
		1986	175	2,604	201,794	204,573
Total		1974–75	7,091	48,186	1,234,511	1,289,788
		1979	7,960	113,024	1,417,802	1,538,786
		1986	12,765	94,534	1,416,636	1,523,935

SOURCE: Based on table 6.1.1. *Statistical Yearbook of Indonesia*, 1989, 300–301.

	PERSONS ENGAGED		
Large/ Medium >19 Workers	Small	Household 1–4 Workers	Total
268,388	151,194	1,401,177	1,820,759
294,441	403,517	1,362,762	2,060,720
520,069	318,722	937,800	1,776,591
174,246	55,375	435,124	664,745
227,787	91,402	293,198	612,387
389,072	132,718	238,956	760,746
22,368	41,680	1,644,004	1,706,052
51,221	110,932	735,816	897,969
181,452	106,080	805,394	1,092,926
21,982	8,067	9,478	39,527
29,876	11,931	—	41,807
62,531	21,476	14,680	98,887
83,802	12,422	20,946	117,170
103,803	17,363	—	121,166
245,419	24,906	16,090	286,415
24,597	46,916	263,203	334,716
43,000	133,687	221,113	397,800
80,980	106,063	248,799	435,842
2,060	—	—	2,060
8,247	—	—	8,247
16,894	—	—	16,894
55,867	22,113	55,773	133,753
105,686	49,527	79,447	234,660
181,641	39,577	78,634	299,852
8,394	5,473	70,151	84,018
5,958	8,676	102,497	117,131
13,377	20,602	373,711	407,690
661,704	343,240	3,899,856	4,904,800
870,019	827,035	2,794,833	4,491,887
1,691,435	770,144	2,714,264	5,175,843

Subdirectorate for Metal under the Directorate General for Small Industries conducted such a survey in connection with a planned expansion of the "Foster Father" program. Data from that survey are provided below.[5] Department of Industry surveys tend to produce somewhat larger estimates of the number of enterprises and workers than BPS surveys. It appears that the greater familiarity of Department of Industry fieldworkers with the local village environment results in a more complete enumeration.

The Indonesian Industrial Codes

The Indonesian government has adopted a modified version of the International Standard Industrial Classification (ISIC) originated by the International Labour Organization. Under this system industries are broken down by two-, three-, and five-digit codes. Those two- and three-digit codes which are relevant to metalworking are given here.

37 — Basic Metal Industries
    371 — Iron and Steel Basic Industries
    372 — Non-Ferrous Metal Basic Industries
38 — Fabricated Metal Products, Machinery, and Equipment
    381 — Cutlery, Hand Tools, and General Hardware
    382 — Machinery, Except Electrical
    383 — Electrical Machinery, Apparatus, Appliances, and Supplies
    384 — Transport Equipment
    385 — Professional, Scientific, Measuring, Photographic, and Optical Equipment
39 — Other Manufacturing Industries
    390 — Other Manufacturing Industries

Industrial statistics in Indonesia are published according to these codes, often without any identifying labels, and it is therefore necessary to master the codes to interpret industrial data. Code 37, Basic Metal Industries, refers to the primary extraction of raw metal from ore- or metal-bearing sands or gravels, as well as its secondary processing into forms such as bars, rods, and sheet. As discussed earlier, small-scale native mining and smelting industries died out in the nineteenth century, and government-owned companies took over this function. Some participation from large privately owned companies and corporations was allowed in the later twentieth century, but basically this is a subsector where the participation of small and household enterprises is not approved by the government. Code 37 is therefore often left out of surveys of small and household enterprises, as can be seen from table 8. Yet the survey conducted in 1987 by the Subdirectorate for Metal shows 881 small and household industries in code 37, most of them on Java and Sumatra, and most involved in the secondary processing of iron and steel (see table 10, page 174).

Code 38, Fabricated Metal Products, refers to the production of all types of consumer goods made of metal, except jewelry, decorative items, souvenirs, and musical instruments. Those items are included in code 39 and are lumped together with similar items made of wood, bamboo, horn, bone, and shell. It is therefore very difficult to obtain accurate estimates of the number of metalworking enterprises and smiths under code 39.

Code 381 covers most of the traditional smiths discussed in this book. It includes blacksmiths who make agricultural tools, workman's tools, and knives, as well as coppersmiths who make kitchen wares and brass smiths who make locks, latches, hinges, and the like. Some nontraditional smiths who make goods of sheet metal and metal tubing are also included in code 381. According to the Subdirectorate for Metal survey of 1987, code 381 accounts for 75.3 percent of the small and household enterprises under code 38. The machine industries in codes 381 and 382 account for another 12.3 percent, while Codes 384 and 385 account for the rest. Of the machine industries in codes 381 and 382, nearly three-quarters are engaged in repairing and servicing rather than manufacturing machines. The total number of small and household enterprises engaged in machine manufacture was only 2,164 nationwide. The relatively small number of machine industries is generally taken as a sign of Indonesia's technological backwardness and overreliance on imported machinery (Weijland 1984, 1–2).

Between the Industrial Census of 1974–75 and the survey conducted by the Subdirectorate for Metal in 1987 there were no changes to the two- and three-digit codes used for metalworking. But the five-digit codes were completely revamped, apparently on the basis of a recommendation by an evaluation team from the World Bank in 1979. The number of five-digit codes increased from twenty-seven to eighty-two, and the content of the codes changed as well. In some cases it is possible to reconcile the two systems, for example by combining two of the later codes to correspond to a single earlier code, but not always. To take but one example, knife making is combined in the later set of codes with the making of agricultural and workman's tools (code 38111), but in the earlier codes knife making is included with the making of nails, nuts and bolts, and similar items (code 38112). One very serious problem is that BPS did not publish any of its household industry data from 1986 by three- or five-digit codes. Thus it is impossible to construct a complete comparison table at anything finer than the very gross two-digit level used in tables 8 and 9.

Although the survey of the Subdirectorate for Metal only covers a limited number of variables, it is a useful supplement because it combines household and small industries in a single category and breaks down data by five-digit codes. It does not include jewelry making and the other industries under code 39, however, because these fall under the jurisdiction of a different subdirectorate, the Subdirectorate for Handicrafts and Miscellaneous Industries.

Some Conclusions from the Macrodata

Appropriately armed with an awareness of some of the problems, we can begin reviewing the macrodata for possible conclusions. Table 8 provides a time series for the number of enterprises and number of workers, broken down by two-digit industrial code. It indicates that code 38 accounted for 1.5 percent of all enterprises and 1.7 percent of all workers nationwide in 1974–75. By 1986 it accounted for 2.7 percent of all enterprises and 5.8 percent of all workers. Thus code 38 is expanding at a faster rate than the industrial sector as a whole.

Nationwide, household and small enterprises accounted for 99.5 percent of all enterprises and 86.3 percent of all workers in 1974–75. In 1986 household and small enterprises still accounted for 99.2 percent of enterprises, but only 67.3 percent of workers. This sudden drop in the percentage of workers is due only partly to a growth in the average size of medium and large enterprises. Principally it is due to the change in labor force definitions discussed above.

Medium and large-scale enterprises play a more important role in code 38 than they do in the industrial sector as a whole. This is because there are some very large, mainly urban factories which manufacture or assemble machinery, electrical appliances, or vehicles and employ several thousand workers each. Thus the percentages accounted for by small and household enterprises are somewhat lower. In 1974–75 household and small enterprises accounted for 97.4 percent of all enterprises in code 38, and 58.2 percent of all workers. In 1986 these percentages were 96.9 and 39.4.

Within code 38 the number of household and small enterprises more than doubled between 1974–75 and 1986, from 18,389 to 39,421. The number of workers also increased, from 77,886 to 118,211. Despite the change in labor force definitions, the number of workers in household enterprises in code 38 went up, not down. It is probable that code 38 was less affected by this change of definitions than sectors such as food products and textiles which use large amounts of part-time female labor.

Two reasons for the decline in national household industry employment have already been suggested: the change in labor force definitions and the conversion of some household industries into small industries through growth. A third possible reason is the "rationalization" of household enterprises through the adoption of labor-saving technologies. This rationalization is in turn related to the spread of rural electrification. In code 38 there may have been a genuine decline in the average number of workers per household enterprise because of the adoption of such equipment as the blower and gerinda. Further research might show that other subsectors have experienced a decline for the same reason.

Input-output data comparing code 38 metalworking industries with all industries are provided in table 9. Gross output, as the term is used by BPS, includes the value of products made and sold, the value of services rendered, and (for small industries) the profit made from any incidental trading. Input, as the term is used by BPS, includes the value of purchased raw materials and parts, the value of purchased fuel, and the value of services purchased from outside individuals and firms. It does not include wages paid to hired workers. To obtain the figure for value added, inputs are subtracted from gross output. This is a census value added which does not include taxes, interest payments on loans, or depreciation. BPS also provides data on wage payments. In table 9 and subsequent tables, I have subtracted wage payments from value added to obtain a figure labeled "profit to the owner," which is shared by the owner and his unpaid family workers. It corresponds to the Indonesian term *keuntungan* (profit) as it is used by village industry

Table 9: Gross Output, Input Costs, Value Added, and Profit of Metalworking Industries and All Industries, 1974–1975, 1979, and 1986

		METALWORKING INDUSTRIES (CODE 38)				ALL INDUSTRIES			
		Large/Medium >19 Workers	Small 5–19 Workers	Household 0–4 Workers	All Enterprises	Large/Medium >19 Workers	Small 5–19 Workers	Household 0–4 Workers	All Enterprises
Average annual value of gross output per enterprise (000 Rp)	1974–75	347,560	3,057	383	9,992	182,455	3,270	163	1,281
	1979	874,695	5,124	1,335	19,534	581,735	5,317	527	
	1986	3,151,241	21,630	3,310	103,967	2,027,210	23,090	2,482	
Average annual input costs per enterprise, excluding labor (000 Rp)	1974–75	227,000	1,747	191	6,439	115,194	2,169	96	806
	1979	593,680	3,048	614	12,948	373,135	3,659	322	
	1986	2,137,252	11,240	1,811	69,724	1,294,858	14,889	1,593	
Average annual value added per enterprise at market price (gross output minus input costs) (000 Rp)	1974–75	120,560	1,310	192	3,553	67,261	1,100	67	475
	1979	261,015	2,077	721	6,586	208,600	1,657	206	
	1986	1,013,991	10,390	1,499	34,244	732,353	8,201	885	
Average annual value added per enterprise in U.S. $ equivalent (deflated)	1974–75	289,608	3,149	462	8,541	161,685	2,644	161	1,142
	1979	445,349	4,990	1,143	10,437	330,586	2,626	326	
	1986	611,193	8,312	1,199	27,395	585,882	6,560	708	
Average annual value added per enterprise in kg. of rice of medium quality (deflated)	1974–75	1,106,055	12,018	1,761	32,596	617,073	10,092	615	4,357
	1979	1,653,029	12,218	4,241	191,741	1,227,059	9,747	1,211	
	1986	2,824,487	28,942	4,175	95,387	2,039,981	22,844	2,465	

Metric	Year								
Average annual labor costs per enterprise (000 Rp)	1974–75	25,814	—	41	717	13,157	338	8	80
	1979	73,030	868	175	1,758	40,421	620	27	279
	1986	241,862	3,651	399	8,348	147,910	2,431	128	1,609
Labor costs as a percentage of total input costs	1974–75	9.2%	—	21.5%	11.1%	11.4%	15.6%	8.3%	9.9%
	1979	12.3%	28.5%	28.5%	13.6%	10.8%	16.9%	8.4%	11.2%
	1986	11.3%	32.5%	22.0%	12.0%	11.4%	16.3%	8.0%	11.4%
Average annual profit to the owner per enterprise (value added minus labor costs) (000 Rp)	1974–75	94,746	—	151	2,836	54,104	762	59	395
	1979	207,985	1,209	546	4,828	168,179	1,037	179	1,111
	1986	722,129	6,739	1,100	25,896	584,443	5,770	757	5,957
Average annual profit to the owner in U.S. $ equivalent	1974–75	227,765	—	363	6,817	130,058	1,832	142	950
	1979	329,612	1,916	865	7,651	266,528	1,642	284	1,761
	1986	617,703	5,391	880	20,717	467,554	4,616	606	4,766
Average annual profit to the owner in kgs. of medium-quality rice	1974–75	869,229	—	1,385	26,018	496,367	6,991	541	3,624
	1979	1,223,441	7,112	3,212	28,400	989,280	6,100	1,053	6,535
	1986	2,150,777	18,772	3,064	72,134	1,627,975	16,072	2,109	16,593
Inputs as a percentage of gross output	1974–75	65.3%	57.1%	49.9%	64.4%	63.1%	66.3%	58.9%	62.9%
	1979	67.9%	59.5%	46.0%	66.3%	64.1%	68.8%	61.1%	64.2%
	1986	67.8%	52.0%	54.7%	67.1%	63.9%	64.5%	64.2%	63.9%
Labor costs as a percentage of gross output	1974–75	7.4%	—	10.7%	7.2%	7.2%	10.3%	4.9%	6.2%
	1979	8.3%	16.9%	13.1%	9.0%	6.9%	11.7%	5.1%	7.2%
	1986	7.7%	16.9%	12.1%	8.0%	7.3%	10.5%	5.2%	7.3%
Profit to the owner as percentage of gross output	1974–75	27.3%	—	39.4%	28.4%	29.7%	23.3%	36.2%	30.8%
	1979	23.8%	23.6%	40.9%	24.7%	28.9%	19.5%	34.0%	28.6%
	1986	24.5%	31.2%	33.2%	24.9%	28.8%	25.0%	30.5%	28.7%

SOURCE: Based on tables 6.1.1 and 6.1.2. *Statistical Yearbook of Indonesia*, 1989, pp. 300–301.

producers. It does not correspond to the term "profit" as it is used by economists when writing about formal sector industries. This is because nothing has been deducted for the value of the labor expended by the owner and his unpaid family workers.

Table 9 indicates that all types of industries grew rapidly between 1974–75 and 1986. Medium and large industries approximately tripled their value added and profits, but small and household industries grew at similar or even faster rates. If deflated and expressed in U.S. dollar equivalents, average value added for all household industries increased from $161 to $708, and average profit increased from $142 to $606. Value added for code 38 household industries increased from $462 to $1,199, and profit increased from $363 to $880. Small industries experienced similar growth. Average value added for all small industries increased from $2,644 to $6,560, and average profit increased from $1,832 to $4,616. Value added for code 38 small industries increased from $3,149 to $8,312. The labor costs in 1974–75 for code 38 small industries were not published, so it is impossible to determine the increase in profit, but profit levels in 1986 were $5,391. In judging these levels of value added and profit, it should be remembered that rural families usually have several occupations. Thus the income earned from a family-owned industry probably represents only a portion of total family income.

I suggested earlier that metalworking industries are more capital-intensive and profitable than industries making some other types of products. This is confirmed by table 9. Metalworking industries on average require about twice as much working capital for inputs and hired labor as industries as a whole. As a consequence, however, they generate about twice as much value added and profit. The exception is small metalworking industries — those with five to nineteen workers — which spend an average of about 20 percent less for inputs than small industries as a whole, but still manage to generate more value added and profit.

Because rural Indonesian families use a high proportion of their cash income to purchase additional supplies of rice, rice prices are often used as a deflator. The average rural family has about five members and consumes between one and two kilograms of rice per day, depending on the ratio of adults to children in the household. If 730 kilograms is assumed to be the maximum amount needed by an average-sized household per annum, it seems clear from table 9 that household and small metalworking industries generate more than enough income to meet rice requirements, even for landless families which must purchase all their rice. In 1974–75 household industries as a whole still fell short of this goal, but the situation had improved by 1979.

Table 9 gives the value of inputs, labor costs, and profit as a percentage of gross output. The results show that metalworking industries spend proportionately less on inputs and proportionately more on labor than industries as a whole. This is apparently because metalworking industries rely more heavily on hired male workers than other industries and pay relatively high wages to those workers. Metalworking industries also earn proportionately more profits for their owners per unit of gross output, and in this sense are more "efficient." It is interesting to note that household industries are also more efficient in this sense than small, medium, and large industries, presumably because they rely more heavily on unpaid family labor.

Tables 10–12 present the three- and five-digit data that are available on metalworking industries. Blank cells represent data that were never published or collected. Table 10 presents data on the number of small and household industry enterprises and workers for all the three-digit codes used for metalworking, except code 390, which is not shown because it includes an unknown percentage of industries making jewelry and other handicrafts from materials other than metal. The most important of the codes in table 10, from the point of view of this book, is code 381, which contains blacksmithing and other traditional nonmachine industries. The column for the Subdirectorate for Metal survey of 1987 indicates that 74.3 percent of all metalworking enterprises and 74.3 percent of all workers are still to be found in code 381, while only 12.1 percent of enterprises and 10.4 percent of workers are in the machine industry codes of 382 and 383. As mentioned above, the majority of the enterprises and workers in codes 382 and 383 are in fact engaged in machine repair and maintenance rather than production. Within code 381 household enterprises outnumbered small enterprises by about six to one in 1974–75. The number of enterprises and workers in code 381 appears to have approximately tripled between 1974–75 and 1987, although the tendency of Department of Industry surveys to provide a more thorough enumeration should again be mentioned.

The detailed data available for codes 381 and 38111 are given in table 11. Code 38111 is the five-digit code for blacksmithing. In 1974–75 code

Table 10: Number and Percentage of Units and Workers by Selected
Three-Digit Industrial Codes, 1974–1975, 1986, and 1987

| | | INDUSTRIAL CENSUS, 1974–75 | | |
Industry Code	Type of Industrial Product	Small	Household	Small + Household
371	Iron and steel basic industries			
	Number of units	2	—	—
	Percentage of units	0.1	—	—
	Number of workers	21	—	—
	Percentage of workers	0.1	—	—
372	Nonferrous metal basic industries			
	Number of units	4	—	—
	Percentage of units	0.1	—	—
	Number of workers	29	—	—
	Percentage of workers	0.1	—	—
381	Fabricated metal products			
	Number of units	2,265	13,600	15,865
	Percentage of units	76.5	—	—
	Number of workers	16,165	49,531	65,696
	Percentage of workers	73.1	—	—
382	Machinery, except electrical (including repair and maintenance)			
	Number of units	162	—	—
	Percentage of units	5.5	—	—
	Number of workers	1,419	—	—
	Percentage of workers	6.4	—	—
383	Electrical machinery, apparatus, appliances, and supplies (including repair and maintenance)			
	Number of units	63	—	—
	Percentage of units	2.1	—	—
	Number of workers	553	—	—
	Percentage of workers	2.5	—	—

ECONOMIC CENSUS, 1986			SUBDIRECTORATE FOR METAL SURVEY, 1987
Small	Household	Small + Household	Small + Household
0	—	—	475
0	—	—	0.8
0	—	—	2,069
0	—	—	0.8
0	—	—	406
0	—	—	0.7
0	—	—	1,645
0	—	—	0.7
3,598	—	—	45,912
71.7	—	—	74.3
26,473	—	—	182,374
66.9	—	—	74.3
359	—	—	2,190
7.2	—	—	3.5
3,510	—	—	9,351
8.9	—	—	3.8
357	—	—	5,305
7.1	—	—	8.6
3,212	—	—	16,316
8.1	—	—	6.6

Table 11: Selected Economic Data Pertaining to Industrial Codes 381 and 38111, 1974–1975, 1986, and 1987

Item	Industry Code	INDUSTRIAL CENSUS, 1974–75		
		Small	Household	Small + Household
1. Number of enterprises	381	2,265	13,600	15,865
	38111	894	5,090	5,984
2. Number of enterprises using hired labor	381	—	5,192	—
	38111	—	2,793	—
3. Percentage of enterprises using hired labor	381	—	38.2	—
	38111	—	54.9	—
4. Number of workers	381	16,165	49,531	65,696
	38111	5,469	19,800	25,269
5. Number of unpaid family workers	381	3,318	39,769	43,087
	38111	1,401	14,665	16,066
6. Percentage of unpaid family workers	381	20.5	80.3	65.6
	38111	25.6	74.1	63.6
7. Number of hired workers	381	12,847	9,762	22,609
	38111	4,068	5,135	9,203
8. Percentage of hired workers	381	79.5	19.7	34.4
	38111	74.4	25.9	36.4
9. Average number of workers per enterprise	381	7.1	3.6	4.1
	38111	6.1	3.9	4.2
10. Average man-days worked per unpaid family worker per year	381	—	92.3	—
	38111	—	82.2	—
11. Average man-days worked per hired worker per year	381	—	227.0	—
	38111	—	210.5	—
12. Average wages received by hired workers per man-day (Rp)	381	—	264	—
	38111	—	251	—
13. Average wages received by hired workers per man-day in U.S. $ equivalent	381	—	$0.64	—
	38111	—	$0.60	—

	ECONOMIC CENSUS, 1986		SUBDIRECTORATE FOR METAL SURVEY, 1987
Small	Household	Small + Household	Small + Household
3,598	—	—	45,912
1,518	—	—	23,113
—	—	—	—
—	—	—	—
—	—	—	—
—	—	—	—
26,473.0	—	—	182,374
9,433	—	—	82,085
6,489	—	—	—
2,713	—	—	—
24.5	—	—	—
28.8	—	—	—
19,984	—	—	—
6,720	—	—	—
75.5	—	—	—
71.2	—	—	—
7.4	—	—	4.0
6.2	—	—	3.6
—	—	—	—
—	—	—	—
—	—	—	—
—	—	—	—
—	—	—	—
—	—	—	—
—	—	—	—
—	—	—	—

| | | INDUSTRIAL CENSUS, 1974–75 | | |
Item	Industry Code	Small	Household	Small + Household
14. Average wages received by hired workers per man-day in rice equivalent (kgs)	381 38111	— —	2.43 2.30	— —
15. Number of unpaid family workers who work full time (more than 5 hours)	381 38111	— —	73.6% 77.6%	— —
16. Number of unpaid family workers who work part time (5 hours or less)	381 38111	— —	26.4% 22.4%	— —
17. Annual value of materials consumed per enterprise, including fuel (Rp)	381 38111	1,544,076 519,419	198,933 145,809	390,976 201,626
18. Annual value of services consumed per enterprise including rentals and repairs (Rp)	381 38111	23,434 17,132	3,489 2,365	6,337 4,571
19. Annual total value of inputs per enterprise (Rp) (17 + 18; does not include wages)	381 38111	1,567,510 536,551	202,422 148,174	397,313 206,197
20. Annual value of goods produced per enterprise (Rp)	381 38111	2,277,328 1,007,541	365,483 314,193	638,432 417,778
21. Annual value of services rendered per enterprise (Rp)	381 38111	308,243 30,715	23,711 25,001	64,333 25,855
22. Annual profit from trading per enterprise (Rp) (resale of goods in same form as purchased)	381 38111	1,662 1,941	— —	— —
23. Annual total value of gross output per enterprise (Rp) (20 + 21 + 22)	381 38111	2,587,232 1,040,197	389,194 339,194	703,002 443,923

ECONOMIC CENSUS, 1986			SUBDIRECTORATE FOR METAL SURVEY, 1987
Small	Household	Small + Household	Small + Household
—	—	—	—
—	—	—	—
—	—	—	—
—	—	—	—
—	—	—	—
—	—	—	—
8,512,916	—	—	—
3,075,752	—	—	—
475,434	—	—	—
214,018	—	—	—
8,988,350	—	—	3,913,653
3,294,770	—	—	2,512,108
17,750,014	—	—	—
11,939,851	—	—	—
692,593	—	—	—
194,030	—	—	—
63,941	—	—	—
26,809	—	—	—
18,506,547	—	—	9,734,549
12,160,690	—	—	5,593,425

(*Table 11: Continued*)

| Item | Industry Code | INDUSTRIAL CENSUS, 1974–75 | | |
		Small	Household	Small + Household
24. Annual census value added per enterprise (Rp) (23 – 19)	381 38111	1,019,722 503,645	186,772 191,021	305,690 206,197
25. Annual census value added per enterprise in U.S. $ equivalent	381 38111	$2451 $1211	$449 $459	$735 $496
26. Annual census value added per enterprise in rice equivalent (kgs)	381 38111	9,355 4,621	1,714 1,752	1,887 1,892
27. Annual value of wages paid to hired workers per enterprise (Rp)	381 38111	— —	43,088 53,328	— —
28. Annual profit to the owner per enterprise (Rp) (24 – 27)	381 38111	— —	143,684 137,693	— —
29. Annual profit to the owner in U.S. $ equivalent	381 38111	— —	$345 $331	— —
30. Annual profit to the owner in rice equivalent (kgs)	381 38111	— —	1,318 1,263	— —
31. Value of inputs as a percentage of output	381 38111	60.6% 51.6%	52.0% 43.7%	56.5% 46.4%
32. Value of wages as a percentage of output	381 38111	— —	11.1% 15.7%	— —
33. Profit to the owner as a percentage of output	381 38111	— —	36.9% 40.6%	— —
34. Average annual wages per hired worker (Rp)	381 38111	— —	60,029 52,861	— —
35. Ratio of profit to the owner and wages per hired worker	381 38111	— —	2.4:1 2.6:1	— —

ECONOMIC CENSUS, 1986			SUBDIRECTORATE FOR METAL SURVEY, 1987
Small	Household	Small + Household	Small + Household
9,518,198	—	—	5,820,896
8,925,208	—	—	3,081,317
$7615	—	—	$3528
$7140	—	—	$1867
26,513	—	—	14,444
24,861	—	—	7,646
3,057,990	—	—	—
2,129,953	—	—	—
6,460,208	—	—	—
6,795,255	—	—	—
$5168	—	—	—
$5436	—	—	—
17,995	—	—	—
18,928	—	—	—
48.6%	—	—	40.2%
27.1%	—	—	44.9%
16.5%	—	—	—
17.5%	—	—	—
34.9%	—	—	—
55.9%	—	—	—
550,573	—	—	—
481,141	—	—	—
11.7:1	—	—	—
14.1:1	—	—	—

Item	Industry Code	INDUSTRIAL CENSUS, 1974–75		
		Small	Household	Small + Household
36. Percentage of enterprises in inner Indonesia (Java, Bali, Madura)	381 38111	— —	69.1% —	— —
37. Percentage of enterprises in outer Indonesia	381 38111	— —	30.9% —	— —
38. Percentage of workers in inner Indonesia (Java, Bali, Madura)	381 38111	— —	71.0% —	— —
39. Percentage of workers in outer Indonesia	381 38111	— —	29.0% —	— —
40. Percentage of workers who are male	381 38111	— —	— —	— —
41. Percentage of workers who are female	381 38111	— —	— —	— —
42. Percentage of enterprises using power equipment	381 38111	1.5% 0.0%	— —	— —
43. Investment value of machinery and equipment per enterprise (Rp)	381 38111	— —	— —	— —
44. Investment value of machinery and equipment in U.S. $ equivalent	381 38111	— —	— —	— —
45. Annual amount of charcoal used per enterprise (kgs)	381 38111	— —	— —	— —
46. Annual amount of coal and coke used per enterprise (kgs)	381 38111	— —	— —	— —
47. Annual amount of petroleum-based fuels used per enterprise (liters)	381 38111	— —	— —	— —

ECONOMIC CENSUS, 1986			SUBDIRECTORATE FOR METAL SURVEY, 1987
Small	Household	Small + Household	Small + Household
—	—	—	71.4%
—	—	—	67.4%
	—	—	28.6%
	—	—	32.6%
—	—	—	72.2%
—	—	—	67.5%
—	—	—	27.8%
—	—	—	32.5%
93.2%	—	—	—
94.9%	—	—	—
6.8%	—	—	—
5.1%	—	—	—
—	—	—	—
—	—	—	—
1,974,996	—	—	1,321,436
329,980	—	—	761,321
$1580	—	—	$801
$284	—	—	$461
3,295	—	—	—
6,684	—	—	—
447	—	—	—
309	—	—	—
846	—	—	—
131	—	—	—

Item	Industry Code	INDUSTRIAL CENSUS, 1974–75		
		Small	Household	Small + Household
48. Average amount of electricity per enterprise (kilowatts)	381 38111	— —	— —	— —
49. Total number of bank loans outstanding	381 38111	— —	— —	— —
50. Total number of cooperative loans outstanding	381 38111	— —	— —	— —
51. Percentage of enterprises which market entirely within the same province	381 38111	— —	— —	— —
52. Percentage of enterprises which market at least some products in other provinces	381 38111	— —	— —	— —
53. Percentage of enterprises which export at least some products	381 38111	— —	— —	— —
54. Percentage of enterprises which report no serious problems	381 38111	— —	— —	— —
55. Percentage of enterprises which report problems in obtaining capital	381 38111	— —	— —	— —
56. Percentage of enterprises which report problems in supply or price of raw materials	381 38111	— —	— —	— —
57. Percentage of enterprises which report marketing problems	381 38111	— —	— —	— —

ECONOMIC CENSUS, 1986			SUBDIRECTORATE FOR METAL SURVEY, 1987
Small	Household	Small + Household	Small + Household
2,679	—	—	—
278	—	—	—
691	—	—	—
194	—	—	—
73	—	—	—
49	—	—	—
87.5%	—	—	—
88.6%	—	—	—
12.5%	—	—	—
11.4%	—	—	—
1.8%	—	—	—
2.3%	—	—	—
23.5%	—	—	—
27.9%	—	—	—
29.4%	—	—	—
41.6%	—	—	—
21.0%	—	—	—
25.0%	—	—	—
33.1%	—	—	—
25.0%	—	—	—

(*Table 11: Continued*)

| | | INDUSTRIAL CENSUS, 1974–75 | | |
Item	Industry Code	Small	Household	Small + Household
58. Percentage of enterprises which sell at least some products directly to final consumers	381	—	—	—
	38111	—	—	—
59. Percentage of enterprises which sell at least some products through intermediaries	381	—	—	—
	38111	—	—	—
60. Percentage of enterprises which sell at least some products through cooperatives	381	—	—	—
	38111	—	—	—

NOTES: A blank indicates the data were not published and/or not collected.

Code 38111 did not include knife making in 1974–75 but did include it in 1986.

In the 1974–75 Industrial Census full-time work was defined as more than five hours per day. A man-day was one day of full-time work. Part-time days of one to five hours were counted as half-days, two half-days equaling one man-day. Part-time days of less than one hour (nominal participation) were omitted from the computation of man-days.

It is not possible to determine the percentage of enterprises with outstanding bank or co-operative loans since a few enterprises may have more than one loan.

38111 was limited to enterprises making agricultural and workman's tools. In 1986 enterprises making knives and other cutting tools were taken out of code 38112 and added to code 38111. This should be kept in mind when reading the table because some of the increase in the number of enterprises and workers in code 38111 is due to this change in code definitions. Knife-making enterprises tend to be smaller and less well-capitalized than enterprises making agricultural and workman's tools, so that the figures for the average number of workers and the input-output data may also be somewhat affected. Table 11 shows a rapid increase in the number of enterprises and workers for both codes 381 and 38111 between 1974–75 and 1987. The number of enterprises approximately tripled for code 381 and approximately quadrupled for code 38111. The number of workers approximately tripled

ECONOMIC CENSUS, 1986			SUBDIRECTORATE FOR METAL SURVEY, 1987
Small	Household	Small + Household	Small + Household
46.4%	—	—	—
39.7%	—	—	—
64.0%	—	—	—
80.4%	—	—	—
0.9%	—	—	—
1.4%	—	—	—

for both codes. These increases were accompanied by slight declines in the average number of workers per enterprise, from 4.1 to 4.0 for code 380 and from 4.2 to 3.6 for code 38111.

Not surprisingly, table 11 shows that small enterprises rely more heavily on hired labor, while household enterprises rely more heavily on unpaid family labor. In 1974–75 small enterprises in code 381 filled 79.5 percent of their labor needs from hired labor, while household enterprises in code 381 filled only 19.7 percent of their needs from hired labor. The percentages for code 38111 were roughly similar: 74.4 percent and 25.9 percent. The small industry figures from 1986 show a decline of 3–4 percent in the amount of hired labor used, while the household industry figures from that year were not published.

Here we note the problem of classifying family members, usually teenagers and young adults, who are paid wages. This is a new custom, but one which appears to be spreading rapidly. At present it is more common in relatively prosperous villages on Java and Bali than elsewhere. Census forms assume that all family workers are unpaid and that all paid workers are nonfamily, but field observations indicate this is no longer so. It is not clear how family members who are paid wages are currently being classified, and the written instructions for census enumerators contain no clarification on this point.

The only data set which provides information on the intensity of labor is in the household section of the census of 1974–75. This shows that for codes 381 and 38111, three-quarters of the family workers surveyed worked full-time, defined as five or more hours per day. Although they worked full-time on the days when they worked, they apparently did not work continuously throughout the year. This is seen in the figures for average person-days worked per year. Family workers in code 381 averaged only ninety-two days per year, while family workers in code 38111 averaged eighty-two. This contrasts sharply with the pattern for hired workers, who averaged two and a half times as many person-days — 227 for code 381 and 210 for code 38111.

The Subdirectorate for Metal survey of 1987 includes some input-output data, so it is possible to construct a time series for the relevant variables. Table 11 shows that average value added per annum for enterprises in code 381 increased from Rp 305,690 to Rp 5,820,896 between 1974–75 and 1987. Deflated and expressed in U.S. dollars, value added increased from $735 to $3,528. This is nearly a fivefold real increase, truly remarkable in a period of only twelve or thirteeen years. Deflated and expressed in rice equivalents, this is a seven- or eightfold real increase.[6] Average value added is considerably lower for enterprises in code 38111, but it also increased rapidly, from Rp 206,197 to Rp 3,081,317, which is nearly a fourfold increase, from $496 to $1,867. Deflated and expressed in rice equivalents, this is also a fourfold increase.

A breakdown according to enterprise size is only available for the census of 1974–75. It indicates that the difference between codes 381 and 38111 in average value added is in the small industry rather than the household industry segment. Value added for household industries was actually higher in code 38111 than in code 381: Rp 191,021 versus Rp 186,722. This even though code 38111 household enterprises spent considerably less on inputs than code 381 household enterprises did: Rp 148,174 versus Rp 202,422.

Expressed as a percentage of gross output or sales, household enterprises in code 381 spent 52.0 percent on inputs and 11.1 percent on hired labor in 1974–75. The remaining 37 percent went to the owner and his family as profit. Household enterprises in code 38111 spent proportionately less on inputs (43.7 percent) and more on hired labor (15.7 percent), and they took proportionately more as profit (40.6 percent).

Data on the value of wages paid to hired workers are available for the household section of the census of 1974–75 and the small industry section of the census of 1986. It is thus possible to calculate annual profit to the owner for these two sections. For the household section of the census of 1974–75, profit to the owner averaged Rp 143,684 for code 381 and Rp 137,693 for code 38111. These figures are equivalent to $345 and $331. For the small industry section of the census of 1986, profit to the owner averaged Rp 6,460,208 for code 381 and Rp 6,795,255 for code 38111. These figures are equivalent to $5,168 and $5,436. The important point is that code 38111 blacksmithing industries are much more efficient from the owner's point of view than other industries in code 381. They require considerably less working capital for inputs, but generate nearly as much or more value added and profit.

For the household section of the census of 1974–75 and the small industry section of the census of 1986 it is possible to use the wage data to do some additional computations. In 1974–75 hired workers in code 381 household enterprises earned an average of Rp 60,029 per annum, while hired workers in code 38111 household enterprises earned an average of Rp 52,861. These figures are equivalent to $144 and $127. Thus the ratio of profit earned by owners to wages paid to hired workers was 2.4 to 1 for code 381 and 2.6 to 1 for code 38111. This confirms the impression that household enterprises are relatively egalitarian. Dividing the average annual wages paid to hired workers by the average number of person-days worked gives a wage figure of Rp 264 per person-day for code 381 and Rp 251 per person-day for code 38111. These figures are equivalent to to $0.64 and $0.60.

In 1986 hired workers in code 381 small industry enterprises earned an average of Rp 550,573 per annum, while hired workers in code 38111 earned an average of Rp 481,141. These figures are equivalent to $440 and $385. Thus the ratio of profit earned by owners to wages paid to hired workers was 11.7 to 1 for code 381 and 14.1 to 1 for code 38111. These ratios are considerably higher than the ratios of 2.4 to 1 and 2.6 to 1 for household industries, which confirms the impression that small enterprises are less egalitarian than household enterprises.

Some scattered data on other variables are also presented in table 11. It appears that about 70 percent of the enterprises and workers in codes 381 and 38111 are located in Inner Indonesia (Java, Bali, and Madura), with the remaining 30 percent in Outer Indonesia. The density of workers is also higher in Inner Indonesia. Comparing the number of workers in code 381 in 1987 with the national population in the same year shows that the density was 1 to 585 in Inner Indonesia and 1 to 1,287 for Outer Indonesia. For code 38111 the density was 1 to 1,300 in Inner Indonesia and 1 to 2,446 in Outer Indonesia (see also table 13). The percentage distribution of workers by sex is only available for the small industry section of the census of 1986. It shows a large preponderance of male over female workers for both codes 381 (93.2 percent male) and 38111 (94.9 percent male). The percentage of industries using power machinery is only available for the small industry section of the census of 1974–75. Mechanization had scarcely begun in that year, and the percentages were 1.5 percent for code 381 and 0.0 percent for code 38111.

The capital entry or start-up requirements for a rural enterprise consist of the initial outlay of investment capital for machinery, equipment, and workplace, plus enough working capital to purchase at least one batch of raw materials, pay wages to workers one time, and transport the first batch of finished goods to market. Most villagers who start a new enterprise will try to save or borrow a somewhat larger cushion of working capital, enough to purchase one or two months' supply of raw materials. Table 11 gives some data on the investment value of machinery and equipment per enterprise. For 1987 the average investment value was Rp 1,321,436 for code 381 enterprises and Rp 761,321 for code 38111 enterprises, or $801 and $461 in U.S. dollars. If two months' expenditure for inputs is added to these figures, it is possible to estimate that the capital entry requirements for these two codes would be Rp 1,973,712 and Rp 1,180,006, or $1,196 and $715. While this is just a crude estimate, it indicates that the capital entry requirements for blacksmithing enterprises are low in comparison with other metalworking enterprises in code 381. It appears that most of the contrast is in the small industry rather than the household industry section. A similar calculation using figures from the census of 1986 for small industries produces estimates of Rp 3,473,054 for code 381 ($2,778) and Rp 879,108 for code 38111 ($703). Chapter 5 includes a section on rural credit sources and takes up the question of where a villager might obtain start-up capital in these amounts.

The remainder of the data in table 11 pertain to the small industry section of the census of 1986. Some of these data concern fuel consumption. They indicate that code 38111 enterprises use twice as much charcoal on the average as code 381 enterprises, but less of other types of fuels such as coal, coke, petroleum-based fuels (gas, diesel fuel, kerosene), and electricity. If it is assumed that small enterprises in code 38111 experienced relatively few work stoppages in 1986, and operated an average of twenty-five days per month, daily charcoal consumption averaged 22 kilograms per perapen.

Based on the limited data available, it does not appear that government cooperatives play an important role in the activities of metal-working enterprises. Only 2.0 percent of small code 381 enterprises had outstanding loans from cooperatives in 1986, and only 0.9 percent marketed their products through cooperatives. For code 38111 the percentages were only slightly higher, 3.2 percent and 1.4 percent. Thus the important role that the cooperative plays in marketing in Kajar village may be atypical.

Bank loans, mainly from government banks such as Bank Rakyat Indonesia and Bank Pembangunan Daerah, were of considerably more importance. The percentages of enterprises in the small industry section which had outstanding bank loans at the time of the 1986 enumeration were 19.2 for code 381 and 12.8 for code 38111.

The small industry section of the census of 1986 also contains some information on marketing. It shows that the great majority of enterprises in code 381, 87.5 percent, still marketed their products entirely within the province. Another 12.5 percent marketed at least some of their products in other provinces. Exporting to other countries was still relatively uncommon, and only 1.8 percent exported any of their products. The percentages for code 38111 were roughly similar: 88.6, 11.4, and 2.3. The most frequent method of marketing was through intermediaries, and code 38111 enterprises were even more dependent on intermediaries than other enterprises in code 381. While the percentage was 64.0 for code 381, it was 80.4 for code 38111. The next-most common method of marketing was direct sales to consumers, usually out of a marketplace. The percentage of code 381 enterprises which did some direct marketing was 40.4. For code 38111 the percentage was 39.7.

The small industry section of the census of 1986 collected some information on problems faced by enterprise owners. The census forms had spaces for the enumerators to code two problems per owner if necessary, so the percentages in table 11 do not add to 100. Roughly a quarter of the owners reported that they had no major problems. The problems most frequently mentioned by the remaining owners in code 381 were difficulty in obtaining capital (29.4 percent), the supply or price of raw materials (21.0 percent), and difficulty in marketing (33.1 percent). Code 38111 owners were more likely to experience problems with capital and raw materials but less likely to experience marketing problems, perhaps because of their reliance on marketing intermediaries. The percentages for code 38111 were 41.6, 25.0, and 25.0.

Table 12 presents most of the data available on enterprises that make jewelry and musical instruments. The five-digit code used for jewelry making was 39010 in 1974–75. Before the census of 1986 was taken, the code was split in two, 39012 for jewelry made of precious metals and 39013 for jewelry made of base and imitation metals. Similarly, a single code was used for musical instrument making in 1974–75, code 39020. This was later split into code 39021 for traditional instruments such as gamelan sets and 39022 for nontraditional instruments. Comparability between the two censuses has been achieved on table 12 by combining the 1986 codes.

In 1974–75 there were 2,813 small and household enterprises in Indonesia which made metal jewelry. Household enterprises greatly outnumbered small enterprises, by a margin of 24 to 1. These 2,813 enterprises employed 9,688 workers, and averaged 3.4 workers per enterprise. Small jewelry enterprises averaged 8.1 workers while household enterprises averaged 3.3. The number of small jewelry enterprises nearly quadrupled between 1974–75 and 1986, although the average size declined somewhat, from 8.1 to 7.0. Again, the probable cause of a decline in size was the introduction of new mechanical equipment such as polishers and small machines for making metal sheet and wire. Because the survey by the Subdirectorate for Metal in 1987 does not cover code 39 enterprises, it is impossible to construct a time series which includes household jewelry-making enterprises. A comparison of tables 11 and 12 indicates that jewelry-making enter-

Table 12: Selected Economic Data Pertaining to Jewelry and Musical Instrument Making, 1974–1975 and 1986

Item	Type of Product	INDUSTRIAL CENSUS, 1974–75			ECONOMIC CENSUS, 1986		
		Small	Household	Small + Household	Small	Household	Small + Household
1. Number of enterprises	Jewelry	113	2,700	2,813	432	—	—
	Instruments	25	—	—	93	—	—
2. Number of enterprises using hired labor	Jewelry	—	461	—	—	—	—
	Instruments	—	—	—	—	—	—
3. Percentage of enterprises using hired labor	Jewelry	—	17.1	—	—	—	—
	Instruments	—	—	—	—	—	—
4. Number of workers	Jewelry	912	8,776	9,688	3,017	—	—
	Instruments	217	—	—	731	—	—
5. Number of unpaid family workers	Jewelry	240	8,007	8,247	1,032	—	—
	Instruments	45	—	—	186	—	—
6. Percentage of unpaid family workers	Jewelry	26.3	91.2	85.1	34.2	—	—
	Instruments	20.7	—	—	25.4	—	—
7. Number of hired workers	Jewelry	672	769	1,441	1,985	—	—
	Instruments	—	—	—	—	—	—
8. Percentage of hired workers	Jewelry	73.7	8.8	14.9	65.8	—	—
	Instruments	79.3	—	—	74.6	—	—

(*Table 12: Continued*)

Item	Type of Product	INDUSTRIAL CENSUS, 1974–75			ECONOMIC CENSUS, 1986		
		Small	Household	Small + Household	Small	Household	Small + Household
9. Average number of workers per enterprise	Jewelry	8.1	3.3	3.4	7.0	—	—
	Instruments	8.7	—	—	7.9	—	—
10. Annual value of materials consumed per enterprise, including fuel (Rp)	Jewelry	1,367,664	204,891	251,600	11,789,065	—	—
	Instruments	1,847,360	—	—	6,249,785	—	—
11. Annual value of services consumed per enterprise, including rentals and repairs (Rp)	Jewelry	18,274	1,596	2,266	258,222	—	—
	Instruments	129,800	—	—	444,882	—	—
12. Total value of inputs per enterprise (Rp) (10 + 11; does not include wages)	Jewelry	1,385,938	206,487	253,866	12,047,287	—	—
	Instruments	1,977,160	—	—	6,694,667	—	—
13. Annual value of goods produced per enterprise (Rp)	Jewelry	2,343,221	268,481	351,825	16,549,120	—	—
	Instruments	3,274,920	—	—	13,616,925	—	—
14. Annual value of services rendered per enterprise	Jewelry	267,646	87,801	95,026	1,097,079	—	—
	Instruments	24,640	—	—	493,140	—	—

	Type						
15. Annual profit from trading per enterprise (Rp) (resale of goods in same form as purchased)	Jewelry	2,195	0	88	118,755	—	—
	Instruments	0	—	—	3,656	—	—
16. Annual total value of gross output per enterprise (Rp) (13 + 14 + 15)	Jewelry	2,613,062	356,283	446,939	17,764,954	—	—
	Instruments	3,299,560	—	—	14,113,720	—	—
17. Annual census value added per enterprise (16 – 12)	Jewelry	1,227,115	149,796	193,072	5,717,667	—	—
	Instruments	1,322,400	—	—	7,419,054	—	—
18. Annual census value added per enterprise in U.S. $ equivalent	Jewelry	$2950	$360	$464	$4574	—	—
	Instruments	$3179	—	—	$5935	—	—
19. Annual value of wages paid to hired workers per enterprise (Rp)	Jewelry	—	14,821	—	2,011,449	—	—
	Instruments	—	—	—	3,738,516	—	—
20. Annual profit to the owner per enterprise (Rp) (17 – 19)	Jewelry	—	134,975	—	3,706,218	—	—
	Instruments	—	—	—	3,680,538	—	—
21. Annual profit to the owner in U.S. $ equivalent	Jewelry	—	$324	—	$2965	—	—
	Instruments	—	—	—	$2944	—	—

(Table 12: Continued)

Item	Type of Product	INDUSTRIAL CENSUS, 1974–75			ECONOMIC CENSUS, 1986		
		Small	Household	Small + Household	Small	Household	Small + Household
22. Average annual wages per hired worker (Rp)	Jewelry	—	52,036	—	437,756	—	—
	Instruments	—	—	—	637,949	—	—
23. Average annual wages per hired worker in U.S. $ equivalent	Jewelry	—	$125	—	$350	—	—
	Instruments	—	—	—	$510	—	—
24. Ratio of profit to the owner and wages per hired worker	Jewelry	—	2.6:1	—	8.5:1	—	—
	Instruments	—	—	—	5.8:1	—	—
25. Value of inputs as a percentage of output	Jewelry	53.0%	58.0%	56.8%	67.8%	—	—
	Instruments	59.9%	—	—	47.4%	—	—
26. Value of wages as a percentage of output	Jewelry	—	4.2%	—	11.3%	—	—
	Instruments	—	—	—	26.5%	—	—
27. Profit to the owner as a percentage of output	Jewelry	—	—	37.9%	20.9%	—	—
	Instruments	—	—	—	26.1%	—	—

28. Percentage of workers who are male	Jewelry	—	—	—	85.2%	—	—
	Instruments	—	—	—	95.2%	—	—
29. Percentage of workers who are female	Jewelry	—	—	—	14.8%	—	—
	Instruments	—	—	—	4.8%	—	—
30. Investment value of machinery and equipment per enterprise	Jewelry	—	—	—	424,535	—	—
	Instruments	—	—	—	524,409	—	—
31. Investment value of machinery and equipment in U.S. $ equivalent	Jewelry	—	—	—	$340	—	—
	Instruments	—	—	—	$420	—	—

NOTE: This table includes 1974–75 data from codes 39010 and 39020, as well as 1986 data from codes 39012, 39013, 39021, and 39022.

prises are similar to blacksmithing enterprises in many ways. Small jewelry-making enterprises supplied 73.7 percent of their labor needs from hired labor in 1974–75, which is very close to the 74.4 percent figure for small blacksmithing enterprises. Household jewelry-making enterprises only supplied 8.8 percent of their needs from hired labor, however, which is considerably less than the 25.9 percent figure for blacksmithing.

The average gross output of small and household jewelry-making enterprises was Rp 446,939 in 1974–75, while the average value of inputs was Rp 253,866. Thus the average value added was Rp 193,072. That is $464 per annum, which is close to the figure of $496 for blacksmithing.

Wage data are only available for the household industry section of the census of 1974–75 and the small industry section of the census of 1986. Thus it is only possible to calculate profit for these sections. In 1974–75 household jewelry-making enterprises earned an average annual profit of $324, which is again very similar to the figure of $331 for blacksmithing. Wage rates were also similar: Rp 52,036 and 52,861 per worker per annum. Jewelry-making enterprises spent proportionately more on inputs and less on labor than blacksmithing enterprises, because they relied less on hired labor. Expressed as a percentage of gross output, household jewelry-making enterprises spent 58.0 percent on inputs and only 4.2 percent on wages. The remaining 37.9 percent was taken as profit to the owner and his family. The ratio of profit to the owner to wages paid to hired workers was 2.6 to 1, which is identical to the ratio for blacksmithing.

Small jewelry-making enterprises experienced acceptable rates of growth in value added between 1974–75 and 1986, but did not achieve the rates experienced by small blacksmithing industries. Real value added in U.S. dollar equivalents in small jewelry-making enterprises nearly doubles, from $3,179 to $5,935. During the same period real value added in small blacksmithing enterprises increased nearly sixfold, from $1,211 to $7,140. Thus although average value added was much higher in small jewelry-making enterprises in 1974–75, by 1986 it was lower.

A lower growth rate in value added for small jewelry-making enterprises translated into lower profit to the owner and lower wages paid to hired workers by 1986. By 1986 average profit to the owner was $2,965, and average wages were $350. This compares with $5,436 and

$385 for small blacksmithing enterprises. The ratio of profit to the owner to wages to hired workers was 8.5 to 1 for small jewelry-making enterprises versus 14.1 to 1 for small blacksmithing enterprises. Profit to the owner as a proportion of gross output was only 20.9 percent for jewelry-making versus 55.9 percent for blacksmithing.

The jewelry-making industry employs proportionately more female labor than industries in code 381. Some of the women work as polishers, while others make and assemble pieces of jewelry using small, handheld blowtorches. Of the 3,017 workers employed in small jewelry-making enterprises in 1986, 447, or 14.8 percent, were women.

Small jewelry-making operations owned an average of $340 worth of machinery and equipment in 1986. Using the method described above for code 381 industries, the estimated capital entry requirement for a small jewelry-making enterprise was Rp 2,432,416 in 1986, or $1,946. This is much higher than the estimated requirement for a small blacksmithing enterprise of Rp 879,108, or $703.

There are no data available on household enterprises which make musical instruments. There are some data on small enterprises which make such instruments, however, and it is available for both the 1974–75 and 1986 censuses so that a time series can be constructed. In 1974–75 there were 25 small enterprises in the country which manufactured musical instruments. Most of these were engaged in the production of gamelan orchestra sets. They employed 217 workers, or an average of 8.7 workers per enterprise. A high proportion of these workers, 79.3 percent, were hired, while only 20.7 percent were family workers. By 1986 the number of enterprises and workers had more than tripled. The average number of workers had gone down slightly, to 7.9, and the percentage of hired workers had also gone down slightly, to 74.6.

Because musical instruments are so large, the average expenditure on raw materials and other inputs is high. In 1974–75 small musical instrument enterprises spent an average of Rp 1,977,160 per annum on inputs, produced goods worth Rp 3,274,920, and generated value added worth Rp 1,322,400. Value added was $3,179, which was higher than any other category of metalworking enterprises in that year. Between 1974–75 and 1986 average value added in small instrument enterprises nearly doubled, to Rp 7,419,054, or $5,935. Although this is an acceptable rate of growth, these enterprises were outstripped by small enterprises in code 381, which generated an average value added in 1986 of Rp 9,518,198, or $7,615.

There are enough wage data to do a profit calculation for small instrument-making enterprises in 1986. Owners of these enterprises earned an average of Rp 3,680,538 per annum, or $2,944. They paid very high wages to their workers, averaging Rp 637,949 per annum, or $510. These were the highest wage levels of any category of metal-working enterprises in that year. Expressed as a share of gross output, the profit taken by owners was relatively low, 26.1 percent. The ratio of profit to the owner to wages to hired workers was also relatively low in comparison to other types of small enterprises, 5.8 to 1. Wages were high because the labor force consists almost entirely of adult men with high skill levels. Only 4.8 percent of the workers employed in small instrument-making enterprises in 1986 were women.

The average small instrument-making enterprise owned machinery and equipment worth Rp 524,409 in 1986. This is $420, which is higher than the investment value for blacksmithing and jewelry-making enterprises but considerably lower than for nontraditional enterprises in code 381. Capital entry requirements for small instrument-making enterprises can be estimated at Rp 1,640,187 in 1986, or $1,312.

As noted earlier, employment in small and household metalworking enterprises was estimated at about 200,000. By combining the figures for codes 37 and 38 in the survey by the Subdirectorate for Metal for 1987 and the economic census figures for code 39 from 1986, it is now possible to produce a revised estimate:

— code 371 and 372 industries (basic metal industries): 881 enterprises and 3,714 workers;

— code 381 industries (fabricated metal products excluding machinery, transport equipment, and scientific equipment): 45,912 enterprises and 182,374 workers;

— code 39012 and 39013 industries (jewelry-making): 432 small enterprises and an estimated 8,439 household enterprises, 3,017 workers in small enterprises and an estimated 26,328 workers in household enterprises;

— code 39021 and 39022 industries (musical instrument making): 93 small enterprises and an estimated 558 household enterprises, 731 workers in small enterprises and an estimated 2,193 workers in household enterprises;

— other code 390 industries (decorative objects of metal): an estimated 651 enterprises and 2,924 workers;

— total: an estimated 56,966 enterprises and 221,281 workers.

Estimated figures are based on the assumption that metalworking enterprises in code 39 follow the same general patterns as enterprises in code 381.[7] Persons who play supporting roles—for example metal or charcoal suppliers, charcoal makers, or tool traders—are not included. It is not clear whether BPS enumerators place tinkers and cutlers in the industrial sector or the service sector. If they are placed in the service sector, they are also excluded from the above estimate.

Table 13 gives the number of enterprises, number of workers, and density of workers, by province, for codes 381 and 38111. Two density measures are used: the ratio of metalworkers to the total population and the ratio of metalworkers to the working population. In terms of absolute numbers, table 13 shows that there are more code 381 smiths in Central Java than in any other province. Central Java is followed by East Java, West Java, South Sumatra, Jakarta, Bali, North Sumatra, and South Sulawesi, in that order. For code 38111 there are more smiths in East Java than any other province, followed by Central Java, West Java, Bali, South Sumatra, West Nusa Tenggara, South Sulawesi, and North Sumatra, in that order.

The large number of smiths in South Sumatra comes as something of a surprise, since there are no major mines in that province and it is not historically famous for its metalworking industries. There are 16,605 smiths working in code 381 enterprises in the province, of which 6,372, or 38 percent, are traditional blacksmiths. The Subdirectorate for Metal survey of 1987 indicates that most of the remaining smiths are employed in nontraditional industries which make kitchen wares, structural metal products, and furniture from aluminum and other metal sheet and tubing. Apparently there has been a growth of these nontraditional industries in the province in recent years.

When we compare code 381 with code 38111, some interesting differences between provinces appear. The capital city of Jakarta has 1,396 metalworking industries in code 381, but only 8 of them (less than 1 percent) are code 38111 blacksmithing industries. Central Java, with a concentration of casting and spare-part industries, also shows a low ratio of code 38111 to code 381 enterprises (29 percent), as does South Sumatra (35 percent). On Bali, on the other hand, 2,990 of the 3,111 industries in code 381 (96 percent) are blacksmithing industries.

The average number of workers per enterprise also varies significantly by code and province. The largest enterprises are found in South Sumatra province, where code 381 enterprises have an average of 5.4

Table 13: Density of Employment in Code 381 and
Code 38111 by Province, 1987

	CODE 381			
	Number of Enterprises	Number of Workers	Ratio of Workers to Total Population	Ratio of Workers to Working Population
1. Jakarta	1,396	7, 114	1:1195	1:376
2. West Java	5,126	21,802	1:1486	1:575
3. Central Java	12,367	54,756	1:509	1:228
4. Yogyakarta	855	3,274	1:928	1:464
5. East Java	9,925	37,794	1:851	1:405
6. Bali	3,111	6,888	1:395	1:225
Total, Inner Indonesia	32,780	131,628	1:811	1:350
7. Aceh	836	3721	1:848	1:344
8. North Sumatra	1,678	5,770	1:1,716	1:729
9. West Sumatra (Minangkabau)	1,039	2,866	1:1,331	1:495
10. Riau	175	817	1:3,329	1:1,121
11. Jambi	200	642	1:2,935	1:1,120
12. South Sumatra	3,056	16,605	1:345	1:133
13. Bengkulu	291	748	1:1,374	1:732
14. Lampung	420	1,756	1:3,733	1:1,560
15. West Nusa Tenggara	652	2,614	1:1,209	1:513
16. East Nusa Tenggara	410	1,024	1:3,157	1:1,659
17. East Timor	91	303	1:2,225	1:1,248
18. West Kalimantan	276	780	1:3,827	1:1,575
19. Central Kalimantan	297	751	1:1,593	1:1,604
20. South Kalimantan	676	1,754	1:1,353	1:595
21. East Kalimantan	274	885	1:1,864	1:824
22. North Sulawesi	856	1,776	1:1,351	1:593
23. Central Sulawesi	166	538	1:3,016	1:1,295
24. South Sulawesi	1,213	5,284	1:1,293	1:446
25. Southeast Sulawesi	357	1,353	1:896	1:339
26. Maluku	101	522	1:3,289	1:977
27. Irian Jaya	70	237	1:6,173	1:2,913
Total Outer Indonesia	13,132	50,746	1:1,287	1:527
Total Indonesia	45,912	182,374	1:942	1:399

NOTE: The working population is defined as those persons who worked during the week prior to the census enumeration. It is 97.19% of the economically active population, the remaining 2.81% consisting of persons who were looking for work.

SOURCES: Subdirectorate for Metal (Department of Industry), *Data on Small Industries*, 1987; BPS, *Statistik Indonesia 1989*, tables 3.1.2. and 3.2.3., pp. 44–45 and 60.

Number of Enterprises	Number of Workers	Ratio of Workers to Total Population	Ratio of Workers to Working Population
		CODE 38111	
8	44	1:193,152	1:60,771
2,998	11,745	1:2,759	1:1,067
3,583	15,168	1:1,838	1:824
296	1,174	1:2,587	1:1,293
5,713	20,701	1:1,554	1:739
2,990	6,553	1:415	1:236
15,588	55,385	1:1,927	1:832
595	2,393	1:1,318	1:535
712	2,442	1:4,055	1:1,723
524	1,463	1:2,607	1:970
86	363	1:7,492	1:2,524
148	495	1:3,806	1:1,453
1,083	6,372	1:899	1:347
164	436	1:2,357	1:1,256
200	691	1:9,487	1:3,964
512	1,988	1:1,589	1:675
374	839	1:3,853	1:2,025
90	292	1:2,309	1:1,295
174	419	1:7,124	1:2,931
251	608	1:1,968	1:845
538	1,317	1:1,803	1:792
114	265	1:6,226	1:2,751
675	1,301	1:1,844	1:810
93	275	1:5,900	1:2,534
857	3,522	1:1,940	1:670
222	678	1:1,722	1:677
75	404	1:4,249	1:1,288
38	137	1:10,679	1:5,040
7,525	26,700	1:2,445	1:1,002
23,113	82,085	1:2,096	1:887

workers and code 38111 enterprises have an average of 5.9 workers. Enterprises also average more than five workers each in Jakarta and Maluku. In Bali, by contrast, the average number of workers per enterprise is 2.2 for both codes. Enterprises also average less than three workers each in West Sumatra, Bengkulu, East Nusa Tenggara, West Kalimantan, Central Kalimantan, South Kalimantan, and North Sulawesi.

Density figures are also revealing. The highest density for code 381 is found in South Sumatra, where 1 out of every 133 working persons is employed in a metalworking enterprise. This is an astoundingly high density, especially when it is considered that some working persons are women. The density for working males would undoubtedly be much higher. Bali and Central Java also have very high code 381 densities of 1 in 225 and 1 in 228. The lowest density, not surprisingly, is in the province of Irian Jaya, where stone tools were used by the population of most districts until recent years. Low densities are also found in East Nusa Tenggara, West Kalimantan, Lampung, Central Sulawesi, and East Timor.

The density figures for code 38111 reveal a rather different pattern. The highest density by far is in Bali, where 1 of every 236 working persons is a blacksmith. Since the rate of female participation in the labor force is very high in Bali, this figure would have to be approximately halved to obtain the density for working males. In other words, approximately 1 of every 118 working males in Bali is a blacksmith. The provinces of South Sumatra, West Nusa Tenggara, Aceh, South Sulawesi, Southeast Sulawesi, North Sulawesi, East Java, Central Java, South Kalimantan, and Central Kalimantan also have high densities. As in Bali, the female labor force participation rates are very high for the four provinces on Java, which would tend to depress the density ratios in comparison with the provinces in Outer Indonesia. Low densities for code 38111 are found in Jakarta, Irian Jaya, Lampung, Riau, West Kalimantan, East Kalimantan, Central Sulawesi, and East Nusa Tenggara.

The density figures for code 38111 may reveal something about historical patterns of dispersion. First, it is interesting to note that there are blacksmithing enterprises in every province of Indonesia. This suggests that the industry is an ancient one which had time to spread into every corner of the archipelago, with the exception of some parts of Irian Jaya. Second, the plotting of high-density provinces on a map suggests that there were six major regional centers of metalworking:

Center 1: East Java, Central Java, Bali, and West Nusa Tenggara
Center 2: South Sulawesi and Southeast Sulawesi
Center 3: South Kalimantan and Central Kalimantan
Center 4: Minangkabau, Bengkulu and South Sumatra
Center 5: Aceh
Center 6: North Sulawesi

The part of West Nusa Tenggara which should be included in center 1 is probably limited to the western part of Lombok island, where there is a large Balinese outlier population.

Center 1 was a major importer of metals from other provinces, while Centers 2, 3, and 4 were major exporters. Aceh and North Sulawesi were smaller regional centers which depended on a combination of metals from their own mines and imported metals. Center 1 is associated with the Majapahit dynasty in the late historical period, which had strong trade relations with centers 2 and 3, succeeding at times in extending hegemony over them. Center 2 is also associated with the smaller historical kingdoms of Luwu and Banggai. Majapahit also had dynastic and trade relations with center 4, and attempted to extend its hegemony over this center for a time, beginning in the fourteenth century. At an earlier period center 4 was associated with the kingdom of Srivijaya, centered in South Sumatra around Palembang. Although the majority of metalworking enterprises in South Sumatra province are nontraditional, the density of code 38111 blacksmithing enterprises is still the second-highest in the country. One hypothesis in need of further testing is that the blacksmithing communities in South Sumatra arose in response to Srivijaya's need for weapons and tools, and they imported their iron from West Sumatra and Bengkulu.

Summary of Conclusions

At this point it would be well to summarize some of the major conclusions that can be derived from the macrodata.

There has been a gradual shift of labor out of the agricultural sector and into other sectors of the rural economy, including small and household industries. This shift amounts to about 11.6 percent between 1971 and 1985. It is part of a longer-term trend which began about 1960.

The Industrial Census of 1974–75 used a very generous labor force definition that included anyone who worked at all, no matter how few the hours. Subsequent surveys, such as the Economic Census of 1986, used much tighter definitions which excluded many part-time family workers. Since the majority of part-time family workers are rural women, published time series give the impression that there was a great rush of part-time female labor into the rural industrial sector in the mid-1970s, followed by a great rush out again in the 1980s. This is largely a statistical artifact, possibly exacerbated by the crop failures of 1973–75 due to the wereng rice pest. The true underlying pattern seems to be stable but relatively rapid growth in industrial employment, also starting around 1960, with growth in male employment somewhat exceeding growth in female employment in rural areas. Using the tighter definitions, employment in household industries increased from about 2.1 million in 1964–65 to about 2.7 million in 1986. Use of a looser definition would add approximately a million part-time workers to each of those totals (see note 2, and table 8).

Metalworking industries rely largely on full-time male labor. Therefore the statistics for these industries are less affected by changes in labor force definitions. These statistics show that the number of small and household metalworking enterprises, as well as the number of workers employed in these enterprises, approximately tripled between 1974–75 and 1987. For enterprises in code 381, the industrial code which includes blacksmithing and other base metal industries making utilitarian goods, the number of enterprises increased from 15,865 to 45,912. The number of workers increased from 65,696 to 182,374. Although the data for other metalworking codes are not as complete, industries making jewelry, musical instruments, and ornamental objects of metal appear to have experienced similar or even more rapid increases.

Metalworking industries are more capital-intensive than other industries. They spend more on inputs and labor, and as a consequence generate more value added and profit for their owners. Household and small industries as a whole spent an average of $2,158 on inputs and labor in 1986, which generated average value added of $1,075 and average profit of $875. In contrast, household and small industries in code 38 spent an average of $3,059 on inputs and labor, which generated average value added of $2,105 and average profit of $1,455.

Household and small metalworking industries generate more than enough income to meet rice requirements, even for landless families which must purchase most of their rice. Assuming that the maximum amount of rice needed by an average-sized household of five persons is about 730 kilograms per year, the owners of household metalworking enterprises earned three times their rice requirement in 1986, and the owners of small metalworking enterprises earned twenty-two times their rice requirement. These households usually have other sources of income as well, for example from income-generating activities carried out by the female members of the household.

Household metalworking industries meet most of their labor needs from unpaid family labor, while small metalworking industries meet most of their needs from hired labor. Household enterprises in code 381 used about 80 percent family labor and 20 percent hired labor in 1974–75. These percentages were reversed for small enterprises.

The average size of code 38111 blacksmithing enterprises declined slightly between 1974–75 and 1987, from 4.2 to 3.6 workers. This is probably due more to the "rationalization" of enterprises through the introduction of small low-wattage machinery than to the change in the labor force definition. Although the data are not complete, it appears that jewelry- and musical instrument–making enterprises experienced similar declines, and for the same reason.

Time series indicate that there was an enormous across-the-board increase in real value added for all sizes and types of industries between 1974–75 and 1986, giving some support to proponents of the "pull" theory. This value added is not affected by changes in labor force definitions, as long as it is expressed in value added per enterprise rather than per worker. Value added increased at an even faster rate for code 381 and code 38111 metalworking industries than for industries in general. Average value added for small and household industries in code 381 increased nearly fivefold, from $735 to $3,528. The highest rates of increase were for small blacksmithing enterprises, those employing five or more workers, which experienced nearly a sixfold increase, from $1,211 to $7,140. Small jewelry- and musical instrument–making enterprises experienced lower but still acceptable rates of increase of one and a half or two times.

Traditional metalworking enterprises such as blacksmithing, jewelry making, and musical instrument making are relatively egalitarian, in that a high proportion of the gross output goes for wages, and the ratio of profit to the owner to wages to hired workers is relatively low. Apparently there is some wage expectation carried over from historical share systems that keeps the ratio at about 2.6 to 1. As enterprises grow in size and there are fewer disruptions due to cash flow problems and seasonality, incomes for hired workers also increase, but incomes for owners increase at a much faster rate, so that the gap widens and the industries become less egalitarian.

There is very little in the way of available data on wages in metalworking industries, and particularly on wages per man-hour. What data there are indicate that wage laborers who work in small enterprises are better off than those who work in household enterprises. Wage laborers who worked in code 381 household enterprises in 1974–75 earned the equivalent of $144 per annum, or $0.64 per person-day. This was enough to purchase only 551 kilograms of rice per annum. Thus if these workers were heads of household, they may not have met their household's rice requirement. Wage laborers who worked in small enterprises in 1986 earned an average of $440 per annum, which was enough to buy 1,534 kilograms of rice per annum, or more than twice the rice requirement for a household. The macrodata are not fine enough to distinguish between categories of workers, for example between empu, who are likely to be heads of mature households with high rice requirements, and panjak, who are likely to be single or just starting new households.

Code 38111 blacksmithing enterprises are remarkably efficient from the owner's point of view compared with other types of metalworking industries. They require less capital investment in machinery and equipment and less working capital, but they generate as much profit or more to the owner and his family. In 1986, for example, small blacksmithing enterprises had an average investment of only $264 in machinery and equipment and spent an average of $4,340 per annum for inputs and labor. In contrast, code 381 enterprises had an average investment of $1,580 in machinery and equipment, and spent an average of $9,637 for inputs and labor. Yet blacksmithing enterprises earned more profit: $5,436 compared to $5,168 for code 381 enterprises. Remembering that code 38111 is subsumed under code 381, this contrast would be even sharper if blacksmithing enterprises were compared with nonblacksmithing enterprises. The estimated capital entry requirement for starting a small code 38111 enterprise in 1986 was $703, versus $2,778 for code 381.

Blacksmithing is still the most important metalworking industry in Indonesia. The total number of small and household metalworking enterprises was estimated at 56,966 for 1987, which includes all the industries that can be accounted for in codes 37, 38, and 39. Of this number 23,113, or 40.6 percent, are in code 38111. Nonblacksmithing enterprises in code 381 account for another 40.0 percent. These include traditional casting industries as well as a variety of industries making kitchen wares and other utilitarian products out of metal sheet and tubing. The machine enterprises in codes 382 and 383 account for another 13.2 percent, but nearly three-quarters of these enterprises are actually engaged in machine repair and maintenance rather than production.

There are not enough published data to construct time series on the important issues of intensity of labor and the ratio of hired to family workers. What data there are indicate that hired laborers in household enterprises put in about two and a half times as many person-days per year as unpaid family laborers. The ratio of hired to family labor appears to have declined by 3–5 percent in small enterprises between 1974–75 and 1986, but the issue is obscured somewhat by the growing tendency to pay wages to family members.

Approximately 70 percent of the metalworking enterprises and workers in codes 381 and 38111 are located in Inner Indonesia, with the remaining 30 percent in Outer Indonesia. The density of workers, expressed as a ratio of metalworkers to the working population, is more than twice as high in Inner Indonesia. Some Outer Island provinces have high densities, particularly those which had traditional mining and smelting industries, or which exercised political control over mining and smelting sites. By far the highest density of metalworkers today is on Bali. The pattern of density for code 38111 supports the hypothesis of a late historical dispersion out of East Java toward Bali in the east and Central Java in the West.

The most important government intervention appears to be bank credit. The percentage of small enterprises in code 381 which had outstanding bank loans was 19.2 in 1986. In contrast, cooperatives appear to be relatively unimportant. Only 2–3 percent of small enterprises in code 381 had outstanding cooperative loans or marketed their products through cooperatives.

The macrodata confirm the impression that blacksmithing enterprises are heavy users of charcoal, consuming an average of 6,684 kilograms per perapen per year.

The most frequent method of marketing for small metalworking enterprises is through intermediaries, followed by direct sales to consumers in the marketplace. Blacksmithing enterprises rely even more heavily on intermediaries than other metalworking enterprises do. Most marketing is done within the province, but 12.5 percent of small code 381 enterprises market some of their products in other provinces. Exporting is still rare for code 381 enterprises but may be more common for code 39 enterprises such as jewelry and musical instrument making.

The three problems most frequently reported by small metalworking enterprises are difficulties in marketing, difficulties in obtaining capital, and the supply and price of raw materials.

In 1974–75 jewelry making enterprises closely resembled blacksmithing enterprises in terms of their input-output structure. The average value added for small and household jewelry-making enterprises was $464, compared with $496 for blacksmithing enterprises. Average profit to the owner for household jewelry-making enterprises was $324, compared with $331 for blacksmithing. By 1986 a significant gap had opened between the two industries because of lower growth rates in value added in jewelry making.

Most of the musical instrument–making enterprises in code 39 produce gamelan sets. These enterprises are characterized by their large size, high average expenditures on inputs, and very high wage levels. In 1974–75 average value added in small instrument-making enterprises was $3,179, which was higher than any other category of metalworking enterprises. Again, however, relatively low growth rates meant that instrument-making enterprises were outstripped by code 381 enterprises by 1986.

CHAPTER 5

Government Interventions

This chapter describes several types of government interventions which af-fect rural industries, particularly those interventions aimed at the metal-working subsector. I begin with the regulatory environment: policies which govern the import of potentially competing manufactures, export promo-tion, and the granting of industrial licenses. Next I take up the Depart-ment of Industry and its extension programs for rural industries. There follows a section on government banks operating in rural areas, and credit programs which make loans for nonagricultural enterprises. Finally, there is a comment on government rice price supports and fertilizer subsidies, and their indirect effect on rural industries.

The Five-Year Plans

UNDER THE OLD ORDER REGIME of President Sukarno, the govern-ment pursued a strongly interventionist and inward-looking strategy of industrial development which gave priority to state-owned enter-prises. A large number of private domestic and foreign enterprises were nationalized during this era (Poot, Kuyvenhoven, and Jansen 1990, 3–4). This strategy was officially abandoned after the New Order government of President Suharto took over in 1966, but protection-ist and interventionist sentiments are still found among government officials at all levels of the bureaucracy.

Since 1969 the New Order government has prepared and published a detailed development plan for every five-year period. These plans, known by the acronym REPELITA, outline the government's development philosophy and strategy for every sector of the economy, including the industrial sector. A review of these plans indicates that there has been a broad shift from a strategy in the 1970s which emphasized import substitution and the protection of domestic industries to the current strategy which emphasizes export promotion and deregulation.

The main rationale for the import substitution strategy of the 1970s was the need to save foreign exchange. It was felt that this could be done by actively assisting import-competing industries—domestic industries which produced goods that could replace imports. Principally these were industries which produced consumer goods. One way of assisting them was with favorable credit policies, including credit subsidies; another was protectionist trade measures. A further rationale for the import substitution strategy was to preserve jobs in domestic industries.

Beginning about 1983 the government came under heavy pressure from the World Bank and other foreign assistance agencies to dismantle protectionist policies and permit free trade.[1] It was argued that foreign exchange should be earned by actively promoting exports rather than discouraging imports, and that deregulation would force domestic industries to become more efficient and competitive. Many senior Indonesian officials and economists had become convinced of the economic wisdom of such a course. However, the government still regarded small and household industries as a special case. It was feared that removing the protections for these industries would cause widespread unemployment in rural areas, which could have led to political unrest. Accordingly, much of the protectionist legislation which covers these industries has been left in place.

The REPELITA plans need to be understood as both economic and political documents. They outline the strategy of central government planners for developing the economy of the nation, but at the same time they must address the political concerns of the Indonesian people. Over the years these concerns have varied, but they have included employment creation, equitable distribution of the benefits of economic growth, protection for economically weak entrepreneurs, and preferential treatment for pribumi (Malay) over non-pribumi (non-Malay, usually Chinese) people.

Under REPELITA I, which covered the period 1969–70 to 1973–74, industrial development was supposed to focus on industries supporting the agricultural sector through the provision of inputs or the processing of output. Priority was also given to industries which generated badly needed foreign exchange — either through import substitution or exporting — as well as domestic raw-material-processing industries, labor-intensive industries, and industries contributing to regional development. Little priority was given to the development of small-scale enterprises.[2]

Under REPELITA II (1974–75 to 1978–79) creation of employment was introduced as the most important objective. There was also a preference for industries which processed domestic raw materials or promoted linkages with agriculture or infrastructure, and an emphasis on favoring pribumi entrepreneurs. In general, a tendency could be noted toward a return to interventionist measures, such as restrictions on imports to protect domestic industries and the tightening of rules on foreign investment. During this period foreign exchange became less of a concern because of worldwide increases in the price of oil, which benefited Indonesia as an oil-exporting nation.

During the late 1970s the government's Green Revolution program was heavily criticized for having exacerbated class differences in rural areas. The government responded to this criticism in REPELITA III (1979–80 to 1983–84) by placing a new emphasis on equity (pemerataan). The goal of economic growth was not to be abandoned, but growth would be accompanied by a more equitable distribution of economic benefits. The most important industrialization objectives were the promotion of economically weak entrepreneurs, orderly (i.e. politically stable) economic development, development of a broad industrial base, and the promotion of labor-intensive exports. The development of small-scale enterprises was given priority for the first time because it was seen as a means to achieve the equity goal. Credit was made available to small-scale enterprises at lower than market rates.

In REPELITA IV (1984–85 to 1988–89) pressures on the Indonesian government to deregulate and privatize became clearly visible. A major goal was to lay the foundation for the industrial sector to become equal in size to the agricultural sector. Another goal was to decrease dependence on oil revenues. Previous objectives which were reiterated included employment creation, promoting exports, import substitution, regional development, and the processing of domestic natural resources. Priority was given for the first time to the development of the machine industry. The development of small-scale enterprises was again emphasized. In REPELITA IV there was also a new emphasis on the private sector. Foreign private investments were preferred in export and high-technology industries, but with the ultimate goal of Indonesian ownership of a majority share. For the first time attention was given to some of the constraints on industrial growth, and there were proposals to improve import and export regulations, the efficiency of domestic production, the operation of capital markets, and the availability of credit. The protection of domestic industries and market regulation were not abandoned as policy options, however.

In REPELITA V (1989–90 to 1993–94) the idea of economic takeoff championed in the 1960s was revived, and preparing Indonesia for takeoff, supposed to occur during REPELITA VI, was seen as a major goal. By the time of takeoff the industrial sector would be the main engine of the Indonesian economy. Under REPELITA V there was a new emphasis on promoting export-oriented manufacturing through the further removal of trade constraints. The development of small-scale industries continued to be important, but was to be accomplished by the formation of linkages with large- and medium-scale industries. Small-scale industries were to be included in the export promotion effort for the first time. Credit subsidies were removed in order that government banks could become profitable, but credit was made available at market rates in rural as well as urban areas.

The Regulatory Environment: Imports

The Indonesian government produces a tariff book which lists all types of imported manufactures and breaks them down according to two-digit, four-digit, and nine-digit codes. The code descriptions, which are standardized internationally according to the SITC commodity groups, are in English and do not correspond very well to Indonesian tool types. Beside each type of manufacture in the tariff book are columns which list any tariff, tariff surcharge, value-added tax, or luxury tax which must be paid by importers, as well as any restrictions placed on imports. The two-digit code for hand tools and cutlery is 82. Under code 82 are fifteen four-digit codes:

82.01 — Hand Tools Used in Agriculture, Horticulture or Forestry

82.02 — Hand Saws, Blades for Saws of All Kinds

82.03 — Files, Rasps, Pliers, Pincers, Tweezers, Metal Cutting Shears, Pipe-Cutters, Bolt Croppers, Perforating Punches and Similar Hand Tools

82.04 — Hand Operated Spanners and Wrenches; Interchangeable Spanner Sockets

82.05 — Hand Tools Not Elsewhere Specified or Included; Blow Lamps, Vises, Clamps, Anvils, Portable Forges, Grinding Wheels

82.06 — Tool Sets

82.07 — Interchangeable Tools for Hand Tools, Whether or Not Power-Operated, or for Machine Tools, Including Dies for Drawing or Extruding Metal, and Rock-Drilling or Earth Boring Tools

82.08 — Knives and Cutting Blades, for Machines or for Mechanical Appliances

82.09 — Plates, Sticks, Tips and the Like for Tools

82.10 — Hand Operated Mechanical Appliances, Weighing 10 Kilograms or Less,   Used in the Preparation, Conditioning or Serving of Food or Drink

82.11 — Knives with Cutting Blades, Serrated or Not (Including Pruning Knives, Other Than Knives of Heading No. 82.08 and Blades Therefor)

82.12 — Razors and Razor Blades

82.13 — Scissors and Shears

82.14 — Other Articles of Cutlery; Manicure or Pedicure Sets and Instruments

82.15 — Spoons, Forks, Ladles, Skimmers, Cake-Servers, Fish Knives, Butter-Knives, Sugar Tongs and Similar Kitchen and Tableware

The greatest degree of protection is enjoyed by industries in code 82.01, which manufacture hand tools used in agriculture, horticulture, and forestry, such as spades, shovels, hoes, pitchforks, rakes, hatchets, axes, adzes, grass shears, and sickles. The tariffs and taxes charged on products in this code total 50 percent of the value of the product in most cases. This of course means that the product will have to be retailed for a considerably higher price and will therefore be less competitive with local manufactures.

Some of the tools covered by code 82.0 may only be imported by state-owned companies. Generally the companies which import such tools are those under the supervision of the departments and directorates of forestry, plantations, and transmigration. Most of these tools are distributed free of charge to villagers who work in government forests or on government-owned plantations, or who have agreed to participate in the government's transmigration scheme. The types of tools imported by state-owned companies are similar in most cases to those made by local blacksmiths, and could just as well be ordered from blacksmithing villages such as Kajar. A common complaint of blacksmiths, in fact, is that state-owned companies prefer to either import the tools they buy or order locally made tools through urban dealers. The reasons why state-owned companies seldom deal directly with blacksmithing villages are complex and may have to do with factors of quantity, standardization, packaging, and convenience. Village smiths generally assume that importers and dealers provide kickbacks to government officials in charge of procurement. Since many of these importers and dealers are ethnic Chinese, this suspicion unfortunately tends to exacerbate anti-Chinese sentiment.

State-owned companies have a monopoly on importing tools in seven of the nine-digit codes under code 82.01. The total value of tools in these codes imported by state-owned companies in 1989 was Rp 228 million, or $130,338. This very small amount does not even equal the value of the annual production of a single village. The average blacksmithing enterprise which makes pacul (spades/hoes), for example, finishes twenty tools a day. If it operates more or less continuously, for three hundred days a year, that amounts to six thousand tools annually. If each tool is displaced by an imported tool worth $3.00, the total number of smithies displaced is only seven or eight. Of course state-owned companies are not limited to importing tools in the categories for which they hold a monopoly. If they import tools in other categories, the amount of damage to indigenous blacksmiths may be much greater.

The government's stated aim in imposing a high tariff and import restrictions on code 82.01 imports is to assist indigenous blacksmiths. This being so, it should be observed that the coverage is inadequate to achieve that purpose. The three general categories of products made by most blacksmithing villages are agricultural tools, workman's tools, and knives. Only agricultural tools fall under code 82.01. Most workman's tools (hammers, chisels, planes, crowbars) fall under code 82.05 and are protected by tariffs and taxes amounting to 30 percent. Fixed-blade knives such as those made by village smiths fall under code 82.11 and are protected by tariffs and taxes amounting to 30–40 percent. Other types of items commonly made by village smiths are pliers, tweezers, scissors, and shears. These fall under codes 82.03 and 82.13 and receive protection of 20–40 percent. There are no restrictions on the import of any of these items, and private companies may import them in any quantity they desire.

Not all the code 82 imports compete with traditional products. Blacksmiths are able to make saws, and sometimes do for home use, but the teeth of the saw blade must be hand-filed and this is too time-consuming to make the saws profitable. Thus the importation of products in code 82.02 does not affect local markets very much. Similarly, blacksmiths can make files and rasps by hand, but again, the procedure is time-consuming and the resulting product is not very satisfactory. If blacksmiths make files and rasps, it is generally for their own use to avoid purchasing the expensive imported types. Obviously blacksmiths do not make the mechanical appliances used in food processing industries listed under code 82.10. Neither do they make the razors and razor blades listed under code 82.12. In between products which definitely compete and those which definitely do not is a gray area of products which village blacksmiths might learn to make if they had samples to copy and firm orders. Examples would be the interchangeable blades used for machinery listed under code 82.08.

Some of the products listed under code 82 do not compete with those made by blacksmiths but do compete with those made by other types of smiths. Examples would be nonelectric flat irons (code 8205.51.100) and kitchen wares of all types (code 82.15). The former are a common product of iron-casting smiths in Central Java, and the latter are made in many districts by smiths who work with sheet aluminum and other metal sheet.

The total value of products imported under code 82 in 1989 was Rp 135.6 billion, or $77,466,690. The five most important types of imports were:

— rock drilling or earth boring tools with working parts ($18.1 million);
— blades for mechanical saws such as band saws, chain saws, and circular saws ($7.9 million);
— knives and cutting blades for woodworking machines and appliances ($5.9 million);
— spanners and wrenches ($4.9 million);
— pliers, pincers, tweezers, and similar tools ($2.1 million).

The first two types do not compete with village-made products, the last type definitely does, and the third and fourth types are in the gray area mentioned above.

In contrast, the total value of all the types of knives imported under code 82.11 was only $0.6 million. Similarly, the total value of all the types of kitchen wares imported under code 82.15 was only $0.9 million. It appears that importers do not find it profitable to bring in a foreign-made product if there is a less expensive domestically made alternative already on the market. This implies that village metalworking industries are already competing reasonably well with imports.

It is interesting to note that blacksmiths would actually benefit from a lowering of tariffs and taxes on several types of tools which they use as capital goods in production. These include files, rasps, vises, clamps, and the like, anvils, portable forges, and hand- or pedal-operated grinding wheels with frameworks.

Files and rasps are of course used in finishing work. Vises and clamps can be used, in place of the buffalo horn rack, to hold tools in place while they are being filed. Portable forges and grinding wheels are needed by tinkers and cutlers. Certain types of drills, punches, and stamps may also be used as capital goods. Of all of these items files are the most important, because the expense of frequently replacing imported files cuts significantly into profits for blacksmiths. Lowering the tariff and taxes on imported files, which currently amount to 50 percent, should be a priority.

My estimate of the value of imports which directly compete with products commonly made by village smiths is Rp 28.9 billion, or $16,551,256. This is 21.4 percent of the total. This estimate includes simple hand tools, handheld knives, flat irons, scissors, shears, and kitchen ware other than enameled. It excludes all types of saws, files, rasps, vises, clamps, forges, grinding wheels, rock- and earth-drilling tools, interchangeable blades for machinery, food-processing appliances, razors, razor blades, manicure and pedicure sets, tool sets, and enameled kitchen ware. Village smiths could conceivably make some of these items, but they do not commonly do so, either because they lack the necessary skills and equipment or because there is so much finishing labor involved (particularly hand filing) that commercial production would not be profitable.

It was estimated above that the impact of goods imported by state-owned companies was negligible, and probably displaced only seven or eight smithies. Using the same method of estimation, the total number of smithies displaced by imports, both by state-owned and private companies, is about 2,759. Since the average number of smithies in a smithing village is about forty, the approximate number of villages displaced is sixty-nine. If the average smithy has four workers, then the approximate number of workers displaced is 11,036. Most of this displacement is through allowable imports by private companies. These are of course crude estimates. Losses due to competition from imports may be spread out over a much larger number of smithies and villages, and may be reflected in lower profits per smithy rather than actual displacement.

Tariff code 82 roughly corresponds to industrial code 381 (fabricated metal products), discussed in chapter 4. According to table 11, there were 45,912 small and household metalworking enterprises in code 381 in 1987. If 2,759 enterprises were displaced, this represents about 6 percent of the total number of code 381 enterprises nationwide. Similarly, table 11 indicates that there were 182,374 workers in code 381 in 1987. If 11,036 workers were displaced, this again represents about 6 percent of the code 381 workers nationwide. Thus it appears that competition from imports has a significant but not a devastating impact on small and household metalworking enterprises.

Another method of estimating displacement is by looking at the gross output figures for code 381 enterprises in table 11. The average gross output for a single code 381 enterprise was Rp 9,734,549 in 1987. If the value of imported products which compete directly with those made by village smiths is Rp 28.9 billion, this gives an estimate of 2,969 enterprises displaced. Thus the two estimates tally fairly closely.[3]

It has been noted that Indonesia's capacity for producing machinery is still weak. Machinery and other metal products account for a very high proportion of total Indonesian imports, about 45 percent. The total value of machinery and metal products imported in 1983 was Rp 7,420.0 billion, or $7.4 billion. Hand tools and cutlery in tariff code 82 accounted for less than 2 percent of this amount. Over half the machinery imported is used by the manufacturing sector itself, mainly large- and medium-sized firms, while another quarter is used by the construction sector. According to figures from BPS and the Department of Industry, imports supplied 68.4 percent of the domestic demand for nonelectrical machinery and 55.2 percent of the demand for electrical machinery in 1983. While those percentages are high, they are down considerably from 1975, indicating that Indonesia's capacity to produce machinery is growing. Japan supplies more of Indonesia's machinery imports than any other country, 49.6 percent in 1980, while the European Economic Community and the United States supply most of the rest (Poot, Kuyvenhoven, and Jansen 1990, 409–12).

When considering the effect of trade policies on domestic industries, it is well to remember that there are imported inputs as well as imported outputs. For rural metalworking industries the primary inputs are charcoal and metal. Charcoal is produced domestically and is therefore not affected by import policies. Most of the metal used by blacksmiths and brass smiths is scrap which dates from the colonial and Second World War eras. Again, the supply and price of this scrap are not affected by current import policies, but it is possible that Indonesian blacksmiths would prefer to use new iron and steel if the prices were lower. The exclusive use of scrap iron and steel as raw materials dates from the period of the Japanese occupation. Before the Japanese occupation Indonesian blacksmiths used new metal bars which were imported, primarily from Europe. These bars were commonly sold by Chinese shopkeepers throughout Indonesia. Of course blacksmiths probably did a fair amount of recycling, but new metal in the form of bars was at least affordable at that time.

The primary importer of steel and producer of new bars, rods, and sheet is the giant government facility P. T. Krakatau Steel, located at Cilacap on the south coast of Central Java. Krakatau Steel has a monopoly on steel imports, and the World Bank has estimated that domestic steel prices exceed international prices by 25 to 50 percent (World Bank 1985, cited in Poot, Kuyvenhoven, and Jansen 1990, 445). The bulk of steel imports now comes from Japan, with smaller amounts from Singapore, the United States, France, and Germany (Central Bureau of Statistics 1989a; Central Bureau of Statistics 1989b). Krakatau Steel has been selected under the Foster Father program for a number of blacksmithing villages, including Kajar, and attempts have been made by the Department of Industry to develop supply linkages. These attempts have been rejected by village blacksmiths because of the gap in price between new metal from Krakatau Steel and comparable forms of high-grade scrap such as rails and reinforcement rods. If the monopoly granted to Krakatau Steel were withdrawn, and the free import of steel by the private sector permitted, it is possible that village blacksmiths would benefit from lowered prices on new steel.

The Impact of Smuggling

Village blacksmiths often complain that there are smuggled as well as legally imported tools on the market. There is of course no visual difference between the two, but reports of smuggling reach the ears of blacksmiths through contacts with market traders and other intermediaries. Smuggling is common along all the coastlines of Indonesia, but particularly the east coast of Sumatra and the north coast of Java. Smuggled tools generally come from other Asian countries, particularly China, Taiwan, Singapore, and Malaysia. Since no tariffs or taxes are paid on these tools, they can be marketed more cheaply than legally imported tools and are more competitive with domestic products. It is impossible to estimate the volume of smuggled tools on the market in Indonesia, or the impact they have had on domestic enterprises, but officials with the Department of Industry feel that it is considerable (see interview below).

In chapter 3 it was seen that village smiths have three main techniques for dealing with competition from foreign and factory-made products: underpricing, imitating the finish on foreign and factory-made products, and falsifying trademarks such as Schlieper German. Of these techniques underpricing is the most widely used. It should be noted that it is more difficult for village smiths to underprice smuggled tools and still make a profit.

The Regulatory Environment: Exports

In the 1970s there was little effort in Indonesia to promote the export of products made by small and household industries. Although some Asian countries, notably India and the Philippines, organized national handicraft cooperatives and successfully penetrated international markets, it was generally thought that Indonesian handicraft industries would not be able to meet international standards. Moreover, the handicraft market is very fickle, and villages which increased their productive capacity in response to orders from abroad could find those orders drying up a few years later. A frequently cited example was the collapse of the market for Madras textiles. Most industrial consultants advocated that Indonesia concentrate on production for the very large and less demanding domestic market.

Today the climate of opinion has changed. Export promotion is currently the most valued coin in development circles. Furthermore, the government's export promotion efforts have been extended for the first time to include small and household manufacturing industries. Still, it is mainly handicraft industries in code 39—those which make products with some artistic merit—which are being included in the export promotion effort. Enterprises which make utilitarian wares such as agricultural tools have not been included as yet.

The Dutch developed Indonesia as a source of basic raw materials and agricultural products rather than as a source of manufactures. This pattern is still reflected in the composition of Indonesia's exports, in which manufactures play a very modest role. Not only is the share of manufactures in total exports small, but the share of exports in manufacturing output is low. Excluding petroleum refining and basic agro-processing, the share of manufactures in total exports was only 4.8 percent in 1980, and the share of exports in manufacturing output was only 5.2 percent. These percentages increased somewhat in the 1980s, partly as a result of export promotion measures, but they still remain the lowest in Asia. The poor performance of manufactured exports is currently being blamed on the import substitution strategy of the 1970s. In other words, manufacturers are said to have found it easier and more profitable in the 1970s to produce for the protected domestic market, and their international competitiveness eroded as a result (Poot, Kuyvenhoven, and Jansen 1990, 413–15).

Several measures have been used to promote exports, such as eliminating or reducing export taxes, lifting bans on certain types of exports, and granting special incentives to firms which export most of their production. Another measure is currency devaluation, designed to improve Indonesia's trade position in international markets. Major devaluations were made in 1971, 1978, 1983, and 1986. In May 1986 the government introduced a comprehensive "packet" of trade reforms, some of which were aimed at easing customs clearing procedures for imports and exports, and providing export firms with unrestricted access to imported inputs (Poot, Kuyvenhoven, and Jansen 1990, 415, 448–49).

Although manufactured exports have begun to increase in importance, table 11 in chapter 4 indicates that small metalworking enterprises still do very little exporting by themselves. At the time of the economic census of 1986, only 18.8 percent of the small enterprises in code 381 and 2.3 percent of those in code 38111 exported any of their products. The household section of the 1986 census did not collect data on marketing, but undoubtedly the percentages for household enterprises would have been even lower. It is of course possible that exporting is being done by traders and dealers rather than producers, which would not show up on table 11. In other words, traders and dealers may be buying up tools for export from local villages and markets. But there is no ethnographic evidence to support the notion that this practice is common.

Although code 381 enterprises do little exporting, some code 39 enterprises now produce mainly for the foreign market. Most notable among these are the silver jewelry industries of Yogyakarta and Bali. Indonesians prefer wearing gold to silver, and most of the silver jewelry made in Indonesia is either sold to foreign tourists or exported, mainly to the United States and Europe. Designs and proportions have been adapted to foreign tastes. The larger jewelry-making enterprises have retail shops along the roadside where they receive foreign buyers. These buyers are given wholesale discounts from a special price list. Exporting is usually handled through small, locally owned shipping companies which have arisen in Yogyakarta and Bali in response to tourist demand. These companies have export licenses, and they specialize in the packing and shipping of handicrafts and souvenirs. Jewelry items are usually sent by air mail or air freight. The boom in silver jewelry exports is assisted by the absence of tariffs imposed by the United States, as long as they are not set with precious stones.

Gamelan makers have also begun exporting sets of these musical instruments abroad. The principal buyers for these instruments are schools and universities in Europe and the United States.

Production and Trade of Raw Metals

At this point it would be well to analyze the flow of raw metals in and out of the country, and its impact, if any, on small and household metalworking industries. For this purpose metals can be divided into ferrous metals (iron and steel), nonferrous base metals (nickel, copper, tin, and manganese), and precious metals (gold and silver). Indonesia's own mines currently produce ferrous metals and precious metals in relatively small quantities, mainly for domestic consumption. They also produce nonferrous base metals in relatively large quantities, mainly for export. The production figures for 1989 were 137,205 metric tons of iron sand, 1,904,315 metric tons of nickel ore, 328,155 metric tons of copper ore, 131,736 metric tons of tin, 9,076 metric tons of manganese ore, 5,573 kilograms of gold, and 65,470 kilograms of silver (Central Bureau of Statistics 1989a; Central Bureau of Statistics 1989b).

Most mining is under the control of another state-owned company, P. T. Aneka Tambang, which is responsible not only for mining but also for the preliminary processing and marketing of all raw metals and mineral products except oil, gas, coal, and tin. The latter products are controlled by other state-owned companies.

The iron sand (*pasir besi*) produced under the control of P. T. Aneka Tambang is sent to P. T. Krakatau Steel for further processing into such forms as pig iron and iron bars. Most of the finished products are retained for use by domestic industries, but a small quantity is exported, amounting to only 1.4 percent of total ferrous metal production in 1983. The pig iron is exported mainly to Japan and other countries of North Asia, while the iron bars are exported mainly to other ASEAN countries. In 1981 the combined value of these two products was $9.9 million (Poot, Kuyvenhoven, and Jansen 1990, 418, 420, 426–27). Since iron is usually cast in "pigs" (blanks) preparatory to the production of steel, it appears that Indonesia is exporting iron and reimporting steel, particularly from Japan. The value of the iron exported is much less than the value of the steel imported.

In 1975 Indonesia supplied only 6.7 percent of its domestic need for ferrous metals from its own mines, the remaining 93.3 percent coming from imports. By 1983 this situation had changed considerably, and Indonesia was able to supply 37.3 percent from its own mines, relying on imports for the remaining 62.7 percent (Poot, Kuyvenhoven, and Jansen 1990, 411). Most of the ferrous metal imported is in the form of iron and steel tubes. The volume of iron and steel tubes imported in 1988 was 122,500 metric tons, valued at $173 million. Again Japan was the principal trade partner, followed by Germany and other countries of the European Community (Central Bureau of Statistics 1989a). Indonesia also imports ferrous metal in the form of machinery, of course. The volume of machinery imported in 1988 for industrial and commercial purposes only was 178,400 metric tons, valued at $1,299 million (Central Bureau of Statistics 1989a). Since this was only a portion of the total volume of machinery imported, it appears that more metal now comes into the country in the form of machinery than in the form of semifinished products such as tubes and bars.

The mining, processing, and marketing of precious metals are also controlled by P. T. Aneka Tambang. Again, most of these metals are retained for domestic consumption. They are made available to jewelry makers and the general public in various forms such as sheet and wafers. Small jewelry-making enterprises do not purchase these metals directly from P. T. Aneka Tambang but from urban dealers who buy in larger quantity and act as intermediaries.

The pattern for nonferrous base metals is very different. Indonesia produces nickel, copper, and tin in relatively large quantities, but exports nearly 100 percent of production. Nonferrous metals accounted for 26.1 percent of Indonesia's total volume of manufactured exports in 1983 (excluding petroleum and basic agro-products such as rubber), and this percentage is down considerably from previous years. Although the volume of tin produced was less than the volume of nickel and copper, unwrought tin was the most important metal export in terms of value (Poot, Kuyvenhoven, and Jansen 1990, 416–18).

What do these patterns of export and import of basic metals mean for small and household metalworking industries? Blacksmiths, coppersmiths, and brass smiths rely on recycled rather than new metals. At present market prices they could not make a profit if they used new metals. They would conceivably benefit from an elimination of trade restrictions if this caused the price of imported new metals to drop. In other words, they might use some new metals, as they did before the Second World War.

Not all the scrap used by blacksmiths dates from the colonial and Second World War eras. Some of it has been imported more recently. An example is the spring steel from vehicle springs and shock absorbers. Indirectly the price of this type of scrap is affected by the restrictions, tariffs, and taxes on imported vehicles. Of course there is a gap of approximately twenty to thirty years between the time a vehicle is imported and the time its springs and shock absorbers become available as scrap to the village blacksmith. In the very long run, though, blacksmiths might benefit from freer vehicle imports. A similar situation prevails with regard to steel reinforcement rods. The price of these rods may be higher because of monopolies, tariffs, and taxes affecting steel imports. But there may be a gap of decades between the time the steel is imported and used in a building, bridge, or other construction project, and the time that project is demolished and the steel becomes available as scrap.

Musical instrument enterprises use various types of metals, almost all of them recycled, including bronze, brass, and even iron. Although some gongs are still made of cast bronze, nowadays most are made from the heavier types of metal sheet or plate. These are primarily shaped by cold forging, sometimes with the assistance of molds. Secondary shaping techniques may also be used, for example folding, welding, or bolting. The bars on percussion instruments may be cast, but frequently they are made from brass shell casings, cut in strips, and cold-forged. In either case the raw material is scrap. Thus musical instrument makers, like blacksmiths, are little affected by the import and export of raw metals. If they are affected, it is indirectly and in the long run.

Some sheet metal industries use new metals in the form of factory-made rolls of aluminum and zinc. These are probably imported, since Indonesia does not produce these metals in any quantity. Other sheet metal industries use recycled sheet, for example from food tins which they cut open, flatten, and join by folding, welding, or soldering the seams.

Of all the types of small and household metalworking industries, the ones that rely the most heavily on new metals are jewelry-making enterprises. An elimination of monopolies on the production and import of these metals might result in the lowering of prices. But privatizing production could result in domestic shortages if private mining companies chose to export their production rather than making it available locally.

The Regulatory Environment: Investments and Licensing

In addition to policies governing imports and exports, the government has a number of policies involving investments and the granting of licenses for new factories and service sector operations. These policies date from foreign and domestic investment laws passed in the late 1960s.

With the exception of investments in a few sectors (oil, natural gas, coal, and banking), all major foreign and domestic private investments must be approved by BKPM, the national investment board. BKPM assists potential investors with planning and, after appraisal, issues the necessary investment approvals and licenses (Poot, Kuyvenhoven, and Jansen 1990, 234). BKPM prepares an annual list of investment priorities. Formerly this was a "positive list" of businesses in which investment was allowed. In 1989, in keeping with the new move toward deregulation, BKPM adopted a much shorter "negative list" of industries in which investment is restricted in some way. This was updated in 1991. If an industry does not appear on the new negative list, there are no restrictions on investment.

The new negative list of investments takes the form of two attachments to Presidential Decree No. 23/1991, issued in June of that year. These are "Fields of Business Which Are Closed to All Kinds of Capital Investments" and "Fields of Business Which Are Reserved for Small Scale Industries/Business Operations Cooperating with Medium Scale or Large Scale Companies." All the industries listed in attachment I are either completely closed to foreign investment or closed unless certain requirements are met, for example the exportation of at least 65 percent of production. Most of the same industries are also closed to large and small domestic private investment. Many of the items listed are already being made by state-owned enterprises, so that attachment I acts to protect these enterprises from private-sector competition. Some of the items listed are made by individuals who have been favored with a government monopoly license for one reason or another. The phrase "cooperating with medium scale or large scale companies," used in the title of attachment II, refers to linkage arrangements under the Foster Father program (see below).

Attachment I affords protection to some of the machine industries under industrial code 38, for example industries making non-automotive internal combustion engines, heavy construction equipment, and transport vehicles. It also lists industries making two types of steel sheet. It does not list any basic metal industries, or industries making other types of manufactured metal products.

Section II lists all the small and household industries which are still afforded government protection from factory competition. With a few exceptions, these run the gamut of traditional peasant industries and testify to the government's continued commitment to a high level of protection. Included are most of the important food product, textile, coarse fiber, lime, ceramic, metalworking, shell, and leather industries. Missing are the very important brick and roof tile industries, and certain metalworking industries, as noted below.

The items under Section II which relate to metalworking are as follows:

33. Agricultural Implement Industry
    1. hoes (*cankul*)
    2. spades (*sekop*)
    3. plows (*bajak*)
    4. harrows (*garu*)
    5. rakes (*garpu*)
    6. crowbars (*linggis*)
    7. sickles (*sabit/arit*)
    8. weed-removing devices (*koret*)
    9. reaping knives (*ani-ani*)
    10. rat-killing devices (*emposan tikus*)
    11. sprinklers (*alat penyiram*)
    12. hand sprayers (*alat semprot tangan*)
    13. manual paddy threshers (*alat perontok padi*)
    14. manual maize threshers (*alat pemipil jagung*)
    15. manual hullers (*alat penyosoh*)
34. Tool Industry
    1. chisels (*pahat*)
    2. screwdrivers (*obeng biasa*)
    3. hammers (*palu/martil*)
    4. wood planes (*serut/ketam kayu*)
    5. trowels (*cetok semen*)
35. Cutter Industry
    1. kitchen knives (*pisau dapur*)
    2. daggers (*parang*)
    3. axes (*kampak*)
36. Traditional Musical Instrument Industry
37. Handicraft Industries Not Elsewhere Classified:
    1. handicrafts using basic materials of vegetation
    2. handicrafts using basic materials of animal origin

Missing from this list are all the traditional casting industries which make utilitarian products such as locks, hinges, and handles. Also missing are the nontraditional industries which make kitchen wares, containers, furniture, and other items from metal sheet and tubing. Apparently there is free licensing of factories to make these types of products. There is also the rather puzzling question of whether enterprises making jewelry, decorative items, and souvenirs of metal are subsumed under item 37.

Judging from the new negative list and the previous positive list, it would seem that blacksmiths, at least, are fully protected from factory competition. In fact, according to Department of Industry sources, this is not entirely so. The government has occasionally granted licenses to factories making agricultural and other hand tools, in violation of its own policy. These include: Pabrik Pacul, a factory in Pasuruan, East Java, which makes hoes and spades; Boma Bisma Indra, a factory in Surabaya, East Java, which makes tools for the transmigration program; and a factory in Semarang, Central Java, which makes gardening tools, but only for export.

Even granting that blacksmiths are well protected, it is difficult to estimate the dampening effect that the licensing of large, usually capital-intensive factories has on the growth of blacksmithing enterprises. Would they be more likely to learn new techniques and expand into new product types in the absence of such factory competition?

Between 1967 and 1983 BKPM approved $1.6 billion worth of foreign investments in code 38 metal product industries, of which $562 million were actually implemented. Code 38 industries accounted for 17.0 percent of all foreign investments approved and 16.3 percent of all foreign investments implemented. By far the largest investor country was Japan. Basic metal industries accounted for another 27.6 percent of investments approved, but only 9.8 percent of investments implemented (Poot, Kuyvenhoven, and Jansen 1990, 237–38, 243–46).

Before 1976 the industrial subsector which received the greatest amount of foreign investment was textiles. Since that time the relative share of textiles has declined sharply, at the expense of chemicals, basic metals, and metal products. In 1980 there were 812 medium- and large-scale firms manufacturing code 38 products, of which 81 firms had foreign ownership participation. Of the remaining firms, 64 were state-owned and 667 were privately owned. Not surprisingly, the firms with foreign ownership participation were larger in size, employing an average of 383 workers each, compared to 188 for the government-owned firms and 118 for the privately owned firms. They were also more efficient in terms of value added per worker (Poot, Kuyvenhoven, and Jansen 1990, 238–45). Broken down by three-digit industrial codes, 38 of the 81 firms with foreign ownership made nonmachine fabricated metal products in code 381. Another 34 made nonelectrical and electrical machinery in codes 382 and 383, while the remaining 9 made transport equipment in code 384 (Poot, Kuyvenhoven, and Jansen 1990, 244–45).

Surprisingly, there were almost as many state-owned firms manufacturing metal products as there were firms with foreign participation. Of the sixty-four state-owned firms mentioned above, twenty-six made nonmachine fabricated metal products, seventeen made machinery, and twenty made transport equipment (Poot, Kuyvenhoven, and Jansen 1990, 244–45). This raises the question of whether there is a basic conflict of interest in the government's development programs for small and household metalworking enterprises. As a concomitant of pressures to deregulate, there have been increased pressures on directors of public enterprises to show a profit, and it might not be in their interest to encourage the production of competing products.

The general policy trend reflected in the packet of reforms enacted in May 1986 is to relax licensing and other investment restrictions, particularly for companies which export most of their products or have achieved the government's target of majority ownership of shares by Indonesian nationals. Because of the overconcentration of manufacturing industries on Java, higher priority is also given to investment projects on the Outer Islands (Poot, Kuyvenhoven, and Jansen 1990, 235–36).

Technically all large, medium, and small manufacturing enterprises in Indonesia are supposed to be licensed by the government, while household enterprises are free of this obligation. In practice, local government offices usually look the other way where small and even medium enterprises in rural areas are concerned. Obtaining an industrial license is an expensive and time-consuming process, requiring many trips to town and many frustrating encounters with the government bureaucracy. Village enterprise owners will naturally avoid this process if at all possible. A very few owners of village enterprises have licenses because they participated in the now-defunct KIK/KMKP credit program, which required a copy of the license as support documentation on loan requests.

Summary of the Regulatory Environment

The regulatory environment has had a varied impact on small and household metalworking enterprises,

Small and household metalworking enterprises appear to have benefited from protection against competing imports in the form of import restrictions, tariffs, and taxes. Blacksmithing enterprises which make tools used in agriculture, horticulture, and forestry are accorded the greatest degree of protection. It may not be entirely coincidental that blacksmithing enterprises have also enjoyed the greatest increases in the number of enterprises, number of workers, and value added per enterprise. Coverage for small and household industries making other types of metal products is less complete. If it is the government's intention to protect these industries, the heavily protected categories should be expanded to include knives, kitchen wares, and some additional types of workman's tools.

Import restrictions should be eliminated on capital goods needed by small and household metalworking enterprises, particularly files and rasps.

Blacksmiths would benefit if government procurement officers were required to buy their hand tools directly from smithing villages rather than through urban dealers or importers. This would not be difficult since there are blacksmithing villages in every province in the country.

It was estimated that 6 percent of small and household metalworking enterprises have been displaced by imports which have been brought into the country legally. In addition, these enterprises must compete with smuggled imports, which are more competitive in price because they are not subject to tariffs and taxes.

Only one-fifth of the metal products which are legally imported compete directly with products commonly made by village smiths. Importers apparently do not find it very profitable to compete with village enterprises, even in categories such as knives and kitchen wares, which are not heavily protected. The value of imports in these categories is relatively low, because village smiths can regularly underprice imports in the marketplace. The reverse side of this is that village smiths who make knives and kitchen wares cannot raise their prices because of the threat of increased imports, and thus their levels of value added and profit are lower than for blacksmiths.

Village smiths are relatively unaffected by the flow of raw metals in and out of the country. This is because they rely mainly on recycled metals. It is possible that an elimination of the government monopoly on steel imports would cause steel prices to drop so that blacksmiths could use at least some new metal. It is also possible that a reduction of tariffs and taxes on some types of manufactured imports, for example vehicles, would eventually lead to a reduction in scrap prices, but only after a lag of twenty years or more.[4]

Four-fifths of the metal products which are legally imported do not compete directly with products commonly made by village smiths. Yet low tariffs and taxes on these products may have a discouraging effect on the expansion of village smiths into new product types. Village smiths could easily learn to make some of these products, for example interchangeable blades for machinery, if they had prototypes to copy and firm orders.

Small and household metalworking enterprises in code 38 do not appear to have benefited from the government's recent export promotion efforts. Their primary market still consists of farmers and workmen within the region. As of 1986 less than 2 percent of small enterprises in code 38 exported any of their products, and the percentage for household enterprises must have been close to zero.

Small and household enterprises in code 39, particularly those which make silver jewelry and gamelan instruments, are exporting a large proportion of their products. The secret of their export success lies not so much with the export promotion efforts of the Indonesian government as with the activities of foreign traders based in Yogyakarta and Bali, and with favorable terms of trade granted by the United States and the European Economic Community. The willingness of jewelry makers to adapt their designs has also been important.

Small and household metalworking enterprises have also benefited from protective legislation governing the licensing of large and medium-sized factories. Again, coverage is better for blacksmithing enterprises than for other types of metalworking industries. There is a ban on licensing factories which make agricultural tools, other hand tools, and knives. If it is the government's intention to protect village metalworking industries from factory competition, the ban should be extended to include factories which make simple utilitarian products of cast metal, sheet metal, or metal tubing.

There is a surprisingly large number of state-owned firms (sixty-four) which manufacture metal products. These firms are under the Department of Industry and their directors are under considerable pressure from the government to show profits or risk dissolution. Their presence suggests a possible conflict of interest with regard to the Department of Industry's extension programs for village metalworking enterprises. The same question will come up with regard to the Department of Industry's common service facilities in rural areas.

In the realm of metalworking industries, Japan is Indonesia's primary trade partner. Japan supplies more steel, metal products, and machinery to Indonesia than any other country. Japan also imports more of Indonesia's nonferrous metals than any other country. The negative side of this trade relationship is that Japan may try to preserve its markets in Indonesia by preventing domestic industries from expanding their product types. The positive side is that Japan, almost alone among developed nations, has taken a real interest in developing and exporting appropriate technologies which can be used in rural areas of countries like Indonesia. These technologies take the form of small machines and other equipment with a relatively low capacity and low purchase price.

The Department of Industry

Interviews with village industry producers indicate that many — perhaps the majority — have never had contact with a government extension agent or participated in a government development project. This is particularly true of those with smaller and weaker enterprises, or those who live off the main road leading into the village. In stratified villages, where many enterprise owners have dependency relationships with a stronger entrepreneur, contacts with the government are usually channeled through that entrepreneur. If there is an alliance between the entrepreneur and the village administration, as in Kajar, that channeling tendency is strengthened.

That said, the government agency with primary responsibility for providing extension services to rural producers is the Department of Industry. The Department of Cooperatives also has responsibility for assisting with the formation and guidance of village industry cooperatives and pre-cooperatives. The two departments are supposed to work together, so that inputs provided by the Department of Industry, for example credit and raw materials, can be channeled through the village cooperative. As seen in Kajar, this does not always go smoothly, and there can be competition between extension workers of the two agencies. In addition to contacts with these two mainline departments, many village producers have had contact with employees of government banks. The two government banks most active in rural areas are BRI (Bank Rakyat Indonesia, or the People's Bank of Indonesia) and BPD (Bank Pembangunan Daerah, or the Regional Development Bank; see the discussion of rural banking programs below).

The Department of Industry was founded at the beginning of the twentieth century by the Dutch colonial regime. Its purpose at that time was to provide extension services for peasant industries in rural areas, as part of a more comprehensive scheme to improve peasant welfare. To a large degree the department has retained that character. Although it is also involved in industrial planning and licensing for large and medium-sized firms, the bulk of its staff is deployed in rural areas.

The Department of Industry is headed by the minister of industry, who reports directly to the president. Under the minister of industry are four general directorates, one of which is the General Directorate for Small Industries. Under the General Directorate for Small Industries are five subdirectorates: the Subdirectorate for Food (food-processing industries); the Subdirectorate for Chemicals and Construction Materials (including clay and limestone product industries); the Subdirectorate for Clothing and Leather (including textile, ready-to-wear, and leather goods industries); the Subdirectorate for Metal (metalworking industries); and the Subdirectorate for Handicrafts and Other Industries. Authority has been subdivided between these directorates according to the ISIC industrial codes. The Subdirectorate for Metal covers basic metal and metal product industries, i.e. codes 37 and 38. Since there are very few small and household industries in code 37, for all practical purposes the subdirectorate covers code 38. In addition, some service sector enterprises, for example vehicle repair, have been put under the authority of the subdirectorate. These have the ISIC code of 95.

The subdirectorates are vertical divisions based on the ISIC codes. In addition, the department has horizontal, or territorial, divisions. These consist of 27 provincial offices which supervise 241 district (kabupaten) offices. Unlike some mainline departments, for example the Departments of Agriculture and Health, the Department of Industry does not extend down to the subdistrict (kecamatan) level.

Department of Industry Extension Workers

Extension services are provided by field-workers called TPLs (*tenaga penyuluhan lapangan*), who are based at the district offices. Most of these TPLs are men in their twenties with high school diplomas. Typically they were born and raised in the districts where they are working. After being on the job for several years they are promoted to the status of government official (*pegawai negeri*), which gives them a certain level of prestige and security which is highly valued in Indonesia. Although their salaries are very modest they are provided with motorcycles and gas money so that they can make their rounds of enterprises in the district. They are also allowed to take these motorcycles home for personal use after office hours, so this is considered an important perquisite.

In most district offices there are four TPLs. Since there are 241 districts nationwide, that means there are approximately 964 TPLs. In 1988 there were 66,979 villages (desa/kelurahan) in the country, which means that the average TPL was responsible for providing extension services to 69 villages. The Economic Census of 1986 indicates that there were 1,511,170 small and household enterprises in the country in that year. Thus the caseload of the average TPL can be estimated at about 1,568 enterprises. With such a large number of villages to visit, and such a large caseload, it is little wonder that most TPLs developed a pattern of concentrating on a handful of villages—those which are centers of rural industry and which are within easy access of the district office. Within those villages the TPLs concentrate on the larger and more visible enterprises, which are located along the main village roads. During the late 1970s, when I was working with the Department of Industry in Yogyakarta and Central Java, many village roads were still unpaved. These roads turned into a sticky or soupy mixture of clay and rain between October and April, quite impassable by motorcycle. Since then most village roads have been paved, but TPLs still concentrate on villages and enterprises with easy access, and curtail their visits during the rainy season. Mountain villages and villages in more isolated or remote areas may never receive a visit.

Because the salaries of TPLs are low, many try to earn extra money by trading in the products made by industries in their operational area. Strictly speaking, this is a conflict of interest, because it entails bargaining with enterprise owners to obtain lower prices when the TPLs should be helping these owners to increase profits. Trading is generally justified within the department, however, as a way to help enterprise owners expand their markets. Not only are many TPLs involved in trading, but more highly placed officers within the district and provincial offices may do this as well.

There is always the danger that TPLs, who are young, will form patron-client relationships with powerful village entrepreneurs or village officials. The entrepreneur or official, being an older and wealthier man, may come to dominate the TPL and try to dictate certain aspects of the implementation of a project. This is particularly evident in the selection of project participants. If the TPL has consciously or unconsciously relinquished control over the selection of participants, there is little hope that the owners of smaller and weaker enterprises will be included in the project. Experience shows that powerful entrepreneurs and village officials usually try to use credit and other resources distributed through development projects as personal patronage, steering them toward political allies, friends, and relatives.

There is yet another reason why village officials may try to block the participation of poor enterprise owners in development projects. Many projects involve distributing credit in the form of cash, inputs, or equipment. Village officials usually fear that the Department of Industry or the Camat (subdistrict head) will hold them personally responsible if poor enterprise owners do not repay their credits. With better-off owners selected as participants, the risk of non-repayment is reduced. A similar logic often affects the decisions of TPLs and village bank officers.

In addition to TPLs, the Department of Industry has another type of fieldworker, the technical training officer. Technical training officers are funded under an important program within the Directorate General for Small Industries called Bimbingan dan Penyuluhan Industri Kecil (BIPIK, or Training and Guidance of Small Industries), which dates from the 1970s. The main purpose of the program is to introduce village industry producers to new and improved technologies. BIPIK officers are usually university graduates who have received additional training from the Department of Industry at one of its technical centers. Each BIPIK officer specializes in a certain sector, for example metalworking or clay product industries, though some have received training in more than one sector. The technical center which trains officers to work in blacksmithing and other metalworking villages is MIDC (Metallurgy Industry Development Center), at Bandung in West Java. In addition to the technical centers, BIPIK offices at the provincial level maintain their own technical facilities for research, product development, and training. BIPIK officers enjoy higher salaries, more benefits, and more prestige than TPLs. Their caseload is also considerably lighter, because each officer is assigned to one, two, or at most a few villages. Ideally each important industrial village or cluster of villages would have its own BIPIK officer, but budgetary and hiring constraints have made it impossible to achieve this ideal.

Project Planning for Blacksmithing Enterprises

Every provincial office of the Department of Industry has a planning division. This division is responsible for drawing up project proposals and budgets every year. The district offices do not have planning divisions, but provincial planning officers confer with district officers and TPLs before drawing up the plans for projects to be carried out in rural areas. These project plans are called DUPs (*daftar usulan proyek*). Before being implemented they must be reviewed and approved by the Regional Planning Board, or BAPPEDA. The BAPPEDA is a separate agency of the government, under the National Planning Board, or BAPPENAS. Once approved, the funds for implementation can be released by the central government. An approved project plan is called a DIP (*daftar isian proyek*).

A review of DUPs and DIPs nationwide shows that they follow a very similar pattern. First there is a background statement on the weaknesses of rural industries and the problems they face. The background statements describe rural industries in almost wholly negative terms, but stress the need for assisting these industries for the sake of rural employment and welfare. As mentioned in chapter 1, these background statements owe much to the thinking of Boeke and other colonial bureaucrats earlier in the century. Following the background statement is a short work plan giving the specific project aims, the names of the villages where the project is to be carried out, the number of participants, the steps in implementation, the types of equipment or inputs to be distributed, etc. This is followed by a project budget.

In 1980 I had the task of reviewing DUPs and DIPs for two districts in the province of Aceh in North Sumatra, and four districts on the island of Madura in the province of East Java. Below are the workplan sections, slightly edited, from four projects to be carried out in blacksmithing villages, plus a comment at the end of each taken from my field notes. They give an idea of the type of projects typically planned and implemented by the Department of Industry.

1. *Credit subproject for blacksmiths and rencong (Acehnese dagger) makers, Aceh Besar District.* This project provides Rp 1,536,000 ($2,430) in the form of equipment credits to blacksmiths and rencong makers in the villages of Ba'et Sebreh and Lamblang. Six enterprises in each village will be organized into a pre-cooperative or "group" (*kelompok*), making a total of twelve enterprises. Each of the twelve enterprise owners will receive one large sledgehammer (*martil*) worth Rp 5,000; one six-inch rotary edge grinder (*gerinda tangan*) worth Rp 8,000; iron and white iron worth Rp 50,000; horn and ivory (for *rencong* handles) worth Rp 10,000; coconut shell charcoal worth Rp 5,000; and Rp 50,000 as working capital, to cover wages and living expenses until the products are sold. The credit is to be repaid over a three-year period. Payments will be given to the subdistrict office of BPD (Bank Pembangunan Daerah).

COMMENT: Other project aims are mentioned in the workplan, such as to carry out training, help with marketing and promotion, and free the enterprise owners from the hold of intermediaries (*tengkulak* and *ijon*), but there are no budget allocations for trainers or other related inputs. Presumably these aims are to be carried out by the TPLs in the regular course of their duties.

2. *Credit subproject for blacksmiths in Kuala Subdistrict, West Aceh District.* Ten blacksmithing enterprises will be chosen to participate in the project.

Each will receive a rotary edge grinder worth Rp 20,000; 9 kilograms of iron worth Rp 18,000; 180 kilograms of charcoal worth Rp 90,000; money for accumulating stocks (working capital) worth Rp 162,000. The total budget for the subproject is Rp 2.9 million ($4,589).

COMMENT: Nothing is said in the project document about repayment terms or procedures.

3. *Project to train blacksmiths from Bates and Peterongan Villages in Bang-kalan District (Madura)*. At present there are 21 perapen in Bates village employing 75 smiths and 30 perapen in Peterongan village employing 150 smiths. The only product made by these perapen is a type of sickle used for cutting grass. The profit on these sickles is low because they are made from a low grade of scrap iron sheet which the smiths purchase from the city of Surabaya. Each enterprise goes to Surabaya separately to purchase this sheet, so unit transport costs are high. In addition, the smiths still work while sitting in the traditional cross-legged manner. The purpose of this project is to train the smiths to make larger tools such as pacul which are more profitable. Ten smiths from the village will be selected for training and sent for thirty days to live in the village of Kesamben in Blitar District (East Java), where the Margono Blacksmithing Cooperative is located. One or two perapen will be rented in Kesamben, where the ten smiths will be trained in Blitar methods of smithing. During training they will be taught to work standing up, to make pacul and fit them with sockets, and to finish and pack the pacul. On their return to Madura they will be organized into two work groups of five persons each. Each group will be given a set of tools, including files, hammers, and anvils. These two work groups will act as demonstration units (*unit percontohan*) for the rest of the village. A KUD (government cooperative) will be formed which will supply sheet iron to all the enterprise owners. This sheet iron will be obtained from Kamal (the ferry docking station where ships are dismantled). Since companies which dismantle ships must have a license from the Department of Industry, the sheet iron will be requested from one of these companies. Two tons of iron will be supplied to the smiths in the first year as a form of revolving credit. In subsequent years other groups of smiths will be trained. The profit on making sickles is Rp 240–320 per perapen per day, depending on the number of workers. Through this project it expected that profit will increase to Rp 600 per perapen per day. The project will be carried out over four years. The total budget is Rp 7.5 million ($11,867), of which Rp 1,749,000 will be spent in the first year.

COMMENT: When this project was carried out, the district head insisted that the iron must be distributed through the village LSD (Lembaga Sosial Desa, or Village Social Welfare Organization), rather than a KUD. The LSD took a commission of approximately 10 percent, partly as administrative charges and partly as profit. The LSD not only distributed iron but also requested that participants market their products through the LSD.

4. *Subproject for blacksmiths in Somalang Village in Pamekasan District (Madura).* At present there are only four perapen in Somaleng village, employing a total of twelve men. They make sickles and knives. Their production is not continuous but coincides with the market days. The total capital investment per perapen is about Rp 50,000. The purpose of this project is to increase the number of perapen in the village from four to ten, and thereby increase employment from twelve to about forty. New appropriate technologies (*teknologi tepat guna*) will be introduced. The smiths will be organized in a pre-cooperative.

The Department of Industry will provide the equipment to set up six new perapen, including appropriate technologies. It will provide this equipment as well as raw materials through a "feederpoint" system, channeled through the pre-cooperative. Training and marketing assistance will be provided to enable the smiths to break the hold of intermediaries (*mencegah sistem tengkulak*).

The project is to last for four years. The budget for the first year only is Rp 4 million ($6,329), to be allocated as follows: Rp 80,000 for a survey; Rp 380,000 for wages and payments; Rp 1,000,000 for raw materials; Rp 1,400,000 for equipment and machines; Rp 600,000 for training; Rp 540,000 for "operational costs."

COMMENT: This budget is seriously padded. At least 25 percent of the budget will go to department officials.

These projects obviously differ as to quality, and there are serious problems with each one. The second project, for example, does not specify credit repayment terms or procedures, while the fourth has a padded budget. The most serious problem, and one which affects many government development projects carried out in rural areas, is the lack of evidence that villagers have been involved in the planning process. Do the blacksmiths want to accept credit from the government? Do they want to form groups or pre-cooperatives? Do they want to change their work schedules, the types of tools they make, or their methods of working? Do they want to take thirty days off from their work to travel to East Java? These questions are seldom asked before the plan is drawn up by the provincial planning division and approved by the BAPPEDA. It is therefore not surprising that TPLs may face considerable resistance from village producers during the implementation phase. Post-project evaluations carried out by the Department of Industry are very brief, and say little more than whether the project funds were spent.

Critical Analysis of Key Program Elements

A review of Department of Industry DUPs and DIPs indicates that there is a limited range of program elements. Each project workplan takes one, two, or more of these elements and combines them for implementation in a specific village or group of villages. The twelve most common program elements are discussed below and evaluated as to their effectiveness.

1. *Sentra.* The linchpin of the Department of Industry's programs in rural areas is the concept of *sentra*, or "center." A sentra is loosely defined as a cluster of enterprises which make the same or related products. It is also used to mean a village or group of villages where such a cluster exists. In general it is the larger and more important industrial villages such as Kajar and Massepe that are designated as sentra. The four blacksmithing hamlets in Kajar, for example, constitute a sentra. But there is no minimum number of enterprises which must be achieved before the Department of Industry designates the cluster as a sentra. There are a few cases of sentra with only one or two enterprises, but those enterprises are particularly well known for some reason. A village or group of villages becomes a sentra when a specific request is submitted from the district office of the Department of Industry to the head office in Jakarta. Most sentra are rural, but some urban clusters of small and household industries have also been designated as sentra.

At present the national list includes eighty sentra which make code 38 products. According to my estimates, this is only 7 percent of metalworking villages nationwide. But these eighty sentra may account for as much as 15 or 20 percent of code 38 workers, because they tend to be larger than the average metalworking village.[5] The Department of Industry, and particularly BIPIK, focuses its extension services on sentra. A village must be designated a sentra, for example, before a BIPIK extension officer can be assigned to work there. All common service facilities built by the Department of Industry are located at sentra (see below).

Use of the sentra concept enables the Department of Industry to identify major centers of industrial activity in rural areas, and to concentrate scarce resources of personnel and infrastructure where they will benefit the most producers. The disadvantage is that producers who live in villages with smaller concentrations of enterprises tend to be overlooked.

2. *Cooperatives.* There are several levels of rural cooperatives in Indonesia. The largest are the KUDs which the government has organized at the kecamatan (subdistrict) level. These KUDs are to a large extent artificial constructs, in the sense that they are not based on any commonality of interest among the members. Anyone in the subdistrict is potentially a member. A variety of government programs operate through the KUDs, but they are best known for providing inputs to rice farmers. Many KUDs own rice mills and are active in the buying up, milling, and marketing of rice. Some KUDs also provide credit for other agricultural and nonagricultural activities, including petty trade and village industries.

At the next level are cooperatives which are organized according to common interest, such as the blacksmithing cooperative at Kajar. These cooperatives are incorporated as legal bodies and registered with the Department of Cooperatives. Their status as a legal body allows the directors to sign contracts and negotiate other business in the name of the cooperative. Officially these cooperatives are subunits of the KUD, because the government has declared that no rural cooperative can exist as an independent entity. The basis for this ruling is fear on the part of the government that nongovernmental organizations (NGOs) will become politically powerful in rural areas. In practice, however, these cooperatives function almost independently of the KUD. The Department of Industry's acronym for a registered small industry cooperative is KOPINKRA (Koperasi Industri Kecil dan Kerajinan, or Small Industry and Handicraft Cooperative).

Some KOPINKRA are new, and the initiative for their formation has come from the Department of Industry or the Department of Cooperatives. Others are based on organizations which actually predate the KUD system. In Kajar, it may be recalled, the first such organization was a PERPARI cooperative which the blacksmiths were ordered to form by the occupying Japanese forces. Later, in 1962, the villagers formed their own cooperative as a response to the problem of restitusi payments demanded by corrupt police and Forestry Department officers. Still later, in 1969, the villagers incorporated their organization as a legal body and registered it with the Department of Cooperatives in the hopes of obtaining a permit from PJKA to legally buy railroad rails. Then, after the KUD system was put in place in 1973, this cooperative was told that it had to become a unit of the KUD. The alternative would have been disbanding.

Below this middle level of KOPINKRA are a variety of smaller and less formal associations of producers which are simply called "groups" (*kelompok*), or sometimes pre-cooperatives (*pre-koperasi*). The workplans of most Department of Industry development projects require that the participants at least be organized in a group, with a responsible group head or treasurer, and that any project inputs be distributed through the group. Of course if a KOPINKRA already exists in the village, inputs will be channeled through the KOPINKRA.

In some developing countries the industrial cooperative movement has emphasized production: the members of the cooperative work together in a single location to produce goods which they then market together. These cooperatives often come to resemble small worker-owned factories. In Indonesia this is not the case. Producer cooperatives are relatively rare, and most KOPINKRA are supply, credit, or marketing cooperatives. The same holds true for smaller groups and pre-cooperatives. Actual production usually remains in the hands of small individually owned units such as perapen.

Membership in most metalworking cooperatives and groups is limited to perapen owners. Sometimes, as at Kajar, membership also includes hired empu. Unpaid family workers and other hired workers are rarely if ever allowed to become members. The head of a cooperative or group is elected by the members. Usually there are other elected or appointed officers as well, such as a treasurer and a secretary. In well-stratified villages where many of the producers are tied by dependency relationships to a large entrepreneur, that entrepreneur is almost inevitably elected head of the cooperative.

From the Department of Industry's point of view, the principal advantage of working through cooperatives and groups is a reduction of the extension officer's workload. Instead of trying to deal with many scattered enterprise owners individually, the extension officer can limit those with whom he deals day to day to the head of the cooperative and its officers. The cooperative head acts as the local project implementer, distributing inputs, collecting repayments, maintaining financial records, and in many instances selecting project participants.

The Department of Cooperatives provides the members of small industry cooperatives and groups with some motivational training. Occasionally this training catches hold and the members come to think of the cooperative or group as their own, something they can use to improve their own welfare. When this occurs the members can be motivated to expand and improve their enterprises. Motivation works best when it is combined with other program elements, such as the distribution of resources.

The principal disadvantage of working through cooperatives is the risk of financial mismanagement by their heads and officers. The rate of failure due to mismanagement is very high in rural Indonesia, and has led to a widespread distrust of cooperatives among villagers. The situation may be improving somewhat with the establishment of government banks in rural areas. Extension agents can insist that cooperative funds be deposited in a bank where they are safe and earn respectable rates of interest. Once the funds are deposited, a public record of the cooperative's finances is available for inspection at any time.

Even if the head of the cooperative does not misappropriate the funds, there is the danger that he will try to merge his own business with the business of the cooperative, as occurred at Kajar. Any cash or raw material inputs distributed through the cooperative then act to augment his working capital and strengthen his position vis-a-vis weaker producers. Equipment distributed through the cooperative may be retained at the cooperative headquarters, in which case it effectively becomes part of the personal capital assets of the cooperative head. This is particularly so if his home or workplace is used as the cooperative headquarters. On-the-ground inspection of many KOPINKRA, KUD, and other types of organized rural groups indicates that this occurs frequently.

3. *Centers*. The most common program element in Department of Industry workplans is the distribution of resources. These resources are of three basic types: cash to be used as working capital, bulk amounts of raw materials such as scrap iron and charcoal, and productive equipment and machinery such as anvils and edge grinders. The Department of Industry uses the English term "feederpoint" to describe projects which distribute resources. Sometimes the word is also used for the location where the resources are dropped off, usually the cooperative or group headquarters.

Sometimes the Department of Industry distributes resources to village producers without any obligation to repay—as a gift or grant. When this occurs it is usually because the department has received some special project funds from a foreign donor agency. But normally an obligation to repay is written into the workplan. Sometimes this obligation is vigorously enforced and sometimes it is not. If the repayment obligation is enforced, various arrangements are used. Often the participants simply give their repayments to the cooperative or group treasurer. He may keep them at home in a locked cupboard, give them to the Department of Industry field-worker, or deposit them in the local unit of a government bank. Sometimes a workplan stipulates that the credit must be "revolving": the repayments made by the first group of participants are loaned out to a second group of participants, the repayments made by the second group are loaned out to a third group, and so on.

In a village where resources are scarce, enterprise owners will obviously be attracted to feederpoint projects. It is safe to say that without feeder-points the Department of Industry would have trouble gaining the attention or cooperation of enterprise owners. Feederpoint projects are popular with Department of Industry officials in the regional and district offices. First, they are relatively easy to implement. Any resources to be distributed can be requisitioned or purchased and dropped off to the cooperative office in a day or two. Then the official can make out a report saying that the project has been implemented. Second, feederpoint projects offer opportunities for officials to supplement their modest salaries by obtaining commissions (*komisi*) from dealers of raw material, equipment, and machinery. Generally the dealer is asked to quote a full or undiscounted price on the items to be purchased. The official then bargains for a discounted price, with the understanding that the dealer will supply him with a receipt for the larger amount. The difference is pocketed as a commission or kickback. Generally these commissions are held within reasonable bounds and amount to no more than 10 or 15 percent of the full price. It should be understood that the taking of commissions is not limited to the Department of Industry. It is a common practice in Indonesia, found in nearly every public and private institution. Even if an official does not ask for a commission, the dealer may offer it to develop a langganan trade relationship with the official.

Project plans often justify feederpoint projects as a way to "break the hold of intermediaries." Examined more closely, this justification does not hold up. First, there is no real evidence that village industry producers want to sever their ties with intermediaries. Intermediaries perform a number of vital supply, transport, and marketing functions, and there is a recognition in rural areas that intermediaries deserve a fair profit for their services. When village industry producers try to perform supply, trans-port, and marketing functions on their own, it cuts heavily into production time and generally results in lower rather than higher earnings. Of course producers will complain if an intermediary becomes greedy and tries to cut too deeply into their profit margins, but competition between intermediaries usually prevents this. Producers also realize that government projects have a finite lifetime, lasting one, two, or at most a few years. It would be foolish for them to sever ties with their intermediaries because of a government project. Therefore, government credit distributed through feederpoint projects is usually used to augment rather than replace credit from intermediaries.

Second, there is no real evidence that raw materials, equipment, and machinery supplied by feederpoint projects are significantly cheaper than those supplied by intermediaries. Occasionally they may be more expensive, in which case village industry producers will naturally feel some resentment at being pressured to participate. Even working capital supplied through feederpoint projects may carry disguised interest charges in the form of cooperative dues and administrative fees.

Feederpoint projects are often used to introduce or disseminate new technologies. This can work well if the technologies are acceptable to the producers and if the department makes them available at or below the outside market price. But technology projects can backfire if planning officers fail to consult with producers, as often occurs. In 1978, for example, the Central Java office of the Department of Industry imported a large number of European tanged anvils for distribution through feederpoint projects. These anvils were made of a very superior grade of steel, and the tanged shape meant that they had a larger working surface than the Indonesian nail-shaped anvil. Nonetheless, blacksmiths throughout the province refused to accept these anvils, and the Central Java office was left with a storeroom full of anvils which it had to write off. The next year I was asked to investigate the situation and found that the principal barriers to acceptance of the tanged anvil were cultural and symbolic, not economic: blacksmiths did not want to give up the nail-shaped anvil because of its importance as a lingam symbol.

Feederpoint projects are expensive to carry out. Even when resources are distributed as a form of non-revolving credit, there are significant "leakages," so that relatively little money comes back to the Department of Industry to use in subsequent projects. In fact, DUPs and DIPs do not acknowledge the existence of any repayments from previous years. During the 1970s, when the government had ample oil revenues, feederpoint projects were very popular. After the decline in oil prices in 1984, the government was forced to cut back on the number and size of these projects.

4. *Common service facilities*. The Department of Industry has built com-

mon service facilities in many of the small industry sentra around the country. The department's term for a common service facility is UPT (*Unit Pelayanan Teknis*, or Technical Servicing Unit). Of the eighty sentra which make code 38 metal products, forty-eight already have UPTs.

The UPTs built in blacksmithing villages are fairly standard around the country. Generally they consist of a small brick and plaster building, equipped with enough electricity to operate high-wattage machinery, plus a supplemental generator. In addition, there are various pieces of productive machinery such as large blowers, electric edge grinders, electric polishers, and electric welding equipment. Sometimes there is casting equipment as well, or less commonly, electroplating equipment.

The concept behind the UPT is giving small industry producers access to machine technology which they could not otherwise afford. Blacksmiths, for example, are encouraged to bring their semifinished tools to the UPT, where they can use the polishers and edge grinders to finish the tools. Smiths who make more complex products such as insecticide sprayers or pumps can bring their metal sheet or scrap to the UPT, where they can use the welding or casting equipment. The UPT is manned by between one and four hired operators, who are low-ranking employees of the Department of Industry. The job of the operator is to maintain the equipment and teach the smith how to use it properly. The smith is charged a small fee, usually per item processed, which is used to offset the costs of operating the UPT and pay the salaries of the operators.

The concept behind the UPT is a good one. But in practice the purpose of the UPT is usually subverted by the operators. Operators begin to supplement their meager salaries by using the UPT equipment to produce their own goods for sale. If they are successful in doing this, they will monopolize the use of the equipment for most of the workday and find ways to restrict the access of village producers to the equipment. Sometimes this is done by requiring that the villager sign up many days or even weeks in advance to use the equipment. At other times the operators raise the fees charged so that it is no longer profitable for villagers to use the equipment. Even if operators do not use the equipment for their own production, they may raise the fees and pocket the difference between the fee set by the department and the fee actually charged. Sometimes officers from the district or provincial office go into partnership with UPT operators to produce goods for sale. When they do, the higher-ranking officer supplies working capital and help in getting government contracts, while the operators actually produce the goods. Sometimes the operators form a patron-client relationship with a private individual, for example a wealthy village-based entrepreneur or the owner of a hardware store in a nearby town that functions in the same way. Not infrequently an operator begins to function as an intermediary by buying up semifinished products from village producers. The products are then finished and marketed by the operator. There are many types of arrangements, but all involve conflict of interest and result in restricted access for village producers to the UPT. Sometimes these arrangements are made without the knowledge of the department, but at other times they are actually countenanced by the department as a way of helping villagers to expand their product types and markets.

5. *Demonstration technology projects*. Closely related to the UPT concept are various types of demonstration technology projects. During the 1970s there was a vogue for these types of projects, fueled by the international appropriate technology movement. E. F. Schumacher's *Small Is Beautiful* was translated into Indonesian and constantly referred to in public statements by higher-ranking Department of Industry officials. In addition, a considerable amount of free donor agency money was available for "aptech," as it was often called.

One type of demonstration technology project is the "demo plot," sites where new technologies relating to a number of industries are constructed or installed. These plots are usually built in urban areas, often at or near the regional or district office of the Department of Industry, and are useful primarily in training extension officers. Another type of demonstration technology project is constructed in rural areas and is used to introduce new technologies to village industry producers. This type usually focuses on a single industry. In the mid-1970s the Department of Industry in Central Java tried to wean clay product and lime industries away from the environmentally destructive use of fuelwood. It did this by building a number of demonstration kilns which burned low-grade petroleum-based fuels. These projects were reasonably successful until the central government withdrew its subsidies on petroleum-based fuels, at which point they became too expensive to operate profitably and fell into disuse. Demonstration technology projects are more common for clay product industries than for metalworking industries.

Sometimes a demonstration technology project is donated to a village cooperative which is permitted to use the technology to produce goods for sale. That can raise the usual problem of domination by the head of the cooperative, but at least the technology is being used productively each day and is available for others to see and emulate. Sometimes the project remains the property of the Department of Industry, in which case the tools are usually kept under lock and key unless a training course is held there, or unless a group of dignitaries visits the village. Some demonstration technology projects have operators, which can cause the same problems as with UPT operators.

6. *Training courses.* Next to feederpoint projects, training courses are the most common type of project. TPLs and BIPIK extension officers are supposed to conduct training as part of their everyday duties. In addition, special training courses are often planned for small industry villages. The acronym used for these courses is DIKLAT (*Pendidikan dan Latihan*, or education and training). The typical course lasts one or two weeks and is attended by ten to twenty producers. Usually the course is conducted in the village, for example at the village meeting house (*balai desa*) or at the cooperative headquarters. Occasionally the villagers are transported to another location, such as the district office or a demonstration technology project in another village. The trainers are usually staff members of BIPIK or one of the national technology development centers such as MIDC. The subject matter of the courses varies. Most are technical, but some deal with such management topics as marketing and bookkeeping.

Department of Industry officials at the provincial and district levels like the DIKLAT projects because like feederpoint projects they are relatively easy to implement. Once the course is over, an evaluation can be written attesting that the project has been successfully completed, and there are no messy details which carry over into the next budget period. The budgetary allotments for training augment the salaries of trainers, extension workers, and other officials involved in implementing the project. The value of DIKLAT projects of course depends on the quality of the trainers and the usefulness of the subject matter. Unfortunately many trainers are careless in their preparation, secure in the knowledge that villagers will never raise a complaint to the authorities. Often the villagers who are asked to attend DIKLAT know more than the trainers, but they are too polite to say so.

Private conversations with village industry producers indicate that they consider DIKLAT to be an imposition. There are at least three reasons for this. First, producers feel that they learn very little that is useful from DIKLAT. Second, DIKLAT are usually held during the day, so that producers who are asked to attend lose valuable work time and income. Projects should build in some compensation for lost work time in the form of per diem fees for participants, but they do not always do so. Third, if the DIKLAT is designed to introduce a new production process or technology, the participants are usually asked to provide their own raw materials to work on during the course. If the products made turn out to be unsalable, as often occurs, the risk falls on the participants. Again, raw materials should be included in the DIKLAT budget, but they seldom are.

Participants for DIKLAT are usually rounded up by the TPL or the BIPIK officer, assisted by village officials or the head of the cooperative. Busy enterprise owners often avoid attending by sending one of their grown-up children. In metalworking villages, for example, perapen owners often send a grown-up son who works as a panjak. This can work out well if the son is actually involved in the enterprise, because the literacy and numeracy levels of younger villagers are higher than those of their parents. Thus the son may be able to absorb the training materials more easily. During the son's absence the perapen can continue production by making smaller tools which require fewer panjak, or by hiring another panjak as a temporary replacement.

7. *Study tours.* Closely related to DIKLAT are study tours. They differ in that they involve a villager-to-villager transfer of skills and knowledge rather than a trainer-to-villager transfer. There are two basic types of study tours, the technology tour and the marketing tour. In the technology tour a group of producers is transported from a village that the department considers technologically more backward to a village that is technologically more advanced. The participants live in the new village for an extended period, usually one to three months, during which time they are supposed to learn new skills from their host villagers. As already mentioned, blacksmiths are often sent on study tours to iron-casting villages such as Batur, or to another blacksmithing village where the Department of Industry has set up a demonstration iron-casting project.

The villager-to-villager approach to learning new technologies works well if the host villagers are accepting of the project. For them to be accepting, two conditions must be met. First, they must be rewarded financially or psychologically for the time and effort they put into training the newcomers in their midst. The financial reward usually consists of daily payments to host enterprises, plus free use of the labor of the trainees. Psychological rewards may include praise and recognition by government officials, plus access to other opportunities such as participation in fairs and exhibitions. The second condition which must be met is a negative one: the host villagers must not feel that they are training potential competitors. If they do, they may succumb to pressure from the Department of Industry to accept the newcomers, but then will collaborate to withhold some of their most important trade secrets, making the transfer of technology incomplete. Usually distance determines whether the host villagers feel threatened. If the newcomers are from a neighboring district and compete in some of the same marketplaces, the host villagers will feel more threatened than if the newcomers are from a distant district or another island.

Another type of study tour is the marketing tour. The marketing tour is usually shorter, lasting from a few days to two weeks. During the tour the participants are usually put on a bus and taken to see the marketplaces and stores where their own products and the products of their competitors are retailed. Because many producers rely entirely on intermediaries to retail their products, they are ignorant of the retail prices charged by these intermediaries. The marketing tour is designed to remedy this situation and strengthen the bargaining position of the producer by providing him with better market information. Ideas for technological improvements and new product types can also be obtained by examining products made in other villages.

8. *Mini-industrial estates.* In the 1970s and early 1980s the Department of Industry constructed a number of mini industrial estates called "LIK" (Lingkungan Industri Kecil, or "small industry environments"). These LIK, based on models developed largely in Africa, usually consisted of large cement buildings divided into workspaces which could be rented out by producers. Most LIK were built on the outskirts of large towns where a plentiful supply of electricity was available. Presumably producers would be motivated to rent space in the LIK so that they could make use of electrically powered technologies. Other inducements were added in the way of running water, new machine technologies available for use, etc.

Conversations with Department of Industry officials indicate that the LIKs are underutilized. The installation of electricity in most villages in the mid-1980s rendered the LIK concept largely obsolete. In addition, the rents charged for workspaces in the LIKs are high by village standards, certainly higher than the cost of working out of one's own house yard. Those LIKs which are still used are occupied mainly by urban-based enterprises, commonly machine and repair shops. No new LIK are planned.

9. *Urban salesrooms and emporia.* The Department of Industry attempts in various ways to promote the sale of products made by village producers, including blacksmiths. One way is through urban salesrooms, where buyers can see various products on display. If a buyer is interested in a particular product, department officials will facilitate contact with the producer,

often by accompanying the buyer to the village. These urban salesrooms are modest affairs, usually located in a room adjoining the department's provincial office. Often they do not retail goods at all but just maintain permanent displays of products made in the province. The net impact of these salesrooms on total sales of small industry products is virtually nil.

Of much greater importance is the government-owned Sarinah Jaya handicraft trading corporation, which operates out of the Sarinah chain of department stores. Sarinah Jaya, set up by an Italian consultant in the late 1960s, resembles in concept the mighty national and regional emporia on the Indian subcontinent, such as those run by the Cottage Industries Corporation of India and the Punjab Small Industries Corporation of Pakistan. Sarinah Jaya retails goods directly to customers who visit the Sarinah stores, and it also wholesales and exports goods in bulk. It handles only handicrafts, not utilitarian products such as agricultural tools. But these handicrafts include many products made by metalsmiths, including cast bronze statues, souvenir keris, and silver jewelry. The wholesale marketing of handicrafts in Indonesia largely shifted to Bali in the 1980s, where it operates entirely through private arrangements between foreign buyers and Balinese producers and traders. In the Jakarta area, though, Sarinah Jaya remains the most important retail and wholesale outlet for handicrafts.

In many developing countries emporia are owned by large government-sponsored handicraft cooperatives. Sarinah Jaya is not organized as a cooperative but rather contacts handicraft villages all over Indonesia and offers to market their goods. Often modifications in product design are suggested to make the product more salable. Some goods are purchased outright, while others are accepted on consignment.

10. *Industrial shows and fairs.* The Departments of Industry and Trade also promote Indonesian products through industrial shows and fairs. These shows and fairs are organized at various levels — national, regional, and local. Some focus on handicrafts, others on utilitarian products, for example machines and tools related to agriculture. Department officials select the producers who are allowed to participate in these fairs, and inevitably there is a tendency to select the same producers year after year — those with larger enterprises or a special reputation for craftsmanship. Pak Sastro, for example, is always asked to attend industrial fairs in the Yogyakarta area, and sometimes national fairs as well. Since producers usually man their own booths or display tables at fairs, the fairs provide useful opportunities to make direct contacts with new customers.

The Indonesian government also participates in some industrial shows and fairs abroad. Sometimes skilled village industry producers are sent abroad for a few weeks or months to give demonstrations at fairs. Thus it is not unusual to come across a villager who reports having spent a few cold and puzzling weeks sitting in a fairground in Japan or Germany, cutting out wayang puppets, waxing batik cloth, or tracing repoussé designs on silver.

11. *"Upakarti" awards.* Although not strictly a program element, this government award may be mentioned. It is modeled after the "national treasure" program which has been used effectively in Japan to promote the preservation of traditional handicrafts. The village industry producer who is selected to receive an Upakarti is called to the palace in Jakarta and presented with a large, beautiful trophy by the president. Being able to install such a trophy in one's living room back in the village, together with a color photograph of the recipient shaking hands with the president, brings tremendous prestige.

12. *Bapak Angkat.* The Foster Father program has been in existence in Indonesia for several decades, but in recent years it has taken on a new importance and new functions. This has occurred because of cutbacks in funding for other types of rural development projects because of declining oil revenues. Originally the Foster Father program was designed to promote production linkages between large and small enterprises. Such linkages could be backward linkages, as when blacksmithing villages received steel blanks from the Krakatau Steel plant, or forward linkages, as when a vehicle plant gave casting smiths an order for component or spare parts. Generally the linkage model of development works best in the metalworking sector, and not as well in other sectors such as textiles and wood products. In development literature the model is usually associated with Japan, where large numbers of rural workshops turn out component parts, spare parts, and hand tools for factories.

Formerly the Foster Father firm acted as a supplier or buyer to the village-based firm but did not play any other role. Then the Indonesian government asked Foster Father firms to take on new responsibilities, such as arranging for credit through a government bank, or providing technical or managerial training. Sometimes Foster Father relationships are between a single village enterprise and a single large factory or firm, but often the large factory or firm is asked to provide assistance to a number of village-based enterprises. To facilitate the channeling of assistance, the village-based producers may be organized into a cooperative or group.

As envisioned by the government, village-based firms will derive a number of potential benefits from participating in the Foster Father program, including access to raw materials and fuel of higher quality or at lower prices, orders for new products, transfer of skills and technologies, and better access to formal-sector credit. There are certain dangers inherent in the program which have not been sufficiently acknowledged by the government. These dangers arise because the Foster Father firm is larger and more sophisticated, and may try to subvert the program to its own ends. It may try to undermine the independence of the village-based firms (if they were independent to begin with, which is not always the case), or exploit the village-based firms as a source of cheap labor. If credit is involved, the Foster Father firm may misuse credit facilities in various ways. An example will help to make this clear. In 1992, while doing survey work for Bank Rakyat Indonesia, I encountered several corruption cases involving Foster Father firms. In one typical case the Foster Father owned a large machine-embroidery enterprise which made use of put-out labor. He arranged loans of Rp 250,000 each through the local village unit of BRI for forty of his put-out workers. Interviews with some of these workers revealed that they had only received Rp 190,000 each, while the Foster Father had pocketed the remaining Rp 60,000. Since the workers had individually signed the loan agreements with BRI, they were legally responsible for paying off the full amount, plus interest.

There is another problematic aspect to the Foster Father program. Many of the private firms enrolled in the program are owned by ethnic Chinese. This may be simply because ethnic Chinese dominate the industrial sector at the higher levels. Yet it appears that participation in the Foster Father program is not always voluntary but is rather a way that the government has of putting pressure on Chinese firm owners to share their wealth with small pribumi (ethnic Malay) entrepreneurs.

Interview with Head of the Subdirectorate for Metal

In September 1991 I conducted an extended interview with Ir. Felik Lengkong, head of the Subdirectorate for Metal, and two of his staff members. This interview provided a good deal of information on Department of Industry programs, as well as some important clues about the future of small and household metalworking industries as seen through the eyes of department officials.

Ir. Lengkong believes that blacksmiths and other metalworkers are better off now than before. He does not take sole credit for this, but says it is largely due to greater market demand, better transport, and expanded marketing networks. He does note that there is a problem with competition from tools smuggled in from other Asian countries. Ir. Lengkong is a firm believer in the concept of takeoff and is confident that Indonesia's metalworking industries will be able to achieve takeoff during the REPELITA VI, as planned by the government. He defines takeoff as the ability of an enterprise to be independent (*mandiri*) and stand on its own feet without help from the government.

Although the removal of protective import legislation is justified on the grounds of assisting export industries, Ir. Lengkong admits that small and household metalworking industries in code 38 have not been included in the current export drive. Mercedes-Benz once ordered some components for its buses from local enterprises, and the buses were then assembled in Indonesia and exported, but Indonesian-made components and spare parts are not being exported directly.

The subdirectorate has been active in promoting the use of new metalworking technologies such as mechanical blower and gerinda. The staff members are aware of the dangers of displacing human workers with these machines, but do not regard this as a problem for two reasons. First, the market for metalworking industries is still expanding rapidly, so that many smithing villages are actually experiencing a shortage of skilled labor. Second, the newfound prosperity of some metalworking families means that they are keeping their sons in school longer rather than putting them to work in the perapen. Once these boys have graduated from high school, they prefer to look for white-collar jobs rather than work as smiths. Thus the proportion of boys from smithing households who are following their fathers into the trade is declining.

The subdirectorate is currently trying to develop a forging machine (*mesin tempa*), also referred to by the English name of "springhammer," which would replace the labor of the hammer swingers. An operator stands or sits in front of the machine, inserts a metal blank, and steps on a foot pedal, releasing a spring which hammers the blank. A prototype for the springhammer was donated to the subdirectorate by JAICA, the Japanese Industry Cooperation Agency, which has an office in Jakarta. There have been some problems in copying the prototype because early models used scrap steel from automobile springs, which did not strike with the correct force. Newer models are using springs special-ordered from a spring factory. So far six springhammers have been produced in a blacksmithing village in Sukabumi district, West Java, under the supervision of the directorate. Five of the machines were sold to a large government-owned plantation, PTP 12, which is using them to produce tools for distribution to their plantation workers. PTP 12 acts as the Foster Father to the blacksmithing village which produced the machines. The sixth machine is being kept by the district headman.

According to the subdirectorate, the cost of a springhammer is Rp 6 to 7 million, plus another Rp 200,000 for the cement foundation. It is not clear whether this cost includes a profit margin. In addition, the springhammer requires 600 watts of electricity. This can either be supplied by two additional units purchased from PLN, the government electricity utility, or by an electric generator. Either option adds about Rp 2 million to the price, bringing the total price to about Rp 8.2–9.2 million ($4,173–4,682), which is nearing the upper limit of what would be affordable even by the largest village-based entrepreneurs.

A springhammer would enable the empu to work alone without the help of any hammer swingers. Since most smithies have two to three hammer swingers, the number of workers displaced is potentially greater than with the blower or gerinda. The subdirectorate therefore plans to restrict the distribution of the springhammer to "areas where the market is elastic." But once a successful model has been produced, it is unrealistic to expect that the subdirectorate will be able to control its spread. Because of its cost, the springhammer will probably disseminate in the same pattern as the electric generator and other larger pieces of capital equipment such as large gerinda and trucks. One or a few of the wealthier enterprise owners in each smithing village will be able to afford it, while the remainder continue to rely on human labor.

The subdirectorate is also trying to introduce iron-casting technology to a number of traditional blacksmithing villages. It has donated cupolas or the smaller tungkik to these villages, or asked a Foster Father to donate the technology. Massepe village in South Sulawesi has received both a cupola and a tungkik from Tonasa Cement Factory. In return, the village cooperative is expected to produce spare parts for Tonase's machinery as a subcontractor. One or two cupola or tungkik have also been received by blacksmithing villages in West Java, North Sumatra, and Lampung. The net impact of these equipment donations is small, and iron casting on a commercial scale continues to be confined to Tegal and Klaten districts in Central Java.

Currently the subdirectorate is putting most of its eggs in a single basket, the Foster Father program. Other programs, notably the industrial estate program, are being phased out for budgetary and other reasons. In February 1991 the government announced the start of a National Movement for the Formation of Linkages (Gerakan Nasional Keterkaitan Linkages), with a national target of ten thousand linkages to be formed in all industrial sectors. By September, when I conducted my interview, Ir. Lengkong had participated in twenty-eight ceremonies all over the country to formalize the relationships between 292 "Foster Fathers" and 365 small metalworking enterprises and cooperatives.

Rural Banking Programs and Their Impact

It is probable that rural banking programs have had a greater impact than Department of Industry programs on smithing villages. The most important of these programs at present are operated by two government banks: BPD (Bank Pembangunan Daerah, or Regional Development Bank) and BRI (Bank Rakyat Indonesia, or People's Bank of Indonesia). Both banks make small loans available for activities unrelated to rice cultivation, including petty trade, rural industries, small livestock operations, and small service sector operations. Both charge market interest rates, which are high by western standards but considerably lower than the informal rates traditionally charged by moneylenders, or the hidden interest rates charged by intermediaries (discussed in chapter 2).

Modern rural banking programs began in the early 1970s with the BIMAS subsidized credit program for rice inputs. This program was part of a larger extension package designed to encourage rice farmers to adopt Green Revolution technologies, particularly the use of chemical fertilizer. It was operated through a nationwide network of rural banks established by BRI. These banks, called Unit Desa (Village

Units), were usually located at the subdistrict level. Each bank was staffed with four to eight officers, most of whom were young people with high school diplomas from the local area.

The BIMAS program eventually suffered high losses because of a poor repayment rate. A black market for fertilizer and other inputs arose, which operated among market sellers and small shopkeepers. Eventually it became clear that the informal sector was capable of effectively supplying rice inputs on credit, and the credit component of the BIMAS program was phased out by mid-1984. Rather than disband their nationwide network of Unit Desas and staff, BRI decided to start a new rural credit program which would focus on activities unrelated to rice cultivation. This program, called KUPEDES (Kredit Umum Pedesaan, or General Rural Credit), is now thought to be the world's largest rural credit program. The first KUPEDES loans were made in February 1984, and as of the end of 1991 10.1 million loans totaling Rp 5,457 billion, or about $3.1 billion, had been lent out, for an average loan size of Rp 540,297 ($309).

KUPEDES is a "demand" credit program: although sometimes fieldworkers attempt to publicize the program by giving speeches at village meetings and visiting enterprise owners in their homes, in general villagers must take the initiative to come into the Unit Desa and apply for a loan, and to make decisions concerning the size of the loan request and the repayment terms. This program contrasts with an older generation of "supply" credit programs, popular during the Sukarno era, which operated through mainline departments such as the Department of Industry. In a supply credit program the department fixes the number of loans to be made in each village, the size of the loans, and the repayment terms. Generally these are standardized so that all loan recipients receive the same amount, regardless of need. Loan recipients are selected by department field staff, usually in cooperation with village officials. Evaluations of supply credit programs indicate that subjective criteria often influence the selection of participants, who tend to be friends, cronies, and allies of village officials. The deserving poor whose enterprises might benefit from a loan are often excluded.

Two types of loans are available under KUPEDES: working capital loans and investment loans. Working capital loans are usually used for raw materials, fuel, and wage payments, while investment loans are used for buildings, vehicles, machinery, or equipment. In the early years of the program a lower interest rate was charged on investment loans owing to a subsidy from the World Bank. It was hoped that this subsidy would encourage villagers to invest in new technologies. It did not have the desired effect, and the demand for investment loans remained very small in comparison with the demand for working capital loans. Eventually the subsidy was withdrawn, and the interest rate on the two types of loans was equalized at 1.5 percent per month. This compares with rates of 10–30 percent per month on informal credit from moneylenders and intermediaries.

There is no minimum loan for KUPEDES, but loans of less than Rp 200,000 (about $100) are rare. Originally there was a "ceiling" of Rp 1 million (about $500), but this was moved up in stages to Rp 3 million, 10 million, and 25 million. Even so, approximately 95 percent of the loans are for Rp 5 million or less.

To qualify for a loan under KUPEDES the borrower must have an established enterprise. Villagers who do not own an enterprise—for example those who live entirely from wage labor, pensions, or remittances from relatives who live outside the village—do not qualify. Since such persons often constitute the poorest segment of a village, KUPEDES excludes some of the rural poor. Remembering, however, that most rural Indonesian households have multiple occupations and income sources, there is usually at least one enterprise that qualifies for a loan. Consider a rural poor household where the father and son work as wage agricultural laborers, the mother works as a vegetable seller in the marketplace, and the daughter earns piece rates in a garment factory. The father, son, and daughter will not qualify for a loan, but the mother will because market trade is considered an enterprise.

To qualify for a KUPEDES loan, the borrower is also required to provide some type of loan guarantee. The guarantee preferred by Unit Desa officers is a legal land certificate from the government's Land Registry Office (BPN, or Badan Pertanahan Nasional). But clearing land certificates is a difficult, frustrating, and expensive process, involving many trips to town, confusing encounters with indifferent government officials, and numerous under-the-table payments. Better-off villagers who are literate and have some experience in dealing with government institutions can usually manage to clear their certificates in a reasonable length of time (two or three months), while poorer and less sophisticated villagers give up in frustration or wait for years with no result. In lieu of a land certificate other types of land documents may also be used, such as a "letter C" certificate issued by the subdistrict (kecamatan) office. Still, the larger loans are reserved for villagers with certificates from BPN. The land used to guarantee the loan need not be irrigated sawah. Dry fields, house plots, and other types of land may also be used. The value of the land used to guarantee the loan must exceed the value of the loan, which also creates a bias in favor of large landowning households.

KUPEDES regulations also permit the use of fiducia (movable assets such as vehicle registration papers, machinery, or buildings) to guarantee loans. Yet in practice Unit Desa officers are often reluctant to accept fiducia as the sole guarantee of a loan, although fiducia may be used as a supplemental guarantee so that the borrower can qualify for a larger loan than would be otherwise available.

KUPEDES is a nationwide program, available in nearly every subdistrict in the country. Somewhat more limited in geographical coverage, but also important, are the programs run by BPD. These are found in seven of the more densely populated provinces in the country. Unlike KUPEDES, which is centralized, the BPD programs are decentralized and vary somewhat from province to province. The best-known is the pilot BKK (Badan Kredit Kecamatan, or Subdistrict Credit Institution) program. BKK and the other BPD programs differ from KUPEDES in having a smaller average loan, shorter repayment terms, easier application procedures, and somewhat easier guarantee requirements.

In addition to rural credit programs, large entrepreneurs such as Pak Sastro may qualify for loans from urban banks. These banks may be either government-owned or privately owned. The ceiling on urban bank loans is much higher than on rural bank loans, and the interest rates are lower. The number of villagers who take out urban bank loans is still very small.

It is possible to make some generalizations about the impact of rural credit programs on metalworking villages.

—Perapen owners obviously meet the loan requirement of owning a productive enterprise, but hired workers in the perapen may not. Hired workers who do not meet this requirement may qualify for a loan through a family member, for example a wife who owns a trading enterprise.

—Because of the guarantee requirements, there is a credit bias in favor of landowning households. In dry-zone villages such as Kajar, nearly every household will own enough land to guarantee a loan. In more densely populated lowland villages such as Batur, many households may have difficulty meeting the guarantee requirements. Employment status and land-owning status are often linked. In other words, the proportion of pera-pen owners who own land is generally higher than the proportion of hired workers who own land.

—Dependent perapen owners have less need of bank loans than independent perapen owners. On the other hand, a bank loan may enable a dependent perapen owner to become independent.

—In taking out bank loans, perapen owners must consider their income, which determines their capacity to repay. Most KUPEDES loans are for one to two years, with monthly repayment schedules. The repayment schedule must leave enough from perapen profits for the owner to cover working capital expenses and support his household. For this reason, smaller and weaker perapen owners usually take out smaller loans, while larger and stronger owners take out larger loans.

—As discussed in previous chapters, capital is the engine of stratification. Smaller and weaker perapen owners use their loans as working capital. Larger owners and empu pedagang use their loans to hire additional workers or purchase raw materials which are given out on credit to dependent owners. Using bank funds to purchase raw materials which are given out on credit is a type of relending. In other words, it only benefits entrepreneurs to engage in this practice if they charge a hidden interest payment on materials given out on credit which exceeds the bank interest rate. Empu pedagang who own warehouses can use bank loans to stockpile iron or charcoal when it is cheap, for resale or relending to smaller enterprise owners when the price goes up.

—Small pieces of equipment which cost less than Rp 200,000 are usually financed out of perapen profits rather than bank loans. Large pieces of equipment such as diesel engines and large gerinda are often financed with bank loans. Vehicles may either be financed with bank loans or purchased on credit from vehicle dealers.

—The ceiling on rural bank loans is often too stringent if compared with the working capital needs of metalworking industries. The average daily working capital requirement of a perapen in Kajar was approximately Rp 55,000 in 1991, for example. A one-year loan of Rp 200,000, which would be quite suitable for many rural enterprises, would be ludicrously inadequate for a perapen owner and not worth the effort of filing an application. Most perapen owners need loans of at least Rp 3,000,000 ($1,500).

A Note on Rice Price Supports and Subsidies

Because rice is such an important part of the Indonesian diet, the government has long had a policy of subsidizing rice inputs and controlling rice prices, exports, and imports. This policy is designed both to protect the producers of rice—rural farmers—and the consumers of rice, including the rural and urban poor. During the colonial and Sukarno eras bans on exports were periodically enforced, both as a reaction to scarcity caused by harvest failure and in a effort to keep rice cheap enough that the average Indonesian could afford to continue eating it. When international rice prices were higher than the domestic price, the government reacted by banning exports. Conversely, when international prices were lower, the government banned imports to prevent farm incomes from dropping.

Government interventions in the markets for rice and rice inputs continued during the Green Revolution period of the 1970s and 1980s. Although most of the inputs came to be distributed through the activities of private traders rather than the KUDs, the government continued to subsidize fertilizer to keep prices low and encourage its adoption. The most important fertilizer is urea, and the ratio of urea to paddy prices has steadily declined, partly as a result of the construction of government factories to produce urea domestically (Booth 1988, 149–50).

BULOG, the National Logistics Agency, buys up rice from the KUDs and maintains large reserves. It also sets farm-gate floor prices for rice so that the increase in supply owing to Green Revolution technologies will not cause rice prices to plummet as they undoubtedly would do if the situation were left to the play of market forces. BULOG also has sole charge of rice imports and sets prices on these imports. This twin policy of regulated imports and domestic procurement has effectively insulated domestic rice prices from international price movements (Booth 1988, 155).

There is a close connection between the agricultural and industrial sectors of the rural economy. This is particularly true for blacksmiths, who make the hand tools used by farmers. If farmers' incomes are high, farmers will buy more tools and pay more for the tools they buy. If rice is being planted and harvested more frequently, as occurs with the new rice varieties, tools will wear out faster and have to be replaced more often. In addition, high farm incomes result in more rural construction, such as the building of houses, work sheds, and animal pens. Therefore blacksmiths who make workman's tools also benefit. Other rural metalworking industries, for example those which make knives and kitchen equipment, will also benefit from increased farmer incomes and an expanded market.

One might ask what would happen to rural metalworking industries if the government deregulated the rice sector. If deregulation resulted in a drop in farmers' incomes, it is very likely that metalworking industries would also be adversely affected. The same could be said of many other nonagricultural sectors of the rural economy. A move in that direction occurred in 1987–88, when the government substantially reduced the fertilizer subsidy (Booth 1988, 158).

CHAPTER 6

Conclusions and Development Implications

In this chapter I return to some of the issues raised in the Introduction, and reconsider them in the light of the material presented in the intervening chapters.

WE CAN BEGIN BY ASKING whether the Indonesian industrial sector is still dualistic. As early as 1910 Boeke used this term to characterize the Indonesian economy, meaning that there was a gap between capital-intensive enterprises along western lines and the more labor-intensive peasant enterprises. The data presented in chapter 4 indicate that this characterization is still pertinent today. In the industrial sector the gap falls between large and medium industries on the one hand, and small and household industries on the other. The average size of large and medium enterprises in code 38, for example, was 143 workers in 1986, while the average size of small and household enterprises was 3 workers (see table 8, pages 164–65). Other economic measures such as gross output, value added, value added per worker, and profit show a similar bifurcation.

BPS currently uses separate surveys for small and household industries. These surveys only partially overlap, and incomplete publication of the data that are collected complicates comparisons and the construction of time series. Nonetheless, the published data indicate that there is only one important qualitative difference between small and household industries, namely the proportion of unpaid family to hired labor. In code 381, for example, small enterprises filled 80 percent of their labor needs from hired labor and only 20 percent from unpaid family labor in 1974–75. For household enterprises these percentages were reversed (see table 11).

The ethnographic data presented in chapter 3 indicate that small and household metalworking industries coexist within the same villages and form a single socioeconomic and cultural complex. With the exception of some casting industries established by the Dutch in Central Java — for example at Batur hamlet — there do not seem to be any large or medium-sized metalworking enterprises in rural areas.

The second question is whether dualism is caused by cultural or rather economic factors. Boeke's theory was not controversial because it pointed to a gap between the western and native economic spheres. This gap had been recognized by colonial authorities in charge of native welfare as early as the 1890s. Rather, Boeke's theory was controversial because it pointed to cultural differences as the primary cause of this gap. Natives, he wrote, value social over economic needs, have limited rather than unlimited economic needs, are uninterested in capital accumulation, prefer cooperation to competition, lack organizational ability and work discipline, place no value on their own time, and are incapable of calculating profits rationally.[1]

The ethnographic data presented in this book lend very little support to these notions. Rather, a quite different picture emerges of village industry producers who are intensely interested in profits and spend a good deal of time and thought trying to maximize those profits. Profit calculations, generally quite rational and accurate, dominate daily conversation in the perapen and in the coffee shops. Every producer is keenly aware of fluctuations in the prices of factor inputs of scrap, fuel, and hired labor, and how they affect profit margins. Economic arrangements which allow profits to be shared among producers, hired workers, and intermediaries are another area of great concern. Producers within the same village may choose to cooperate, for example in sharing an order too large for one perapen to fill, but only when cooperation has clear economic benefits. The moribund condition of most government-sponsored cooperatives, described in chapter 5, indicates that cooperation is not automatic. Work discipline in the perapen is high, and there are production targets which workers are expected to meet. When there is a large order to fill, workers are asked to put in overtime hours. Work stoppages generally have economic causes — for example a shortage of raw material supplies or working capital—rather than cultural causes. Where the industrial sector interacts with agriculture or another sector, the allocation of scarce resources of capital and labor is done with great deliberation. Villagers do not "run off" to their rice fields during the planting and harvesting periods because they lack work discipline, as Boeke claimed, but because relatively small inputs of labor in the agricultural sector during those critical periods can have a big payoff.

Of course there is an important cultural dimension to rural industries, and particularly to metalworking industries, but this dimension generally coexists with the economic dimension and does not conflict with it. After all, the two dimensions evolved together over a period of at least two thousand years. Occasionally cultural associations may lead to conservatism in the adoption of new technologies or working methods. As described in chapter 5, smiths in Central Java refused to accept European tanged anvils on credit because they did not conform to the cultural expectation that an anvil must be shaped like a lingam. But such examples are relatively uncommon.

It would appear that the principal cause of dualism in the Indonesian economy is differential access to capital. Lack of information and suitable technologies may be secondary causes, but the ethnographic data indicate that many rural smiths have spent a stint working in a large urban machine shop or foundry. Should they return to their villages they would not attempt to replicate these machine shops or foundries; that is due more to lack of capital than lack of information. A large village entrepreneur such as Pak Sastro may have made a considerable investment in equipment by rural standards, perhaps amounting to $20,000.[2] Yet this pales in comparison to the hundreds of thousands of dollars needed to set up a large machine shop or foundry, or the millions of dollars needed to set up a modern, western facility. The rural banking programs described in chapter 5, while very useful in raising the incomes of smithing households, do not make a dent in the dualistic gap.

The nature of forging, and the maximum of three hammer swingers who can be used at a time, have limited the perapen work group to a maximum of seven or eight men. Expansion takes place by replicating units rather than expanding the size of existing units. Hence the metalworking sector tends to be fairly atomized. This is not inevitably so in rural industries. In some subsectors, notably textiles and basketry, quite large units are to be found. These units are generally organized according to the put-out system, so that workers make semifinished products in their own homes, and then turn them over to the enterprise owner for finishing. Using a put-out system obviates constructing a large and expensive factory building. Such a building would not only be expensive to build but would attract the unwanted attention of tax collectors and licensing and regulatory agencies. Put-out operations often employ several hundred workers and thus would qualify by BPS definitions as "large enterprises," except that they are seldom recognized as single units by census takers. The point is that there is nothing in rural Indonesian culture which limits the size of enterprises. Rural enterprises are smaller on the average because they are less well capitalized.

Are village industries dying out in Indonesia? Boeke predicted that contact between the two spheres of a dualistic economy would inevitably lead to destruction of native industries, which would be unable to compete with imported, factory-made products from the West. Large factories established in Indonesia and modeled after those in the West would also compete with native industries and, being capital-intensive, would employ relatively little of the displaced labor. Native industries would be unable to compensate by developing export markets because, according to Boeke, their products are low in quality. Thus deprived of any markets, they would die out.

This argument, made by Boeke as early as 1910, seems very persuasive. Yet history has a way of making fools of us all, and the reality is that native industries have not died out. The data presented in chapter 4 indicate that there were approximately 1.5 million small and household industries in 1986, employing approximately 3.5 million people. This is a conservative estimate of employment because the labor force definition used in 1986 excluded perhaps a million part-time family workers.

Between 1974–75 and 1986 the number of small and household enterprises increased from 1.3 to 1.5 million (see table 8). If corrections are made for the use of different labor force definitions, the number of workers appears to have increased from 4.2 million to about 4.5 million. Scholars who have ignored the change in definitions have written about a sharp decline in employment in household industries, particularly in the number of female family workers. But the true pattern would appear to be one of stable but relatively rapid employment growth for both household and small industries.[3]

Metalworking industries rely mainly on full-time male workers, and hence the statistics for these industries are less affected by changes in labor force definitions. In addition, these industries seem to have grown at rates more rapid than the industrial sector as a whole. For code 381 metalworking industries the number of enterprises and the number of workers approximately tripled between 1974–75 and 1987 (see table 11). The fastest rate of increase was for code 38111 black-smithing industries. The number of blacksmithing enterprises approximately quadrupled during these years, though the number of workers only tripled. This discrepancy is due to a decrease in the average size of blacksmithing enterprises, from 4.2 to 3.6 workers. The ethnographic evidence in chapter 4 indicates that this decrease was caused by rural electrification and the replacement of labor by small low-wattage machinery.

Given the persuasiveness of Boeke's argument, it seems important to ask why village industries have not died out. To answer this question, both the supply and demand sides of the issue must be considered. On the supply side, village industries have not died out because villagers need nonagricultural income. Natural population increase has exceeded rural-to-urban migration, resulting in a declining land-person ratio. In addition, there seems to have been an increased skewing of land ownership and control in the 1970s and 1980s, not only through outright sales of land but also through rental and pawning arrangements. In lowland Java the proportion of households which neither own nor control sawah has increased from about one-third earlier in the century to over one-half.

The ethnographic evidence indicates that villages with large concentrations of industries are generally not self-sufficient in the production of starchy staples. Some of these villages, for example Kajar and Massepe, are in dry-zone areas where water is not available for irrigation and the per-hectare productivity of the land is low. Other villages, for example Sungai Puar and Batur, are in more fertile areas, but the villages themselves have unusually high densities and little land available for agriculture within their boundaries. In either case these industrial villages must purchase most of their food, and they earn the money to do so by making durable goods for sale.

The survey forms for the Industrial Census of 1974–75 and the industrial section of the Economic Census of 1986 did not include questions on land holdings or agricultural income. Thus it is not possible to determine whether there is a statistical relationship between these variables and the incidence of industrial activity. The ethnographic evidence presented in this book strongly suggests that there is such a relationship, but it remains to be confirmed at the national level.

The question of why village industries have not died out must also be examined from the demand side. Here it is useful to distinguish between two broad groups of industries, which can be referred to for convenience as "utilitarian industries" and "handicraft industries." The first group produces utilitarian wares, principally for sale to other villagers and low-income urban dwellers. The second group produces objects considered to have artistic merit, principally for sale to middle- and upper-income urban dwellers and tourists. In the metalworking subsector utilitarian industries are grouped under code 38. They include those industries which make agricultural tools, workman's tools, kitchen utensils, and machinery. Handicraft industries are grouped under code 39, and include those which make jewelry, musical instruments, statues, and souvenir keris.

The demand for products made by utilitarian metalworking industries has increased for two reasons: natural population increase and improved levels of rural prosperity. Because of natural population increase more food must be produced, which has led to agricultural intensification and an expansion of the area under multicropping. In the absence of agricultural mechanization there are more farmers working the land, and these farmers must plant, weed, harvest, and repair irrigation canals more often than their ancestors did. Thus they must replace their agricultural tools more frequently. Similarly, natural population increase has led to a demand for more housing and other types of construction. Thus woodcutters, stonecutters, carpenters, masons, and other kinds of workmen must replace their tools more frequently. Improved levels of prosperity mean that both farmers and workmen have more money to spend on tools. They replace worn-out or broken tools more quickly, and are willing to pay a little more to get tools of higher quality.

The demand for products made by handicraft industries doing metalwork has also increased in recent years, but for very different reasons. These industries have always relied heavily on outside patrons. This is because they use expensive raw materials such as gold, silver, and bronze, and production methods which are very labor-intensive such

as pamor and repoussé. During the Late Historical period these industries were patronized by members of the various regional courts, and
by wealthy Indian, Arab, and Chinese merchants. During the colonial
period the role of patron was largely taken over by the Dutch. Colonial officers and their wives ordered swords, pistols, tea sets, dinner
sets, and jewelry in large quantities, often demanding that designs be
modified to suit European tastes. Indonesian aristocrats and Chinese
merchants provided some additional patronage, although the Chinese also imported their own goldsmiths. During the chaotic period
between the outbreak of the Second World War and the end of the
Sukarno era, handicraft industries suffered from a loss of patronage.
Sukarno forcibly evicted the Dutch in 1956, and foreigners did not
begin to reenter Indonesia in large numbers until political and economic stability had been reestablished in the early 1970s.

Today new groups of patrons have emerged to fund a revival of Indonesian handicrafts. These patrons include wealthy Indonesian government officials, military officers, and their wives; resident foreigners
associated with joint-venture firms, diplomatic missions, and aid
agencies; foreign tourists; and foreign handicraft buyers who mainly
reside in Yogyakarta and Bali. Among the foreign groups Americans,
Europeans, Japanese, and Australians now predominate. Once again
Indonesian craftsmen are being asked to modify their designs to suit
the tastes of foreign patrons. In recent years, for example, Balinese
blacksmiths have become adept at making copies of samurai swords,
because they often get commissions for such pieces from Japanese
customers.

The natural population increase and improved levels of prosperity
in rural areas that stimulated demand for utilitarian products had
little influence on the demand for handicraft products. Handicraft
demand began to increase during the same period, coincidentally,
because Indonesia officially reopened its doors to foreigners in 1967,
began to encourage foreign participation in joint-venture enterprises,
and began to actively promote tourism.

Are "push" or "pull" factors responsible for the growth of village
industries? Many of the supply and demand issues discussed above
also pertain to the push-pull debate that has occupied Indonesianists
in recent years. Briefly stated, proponents of the "push" hypothesis
argue that incomes per hour of labor are higher in the agricultural sector than in such nonagricultural sectors of the rural economy as trade

and industries. It follows that villagers will only leave the agricultural sector if they are pushed out, for example by loss of their land, or by the loss of traditional opportunities to earn agricultural income from such arrangements as sharecropping, share harvesting, and pounding rice for shares. Proponents of the "pull" hypothesis, on the other hand, argue that villagers are being pulled into nonagricultural activities by new economic opportunities. These economic opportunities are the result of increased levels of prosperity in rural areas, and of investment linkages between the agricultural and nonagricultural sectors.

It is interesting that the Green Revolution is cited as a primary cause by proponents of both the push and pull hypotheses. Both groups would agree that the Green Revolution has led to an approximately threefold increase in rice yields and considerable rice surpluses. Proponents of the push hypothesis point out that a disproportionate share of these surpluses was garnered by large landowning families. These landowning families used their rice income to acquire control over additional land through purchase, rental, and pawning arrangements. They have also tended in recent years to "rationalize" their enterprises and increase their profit margins by substituting relatively small amounts of hired labor for larger amounts of traditional share labor. In many cases they have invested in labor-saving technologies such as rice mills. All these activities have resulted in reduced opportunities to earn rice income for poorer groups in the village.

Proponents of the "pull" hypothesis credit the Green Revolution with increased levels of prosperity in rural areas. Farmer incomes have gone up because of increased yields, combined with rice price controls and subsidies on inputs. Since nonagricultural enterprises market most of their products in rural areas, farmers' prosperity has indirectly benefited these enterprises as well. Furthermore, many farmers have used their rice surpluses to invest in new nonagricultural enterprises.

The ethnographic data in this book demonstrate a fallacy in the "push" argument, namely its assumption that incomes per hour of labor are always highest in agriculture. This cannot be assumed but must be determined empirically for any given village. In Kajar and the other metalworking villages, labor productivity in agriculture is low for one of two reasons. Either the quality of the agricultural resource base is poor (rocky soils, lack of water for irrigation, etc.) or there is a shortage of agricultural land within the boundaries of the village because of overcrowding. Overcrowding leads to high rates of landlessness, or a highly fragmented pattern of holdings. Fragmented holdings tend to yield low incomes per hour of labor because of the law of declining marginal returns to labor under conditions of agricultural intensification (Boserup 1965). In villages where labor productivity is low in agriculture for any reason, labor productivity in nonagricultural activities is likely to be higher.

The pattern of economic activity in any given village is the result of economic choices made by individuals and households. Although every activity has capital and skill entry requirements, and these are higher for some activities than others, Indonesian villagers are fairly free to shift their scarce resources of capital and labor between sectors to maximize their incomes. Not surprisingly, therefore, wet-rice agriculture is the most profitable activity in wet-rice villages, and small industry is the most profitable activity in small industry villages. This seems an obvious point, but one which has frequently been overlooked by scholars who have based their conclusions entirely on ethnographic studies of wet-rice villages.

The best measure of the relative profitability of the agricultural and nonagricultural sectors may be the wage rates paid to hired labor. If a village is experiencing a shift of labor out of agriculture, a comparison of wage rates will indicate whether push or pull factors are at work. If agricultural wage rates are higher, the shift can be attributed to push factors. Conversely, if nonagricultural wage rates are higher, the shift can be attributed to pull factors. In Kajar wages paid to adult male workers in the perapen are higher than wages paid to adult male agricultural laborers (see table 3). The same holds true for the other villages for which wage data were available.

These wage data are buttressed by interviews with individual perapen owners. They generally agree that income from smithing exceeds income from agriculture, and that perapen owners are wealthier on average than farmers. Smithing is considered the "main activity" (pokok), while agriculture is considered the "side activity" (samben/sambilan).

Labor allocation patterns are also indicative of relative priorities. Smiths in Kajar perform no agricultural labor, for example. Instead they have turned the agricultural sector over to the women of the village, who supplement their own labor with hired labor from neighboring villages. A very similar pattern is seen in the matrilineal village of Sungai Puar, where women not only manage the rice fields but also own them. Women supplement their own labor with the labor of sharecroppers and hired workers, leaving the men free to devote most of their time to smithing. Men may plant a vegetable crop on their wife's land after the rice harvest is over, but the proceeds from the sale of this crop are used to buy scrap iron and fuel. Similarly, smithing families in Massepe village who own agricultural land usually sharecrop it out.

Case studies of individual metalworking villages indicate that push factors may have been more important in the 1960s and early 1970s, but that pull factors later became more important. In addition to push and pull factors, historical factors have played a role. In Kajar, for example, expansion occurred in three stages. The first stage was a forced expansion under the occupying Japanese army (1942–45), which needed forged weapons for its troops. The second expansion occurred in the early 1960s and was associated with a severe famine (jaman gaber) that lasted for two or three years, during which time the villagers needed cash to purchase food from the lowlands. The third expansion began around 1972 and is attributed by the villagers to an improved market. Another famine, somewhat less severe, in 1975–76 also gave a "push" to this expansion. Other villages show a similar pattern of expansion in response to agricultural crisis before the Green Revolution, and expansion in response to expanding market demand in recent years.

The data in chapter 4 provide an additional clue to the solution of the push-pull debate, in the form of statistics on value added per enterprise in the industrial sector. If the number of enterprises was increasing, but value added per enterprise was on the decline, this would provide support to the push hypothesis. It would mean that villagers were being forced into economic activities that were less and less desirable. Conversely, if the number of enterprises was increasing and value added per enterprise was also increasing, it would provide support to the pull hypothesis. Chapter 4 shows that real value added for code 381 utilitarian metalworking industries increased by 4.8 times between 1974–75 and 1987. During the same period real value added for code 38111 blacksmithing industries increased by 3.8 times.

The published data for handicraft industries in code 39 are not complete, but the increase for small jewelry-making enterprises was 1.6 times and for instrument-making enterprises 1.9 times.

In an observation that is relevant to this push-pull debate, Mukhopadhyay has claimed that the rural industrial sector has a sharp bimodal structure. Industries in the first group, which he terms the upper sector, use more sophisticated technology and rely primarily on hired labor. They operate more or less continuously and are concerned with generating surpluses and with growth. Industries in the lower sector, on the other hand, use primitive technologies and rely primarily on unpaid family labor. Their activities are often seasonal and they cater mainly to a local market. According to Mukhopadhyay the upper sector responds to market demand for output, whereas the lower sector responds to the supply side of the labor market. An expansion in the upper sector can be seen as a sign of progress, rural development, and equalization of incomes, but an expansion in the lower sector is usually associated with increased landlessness, unemployment, and poverty. In countries where the incidence of landlessness is high—for example Bangladesh, India, Pakistan, and the Philippines—employment in the lower sector is also high. On the other hand, the lower sector employs relatively few workers in countries such as Korea where landlessness is less pressing. The two sectors are differently linked to agricultural production. Years of good harvests imply steady growth for the upper sector and stagnation for the lower, whereas years of bad harvest cause stagnation in the upper sector and overcrowding in the lower one (Mukhopadhyay 1985, 966, paraphrased from Weijland 1989a, 7–8).

While I would tinker with Mukhopadhyay's framework a bit, his basic point seems valid, namely that expansion in the rural industrial sector is healthier when it is results from an increase in market demand than when it results from labor oversupply. Expansion which results from an increase in market demand produces enterprises which are well capitalized, can produce continuously, can purchase new technologies, and can pay wages to hired laborers. Expansion which results from labor oversupply, on the other hand, is associated with undercapitalized enterprises which operate intermittently, cannot afford new technologies, and cannot pay wages.

What is the composition of the rural industrial labor force? Numerous authors from Boeke on have characterized the rural industrial labor force as consisting predominantly of unskilled female family workers. The productivity of these workers is low, it is said, because of the simple technologies they use and their ability to work part-time or seasonally. The accuracy of some of these statements is in doubt — the Population Census of 1980 showed that there were slightly more men than women in rural industries, for example (see table 6). A more important point is that this characterization of the labor force is too general, and obscures important differences in the types of workers and industries found in rural areas.

This book deals with a subset of rural industries which have traditionally used a very different type of labor force. Over 90 percent of the labor used in metalworking industries is male, and the cultural material indicates that there has always been a strong association between metalworking and male symbols and ancestors. There is a taboo on women entering the perapen, although this taboo may be set aside when there is a shortage of labor. Women are occasionally used as bellows workers in blacksmithing enterprises, and more commonly as polishers in copper-, bronze-, and silverworking enterprises. The only metalworking industry which uses a significant amount of female labor is jewelry making. In small jewelry-making enterprises about 15 percent of the workers are female (see table 12).

Both capital and skill entry requirements are relatively high in metalworking industries. In the blacksmithing industry a boy generally undergoes an apprenticeship of several years as a bellows worker before he graduates to the more highly paid and physically demanding work of a hammer swinger. A hammer swinger must have at least ten more years of experience before he is entrusted with the position of empu or master smith. Some of the decorative metalworking techniques described in chapter 3 require not only experience and skill but artistic ability as well. These would include techniques to produce weapons with fine pamor work, cast bronze statues using the lost-wax method, and silver and gold ceremonial vessels with repoussé or chasing.

In Kajar and the other villages described in this book metalworking is the full-time occupation of most men. Work generally begins around 8:00 a.m. and continues until the production target for that day is completed, usually about 4:00 or 5:00 p.m. The larger and better-capitalized enterprises which rely mainly on hired labor tend to work continuously year-round. The smaller and less well-capitalized enterprises may suffer frequent work stoppages because of cash flow problems. At the national level the data in chapter 4 indicate that hired workers in metalworking enterprises average more than twice as many person-days of work per year as unpaid family workers (see table 11).

Metalworking enterprises constitute just a small proportion of the small and household enterprises nationwide. Code 38 industries account for about 3 percent of the total, and the handicraft industries in code 39 for perhaps another 1 percent (see table 8). Metalworking enterprises are however typical of a larger group of industries which rely on a predominantly male labor force and are relatively well capitalized. These include woodcarving, stone carving, sawmilling, furniture making, house building, boat building, lime burning, and some of the leather goods industries. At the opposite end of the spectrum is a group of industries which fit the stereotype in that they rely mainly on part-time female labor. Some of this labor is unpaid family labor, but much of it is poorly remunerated piece-rate labor organized in workshops or put-out operations. These include the various textile, garment, and soft-fiber matting industries which have traditionally been associated with women. Some tobacco and food-processing industries fall in this group as well. At the end of chapter 2 I suggested that there is yet a third group of industries which use a mixed male and female labor force and tend to be intermediate in terms of capitalization and profitability. These are the clay product industries, the hard-fiber basketry industries, and those food-processing industries which require somewhat more capitalization. The reasons why different industries use a different type of labor force are not entirely clear. Cultural associations rooted in myth and tradition have already been mentioned. Differences between men and women in physical strength, access to capital, and responsibility for household chores seem to be important as well (Sutoro 1982).

Does the survival of village industries depend on protectionist policies? As described in chapter 2, there are three basic metalworking subsectors—mining, smelting, and smithing. In Indonesia all three of these subsectors were in the hands of the small-scale indigenous economy for at least two millennia, from the beginning of the Early Metal Age until about 1800. Toward the end of this long period native mining and smelting had to compete with unrestricted imports of European bar metal and foreign coinage. In addition, the colonial authorities attempted to ban native mining and smelting, and bring these activities under the control of state-owned companies which introduced technologies which were more capital-intensive. This policy was continued by the postcolonial Indonesian government and remains in place today. As a result of unrestricted imports and a government takeover, native mining and smelting died out. With the exception of a little individual panning for gold and tin, the last ethnographic reports of native mining and smelting operations date from the mid-1800s.

Although native mining and smelting died out, native smithing managed to hold on. The reasons for this are not entirely clear. The Europeans exported not only bar metal to Indonesia but also agricultural and workman's tools. The influence of these European tools can still be seen in the names and forms of some tools made by Indonesian smiths today, for example the different types of drills (*bor*). In general, however, native smithing probably held on because of the preference of local customers for local forms. The agricultural conditions of Indonesia are vastly different from those of Europe, and farmers would naturally have preferred to continue using the types of tools with which they were familiar. The same probably held true for carpenters and other workmen. Tool types are not uniform even within Indonesia, and there is considerable regional variation. Farmers on the Outer Islands, for example, prefer heavier hoes and spades than are used on Java because their soils are denser. A highly dispersed rural-based industry is in a much better position to respond to this pattern of variable demand than a factory abroad. In addition, the villager who buys a locally made tool knows that it can be easily returned to a local smith for repairs, whereas a local smith might not be willing or able to repair an imported tool.

The Dutch also made some attempt to set up metalworking factories in Indonesia. These were limited to casting foundries such as those in Batur hamlet. The foundries produced replacement parts for machinery such as sugar mills and locomotives, but not agricultural or workman's tools. Tools made of cast metal are brittle and not as durable as forged tools. Both in Europe and in Indonesia forging was done by small work groups in the nineteenth century. Thus it was not as amenable to factory organization.

Given the historical fact that native mining and smelting died out, is it possible to be entirely sanguine about the fate of native smithing? I do not think so. Despite a remarkable increase in the number of smithing enterprises in recent years, these enterprises are still potentially vulnerable to competition from imports and factory-made products. This is particularly true of blacksmithing and the other code 38 industries which make utilitarian products. There now exist capital-intensive technologies which permit the mass production of machine-forged tools under factory conditions. These technologies are well-known in the West and in Japan. It is interesting to note that the handicraft industries in code 39 are actually less vulnerable to government deregulation. This is because Indonesia has no need of importing handicrafts, and because handicrafts by their very nature are not in competition with factory-made items.

The available data allow us to estimate the displacement of code 381 industries by imports, given current levels of protection. In chapter 4 it was estimated that imports had displaced about 2,759 enterprises, or the equivalent of 69 villages with 40 perapen each. This is a significant number, but amounts to only 6 percent of the code 381 enterprises nationwide. Thus it is probably accurate to say that the impact of imports at current levels of protection is significant but not devastating.

The available data unfortunately do not allow us to estimate the displacement that would occur if import protection were withdrawn. To make such an estimate one would need to know the relative importance to customer demand of price versus other factors such as the form of tools and the ease of repairs. If import protection were withdrawn, imported tools could be sold at prices more competitive with local tools. Assuming that price is an important determinant of demand, the result would probably be an increased volume of tool imports and increased displacement of rural industries. The extent of this hypothetical displacement is difficult to determine.

The withdrawal of licensing protection is probably a bigger threat than the withdrawal of import protection. It would be relatively easy for factories based in Indonesia to adapt the form of their tools to local demand. The existence of state-owned and privately owned factories may already be having an inhibiting effect on the expansion of small and household enterprises into new and more complex product types.

One very hopeful sign in recent years is the willingness of village smiths to adopt new machine technologies. These technologies might open the way for a more dispersed pattern of development that would allow production to remain in rural areas, where it contributes directly to rural prosperity.

Are Indonesian villages homogeneous? Both Boeke and Geertz subscribed to the notion that Indonesian villages are homogeneous collections of poor households which share their poverty. Careful studies of Javanese wet-rice villages carried out by White, Stoler, and others in the 1970s refuted this notion, and pointed instead to a considerable degree of internal stratification. Generally at least three strata can be discerned in wet-rice villages:

1. Wealthy largeholder families who have access to the product of a considerable amount of land through ownership, through usufruct rights (in the case of village officials), and through rental and pawning arrangements. These families generally do not farm their own land but either give it out to smallholder families under sharecropping agreements or farm the land with the use of hired labor. Sometimes these families also grant *bawon* harvest shares to women from smallholder families who assist with the harvest, although this has become less common in recent years.

2. Smallholder families who own smaller plots of land which they farm themselves, sometimes with the help of a small amount of hired labor or the help of neighboring households obtained through gotong royong labor-sharing arrangements. Sometimes these families also obtain rights to farm other plots of land through sharecropping arrangements with largeholder families, or rights to earn bawon income through share-harvesting arrangements.

3. Landless and near landless families who work as wage agricultural laborers. Generally these families are excluded from the more lucrative sharecropping and share-harvest arrangements.

The ethnographic data in this book indicate that stratification in the agricultural sector is paralleled by stratification in the rural industrial sector. Metalworking villages tend to be divided into two, three, four, or even more strata. Metalworking villages with many perapen tend to be more complexly stratified than those with small numbers of perapen.

An unstratified or "homogeneous" system in a metalworking village would mean that none of the perapen use hired labor. Today this is relatively uncommon. In most metalworking villages the smaller and less well-capitalized perapen may rely entirely on unpaid family labor, but the larger and better-capitalized perapen generally supplement family labor with hired labor.

In a large and well-stratified metalworking village there will be at least four strata, consisting of raw material and tool traders (and their family members, who assist with enterprise management); independent perapen owners (and their family members, including any unpaid family workers); dependent perapen owners (and their family members, including any unpaid family workers); and hired workers (and their family members). In villages with two-stage production systems, such as the copperworking village of Jolotundo, there may be more than four strata.

The macrodata provide a little additional information on the subject of stratification, in the form of the ratio of profits earned by perapen owners to wages earned by hired workers (see analyses of tables 11 and 12). The highest ratios are found in "small" enterprises with five or more workers. For these enterprises the ratios in 1986 were 11.7 to 1 for cutlery and hand tools (code 381), 14.1 to 1 for blacksmithing (code 38111), 8.5 to 1 for jewelry making, and 5.8 to 1 for musical instrument making. Thus it appears that blacksmithing is the most skewed of all the metalworking industries. But it should be remembered that "small" enterprises are greatly outnumbered by household enterprises, and that the ratios are much lower for household enterprises.[4]

Having stated that Indonesian villages are stratified rather than homogeneous, one must acknowledge that homogeneity is a relative concept. In 1986–87 I worked on a credit project for artisan castes in the Pakistani Punjab. Villages in the Punjab are divided into three distinct classes. At the top is a hereditary class of feudal landowners referred to by the English term "landlords." Each village is dominated by one or a few landlord families who live in elegant hilltop villas equipped with all the modern conveniences. They drive luxurious automobiles, vacation in mountain resorts, send their children to the best universities, and not infrequently travel abroad. On average these families own about 250 hectares of land each, usually a combination of irrigated rice fields and unirrigated wheat fields. Their farming methods are capital-intensive and include the use of large tractors and other mechanical equipment.

Below the landlord class in Pakistan is a middle class of smallholders who farm tiny plots but are proud of their status as members of several farmer castes. They live apart from the landlords in their own walled-in mud compounds. Their farming methods are more labor-intensive.

Below the smallholders is a third class, made up of the various artisan castes, including blacksmiths, potters, weavers, and leather workers. The artisans are all landless and their status is that of untouchables or near-untouchables.[5] Members of the upper two classes will not, for example, share a meal with the artisans or sit on the same bench with them. The artisans have their own residential areas which generally are not walled in. Traditionally the artisans were not allowed to sell their products on the open market. Their status was that of indentured servants of the landlord. The landlord provided them with raw materials and decided the number and kind of products they would make each season. In exchange, the artisans were given a small share of the grain harvested from the landlord's fields. Artisans could also be sent to work in the fields if the landlord needed additional agricultural labor.

This traditional system still prevails in more isolated areas of the Punjab but has begun to change in areas along the main roads and near towns. Many artisans have severed their ties with the landlords and are instead buying their raw materials and selling their finished products in the open marketplace. The *lohari*, or members of the black-smithing caste, who were among the first to sever their ties with the landlords, have done very well financially by purchasing small metal-bending machines, drills, and other tools to manufacture tractor tines and other replacement parts for agricultural equipment. Their rise in economic status has not been accompanied by a rise in social status, so a rigid three-class system remains in place.[6]

In comparison with villages in the Pakistani Punjab, villages in Indonesia are certainly more homogeneous. Village officials and other large landholders in Indonesian villages generally do not control more than twenty hectares of land each. Some social scientists have referred to the various economic strata in Indonesian villages as "classes," and to the process of economic differentiation as "intra-village class formation." I have avoided the term "class," because it implies a degree of social separation that does not yet exist in Indonesian villages. Obvious class markers such as differences in speech patterns and dress styles are absent or relatively subdued. Wealthy villagers such as Pak Sastro take care to dress simply, behave mod-

estly, and interact with everyone in the village in a friendly and courteous manner. Ostentatious displays of wealth are avoided. To take
one example, a wealthy villager might purchase a utilitarian vehicle
such as a truck or minivan, but would be embarrassed to own something so citified as a luxury sedan.[7] Within the village there are no
taboos or barriers to interaction between groups. Speech patterns are
uniform, and everyone participates in a common cycle of rituals and
ceremonies. Moreover, there is still a considerable degree of upward
mobility, in that a hired worker may reasonably aspire to become an
enterprise owner one day.

The Javanese have historically distinguished between *wong cilik*,
or poor commoners, and *wong gedong*, or wealthy residents of court
towns. Today the term *wong cilik* refers both to villagers and to rural-
urban migrants living in urban *kampungs*. Wong gedong or wong
gedongan, on the other hand, refers to the privileged urban class
which today consists mainly of high-ranking government officials, big
businessmen, and professionals, plus their families. Sometimes resident foreigners are also included among wong gedong. It would seem
that the class break in Indonesia still falls between these two broad
groups, and not yet between the strata of an economically stratified
village such as Kajar. Some social scientists have also tried to identify
an emerging middle class in urban areas.

Do Indonesian villagers share their poverty? Both Boeke and Geertz
linked the concepts of "homogeneity" and "shared poverty." To them
"shared poverty" really has two meanings. First, it means that social
needs are given priority over economic needs. In a village where everyone is poor, disaster is avoided by giving assistance to one's neighbors
and receiving assistance in turn. Second, shared poverty means that
there are leveling mechanisms within the village — customs and practices which enable poor villagers to exert pressure on wealthier villagers to redistribute some of their wealth. The examples of shared
poverty which Boeke and Geertz cite for Java come mainly from the
agricultural sector and include sharecropping (bagi hasil), share harvesting (bawon), and labor sharing arrangements (gotong royong).

As used by Boeke and Geertz, shared poverty is a derisive term.
By preventing wealth accumulation, shared poverty interferes with
the growth of an entrepreneurial class and hence with development
along capitalist lines. Geertz, who associated shared poverty with
"agricultural involution," has been criticized by more recent authors

for reviving Boeke's concept of shared poverty. Historical studies of the colonial era have revealed that there was a considerable degree of intravillage stratification which was based partly on differential rights to land and partly on proximity to the colonial authorities. Then as now, an élite group of villagers exercised a gatekeeping function and controlled access to resources and opportunities coming into the village, as well as delivery of corvée and tax payments from villagers to the colonial authorities. Members of this élite group often used their position to enrich themselves at the expense of other villagers. Stratification was particularly in evidence in the early decades of the twentieth century, before the Depression of the 1930s.[8]

White has also pointed out that conflict between landowning and landless groups over land reform was in large part responsible for the abortive coup of 1965 and the subsequent slaughter of communist supporters in rural areas. As Benjamin White notes (1983, 19), these chaotic events occurred just two years after the publication of *Agricultural Involution*. Stoler and Hart have questioned whether share arrangements in agriculture are actually evidence of shared poverty. They argue that agricultural labor markets in rural areas are not competitive. Stoler argues that an alliance between largeholder and smallholder groups has acted to exclude the landless poor from more lucrative opportunities to earn income from sharecropping and share harvesting (Stoler 1977a; Stoler 1977b; Hart 1986).

Whether shared poverty existed before 1965 is almost a moot question at this point. Almost every scholar would admit that share arrangements have been on the decline in recent years, as large landholders have begun to rationalize their enterprises. Furthermore, social prohibitions on conspicuous consumption may be starting to break down as villagers are exposed to new types of consumer goods through television and visits to city stores and marketplaces.

Evidence was presented in chapter 2 that share systems were once common in rural metalworking industries. These systems involved dividing among the members of the perapen work group the proceeds from the sale of tools or other products made, according to a fixed ratio. Perapen owners who worked as their own empu received the largest share, and the bellows worker received the smallest share. Many elderly smiths on Java remember these share systems, and share systems are still found in a few smithing villages on the outer islands. But they have largely been replaced by systems which use wage labor, paid either daily or by piece rates. Since the share of the proceeds which goes to the perapen owner is larger under a wage system, this replacement can be seen as a type of "rationalization." It is analogous to the replacement of share harvest labor with hired harvest labor.

Similarly, the 1980s saw the beginnings of rationalization through mechanization. Perapen owners can increase their share of the proceeds by replacing their bellows worker with a blower, and replacing one of their filers with an electric gerinda. This replacement is analogous to the replacement by mechanical rice mills of female workers who formerly hand-pounded rice for shares.

Work orders which come into a smithing village are often shared between perapen, and this practice could be taken as an instance of shared poverty. Yet closer analysis reveals that there are two very different situations under which a work order is shared. In the first, the work order is received by an ordinary perapen owner. If it is too large for him to fill in the time designated by the customer, he will share it with other perapen owners, giving first priority to his close relatives, friends, and neighbors. Sometimes he takes a small commission as his fee for coordinating the order, and sometimes he does not. In either case there is the clear expectation that the relatives, friends, and neighbors who shared in his order will repay the favor at some time in the future by sharing orders with him. Thus the system is mutually beneficial and analogous to the gotong royong labor-sharing arrangements used in agriculture. In the second type of situation the work order is received by an empu pedagang, sometimes in his capacity as head of a government cooperative. In this case the order is divided among all the perapen owners who are dependent on him for raw materials and marketing. Independent perapen owners are usually excluded from participating in the order as the price of their independence. The empu pedagang takes his usual profit margin, and the result is a marginal increase rather than a decrease in the degree of stratification.

Chapter 3, on Kajar village, includes some discussion of the relationship between Pak Sastro and the other villagers. To a certain extent the villagers of Kajar are able to put pressure on Pak Sastro to redistribute some of his wealth. This is most evident at the time of village festivals, when he is expected to finance a large share of the food and entertainment, and make his house, yard, and vehicles available to the organizers. Even during other periods he is expected to make small out-of-pocket loans to widows and the destitute, to make his vehicles available if someone needs to be taken to the hospital, to provide wage jobs for younger people who can claim some familial relationship, to lend dishes and glassware to villagers whose children are getting married, and to share the use of his television set with the rest of the village. In private conversation Pak Sastro complains about these pressures, but it is difficult to estimate how far they actually cut into his profits. It is doubtful that they result in a net transfer of more than 5 or 10 percent.

What are the causes of rural stratification? The Green Revolution has been blamed for increasing rural stratification. Large landholders, it is argued, were in a position to garner a disproportionate share of the rice surpluses generated by the new technologies. White has suggested that failure to implement land reform before the Green Revolution is also at fault. If the Green Revolution technologies had been introduced on a reformed agrarian base, the rural population would have shared more equitably in the benefits (White 1989).

Linking the issue of stratification too closely with land reform ignores the presence of other important capital assets in rural areas. In her study of a Central Javanese village (1978), Hart found that the economic position of a household could not be accounted for by its ownership of rice fields alone. The ownership of fish ponds was also important. In consequence, she developed the concept of "asset classes" as a better measure of a household's economic position (Hart 1978; Hart 1986). When applied to industrial villages, this concept would require that such non-land items as workshops, storerooms, vehicles, diesel generators, and machinery also be considered. In and of itself, land reform would not necessarily produce equity in an industrial village.

Another view is that stratification is the inevitable result of increased capitalization in rural areas. In a classic study Van der Kolff (1936) revisited some villages in East Java that he had studied in 1922. These villages had undergone decapitalization during the Depression owing to the collapse of the international commodities market and the loss of opportunities to earn plantation wages. Van der Kolff found that decapitalization had been accompanied by a return to barter in the marketplace and to "precapitalist" labor sharing arrangements that did not require the use of money capital.[9]

In the ethnographic portion of this book I put forth a view that resembles Van der Kolff's by suggesting that capital is the engine of stratification in the rural industrial sector. In metalworking villages which use no wage labor, the result is an unstratified system. If capital is used as wages, the result is a two-stratum system divided between households which pay wages and those which receive them. If capital is used as both wages and credit, as is usual in the larger industrial villages, two more strata are added—those who give credit and those who receive it. The usual result is a four-stratum system.

Any hypothesis that purports to explain the cause of stratification must take into account that stratification in nonagricultural sectors of the rural economy parallels stratification in the agricultural sector. One explanation that has been suggested is the existence of investment linkages between sectors. In other words, landholders may invest part of their income from the sale of agricultural surpluses in nonagricultural enterprises. Alternatively, investment capital may be raised through the sale, rental, or pawning of a piece of land, or by using the land to guarantee a bank loan.

The ethnographic data in this book provide some weakly positive support for this explanation. In general, raw material and tool traders are largeholders, perapen owners smallholders, and hired workers landless. But there are so many exceptions to this rule, particularly in the form of perapen owners who are landless, that it may be well to look for other explanations. One such explanation is parallel uses of capital.

In the village industry sector capital is used as wages and as credit. In the agricultural sector capital is used as wages, as credit, and also as rent. Rent is not common in the village industry sector but occasionally occurs. Seamstresses in put-out garment enterprises, for example, are sometimes forced to rent their sewing machines from the owner of the enterprise, and the rent is deducted from their piece rates. In metalworking enterprises an unused perapen or piece of equipment will occasionally be rented out.

Share systems have almost died out in the village industry sector, having been replaced by wage systems. Change has proceeded more slowly in the agricultural sector, but share systems are also becoming less common and are being replaced by wage systems. Credit in the village industry sector usually takes the form of raw materials given out to dependent producers. Credit in the agricultural sector takes the form of cash given out for land received in pawn. As has been mentioned, capital may also be used in the agricultural sector to rent land. These parallel uses of capital, it is suggested, have produced similar patterns of stratification, even where direct investment linkages between the agricultural and village industry sectors are absent.

Is it possible to have growth with equity? Recent development debates have centered on whether it is possible or even desirable to combine economic growth with equity. Although the Indonesian government is politically committed to equity, many economists and consultants privately admit their misgivings. As we have seen, equity in rural Indonesia has historically been associated with periods of decapitalization and impoverishment. Furthermore, equity in the industrial sector would seem to imply atomization, the proliferation of micro-enterprises, the return to more labor-intensive methods of production, and the return to a labor force consisting entirely of unpaid family workers. The growth of larger, more stable, and better-capitalized rural enterprises would seem to imply some degree of stratification and the emergence of a class of rural entrepreneurs.

In one development report I suggested that rural development efforts should focus on raising the subsistence floor rather than achieving absolute equity (Sutoro 1990). Raising the subsistence floor means raising the real incomes and improving the standard of living for the poorest groups in the village. In industrial villages, the focus should be on hired workers and the poorer enterprise owners.

The ethnographic data in this book indicate that hired workers in large and well-capitalized perapen earn more income per year than hired workers in the smaller and less well-capitalized perapen. This is because large and well-capitalized perapen can afford to use the better grades of scrap metal and to make the larger types of tools which generate higher profits. They can therefore afford to pay higher wage rates. In addition, large and well-capitalized perapen suffer relatively few work stoppages and are able to operate continuously throughout the year. If they do suffer a work stoppage it is likely to be short, and the perapen may be able to continue paying daily wages during the period of the stoppage to avoid losing their workers to other perapen. Small and less well capitalized perapen, on the other hand, earn lower profits, pay somewhat lower wage rates, and suffer more frequent and longer work stoppages because of cash flow problems. During these work stoppages they may be forced to let their workers go.

The ethnographic data also indicate that dependent perapen owners sometimes earn more than independent perapen owners. If the independent perapen owner's capital position is weak, he will be forced to use low-grade scrap and make less profitable products. He may lose income to frequent work stoppages. He may be unable to expand because he cannot afford to pay wages. He may be unable to purchase new technologies for the same reason. If, on the other hand, the weak perapen owner forms a dependency relationship with an empu pedagang, he will receive a continuous supply of higher-grade scrap on credit. His work stoppage problems will be over. His own capital will be freed up for use as wages or the purchase of new technologies. Of course he will lose some income on each tool made to the empu pedagang, but this may be more than compensated for by a higher volume of production and the higher market value of the tools made.

Finally, it should be noted that average earnings for smiths are considerably higher in large and well-stratified villages such as Kajar and Massepe than in small and less-stratified villages. The reasons for this are complex but have to do with economies of scale, which reduce the unit price of inputs and transport, better servicing by intermediaries, which leaves smiths free to spend more time on production, and competition between the perapen for skilled workers, which keeps wage levels high.

Does this mean that the government should deliberately foster stratification in village industries? I do not think so. As discussed in chapter 5, many government programs inadvertently foster stratification by channeling resources through village officials or through a village cooperative controlled by an empu pedagang. Programs which link credit to guarantee requirements can also have this effect. The better programs channel resources directly to poor enterprise owners to improve their capital position. Wage laborers in poor enterprises will also benefit indirectly from such programs, for all the reasons already given above. Programs which target wage laborers directly, for example by providing them with credit to set up their own enterprises, are usually a mistake, because they result in atomization of the industry.[10]

Is entrepreneurship a limiting factor in the growth of rural industries? There was considerable concern in the 1960s that peasant societies would not be able to provide the entrepreneurship needed for economic development. Most consultants and planners of the time were adherents of the modernization school, which viewed peasant culture as a barrier to economic development. One of the presumptions of the modernization school was that peasants do not make good entrepreneurs because they engage in poverty sharing, value social over economic needs, and do not respond to economic incentives. It follows that credit and other inputs channeled to rural areas will be wasted unless some effort is made to change these attitudes and values. This can best be accomplished, it was argued, through extension and training programs.

The ethnographic data in this book indicate that entrepreneurship is in plentiful supply in rural Indonesia. Since the number of enterprise owners who have received industrial extension or attended training courses is actually very small, it would appear that entrepreneurial attitudes are a part of the traditional culture. Such attitudes emerge whenever villagers are given access to capital in adequate amounts. In the larger metalworking villages such as Kajar, there are two groups that could be described as entrepreneurs: the raw material and tool traders, and the independent perapen owners. Dependent perapen owners cannot be considered entrepreneurs because they do not perform the entire range of management functions.

Raw material and tool traders are always the wealthiest people in a large metalworking village. In some villages, for example Kajar, there is only one such person and he is able to establish a near-monopoly over the supply of inputs on credit. In other villages, for example Massepe, there are several, and they compete for credit relationships with dependent perapen owners. Raw material and tool traders may own some equipment and carry out finishing operations on their own premises. But their basic economic strength comes from the use of capital as credit.

Independent perapen owners, on the other hand, derive their economic strength from the use of capital as wages. They are numerous in most large metalworking villages. Unlike raw material and tool traders, independent perapen owners are directly involved in all phases of production. They can be considered entrepreneurs because they perform the entire range of management functions, but it is clear that the use of capital as wages does not generate profits of the same magnitude as the use of capital as credit.

This distinction between two types of entrepreneurs — credit-based and wage-based — appears to hold true for all village industries in Indonesia. In designing development projects, some thought should therefore be given to the type of entrepreneurship the project will foster. Many projects intentionally or inadvertently promote credit-based entrepreneurs. But I favor projects directed at wage-based entrepreneurs, because they use their capital productively, and because projects of this sort represent a reasonable compromise between the goals of growth and equity.

What does the future hold for rural industries? It is impossible to predict with accuracy what the future holds for village industries in Indonesia. It is only possible to mention certain variables that bear watching. The most important of these are deregulation and mechanization. The Indonesian government is under considerable pressure from the international aid community to deregulate the industrial sector. Deregulation of large and medium industries is already well under way, but the government has thus far shown resistance to deregulating small and household industries. Many officials are concerned that deregulation might result in the loss of jobs and income in rural areas, at a time when equity is a sensitive political issue. They are also concerned that deregulation would strengthen the hand of the Chinese minority group at a time when there is political pressure to assist pribumi enterprises. Most of the urban machine shops and foundries, for example, are owned by ethnic Chinese, and they would be in the best position to set up tool factories if licensing were deregulated. Although there is resistance within the government to deregulating small and household industries, my interview with Ir. Felik Lengkong indicates that this resistance is crumbling. If change continues in the same direction, it is probable that the forces of deregulation will strengthen.

As stated above, it is impossible to estimate the degree of displacement that will accompany deregulation. The protection currently offered by the regulatory environment may be largely illusory. There may already be, for example, considerable quantities of smuggled tools on the market. There may also be illicit production of tools in medium-sized urban workshops which either goes undetected or is ignored by local government officials. In the incident that comes to mind, described in chapter 3, a Chinese tool trader from Semarang "stole" more than thirty workers away from Kajar village and set up a competing workshop to produce agricultural tools, which he then sold to the government transmigration program. Many of the state-owned companies and common service facilities operated by the Department of Industry may actually be competing with rural smiths.

Most authors have assumed that small and household industries have no competitive advantages. Yet Dewey observed in the 1950s that peasant industries in Java survived wherever they could compete in price or desirability with western imported goods, which they often could do (Dewey 1962, 198). Rural metalworking industries appear to have at least five competitive advantages: proximity to the rural consumer, familiarity with local tool forms, product durability (particularly if the smith can afford to use the better grades of scrap), low prices, and the willingness and ability to make repairs. Given these advantages, which are often overlooked, village metalworking industries may survive deregulation without excessive displacement.

The government of Indonesia is uncomfortable with the idea of open competition and conflict between large and small enterprises. This discomfort underlies the revival of the Foster Father program, which tries to establish mutually beneficial noncompetitive linkages. So far the number of small metalworking enterprises and cooperatives enrolled in the program is only 365, but if the program is deemed successful it will probably be expanded in the future. It is too early to evaluate the program, but potential impacts are both positive and negative. The impacts will be positive if new technologies are transferred to the smaller firms, and if the smaller firms retain their status as independent producers. The impacts will be negative if the smaller firms are forced into a dependency relationship. Pressures to deregulate are also having an impact on the agricultural sector. Any change in agricultural subsidies or price controls which has a negative impact on farmer incomes will also affect the market for products made by rural smiths.

The 1980s saw the installation of electricity in most rural areas, and the beginnings of mechanization in metalworking industries. The potential impact of this change is profound, as it affects not only the socioeconomic organization of smithing but also its cultural and symbolic content. Smithing is an ancient occupation which has sacred associations. The smith is thought to act as an intermediary between the village community and its male ancestors and gods. Forging metal blanks is seen as akin to the forging of new souls or the reforging of the souls of the dead. The perapen with its furnishings — including the bellows, the anvil, and the quenching trough — functions as a small temple or ceremonial center where this sacred activity takes place.

Given the symbolic associations of the perapen, one is forced to wonder whether mechanization will result in the desacralization of smithing as an occupation. Although the mechanical blower performs the same function as the Malay bellows, that of forcing air into the fire hearth, it is totally unlike the bellows in structure and appearance. It seems unlikely that the symbolic associations which adhere to the bellows can be transferred to the blower.[11] Similarly, one can only wonder what will happen if the anvil, the most sacred of the objects in the perapen, is replaced by a springhammer or forging machine.

The potential socioeconomic effects of mechanization are no less profound. If the bellows worker is replaced by a blower, one of the filers by a gerinda, and the hammer swingers by a springhammer, the size of the perapen labor force will be drastically reduced. With mechanization, two men (one to operate the springhammer and one to operate the gerinda) could perform the work that has traditionally been done by a group of four to seven men. At present prototypes of the springhammer are still being developed, and the Department of Industry is attempting to limit their diffusion. We can expect, though, that a commercially viable model will be available in the next ten years, and that efforts to limit its diffusion will fail. Thus far the negative employment effects of adopting the blower and gerinda have been masked by an expanding market. Although the average size of a perapen has declined somewhat, the number of perapen has greatly increased and absorbed the labor displaced by mechanization. It may not be so easy to absorb the labor displaced by the springhammer, since hammer swingers account for about half the labor force in blacksmithing. The effect of mechanization on stratification will depend to a large extent on access to electricity and investment credit from banks. The government currently subsidizes the first unit of electricity that a village household purchases, which amounts to 150 watts. This is enough to power the smallest models of blower and gerinda sold, but not enough to power the larger models. Ordinary perapen owners are investing in small models, which can be purchased for under Rp 100,000 ($50). They are usually able to save the purchase price out of their profits, without resorting to a bank loan. Wealthy empu pedagang and a few of the independent perapen owners, on the other hand, are investing in larger models of blower and gerinda. These models are powered by a diesel engine or by extra unsubsidized units of electricity purchased from the government. These large technologies, which cost in the millions of rupiah, are often purchased with the assistance of government bank loans.

Mechanization may create problems of labor displacement and increased stratification in the future. But it offers the best hope that village metalworking enterprises will continue to be competitive and survive. The willingness of village smiths to adopt new technologies must therefore be considered a positive sign for the future. If metalworking and other industries remain in rural areas, they will continue to contribute directly to the prosperity of rural communities. A dispersed pattern of development, with well-capitalized rural industries that have increased their productivity by adopting small-machine technologies, probably offers the best hope for the future.

Recommendations for Improving the Macrodata Base

The macrodata base available to scholars, industrial planners, and policymakers has steadily improved in the years since independence, in quantity and quality. Nonetheless there are still shortcomings in the data which make comparisons and the construction of time series difficult. The following suggestions are therefore offered.

1. The ethnographic data in this book indicate that small and household industries in rural areas form a single socioeconomic and cultural complex. It would therefore be preferable to use the same survey forms and the same reference periods when surveying these two segments of the industrial sector. At present different forms are used, with only partial overlap, which means that there may be problems of comparability even within the same industrial census.

2. If possible, all the data collected in future surveys of small and household industries should be published by the five-digit ISIC industrial codes;

all the data should at least be published by the three digit codes. The gaps in tables 11 and 12 show the negative effects of incomplete publishing.

3. The construction of time series has been made difficult by changes in the definitions of enterprise by size (large, medium, small, and household), the definition of labor force participation, and the content of the five-digit ISIC codes. Further changes should be avoided, apart from a return to the more inclusive definition of labor force participation used in the Industrial Census of 1974–75, because it is impossible to estimate with any accuracy the number of part-time workers who were excluded by the tighter definition used in 1986. A more inclusive definition can be supplemented by questions on the intensity of participation.

4. Some basic questions on the amount and type of land owned and cultivated should be included in future industrial censuses. Their inclusion would enable researchers to draw some conclusions about the relationship between the agricultural and industrial sectors.

5. Questions on person-days worked and wages paid to hired workers should be included in every survey. This would enable researchers to calculate wages per person-day, and to convert value added figures to profit figures.

6. Data on the gender division of the labor force in small and household industries should be published. At present these data are only available for the small industry section of the census of 1986.

Recommendations for Revising Import and Licensing Regulations

In the same vein, several recommendations are offered for revising import and licensing regulations. These recommendations are limited to regulations which affect small and household metalworking enterprises.

1. In making policies a distinction should be drawn on the basis of market orientation between utilitarian industries and handicraft industries. Utilitarian industries produce for a market that is largely rural, local (within the province), and low-income. Thus far these industries have not been included in the government's export promotion effort, and there is considerable doubt whether there would be an overseas demand for their products if they were included. Handicraft industries, on the other hand,

produce for a market that is largely urban and middle- to upper-income, and that includes a large proportion of foreign tourists and resident foreigners. There is a considerable overseas demand for the products of Indonesian handicraft industries and they are being included in export promotion efforts.

2. Legislation which protects utilitarian metalworking industries should be left in place. This is because there are no clear benefits to be gained by repealing it, and there is an unknown risk of displacement. Advocates of deregulation usually justify it on two grounds. The first is that deregulation is a necessary prerequisite to the negotiation of favorable trade agreements with other governments. As mentioned by Ir. Felik Lengkong, there is a fear that Taiwan will ban the import of products from Indonesia if Indonesia bans the import of products from Taiwan. But since utilitarian metalworking industries produce almost entirely for a domestic market, they seem to have little to gain from trade agreements with overseas nations. The second justification is that deregulation makes industries more competitive and forces them to be more efficient. Increased competition from imports and factory-made products might have the opposite effect, however. Perapen owners might be forced to lower their prices and accept smaller profit margins. They would then be unable to afford the electrical installations and small labor-saving machinery that mean greater efficiency.

3. Tariffs and taxes should be eliminated on capital goods that are needed by small and household metalworking enterprises. The most important of these are files, which must be frequently replaced, and which now carry tariffs and taxes amounting to 50 percent. Tariffs and taxes should also be lowered or eliminated on rasps, vises, clamps, anvils, portable forges, and hand- or pedal-operated grinding wheels.

4. At present blacksmithing and the casting industries which use copper and copper alloys are all recycling industries. They depend entirely on scrap metal and are unable to afford new metal. The available ethnographic data indicate that this was not always so. Before the Japanese occupation Indonesian smiths were more fully integrated into the world market economy than they are today. This is because they used a considerable amount of new bar metal, imported primarily from Europe. Today the government controls metal imports and it has a monopoly on the import of iron and steel, resulting in domestic prices 25–50 percent higher than international prices (Poot, Kuyvenhoven, and Jansen 1990, 445). If the government gave up its monopoly, and the private sector were permitted to become involved

in iron and steel imports, village smiths might resume using new metal for some purposes. Even with the continuation of a monopoly on iron and steel, blacksmiths might resume using new metal if Krakatau Steel lowered its prices.

Recommendations for Improving Extension Programs

The following six recommendations are offered for improving extension programs, particularly those of the Department of Industry. Although the examples used are taken from metalworking industries, the first five recommendations would also apply to other types of industries.

1. Salaries for Department of Industry field-workers and operators should be increased, and a ban imposed and enforced on activities which involve a conflict of interest. These would include trading in raw materials or finished products, and using the department's common service facilities to set up a personal business.

2. An effort should be made to bring extension services to a wider group of perapen owners. As the caseload of the ordinary field-worker is very high, this may involve increasing the number of field-workers. At present extension tends to be channeled through an élite group consisting of village officials, heads of cooperatives, and empu pedagang. This usually has the unintended result of strengthening the capital position of this élite group. Many ordinary perapen owners have never had direct contact with an extension agent or participated in a project funded by the Department of Industry.

3. Every effort should be made to involve perapen owners in project planning. This should be done by conferring with them before the drafting of project proposals. No villager should be pressured into participating in a project who perceives it as a waste of his or her time and resources, and no field-worker should be put in the position of having to implement such a project. Equipment to be given out on credit should be seen and approved by the perapen owners before the project is funded.

4. Projects involving credit or group funds should be channeled through the local branch of a reliable bank, such as a BRI Unit Desa or a BPD kecamatan bank. Department of Industry field-workers and cooperative officials are not trained as bankers and should not be asked to function as

bankers—they should not be asked to screen credit applicants, disburse credit, collect credit repayments, or keep credit repayments or group funds at home in their cupboard. Many projects fail because of financial ineptitude or mismanagement.

5. Participants in training courses and study tours lose a great deal of work time. They should therefore be given daily compensation commensurate with their lost earnings. If the perapen owner acts as his own empu, the perapen may have to shut down during the training course. For this reason it is often better to let one of his sons attend the course. If it is a technical training course, the Department of Industry should bear the risk of failure by paying for any raw materials or supplies used.

6. The Department of Industry has repeatedly tried and failed to introduce iron-casting technology into blacksmithing villages. The ethnographic information in this book indicates that their efforts would be more successful if they introduced iron-casting technology into copper-, brass-, or bronze-casting villages. Forging and casting are very different procedures, but casting smiths are usually able to adapt to a variety of metals. At present there are two successful iron-casting centers in Indonesia, both in Central Java, and with a similar history of Dutch involvement during the colonial era. These centers are often held up for blacksmiths to emulate, but historical data on one of these centers (Batur hamlet) indicate that it was previously a bronze- and brass-casting village.

Suggestions for Further Research

Over the years a number of theories have been developed with reference to Indonesia. These theories have been based largely on ethnographic studies of lowland wet-rice villages on Java. Other types of villages, which may have very different ecological adaptations and patterns of resource allocation, have largely been ignored. This book represents an attempt to redress this situation. It focuses on a subset of small industry villages, namely those which make products of metal. Obviously many other studies are needed before enough data have been collected to begin revising theoretical assumptions. Within the industrial sector alone, studies are needed of the very important and varied textile industries, the basketry and matting industries, the clay product industries, the leather goods industries, the food processing industries, and several others. Every researcher obviously brings his or her own agenda to the field, but it is suggested that future studies of non-rice villages give particular attention to two subjects. The first is the pattern of resource allocation between sectors, and changes in that pattern over time because of changes in relative profitability. The second is social and economic stratification and the causes of that stratification, including the uses of money capital.

Other Projects Undertaken by the Author Related to the Present Research

1. From June 1977 through September 1978 the author carried out research on village industries in the Yogyakarta Special Region (D.I.Y.) under a student grant from the East-West Center, Honolulu. The Indonesian sponsor for this research was the Department of Industry's agency for the Guidance and Development of Small Industries (BIPIK). During this research phase a general survey was first made of thirty-five industry villages in the four rural districts of Yogyakarta. Four villages were selected from this larger group and a sample survey was conducted of sixty households in each village. These four villages were the blacksmithing village of Kajar in Gunung Kidul district, the ceramics village of Kasongan in Bantul district, the leather puppet village of Pocung in Bantul district, and the bamboo basketry village of Malangan in Sleman district. The author was assisted in this work by several student surveyors from the Population Institute, Gadjah Mada University. During this phase the author also had occasion to collect some data in an informal way on the silverworking industry at Kota Gede village on the outskirts of Yogyakarta, on brass-bell casting at Ngawen village in Sleman district, and on keris making in Jitar village in Sleman district.

2. In May and June 1978 the author was part of a team working at the ILO's office in Jakarta to write recommendations for the Indonesian government's third Five-Year Development Plan (REPELITA III). The author was responsible for the recommendations on village industries and other rural non-agricultural enterprises. This involved an extensive review of the available English- and Indonesian-language literature, which was compiled by ILO.

3. From October 1978 to December 1980 the author was employed as a rural industries consultant on the Provincial Development Project (PDP I) in Central Java, funded by USAID. Based at the Department of Industry's provincial office in Semarang, the author had as her principal task the setting

up of a credit program for twenty-two small industry villages in the north coast districts of Kudus, Demak, Jepara, Pati, and Rembang. These villages included the blacksmithing village of Hadipolo in Kudus district, the blacksmithing village of Kuniran in Pati district, and the copperworking village of Jolotundo in Rembang district. These villages were visited regularly over the two-year period and evaluated as to the impact of program participation on such variables as enterprise income, employment, and labor productivity. Another task was the annual review of proposals for village industry projects submitted by the Department of Industry's offices in the five districts of Central Java mentioned above. Similar reviews were undertaken for other PDP project areas in Aceh (North Sumatra), Madura, and Lombok. In carrying out this task it was necessary to tour these areas, and data were collected in an informal way from such blacksmithing villages as Ba'et in Aceh and Sen Asen on Madura. Yet another task was the completion of a large-scale baseline survey of village industries and other nonagricultural income-generating activities in Central Java province. This was done with the assistance of social science research institutes at Diponegoro and Satya Wacana Universities. On personal time, revisits were also made to Kajar and other villages in Yogyakarta.

4. From January 1981 to August 1984 the author was employed as a program officer for women and employment at the regional Southeast Asia office of the Ford Foundation in Jakarta. Two days a week were spent working with Dr. Pujiwati Sajogyo of the Center for Development Studies at Bogor Agricultural University on a four-year research project concerning the economic roles of rural women in seven provinces of the Indonesian outer islands. This assignment also included instruction and thesis supervision of master's-level students from outer island universities who were involved in the project. The remainder of the week was spent evaluating grant requests from Indonesian organizations, and monitoring and evaluating projects already funded. Most of these projects focused on women in the industrial sector, ranging from village industry producers to put-out workers to workers employed in large factories. The job required considerable travel, and there were opportunities to visit new blacksmithing and metalworking villages, as well as to revisit Kajar and other villages in the Yogyakarta and Central Java region.

5. From May to November 1986 and from August to November 1987 the author was employed as a cottage industries development consultant, assigned to the Agricultural Development Bank of Pakistan under the Gujranwala Integrated Rural Development Project (GADP), credit component. The larger project was funded by the Asian Development Bank and the author's consultancy was funded by IFAD. The main task was setting up a pilot credit project for artisan-caste villagers in Gujranwala district in the Pakistani Punjab. The blacksmiths (lohari) were one of the castes involved and numerous

visits were made for survey and evaluation purposes to the blacksmithing villages of Jandiala Baghwala and Kaili Shah Pur. Other castes included in the project were potters, weavers, and leather workers. In carrying out this project the author worked closely with the Lahore office of the Punjab Small Industries Corporation. A conference paper compared the blacksmiths of Indonesia and the Punjab, mainly from a development perspective.

6. From September 1988 to 1995 the author was employed as a research coordinator at Bank Rakyat Indonesia (BRI), Jakarta. The work was funded by both USAID and the World Bank. BRI is the principal government bank in Indonesia which carries out programs in rural areas. Its credit and savings programs, which are among the largest in the world, are channeled through a nationwide network of approximately 3,500 village banks. Because there is another government program for rice inputs, BRI's rural credit program (KUPEDES) makes loans principally for nonagricultural enterprises. The author's work at BRI was to carry out policy-oriented research on the rural banks and their customers, assisted by teams of staff researchers from BRI's Department of Planning, Research and Development. One of the first projects focused on village industry loan customers and involved cooperation with district offices of the Department of Industry in four provinces. Another project, a borrower-impact study, required intensive interviews with several hundred customer households. Yet another was a village-based comparative study of customer and noncustomer households. The research sites for these studies were located in the provinces of West Java, Yogyakarta, North Sumatra, South Sulawesi, and Bali. About fifty of the intensive interviews conducted by team members during the course of these surveys were with the owners of blacksmithing or other metalworking enterprises, and the author had access to the interview data. While accompanying research teams to the field the author also had the opportunity to visit a number of new metalworking villages. This was the first time that the author had worked on Bali, where there is a strong smithing tradition. Among the villages visited on Bali were the blacksmithing village of Batu Sangihan in Tabanan district, the blacksmithing village of Delod Pangluk in Gianyar district, the silver- and gold-working village of Celuk in Gianyar district, and the silver-, gold-, brass-, and ironworking village of Kamasan in Klungkung district. Metalworking villages of interest elsewhere included the blacksmithing village of Kersamenak in Garut district in West Java and the blacksmithing village of Massepe in Sidrap district in South Sulawesi. It was also possible during this phase to revisit Kajar and other villages in Yogyakarta. More recently some additional information on Kajar was collected for the author by Made Suarjana, a journalist based in Yogyakarta. In 1991 the author and Made Suarjana made two visits to the iron- and brass-casting village of Batur in Klaten district in Central Java to follow up on a study of Batur done in 1970 by Kuntowidjojo.

NOTES

1. According to the census of population of 1980, 3,337,000 persons working in rural areas gave manufacturing as their primary occupation. The number has probably increased since that time (Poot, Kuyvenhoven, and Jansen 1990, 66, table 3.13; see also tables 5 and 6 in this book and accompanying discussion).

2. Furnivall described the Dutch method as "Let me help you, let me show you how to do it, let me do it for you" (Furnivall 1930, 269).

3. Various versions of these ideas are found in Boeke 1953, 1954, and 1966. In writing these paragraphs I have relied mainly on Boeke 1953, which is actually a combined reprint of books published in 1942 (*The Structure of the Netherlands Economy*) and 1946 (*The Evolution of the Netherlands Indian Economy*). Boeke's views are summarized and critiqued in Koentjaraningrat 1975, 74–85, and Higgins 1955a, 58–78. See also the Introduction and part II of Evers 1980.

4. For trade as something foreign to the Indonesian economy see Boeke 1953, 48–49.

5. For Boeke on Gandhi see Boeke 1966, 167–92. In his article on population (1954) Boeke talks about "village restoration."

6. See Koentjaraningrat 1975, 80–83, for a review of early Dutch, European, and Indonesian criticisms of Boeke.

7. See Koentjaraningrat 1975, 191–209, for a review of studies carried out by American anthropologists in Indonesia after the Second World War.

8. The Dutch word is "cultuurstelsel." Although it became a convention to mistranslate this word as "culture system" in English, it actually means "cultivation system," the phrase now used by some authors.

9. Cane uses row irrigation while rice uses pan irrigation. Planting cane in a rice field therefore involves a total restructuring of the field. Moreover, cane is a fifteen-month crop, whereas rice is a four- to ten-month crop, depending on the variety. See Sajogyo 1976, xxv, and Alexander and Alexander 1978.

10. Some of these articles are collected in part II of Evers, ed., 1980. Evers's useful introduction includes a discussion of the major paradigms that have been used in Southeast Asian social science, namely dual societies, plural societies, loosely structured social systems, involution, and modernization theory.

11. Frank 1973 is a well-known polemic against both the modernization school and dualism. White notes the curious fact that Frank praises *Agricultural Involution* in the same article, and asks: "How can Gunder Frank and Higgins like the same book?" (White 1983, 19). Sritua Arief and Adi Sasono published a book in 1980 which applied dependency theory to Indonesia. In writing the book they had the cooperation of Frank. Wertheim and Giap also contributed an article on Java to a volume edited by Wallerstein on social change in the colonial era. Nonetheless, dependency and world-systems theory have not been popular in Indonesia, perhaps because of their emphasis on the need for social restructuring.

12. This is the opinion of most economists. White, however, disagrees. He sees a "proto–Green Revolution" in the late Sukarno era, and "slow but reasonable growth, at rates slightly ahead of population growth" (see White 1989, 72).

13. These scholars include Alexander and Alexander 1978, 1979, and 1982; Collier 1981b; Elson 1978; Gordon 1978; Hart 1978, 1981, and 1986; Stoler 1977a and 1977b; and White 1973, 1976a, 1976b, 1979, and 1983.

14. Geertz also revisited Java in 1957–58 while he was doing fieldwork on Bali (Geertz 1963b, vii).

15. In December 1989 *Prisma* devoted its entire English-language edition to the subject of takeoff.

CHAPTER 2. *Socioeconomic Organization*

1. See Thorburn 1982, 135, for an illustration of an *ubub patri*. It is interesting to note that *pandai gurinda* (cutlers) existed as early as 1817 and are listed among other occupations in appendix E to Raffles 1965 [1817].

2. A province is roughly equivalent to an American state; a district, also called a regency, is roughly equivalent to a county.

3. Kahn 1980 uses the term "sledgers" to refer to hammer swingers.

4. Kinship in Java, as well as much of Indonesia, is bilateral. Newlyweds may choose to live near the parents of either the bride or the groom, although living with or near the bride's parents (matrilocal postmarital residency) is often favored in villages. Sometimes the choice depends on which set of parents has the most property. Bali, on the contrary, has unique kinship patterns and practices of its own.

5. This information is taken from my field notes while I was working on the PDP I project between 1978 and 1980 in the four north coast districts of Rembang, Pati, Jepara, and Demak. In the villages that I visited, the term *pandega* or pendega is used to mean any member of a boat crew except the captain. Elsewhere along the Javanese coast it may have a more restricted meaning.

6. I have never had difficulty visiting or interviewing blacksmiths in their perapen, because western women are treated as honorary males. In Kajar, for example, I was invited to two selamatan ceremonies which were otherwise attended by men only. At a village wedding, where the men and women were sitting on different sides of the room, I was directed to sit with the men.

7. In a study in 1990 of 192 households receiving "Kupedes" bank loans, I found that children aged twelve or under constituted only 1.5 percent of the total labor force in enterprises owned by the households. All the children employed were unpaid family workers, and there were no instances of hired child labor. The sample of 192 households was drawn randomly from the customer lists of eight village banks in four provinces (West Java, Yogyakarta, Bali, and North Sumatra). The typical Kupedes customer is a household which owns no rice land, depends mainly on nonagricultural enterprises, and guarantees its loan with a house plot (Sutoro, 1990). Kupedes customer households have higher average incomes than noncustomer households in the same villages, so that the overall rates of child labor participation may be higher than 1.5 percent.

8. This example comes from the village of Jandiala Baghwala, one of two blacksmithing villages included in an Agricultural Development Bank of Pakistan credit project in 1986–87. The village is about two kilometers from the market town of Gujranwala on a main road. It is occupied entirely by families from the lohari caste of blacksmiths. Each smithy is owned jointly by the males from an extended patrilineal household, usually a father and his sons or a set of brothers.

9. I learned this from a retired Dutch executive of Shell Oil Company who was born and raised in the "Indies."

10. Dian Desa, an appropriate-technology organization based in Yogyakarta, has developed a commercial coconut shell charcoal which it is producing in Kalimantan. The product is packaged for the overseas home barbecue market and is four to five times more expensive than the teak charcoal being used by smiths (personal communication, Anto Sujarwo, director of Dian Desa).

11. I have developed a simple form with which village banks can conduct cash flow analysis. Use of this form enables the bank officer to determine profit levels and repayment ability at different levels of indebtedness. Examples are found in Sutoro 1988.

12. The exchange rate in August 1991 was about Rp 1,970 to the U.S. dollar.

CHAPTER 3. *Kajar, a Blacksmithing Village*

1. The Indonesian words that are used to explain this belief are *nasib* (fate, destiny) and bakat (talent, inborn ability). Kajar men have the bakat to become smiths because it is their nasib. Outsiders do not have the bakat because it is not their nasib.

2. *Pak* is an honorific which comes from *Bapak*, or "father." It is used for any married man. *Bu* is the parallel term for married women. It comes from *Ibu*, or "mother." The names used in Kajar are typical Javanese names. In daily conversation the name is usually shortened to the first two syllables: Pak Karyo for Karyodirejo, Pak Marto for Martodinomo, Pak Harjo for Harjopawiro, etc. In writing, many Javanese keep the old Dutch spelling for their names. Thus Sastrosuyono can also be spelled Sastrosoejono, Karyodirejo can also be spelled Karjodiredjo, etc. To make matters even more complicated, many Javanese use an "a" in writing their names where they pronounce an "aw" sound, as in the English "law." The "aw" sound is written as "o" in Indonesian. Combining these customs, a name may be written as either "Karjadiredja" or "Karyodirejo."

I considered using a pseudonym for Pak Sastrosuyono but decided that doing so would be pointless. His role in Kajar life is so prominent, and he is so well known to government officials in Wonosari, that any visitor to the area would immediately discover his true name.

3. According to one elderly villager, the edge of the teak forest came to within 1.2 kilometers of Kajar in his childhood.

The houses of Kajar have roofs which resemble the *srotong* and *limasan* styles illustrated in Koentjaraningrat 1985, 135. According to Koentjaraningrat, the srotong style is used by ordinary Javanese villagers, while the limasan style is restricted to descendants of the village founders and village officials. The older houses in Kajar differ from houses in the lowlands in being larger and having siding made of teak rather than plaited bamboo. They often have flat-roofed extensions added onto the sides or back of the house, not illustrated in Koentjaraningrat.

4. Some households had help from the Save the Children Foundation in installing their floors.

5. In writing this description I have used the terms actually used in Kajar, which are a mixture of Javanese and Indonesian terms. One English term is even used ("kepala sosial" for "social welfare officer"). For a more complete description of village administration on Java, which includes all the purely Javanese terms, see Koentjaraningrat 1985, 190–96.

6. The term dukuh is somewhat confusing. It is the Javanese term for hamlet, whereas the Indonesian term is dusun. The longer noun forms, *pedukuhan* and *pedusunan*, can also be used, with the same meaning. The hamlet head is

officially called the kepala dukuh or *kepala dusun* (*kepala* meaning head). In practice, however, this title is usually shortened to *Dukuh* or *Pak Dukuh*. Thus *dukuh* means both the hamlet and the person who heads it. Sometimes *dukuh* is spelled *dukoh*.

7. Sometimes the word "landless" is applied to any household without sawah, even if it owns ladang or other types of dry fields. This usage makes it very difficult to talk about villages in dry zone areas or parts of Indonesia where irrigation systems are not well developed, since it means that every household in the village is by definition "landless."

8. The Central Bureau of Statistics (BPS) conducted a nationwide agricultural census in 1973 which has been widely quoted in academic and development publications. In an effort to obtain some better data on land holdings in Kajar than that provided by the registry of 1936, I contacted the BPS office in Wonosari. They said that Kajar had indeed been in one of the census blocks in 1973, but that all forms had long since been forwarded to the head office of BPS for computer entry. I then contacted the head office in Jakarta but was told that there was a two-year backlog of requests for data from government agencies, and that they could not respond to any individual requests. In frustration, I went back to the BPS office in Wonosari and asked for the name of the field-worker who had collected the census data in Kajar. (Perhaps this imaginary field-worker still had copies stashed away under the bed.) The Wonosari office replied that no field-workers had been used. Instead, census forms were distributed to all the village scribes in the area to be filled out and submitted. I then went back to the village scribe in Kajar, who innocently admitted using the figures from the 1936 registry to fill out the 1973 census forms!

9. Harvests were generally poor on Java between 1962 and 1964. According to Ben White, the widespread social unrest created by food scarcities and rising food prices was a major factor contributing to the collapse of the Sukarno regime (White 1989, 70, 72).

10. The sultan of Yogyakarta is said to be in direct communication with Nyai Loro Kidul, who appears to him spontaneously in times of crisis to help guide the state and people to safety. The Sultan sends *labuhan* offerings to Nyai Loro Kidul every year, as well as to the deities of Mounts Merapi and Lawu (Selo Soemardjan 1962, 18–19). Many people in the Yogyakarta area believe that Nyai Loro Kidul is the true wife of the sultan. They note that the other wives (i.e. the human wives) are never given an official status higher than concubine. There has been a revival of the Nyai Loro Kidul cult in recent years, especially in subdistricts along the south coast. Many women wore green, the color associated with Nyai Loro Kidul, to the coronation of the new sultan, Hamengku Buwono X, in 1989. During the coronation procession through the city the sultan sat in one corner of his horse-drawn carriage,

leaving the seat beside him empty. This was widely taken to mean that Nyai Loro Kidul was riding beside him. Many of the common people who watched the procession claimed, in fact, to have seen her. Despite her connection with the sultan, Nyai Loro Kidul has her negative or destructive aspect, and there are those who associate her with the Indian goddess Durga-Kali. She is said to "take" (i.e. to drown) anyone who is so foolish as to swim in the southern ocean wearing green. Villagers believe that she is responsible for all manner of plagues and pestilence.

11. There are several types of gotong royong labor exchanges in Java. The term formerly used in Kajar for exchanges of agricultural labor was *sambatan*. In his classic study of gotong royong in Kebumen, Central Java (1961), Koentjaraningrat identified seven types, including sambatan and *grodjogan*. Sambatan was the term used for an exchange of labor between households living in the same dukuh for tasks related to the household, such as house-building and repairs, digging wells, and pounding rice in preparation for a feast. Grodjogan was an exchange of agricultural labor between neighboring households, or households with adjacent fields. Koentjaraningrat notes, however, that grodjogan was sometimes known by other names, including sambatan (Koentjaraningrat 1961, chapter 6).

12. Garrett Solyom, who also looked over the collection, feels that some of the stones are more recent.

13. Early writings on the effects of the Green Revolution also talked about intravillage class formation as though villages had been previously homogeneous. Increasing familiarity with historical sources from the colonial era has provided a corrective. According to White, sources from the late eighteenth century point to the existence of three broad agrarian classes: the village officials, the *kuli* (also called *sikep*), and the landless peasants. Various large-scale colonial enquiries conducted in the early twentieth century indicated that landless rates were already 30 to 40 percent. The élite group in this period, consisting of officials, wholesale traders, and a few wealthy peasants, constituted 5 to 10 percent of the population (White 1989, 67–69). The landless rates of 30 to 40 percent are high, but lower than the present rates of 50 to 55 percent in wet rice areas. The rate of 5 to 10 percent for the élite group still holds (Sutoro 1991, chapters 2–4).

14. On the first of *Sura* in the city of Yogyakarta, the palace treasures (*pusaka*), including four lances, palace keris, and other weapons, are taken out and cleaned. They are then carried in a solemn nighttime procession which circles the outer wall of the palace compound (*beteng*) seven times. Silence is maintained and no one is allowed to speak. The pusaka are carried by palace retainers, but the public is allowed to follow them in the procession. A similar ceremony takes place in Surakarta (Solo). The labuhan offerings mentioned in note 10, above, are also sent on the first of Suro. Curiously, there is no men-

tion of any of these events in Koentjaraningrat's list of *Agami Jawi* (Javanese religion) calendrical celebrations. For Islamically oriented *santri* Javanese, the first of Sura is Muharram.

15. *Berdikir* in Kajar appears to be similar to the practice of *dikir* described by Koentjaraningrat (1985, 391). According to Koentjaraningrat, dikir is performed both by *santri* and *Agami Jawi* (i.e. *abangan*) Javanese. Among the followers of mystical santri sects the participants may eventually begin to dance wildly and fall into a trance. Among the Agami Jawi Javanese, however, the ceremony is not continued to the trance stage. Koentjaraningrat says that dikir is performed by the Agami Jawi Javanese mainly in connection with mortuary rituals. The purpose in Kajar is quite different.

16. Personal communication, Nancy Peluso.

17. See Sutoro 1982, 31–40, for a similar case of a bamboo basketry industry which rapidly expanded when the agricultural sector temporarily collapsed. The industry is located in the village of Malangan in Sleman district, north of Yogyakarta. Rapid expansion occurred between 1975 and 1978 when irrigation water to the village was cut off for seven growing seasons because of repairs on the Van Der Wijk canal. In addition, the beginning of repairs coincided with a serious attack of the wereng rice pest.

18. When I visited Kajar in August 1991 Pak Sastro had changed his name from Sastrosuyono to Sastrokadis. I did not have the chance to ask why, but the most usual reason why a Javanese changes his or her name is failure to have a child. Near fatal illness is another common reason. It is believed that a name change will divert the attention of malevolent spirits and bring a change in one's fortune.

19. Again, the difficulty of obtaining accurate information on land ownership must be stressed. Pak Paeran is not listed in the village registry as a landowner at all. However, his maternal grandfather, Gunokaryo, who is long deceased, is still listed.

CHAPTER 4. *Relevant Macrodata*

1. Tables 4–6 are based on labor force data which give the percentage of employed according to their primary occupation. Information on secondary occupations has been collected by the government, but very little of it has been published. The remainder of the tables is based on industrial surveys which attempt to enumerate every industrial establishment, without regard to the percentage contribution that each establishment makes to the total income of the owner's household.

2. According to Booth, agriculture was the primary occupation of more than 70 percent of the labor force prior to 1961. The figures she gives are 74

percent in 1905, 77 percent in 1930, and 72 percent in 1961, with some of the variation due to changes in the criteria for participation. Between 1961 and 1971 there was a sharp decline, from 72 percent to 63 percent. This continued in the following decade, with a further decline to 56 percent (Booth 1988, 31, table 2.1).

3. Poot has attempted to use some of the 1964 data by making several adjustments. His figures show an increase in household industry employment from 2.1 million in 1964 to 3.8 million in 1974–75. The greatest increase was in part-time, rural female employment. Value added per worker also declined for household industries between 1964 and 1974–75 as a result of the large number of part-time workers entering the labor force (Poot 1980; summarized in Poot, Kuyvenhoven, and Jansen 1990, 118–20, and table 4.13). Those trends seem to have since reversed themselves, although the figures for part-time female employment are strongly affected by the labor force definition used. See subsequent discussion in this chapter.

4. Weijland has recently published several articles which focus on the drastic decline in cottage and household industry employment indicated by figures from the census of 1986. She finds the cause to be voluntary withdrawal of females from low-productivity cottage and household industry activities because of rising rural incomes, coupled with increased male specialization (see for example Weijland 1984, 6–7). Rather astoundingly, she fails to note the change in labor force definitions. BPS has specifically stated, however, that the cottage industry employment data from the two censuses "cannot be compared" (Central Bureau of Statistics 1987b, 91).

5. A copy of the Subdirectorate for Metal survey (1987) was kindly provided by Ir. Felik Lengkong, head of the subdirectorate.

6. The government has attempted to control rice prices, so that the increase in rice supply created by the Green Revolution would not cause the market price for rice paid to farmers to plummet.

7. Specifically, it was assumed that:

— the number of metalworking enterprises and workers in code 39 roughly tripled between 1974–75 and 1986, as with code 381;

— the proportion of household enterprises to small enterprises and of household workers to small-enterprise workers was roughly the same in code 39 as in code 381, i.e. six times more household enterprises than small enterprises, and three times more workers in household enterprises than in small enterprises;

— the number of enterprises and workers making decorative objects of metal was approximately the same as the number making musical instruments.

CHAPTER 5. *Government Interventions*

1. An early expression of free trade sentiments vis-à-vis Indonesia is found in World Bank 1983. In this report the bank recommends a rollback of import bans, a gradual reduction in tariffs, adjustment assistance to industries affected by import competition, and anti-dumping legislation to protect domestic industries from unfair competition (cited in Poot, Kuyvenhoven, and Jansen 1990, 448).

2. This and the next four paragraphs rely very heavily on Poot, Kuyvenhoven, and Jansen 1990, 3–6.

3. Neither method of estimation is perfect, of course. The first is preferred because it is based on the number of tools produced or imported, rather than the market value of those tools. However, estimating the number of tools imported assumes that their average value is $3.00, which is approximately correct but unproven. The second method is based on the market value of tools produced or imported. Its weakness is that the gross output figure for domestic products includes both wholesale and retail sales. Most domestically made tools are sold wholesale to intermediaries, who then mark up the price, but some are sold directly to consumers at retail. This gross output figure is compared with the wholesale value of imported tools as stated on bills of sale from overseas suppliers, before tariffs and taxes have been levied, and before the tools have been marked up for secondary wholesaling or retailing.

4. I suspect that some scrap is actually imported, for example brass shell casings. This does not show up on any government list of imports.

5. According to a survey of the Subdirectorate for Metal (1987), there were 45,912 enterprises in code 38. Assuming an average of 40 enterprises per metalworking village, there would have been 1,148 villages, and 80 villages would have represented 7 percent of this total. The number of workers in code 38 was 182,374. Assuming that the 80 larger villages had an average of 100 enterprises and that each enterprise employed 4 workers, there would have been 400 workers in each of these larger villages, or 32,000 workers all told, representing 17.5 percent of total employment.

CHAPTER 6. *Conclusions and Development Implications*

1. See chapter 1 for references.

2. This is the estimated value of one truck, one diesel engine, four pieces of high-wattage electrical machinery, and four equipped perapen.

3. The period of most rapid growth may have been the previous decade, between 1964 and 1974–75.

4. These ratios are very crude indicators of stratification because census

forms distinguish between only two broad groups, enterprise owners and hired workers. In a village with four strata like Kajar or Massepe, dependent and independent perapen owners will be lumped together in the census. Raw material and tool traders may also be counted as enterprise owners if, as is usually the case, they own any machinery used for productive or finishing operations. If they do not own any machinery, i.e. if they strictly limit their activities to trading, they probably fall outside the census altogether.

5. The traditional weavers of India and Pakistan do not make pile carpets. Rather they make a flatweave tapestry carpet called a *durree*, which is woven on a horizontal pit loom. The durree weavers are members of the *julaha* caste and are landless. In the early 1970s some smallholder farmers began to import vertical looms and weaving technology from Iran. Pile carpets in the "Persian Garden" style are woven on these looms, using child labor contracted from poor families who are also from the farmer caste. This is the only exception to the rule that all handicrafts are made by artisan-caste families who are landless.

6. Islam does not in fact permit caste. However, the Islamic groups of the Pakistani Punjab have a system of castes which almost exactly parallel the Hindu castes. The lohari caste has experienced considerable frustration over its continued low social status, despite its obvious newfound prosperity. At one point a national congress of the lohari was held, at which they officially changed their caste name to *Mughul Lohari*, to recall their glorious role as armorers to the rulers of the sixteenth-century Moghul dynasty of north India and Pakistan. This name change was perceived by higher castes as ostentatious, and the loharis have been subjected to ridicule because of it.

7. An exception is Bali, where villagers often buy sedans to rent out to tourists. They obtain these sedans on credit from automobile dealers.

8. For a listing and review of these historical studies see White 1983 and Hart 1986, 32–37.

9. Hart has identified four paradigms of rural development and agrarian change which relate to stratification. She uses the term "neo-Leninist" to describe the paradigm which most closely resembles van der Kolff's. The neo-Leninist paradigm stems from Lenin's analysis of agrarian differentiation in nineteenth-century Russia. According to Lenin the penetration of capitalism in the countryside leads inexorably to the polarization of landholdings and the development of impersonal wage labor relations; hence the disappearance of the peasantry and the emergence of opposing classes of kulaks and proletarians. Neo-Leninist authors who have written about contemporary Java, for example Mortimer and Gordon, differ from van der Kolff in emphasizing the growth of class consciousness and conflict (Hart 1986, 5–6).

10. Yet another approach to the equity issue emphasizes consumption rather than production. According to this approach, which has been gaining

in popularity among international aid agencies in recent years, governments like that of Indonesia should leave production to the free market and concentrate on promoting equity by providing better health services, education, housing, water, and sanitation to the poor. Presumably these services would be financed through income transfers, for example land and corporation taxes.

11. There is one example of such a transfer. During the Balinese festival of Tumpek Landep, offerings must be made to items of iron or steel, traditionally blades and weapons. In recent years the ever-adaptable Balinese have begun to give Tumpek Landep offerings to their cars and machinery, which are also made of iron and steel.

GLOSSARY OF METALWORKING TERMS

Most of the italicized terms in this glossary are Indonesian or Javanese. Nowadays it is not easy to distinguish between these two languages because village smiths on Java use a mixture of terms. Balinese terms are very similar to Javanese, and can be assumed to be the same unless otherwise noted. Where other languages are included, for example Dutch or Torajan, that is noted in parentheses. New spelling is used for Indonesian terms (*j* for *dj*, *c* for *tj* and *u* for *oe*). English terms are not italicized. Definitions of English terms marked with an asterisk (*) are taken from Bronson and Charoenwongsa 1986.

There are more terms in this glossary that relate to smithing than to mining and smelting. This is because native mining and smelting died out in most parts of Indonesia around 1800, and because these crafts were never practiced on Java or Bali to any extent.

This glossary is far from complete. For additional English terms relating to mining and smelting, see Bronson and Charoenwongsa. For additional Javanese terms relating to the casting of bronze gongs see Jacobson and van Hasselt 1907 repr. 1975. For additional Javanese terms relating to keris smithing see Solyom and Solyom 1978. For additional blacksmithing terms in Torajan see Zerner 1981; for additional blacksmithing terms in Minangkabau see Kahn 1980. For terms current in eight Indonesian languages in 1817 see appendix E in vol. 2 of Raffles 1965 [1817].

Garrett and Bronwen Solyom reviewed this glossary and made many useful suggestions.

à cire perdue (Fr.) (adj.): cast by the lost-wax method
alat (n.): tool
alat besi (n.): iron or steel tool
alat pertanian (n.): farm tool, usually made of forged steel (from the root word *tani* = farmer)
alat pertukangan (n.): workman's tool, usually made of forged steel (from the root word *tukang* = skilled worker/artisan)

alloy (n.): a homogeneous mixture of two or more metals* (Indon. *paduan*)

amanreang (Bug.) (n.): smithy (see *perapen*)

amril/ambril/mengamril/mengambril (v.): to polish metal items with any coarse, abrasive substance such as sandpaper (also called *amril*), sand, metal filings, alum, etc.

ani-ani (n.): small, traditional palm-held reaping knife for cutting rice stalks one at a time; a common product of blacksmiths

anneal (v.): to free metal from internal stress by heating and gradually cooling; an entire piece can be annealed, or heat can be applied locally to repair very small holes or fractures that appear in sheet metal work

anvil (n.): tool made of stone or metal which acts as a foundation for metal implements when they are being forged (Indon. *paron* or *landasan*)

apa basi (Minang.) (n.): smithy (relates to *dapur*; see also *perapen*)

api (n.): fire (see also *geni*)

arang/areng (n.): charcoal, used by most smiths as fuel (Bal. *adeng*)

arang batok kelapa (n.): charcoal made from coconut shell; commonly used by Balinese and Acehnese smiths

arang batu (n.): coal (see *batu bara*)

arang besi (n.): slag (Jav. *krawa*)

arang dapur (n.): lit. "kitchen charcoal," i.e. charcoal left over from cooking fires; sometimes bought up and used by coppersmiths for soldering work, or by poor blacksmiths on Madura

arang jati (n.): charcoal made from teak wood, usually branches and stumps; the most common fuel used by blacksmiths, producing a high and steady heat

arit (n.): sickle, a common product of blacksmiths (also called *sabit*)

asam (n.): tamarind; when mixed with water is often used to polish copper

baja/waja/besi baja/besi waja (n.): steel

baja putih/waja putih (n.): nickelous steel, traditionally combined with regular iron or steel to make *pamor* designs on a blade (lit. "white steel"); nowadays the term sometimes refers to stainless steel, an alloy of steel and chromium

bakar/membakar (v.): to burn, heat in a fire

bara (n.): live coals, embers

bara/membara (v.): to be aglow or to smolder; to char or carbonize

batu/watu (n.): stone (high Jav., Balin. *sela*)

batu asah/batu asahan (n.): grindstone, whetstone, used with either oil or water for sharpening or polishing tools; comes in different sizes and grades of fineness (Bal. *batu sangihan*; Dayak *anggong*)

batu bara/batu arang (n.): coal, sometimes used by blacksmiths in west and south Sumatra as fuel, but not commonly used elsewhere

batu besi (n.): iron-bearing ore (Toraj. *batu bassi*)

batu bintang/batu lintang (n.): meteorite (lit. "star stone"); preferred as a source of the nickel or nickelous iron used in mixed metal forging

batu gerinda (n.): small grindstone inside a *gerinda* (edge grinder); must be frequently replaced

Batur/Gunung Batur (n.): active volcano on Bali, held sacred by the *pande* clan of blacksmiths; also the name of a large casting village in Central Java

belakas/blakas (Balin.) (n.): cleaver, sometimes made for ceremonial purposes; used in pairs with *golok*

bellows (n.): a pumping device used to force air into a furnace or fire* (Indon. *ubub*)

Besakih/Pura Besakih (n.): most important temple complex in Bali, on the slopes of Gunung Agung volcano; the complex includes a temple for the *pande* clan of blacksmiths as well as a ceremonial smithy

besalen/besalin/besali (n.): foundry where metal is cast; furnace for melting metal; sometimes used for iron smithy

besi/wesi (n.): iron (Toraj. and Minang. *bassi/basi*; Dayak *besi/sanaman*)

besi baja (n.): steel (see *baja*)

besi batang (n.): bar iron (also called *besi ikat* or *besi lantak*)

besi berani (n.): magnet (also called *batu berani, besi sembrani*)

besi beton (n.): iron or steel reinforcement rods (see *besi proyek*)

besi buda/wesi buda (n.): sacred old iron, dug up from the earth; thought by Javanese to date from the Buddhist period in Central Java

besi cor (n.): cast iron (also called *besi tuang*)

besi ikat (n.): lit. "iron tied in a bundle," i.e. bar iron (see *besi batang*)

besi kuning (n.): lit. "yellow iron," a type of iron used in forging weapons which is thought by some Javanese to have magical properties, including invisibility

besi plat (n.): iron plate, sheet iron (see *plat*; also called *besi lantai, besi lempeng, besi papan*)

besi proyek/besi bangunan (n.): scrap iron recovered from the demolition of old buildings, bridges, etc.; often in the form of reinforcement rods

besi putih/besi pamor (n.): nickelous iron, similar to *baja putih* above

besi tempa (n.): wrought iron, i.e. iron which has been forged or welded

besi tua/besi bekas/besi roso/besi rosokan/besi bahan/besi buruk (n.): scrap iron or steel, used by smiths as a raw material

besi tuang (n.): cast iron (also called *besi cor*)

betel/petel (n.): chisel, used in the process of forging to score the metal or break off small pieces; woodworking chisels are also a common product of blacksmiths, made for sale to carpenters or wood carvers (from the Dutch *beitel*; ref. Zerner 1981)

bijih (n.): ore

bijih besi (n.): iron ore, nodule

bimetallic (adj.): used to refer to a tool made partly from one metal and partly from another, e.g. a dagger with a bronze handle and an iron blade

blacksmith (n.): a smith who works with iron or steel

blast furnace (n.): a furnace used for smelting metal; when used in connection with iron making the term has a special meaning: a smelting furnace that reaches temperatures high enough to produce iron as a liquid* (not commonly used in Indonesia)

bloom (n.): the solid lump of iron that forms in a low-temperature iron smelting furnace*

bloomery (n.): an iron smelting furnace that yields its iron as a solid bloom rather than as a pool or stream of liquid metal; bloomeries are run at lower temperatures than blast furnaces*

blower (from the English) (n.): small piece of electrically powered equipment which provides a blast of air aimed at the fire hearth; is beginning to replace the traditional bellows in some areas

bokor (n.): metal bowl or dish for offerings, usually with repoussé work

bor (Dutch) (n.): drill, e.g. a tool used to drill a hole in metal or wood; comes in two forms, rotary and electrically powered

brass (n.): an alloy of copper and zinc (Indon. *kuningan*)

bronze (n.): an alloy of copper with tin, lead, or arsenic (Indon. *perunggu/gangsa*)

buruh tambang (n.): miner, mine worker (also called *anak tambang*; ref. Dobbin 1983)

cakarwa (n.): poker used to stir the charcoal embers in a smithy

caket (n.): areca nut cutters, with only one sharp edge; made in the same tradition as the *keris*, they are often ornate in form and decoration (also called *kacip*)

Candi Sukuh (n.): fourteenth-century temple on the slopes of Mount Lawu in Central Java; includes a famous relief of a scene in a smithy

cangkul (Indon.) (n.): hoe, a common product of blacksmiths (Jav. *pacul*, Balin. *bangkrak*)

carbonize (v.): to char or burn up

carburize (v.): to infuse with carbon, as when converting iron to steel

cast (v.): to melt metal in some type of crucible and pour it into a mold

celurit (Mad.) (n.): traditional Madurese dagger

cetak/mencetak (v.): to cast in a mold; also to coin (money)

cetakan (n.): casting mold into which liquid metals are poured; things which have been cast

Chinese box bellows/windbox bellows (n.): a type of bellows, originally from China, that employs a double-acting piston—a piston that pumps air out on both the forward and return strokes; windboxes are usually used singly and in a horizontal position; they may be either cylindrical or boxlike* (Indon. *ubub dorong/ubub Cina/puup*)

coke (n.): the solid product resulting from the preliminary burning of coal which still contains enough energy to be used as fuel; used by blacksmiths on Madura (Dutch *steenkool*, Indon. *kokas*)

cor/mengecor (v.): to melt, e.g. metals

crucible (n.): a container for melting metal, usually made of stone or ceramic (Indon. *kowi*)

combustion (n.): the act or process of burning; rapid oxidation combined with heat and usually light

cupola (n.): spout near the bottom of a smelting or melting furnace from which the molten metal is tapped; sometimes a vertical cylindrical furnace for melting iron which is equipped with such a tapping spout (Indon. *kubah/kupola*; see also *tungkik*)

cuprous (adj.): having to do with copper, e.g. "cuprous" objects may be found at an archaeological site

cutler (n.): one who sharpens tools using a grindstone or rotary edge grinder; may also carry out minor tool repairs (Indon. *tukang asah* if a grindstone is used, *pandai gerinda* if a rotary edge grinder is used)

damar/damer/damar batu/damar sela (n.): resin; used in various types of metalwork, especially as a bed for repoussé work; often used in combination with beeswax, pitch, or other materials

dandang (n.) (1): pickaxe used to break up hard earth; a common product of blacksmiths

dandang (n.) (2): rice steamer; a common product of coppersmiths

damascene (n./adj.): a term which has been used variously to refer to crystalline steel (e.g. Indian *wootz*) and mixed metal forging (e.g. Indonesian *pamor*); originally referred to Damascus swords, which were actually made in India

da'po bassi (Toraj.) (n.): smithy (relates to *dapur*; see also *perapen*)

dapur (n.): fire hearth, kitchen; a less frequently used term for smithy or foundry (Minang. *apa*; Toraj. *da'po*; see also *perapen*, *besalen*)

dapur kupola (n.): term used in Batur village for foundry or place where iron casting is done; also called *dapur injeksi* or *dapur furnas*; foundries which use the smaller *tungkik* instead of the *kupola* are called *dapur tungkik*

Dong S'on (n.): North Vietnamese site of early bronze workshops, thought to have been destroyed by Han Chinese in the first century A.D.; probable source of many of the early Indonesian bronzes, including Heger I drums

emas (n.): gold (more commonly spelled *mas*)

emboss (v.): to impress designs in a piece of sheet metal from the back; same as repoussé

empu/mpu (n.): a master smith, head of a work group in a smithy (Minang.

nangkodoh/nangkoda; Bug. *punggawa*); derives from Old Javanese honorific *hampu*, which was also used for other professions such as court poet and religious teacher; also used on Bali for the priest to the blacksmith clan

empu pedagang (n.): an entrepreneur or trader who supplies raw materials to blacksmiths and markets their tools; may not have any smithing skills himself

empu pekerja (n.): a working *empu*; contrasts with *empu pedagang*

filigree (n.): a technique of making jewelry and *keris* fittings from very fine silver or gold wires; jewelry made with this technique

firewall (n.): low wall used in some smithies which protects the bellows worker from the heat of the fire hearth; usually made of brick, stone, or split bamboo

flux (n.): a substance that when mixed with the fuel and ore in a smelting furnace lowers the melting point of the slag produced; examples include lime and iron oxide* (not commonly used in Indonesia)

forge (v.): to work metal by heating and hammering (Indon. *tempa/ menempa*); (n.) place where forging is done, i.e. a smithy (Indon. *perapen*)

forge-weld (v.): to join pieces of metal by hammering together, sometimes after they have been rendered malleable and raised to fusion temperature by heat; in sheet metal work, forge-welding usually involves folding the edges together to form a seam

foundry (n.): place where metal, especially iron, is cast (Indon. *pengecoran/ besalen*)

gamelan (n.): Indonesian orchestra traditionally made up primarily of cast bronze percussion instruments; today sometimes made of cheaper metals (high Jav. *gangsa* = bronze)

gangsa (n.): bronze (also called *perunggu, loyang*)

garu (n.): harrow, used for breaking up the soil after plowing; a common product of blacksmiths

gemblak (n.): smith who casts or forge-welds copper or brass (also called *tukang gembleng/pandai tembaga/pandai kuningan/sayang*)

gembleng/menggembleng (v.): to weld or forge-weld by folding and hammering seams together

geni (n.): high Jav. or Balin. for fire (see *api*)

genta (n.): bells, e.g. priests' bells or cowbells, usually made of bronze or brass cast by the lost-wax method

gerbus (Mad.) (n.): bellows (see *ubub*)

gerinda/gurinda/grinda (possibly from the Dutch) (n.): piece of equipment used for grinding the surface and edges of metal tools; now comes in several forms, rotary and electrically powered; mentioned as early as Raffles 1965 [1817]

giggin (Mad.) (n.): plow tip (see *kejen*)

gild (v.): to gold-plate by fire gilding or covering with a thin layer of gold leaf or sheet (Indon. *sepuh/menyepoh*)

golok (n.): cleaver, chopping knife, a common product of blacksmiths (also called *wedung*)

gong (n.): gong (derives from *gangsa* bronze; Dayak *garontong*)

granulation (n.): a technique of decorating jewelry by soldering small beads of metal to the surface

gunting (n.): scissors or shears, including the shears used to cut sheet metal; a common product of blacksmiths

Gunung Agung (n.): Mount Agung, large and active volcano in northeast Bali (see *Besakih*)

Gunung Besi (n.): lit. "Iron Mountain," a small mountain near Lake Singkarek in Minangkabau highlands; the source of most of the iron used by Minangkabau smiths

gunung berapi (n.): lit. "mountain which has fire," a volcano

hafting (n.): technique of attaching a metal blade to a handle; early Indonesian tools used socketed hafting, which was later replaced by tanged hafting

hematite/haemotite (n.): a reddish brown iron oxide commonly used as an ore

ingot (n.): a piece of smelted metal, often brick or disk-shaped, that has not yet been made into a finished product*

intan (n.): diamond, often used in traditional goldwork; source: Kalimantan (Dayak *hintan*)

kacip (n.): betel nut scissors (see *caket*)

kaleng (n.): old aluminum or tin cans, used as the raw material in recent years for some welding industries

kapak/kampak (n.): axe

karat/karatan (n.): rust (also called *tahi besi*)

karat (n.): carat, modern unit for measuring the purity of gold

karung/karong/karung goni (n.): gunny sack or sack of coarse fibers, used as a container and measure of charcoal

kati (from the Sanskrit) (n.): a unit of weight used by metalsmiths until recent years, equal to about .64 kilograms or 1.4 pounds; now generally replaced by the kilogram

kawat (n.): wire, e.g. gold or silver wire used in making jewelry

kejen (n.): plow tip, plowshare; usually forged but sometimes cast (also called *mata bajak*, *luku*, *luku bajak*)

kelinting (n.): small bells (smaller than *genta*), usually made of brass cast by the lost-wax method

kelongsong peluru (n.): shell casing, commonly used as a raw material by brass smiths (also called *sarung peluru*) *kepeng/keping* (n.): copper coin imported in large quantity from China beginning in the thirteenth century (see *pis bolong*)

keris/kris (n.): a straight or wavy-bladed dagger, formerly used in warfare, but now mainly ceremonial; "real" keris usually have *pamor* (possibly a shortened form of *ke-iris*, from the root word *iris*, to slice) (Dayak *karis*; high Jav. or Balin. *duwung*)

keris buda (n.): a short, straight, and sturdy *keris* of plain iron (i.e. without intentional *pamor*), thought by Indonesians to date from the Central Javanese Buddhist period; possibly a predecessor of later *keris* types

keris Majapahit (n.): a type of *keris*, usually small, with an anthropomorphic handle in the style usually associated with ancestor statues; the handle and blade are made from a single piece of iron; like *keris buda*, they are thought to be an older form; women may carry or wear a *keris Majapahit*

kikir (n.): file used by smiths to hand-file the edge or surface of a tool or weapon; often imported and must be frequently replaced

kikir/mengikir (v.): to file, e.g. the edges of tools (Minang. *kikia*)

kikiran (n.): filings, e.g. iron filings

kodi (n.): twenty of anything, e.g. twenty tools tied in a bundle, ready to be taken to market

kokas (n.): coke, i.e. once-burned coal; used by smiths on Madura as fuel (also called *steenkool*, from the Dutch)

kompor (n.): blowtorch used in silver- and goldsmithing, and in welding; comes in various sizes and can be powered by gas, gasoline, kerosene, or electricity

kowi/kui/kowen (n.): a crucible, usually bowl-shaped and made of clay or stone (also called *pengleburan, takaran*)

krawa (Jav.) (n.): slag (also called *arang besi*)

kubah (n.): furnace used in melting iron to be cast; equipped with a tapping spout or "cupola" near the bottom (also called *kupola*)

kulah/kolah (n.): quenching trough, usually rectangular and made of stone (also called *telawah*)

kuningan (n.): brass (also called *tembaga kuning, loyang*)

kupola (n.): see *kubah*; can be used to refer either to the furnace itself or to the tapping spout

la'bo (Toraj.) (n.): Torajan sword; if made with *pamor* patterns it is called *la'bo to dolo* "sword of the ancestors" (ref. Zerner 1981)

landasan/landasan besi (n.): anvil (more commonly *paron*)

lantak/lantakan (n.): bar of metal (e.g. *besi lantak* or *mas lantak*)

lebur/lebor/labor/melebur/melebor/melabor (v.): to melt or smelt, used of metals

leburan (n.) (1): metal, especially melted or smelted metal (more commonly *logam*) *leburan/leboran/laboran* (n.) (2): furnace used for melting or smelting metals (also *dapur leburan*); the term *laboran* was used in southeast Borneo in the nineteenth century to refer to a cylindrical clay smelting furnace (ref. Schwaner 1853)

lempuyangan (n.): a reddish gold copper alloy, often used as a cover for *keris* sheaths

lamus/kamus (n.): a goat hide bellows, used principally along the north coast of Java for copper, brass, and bronze working

lerak (n.): soapfruit, used in polishing silver

limonite (n.): a yellowish brown iron oxide commonly used as an ore

lingga (from the Sanskr.) (n.): symbolic representation of the penis, usually in metal or stone

linggis (n.): crowbar; probably related to *lingga*

logam (n.): metal

loyang (n.): brass (see *kuningan*)

magnetite (n.): a blackish iron oxide commonly used as an ore

malam (n.): beeswax, used in lost-wax casting as a bed for repoussé work, and in making batik cloth; sometimes combined with resin (called *mal* in Batur village, Central Java)

mandau (n.): Dayak sword or machete, similar to *parang*; may have *pamor* patterns; formerly used for headhunting as well as other purposes

martil (n.): large hammer or sledgehammer

mas/emas (n.): gold; probably from the Sanskrit *masa* (Dayak *bulau*)

mas urai/mas pasir (n.): gold dust; used as money in ancient times

masa (Sanskrit) (n.): a unit of weight formerly used for metals, equal to about 2.4 or 2.5 grams, or 1/16 of a *suvarna*

matres (n.): the material used for forming or building up casting molds; probably derives from the word "matrix"

meranggen/mranggen (n.): workshop or place where *keris* fittings and ornaments are made (see *meranggi*)

meranggi/mranggi/mergongso (Jav.) (n.): craftsmen who make fittings and ornaments for the *keris* (ref. Raffles 1965 [1817]; Solyom and Solyom 1978)

Merapi/Marapi/Gunung Merapi/Gunung Marapi (n.): the name of two sacred volcanos, one just north of Yogyakarta and the other in the Minangkabau highlands of West Sumatra; derives from the *gunung berapi* mountain, or volcano (lit. "mountain which has fire," from the root word *api* = fire)

mesin tempa (n.): springhammer or forging machine, recently introduced by the Department of Industry

metal blank (n.): a tool-sized piece of wrought iron, usually in the form of a bar *mirah* (n.): pinkish ruby, often used in traditional gold work; sources: Kalimantan and Sri Lanka; a variant of *merah* red

mixed-metal forging (n.): the forge-welding of metals of different colors or textures; the resulting metal blank, when shaped into a tool, will exhibit patterns on the blade (Indon. *pamor*; also called pattern welding, forge-welding, damascene, etc.)

monel (n.): stainless steel used to make inexpensive rings, which are sold by the roadside in many cities; formerly scavenged from aircraft downed during the Second World War

Moon of Pejeng (n.): giant cast-bronze drum of the moko type, housed in a temple in the village of Pejeng, Gianyar district, on Bali; thought to have been cast on Bali in the early centuries A.D.

naga (from the Sanskrit) (n.): mythical serpent or snake, a frequent motif on Indonesian metalwork (Jav. *sarpa*)

nangkodoh/nakoda (Minang.) (n.): master smith, head of a smithy in West Sumatra (see *empu*)

nekel (n.): nickel (also *tembaga putih*)

ngaroni (n.): bellows worker in a gong factory; uses the *lamus*, or hide bellows, rather than the Malay bellows (ref. Jacobson and van Hasselt 1975)

onderdil (Dutch) (n.): spare parts for machinery, made of cast metal (also *suku cadang*)

open (from the Dutch) (n.): modern fuel-burning furnace

orang gunung (n.): lit. "mountain people"; usual source of charcoal used by blacksmiths

ore (n.): rock (or earth) that contains enough of one or more metal-bearing minerals to be worth mining* (Indon. *bijih*)

oxidation (n.): the process of combining with oxygen, as during combustion

pacul (Jav.) (n.): hoe or spade, a common product of blacksmiths (Indon. *cangkul*; Balin. *bangkrak*)

padu/memadu (v.): to mix metals, to alloy or weld together

paduan (n.): alloy, two metals welded together

pahat (n.): chisel or engraver, a common product of blacksmiths; used by gold and silver workers for decorative metalwork, by wood carvers, and by stone carvers (small versions are called *tatah*)

palu (n.): hammer or sledgehammer

pamor/pamur (n.): patterns in a steel blade which result from mixed-metal forging and the manipulation of the resulting metal sandwich; also refers to the nickelous iron which is mixed with regular iron to make such patterns; also refers to the magical power that this process gives a blade; original meaning "to mix" or "a mixture"

pamor Bugis/pamor Luwu (n.): nickelous iron from Sulawesi

pamor nekel (n.): pamor from imported or factory-produced nickel; very bright in comparison with other types of *pamor*; the imported *pamor nekel* most commonly comes from Germany

pamor Prambanan (n.): nickelous iron from a meteor which fell near the temple of Prambanan in Central Java in the mid-eighteenth century; a large part of the meteor is now kept in the Susuhunan palace in Surakarta

panca-datu (Bal.) (n.): the five sacred "metals" used in Balinese ceremonies and offerings: gold, silver, copper, iron, and either ruby (*mirah*) or tin

pancagina (Bal.) (n.): the five sacred crafts practiced by Balinese men: ironsmithing, coppersmithing, goldsmithing, wood carving, and painting

pandai/pande (n.): lit. "someone who is clever or skilled," a smith; if used alone, usually refers to a blacksmith

pandai besi/pande besi/pande wesi (n.): blacksmith or iron worker (Toraj. *pande bassi*; Buginese *panre bessi*)

pandai gerinda (n.): a cutler, i.e., one who sharpens tools with a *gerinda* or rotary edge grinder; usually itinerant or works out of a marketplace; mentioned in Raffles 1965 [1817] (also *tukang gerinda*; called a *tukang asah* if a grindstone is used instead of a *gerinda*)

pandai kuningan (n.): a brass smith (also *gemblak/tukang gembleng/sayang/ pandai loyang*)

pandai mas (n.): a goldsmith (also *tukang mas*)

pandai perak (n.): a silversmith (also *tukang perak*)

pandai senjata/pande sanjata (n.): weaponsmith or armorer (no longer used)

panjak (Jav.) (n.): a hammer swinger, of which there are two or three in each of the larger smithies; in Jav. also refers to a gamelan player, singer, dancer, or performer (also *pemukul/tukang pukul*; Minang. *tukang tapo*, Aceh. *pepale*)

panji (Jav.) (n.): lit. "prince," a master smith in a gong workshop (ref. Jacobsen and van Hasselt 1975)

parang (n.): large knife, similar to a machete; a common product of blacksmiths (also *bendo*; Dayak *parang* or *mandau*)

paron (n.): anvil (also *besi landasan/bantalan besi*; Toraj. *tandaran*; old Jav. *paron, parwan, parean, paryan*, etc.)

pasir besi (n.): iron sand; the most common product of modern iron mining and smelting methods

pateri/patri (n.): soldering compound

pateri/patri (v.): to solder

pattern welding (n.): see *mixed-metal forging*

pedang (n.): sword

pelat/plat (n.): sheet metal, metal plate

pelat besi/plat besi/besi lantai (n.): iron or steel plate, often from old ships

pelinggih (n.): place for offerings in a Balinese smithy; from *linggih*, seat

pemandian (Mad.) (n.): Madurese for smithy (from the root word *mandi*, to wash or bathe; the term *besalin* is also used on Madura)

pemukul (n.): hammer swinger (from the root word *pukul*, to hit; also *tukang pukul*; Jav. *panjak*)

penarik kawat (n.): tool used for making gold or silver wire; the traditional tool consists of a wooden board with a series of holes graduated in size; wire is pulled through with a winch and chain (also *penganden*)

pendok (n.): metal covering of the outer part of a *keris* sheath

penempa (n.): less common word for a smith who forges or forge-welds (from the root word *tempa*, to forge)

penganden (n.): see *penarik kawat*

pengarangan (n.): charcoal works or kiln; charcoal making (from the root word *arang*, charcoal)

pengecoran (n.): foundry, place where casting is done (from the root word *cor*, to melt)

pengusaha (n.): enterprise owner, entrepreneur (from the root word *usaha*, effort or enterprise)

penipis perak (n.): small machine to convert silver scrap to sheet; also called *rol perak, mesin pres perak, mesin mengiling perak, gulung perak*, etc.

pepale (Aceh.) (n.): Acehnese for hammer swinger (Jav. *panjak*; Indon. *tukang pukul* or *pemukul*)

per (n.): spring steel, commonly used as a raw material by blacksmiths

per mobil (n.): spring steel from old automobile springs and shock absorbers

per sepeda (n.): bicycle spokes, used as a raw material to make knives and other small tools

perak (n.): silver (also *selaka/salaka*)

perak bakar (n.): silver repoussé work with an oxidized background, popular in the Yogyakarta area

perapen/prapen/perapian (n.): smithy, fire hearth, or forge (from the root word *api*, fire; less commonly called *besalen* or *dapur*) (Toraj. *da'po bassi*; Minang. *apa basi*; Bug. *amanreang*; Mad. *besalen* or *pemandian*)

perarangan (n.): charcoal works or kiln (see also *pengarangan*)

permata (n.): precious or semiprecious stone set in a piece of jewelry (from the root word *mata*, eye)

pertambangan (n.): mining (from the root word *tambang*, mine)

perunggu (n.): bronze (also *gangsa/loyang/tembaga perunggu*)

pesi (n.): the tang of a blade that extends down into the handle

pig iron (n.): iron blanks or rods; smelted iron which has undergone some preliminary forging (similar to wrought iron) *pijar/memijar* (v.): to heat steel until it is red-hot and glowing; to temper steel (Bal. *mijer*)

pikul (n.) shoulder pole used to carry bags of charcoal, bundles of tools, etc.; also used as a measure, e.g. one *pikul* of charcoal, meaning two bags (one on each end of the pole)

pisau/piso (n.): knife (Balin. *teyuk*)

pisau dapur (n.): kitchen knife, a common product of blacksmiths

pis bolong/pipis bolong/kepeng (n.): antique copper or copper alloy coin with a square hole in the center, still used for offerings and images in Bali; imported from China beginning in the thirteenth century (probably the same as *pisis* coins mentioned in early inscriptions; Dayak *pisih*)

piston bellows (n.): a type of bellows, Southeast Asian in origin, made from a hollow tube (usually of wood or bamboo) through which a piston is pushed and pulled, thus forcing air out of the tube and into the fire; such bellows tend to be used in pairs and in a vertical position*

PJKA (n.): *Perusahaan Jawatan Kereta Api*, the government-owned company authorized to auction off railroad rails, one of the most common forms of raw material used by blacksmiths

plat (from the Dutch) (n.): metal plate, usually scavenged from wrecked ships or airplanes downed in the Second World War; commonly used as a raw material by blacksmiths

plat kapal (n.): ship plate

pompa (n.): a less common name for bellows (see *ubub*)

pondok (n.): small shed or shelter for working or sleeping; used in Aceh to mean smithy

potongan (n.): cuttings, e.g. iron cuttings (from the root word *potong*, to cut)

prada/perada/pradah (n.): powdered gold, traditionally imported from China, which is mixed with glue and used to paint designs on cloth; also gold leaf which is affixed with glue

punggawa (n.): used in South Sulawesi for a master smith or large enterprise owner; in Balin. *punggawa* is an aristocratic title meaning "lord" or "prince" (see *empu*; *pengusaha*)

puput (n.): a less common name for bellows (see *ubub*)

Pura Ratu Pande (n.): temple to Balinese smith deity (see *Ratu Pande*)

pusaka (n.): sacred heirloom, treasure, magically empowered talisman, or spirit-inhabited fetish; examples would include a ceremonial *keris*, gong, gold ornament, and sacred textile (Minang. *pusako*)

puup (n.): less common name for bellows; sometimes refers to the Chinese box bellows (ref. Thorburn 1982; see also *ubub*)

quench (v.): to strengthen an iron or steel blade by reheating until it is red hot and then plunging into water or (less commonly) oil; also temper (Indon. *sepuh/sepoh/menyepuh/menyepoh*)

quenching trough (n.): a container, often made of stone, which holds the water or oil used for quenching (Jav. *telawah*)

rangka (n.): framework, skeleton

rasa/air rasa/air perak (n.): mercury, used in mining to separate gold from the crystal and other minerals in which it is embedded; also used in fire gilding

Ratu Pande (n.): clan deity of Balinese blacksmiths; a temple to Ratu Pande is included in the Besakih complex on the slopes of Gunung Agung volcano

refractory (adj.): difficult to melt; said of clay, ore, or metal

rel/reli (n.): railroad rails, a major source of raw material for blacksmiths

rel besi (n.): iron or steel railroad rails

rencong (Aceh.) (n.): traditional Acehnese dagger, said to resemble the Arabic letter for Allah

repoussé (n.): a technique of decorating sheet metal with raised or embossed designs; designs are impressed from the back, usually with small hammers and punches

roasting (n.): the process of heating an ore in an open fire before smelting it in a furnace*

rol aluminium (n.): aluminum available in recent years in rolls of thin, factory-made sheet

rol perak (n.): small machine used by many silversmiths to make silver sheet (see *penipis perak*)

rol seng (n.): zinc available in recent years in rolls of thin, factory-made sheet

rosokan (n.): scrap metal (see *besi tua*)

sabit (n.): sickle, a common product of blacksmiths (also *arit*)

sadur (n.): metal plating

sadur mas (n.): gilding, gold plating (v. *menyadur mas*; more commonly called *sepoh mas*)

sajen (n.): an offering, e.g. offering to the fire hearth

sarung keris (n.): keris sheath

sarung peluru (n.): shell casings, commonly used as raw material by brass smiths (also called *kelonsong peluru*)

sayang (n.): copper or brass smith (also *gemblak/tukang gembleng/pandai tembaga/pandai kuningan*)

sela/sula (n.): old Jav. for "stone"; from Sanskrit *sila* (see *damar seta*)

senapan/senapang/sinapang (n.): rifle, musket, or gun; formerly made by casting smiths

seng (n.): zinc (also called *timah sari*)

senjata/sanjata (n.): weapons, usually of metal

sepuh/menyepuh/sepoh/menyepoh (v.): to temper metal, i.e. to fire-harden

an iron or steel blade by reheating and then quenching it in water or oil;
also to engage in the process of metal plating, e.g. to gold plate a piece
of silver jewelry (Toraj. *sapua*; Minang. *sapuah*); on Java old people or
ancestors are also called *sepuh/sepoh*

sepuh/penyepuh/sepoh/penyepoh (n.): liquid used for tempering metal or
for metal plating

sepuhan/sepohan (n.): items which have been metal-plated; often refers to
gilded jewelry

sepuh mas/sepoh mas (n.): gold plating, gilding, often on a base of silver

serok (n.): charcoal scoop used in the *perapen* for stoking the fire

slag: the residue of smelting, formed mainly from the ore components
that are not converted to metal while in the furnace; slags are liquid at
smelting temperatures—when cool they become more or less glasslike
solids that are often found by archaeologists* (Jav. *krawa*)

slaggery (n.): large pile of discarded slag; used by archeologists to identify
early smelting sites

sledger (n.): term used by Kahn (1980) to refer to hammer swingers in a
smithy (see *panjak*)

smelt (v.): to separate metal from metal-bearing ore by heating the ore,
usually in the presence of carbon monoxide

smelter (n.): one who smelts

smeltery (n.): place where smelting is done

smith (n.): any kind of metal worker who converts already smelted metal
into finished products (Indon. *pande/pandai/tukang*)

smithy (n.): place where forging is done (Indon. *perapen/besalen*)

socketed hafting (n.): technique of hafting whereby a handle of wood or
other material is inserted in a socket in the metal blade; used in early
Indonesian tools and later replaced by tanged hafting

solder (v.): to join two pieces of metal by means of a soldering compound
and the local application of heat (Indon. *pateri*)

soldering compound (n.): powdered mixture used in soldering; differs
according to the types of metal surfaces to be joined: a mixture of
powdered tin and lead is commonly used in repairing pots and pans; a
mixture of powdered copper, zinc, and resin in making copperware; silver
filings in making silver jewelry etc. (Indon. *pateri*)

steel (n.): an alloy of iron and carbon, carburized iron (Indon. *baja*)

steenkool (Dutch) (n.): coke, i.e. once-burned coal; used by blacksmiths on
Madura (also called *steenkolen/kokas*)

stoker (Dutch) (n.): person who keeps a cupola filled with a mixture of scrap
metal and fuel; used in the iron-casting village of Batur, Central Java

suasa/suwasa (n.): an alloy of gold and copper, favored by goldsmiths in
Aceh and North Sulawesi for its reddish gold color; also used for *keris
pendok* on Java

suku cadang (n.): spare parts for machinery, made of cast metal (also *onderdil*)

Sulawesi (n.): large island in Indon. archipelago which historically supplied Java with iron; both this name and the old Dutch name, Celebes, are corruptions of *sela wesi* or *sela besi*, i.e. iron stone or ore

suling (n.): lit. "flute," a tube made of clay or bamboo, through which the wind from the bellows reaches the fire hearth; often used in pairs — if two bamboo *suling* are used they are usually joined by a clay tuyere before they enter the fire hearth

sunglon (n.): special brace used by blacksmiths when filing tools; made from a pair of notched water buffalo horns, or from wood carved in the shape of horns

supit/sepit (n.): tongs, used by the *empu* to hold a tool while it is being forged (Toraj. *sisi*)

suvarna (from the Sanskrit word for gold) (n.): a unit of weight formerly used for metals, equal to 1/16 of a *kati*

Suvarnabhumi/Suvarnadvipa (Sanskrit) (n.): lit. "Land of Gold"/"Island of Gold," ancient Indian names for the Indonesian archipelago

tahi besi (n.): rust (also *karat/karatan*)

tailings (n.): the residual byproduct of commercial mining for metal ores or coal, usually heaped up in the vicinity of the mine; sometimes exploited by local villagers

tajam (adj.): sharp

taji (n.): small blades used for cockfighting; made in the same tradition as the *keris*

tambang (n.): mine; (v. *menambang*)

tambang besi (n.): iron mine

tambang mas (n.): gold mine

Tanah Datar (n.): valley in the Minangkabau highlands that was the source of most of the gold for which Sumatra was famous in the Early Historic period

tatah (n.): small chisel or engraver which is tapped on the end with a small hammer, made by blacksmiths, usually from old bicycle spokes; used for repoussé metal work, perforated leather work (e.g. *wayang* puppets), and wood carving; sometimes refers to metal work which is inlaid or set with gems

tang (n.): the part of a *keris* or other blade which extends down into the handle and is used for hafting (Indon. *pesi*)

tanged hafting (n.): technique of attaching blade to handle by means of a tang; thought to have been introduced from India

tap hole (n.): an opening in the side of a furnace through which liquid slag and metal can be tapped* *tapel* (n.): casting molds

telawah (n.): quenching trough (also called *kulah/kolah*)

tembaga/tambaga/tembaga merah (n.): copper

tembaga kuning (n.): brass (see *kuningan*)

tembaga putih (n.): used to refer to either nickel (also called *nekel*) or pewter (an alloy of tin and lead)

tempa/menempa (v.): to forge or forge-weld (Toraj. *tampa*; Dayak *manabasan*)

tempa Bali (n.): forged metal articles made in Bali

tempa Melaka (n.): forged metal articles made in Malacca, including a type of short *keris*

temper (v.): see *quench*

timah/timah putih (n.): tin

timah hitam/timah budeng (n.): lead (Balin. *timah siam*)

timah sari (n.): zinc (also called *seng/timah rek*)

tinker (n.): one who repairs pots and pans by patching, welding, and soldering (Indon. *tukang patri*)

toko besi (n.): iron scrap yard or hardware store

tombak/tumbak (n.): spear or lance used as a ceremonial weapon in Javanese courts and in temples on Bali

trisula (n.): trident used as a ceremonial weapon in Javanese courts and in temples and courts on Bali (Balin. *tumbak trisula*)

tua tambang (n.): head of a workgroup of miners in Minangkabau (also called *kepala tambang*; ref. Dobbin 1983)

tukang (n.): any kind of skilled worker or artisan

tukang asah (n.): a cutler; one who sharpens tools with a *batu asah* or grindstone; usually works out of the marketplace or goes door to door

tukang besi (n.): a blacksmith (more commonly *pandai besi*)

tukang gembleng (n.): a copper or brass smith (also *gemblak/pandai tembaga/pandai kuningan/sayang*)

tukang gending (n.): a gongsmith, maker of gamelan instruments (also *pande gong*)

tukang gerinda (n.): cutler (see *pandai gerinda*)

tukang kikir (n.): one who files and polishes tools; one of the four main jobs in a smithy

tukang kowi (n.): a worker who melts metal in a crucible in preparation for casting

tukang mas (n.): a goldsmith (also *pandai mas*)

tukang pateri (n.): a tinker or solderer, i.e. one who repairs pots and pans by patching, welding, and soldering; usually itinerant or works out of the marketplace

tukang perak (n.): a silversmith (also *pandai perak*)

tukang pukul (n.): hammer swinger in a smithy (see *panjak*) *tukang sepuh/tukang sepoh* (n.): a gilder

tukang ubub (n.): a bellows worker; one of the four main jobs in a smithy (Mad. *tukang gerbus*; Aceh. *tukang put-put angin*; Bug. *pasau*)

Tumpek Landep (n.): Balinese holiday when offerings are made to iron blades and all things made of iron

tungkik (n.): a small cupola made of oil drums and mounted on a swivel; used for iron casting in Batur village, Central Java (see also *kubah, kupola, dapur kupola*)

tungku (n.): most often refers to a ceramic kiln, but may refer to any type of hearth or fireplace; in Ngawen village (Central Java) refers to an enclosed furnace used for lost-wax casting

tuyere (n.): a tube, often of heat-resistant clay, through which air enters a furnace* (or a fire hearth) (Toraj. *po'poran*; Dayak *langit*, ref. Schwaner 1853)

uang logam (n.): coins, metal currency; once commonly used as raw material by metalsmiths

ubub (n.): bellows, usually the vertical double-piston Malay bellows; related to *puput, put-put, puup*, and the Old Jav. *upup* (Minang. *ambuih*; Toraj. *sauan*; Bugin. *asaung*; Dayak *abudan/baputan*; Mad. *gerbus*; Aceh. *put-put angin*)

ubub dorong (n.): Chinese box bellows (windbox bellows, push-pull bellows; see also *puup*)

ubub putar (n.): hand-turned rotary bellows, used principally in eastern Indonesia, probably invented in the twentieth century; often made of spare bicycle parts

ububan (n.): pair or set of bellows (less commonly *puputan*)

warangan (n.): arsenic, used to bring out the patterns in *pamor* blades

wedung (n.): cleaver or axe, often ceremonial (see *golok*)

weld (v.): to join two pieces of metal by heating and then hammering

wootz (n.): Indian crystalline steel, often mistaken for Indonesian *pamor* (known in India as *ukku*, ref. Solyom 1973)

wrought iron (n.): iron that has undergone some preliminary forging and hence has been partly carburized; usually contains less than 25 percent carbon

yoni (from the Sanskr.) (n.): symbolic representation of the vagina (see *lingga*)

Ann Dunham, Indonesia, and Anthropology —A Generation On

Robert W. Hefner

Director of the Institute on Culture, Religion,
and World Affairs at Boston University, and President
of the Association for Asian Studies, 2009–2010

BASED ON RESEARCH CONDUCTED from 1977 to 1991, S. Ann Dunham's *Surviving against the Odds* bears witness to her knowledge of and affection for the Southeast Asian nation of Indonesia. The book also speaks legions about Dunham's integrity as a cultural anthropologist. Both Indonesia and anthropology have changed since Dunham carried out the core portion of research in the mid-1980s, when I briefly met her in Yogyakarta. Comparing Dunham's Indonesia and the field of anthropology with what both have become today risks putting the reader at an even greater remove from the author's world. But the juxtaposition has the welcome benefit of providing insights into social change in contemporary Indonesia, as well as into Dunham herself, a sensitive observer of the human drama.

The Indonesia to which Dunham traveled in the late 1970s was still in the early years of recovery from decades of turmoil. Having enjoyed a heady period of parliamentary democracy from 1950 to 1957, in the late 1950s Indonesia began a steep political and economic decline. A Muslim-majority country (today 87 percent of the population professes Islam), the Indonesia of those years enjoyed the unusual distinction of having given rise to the largest communist party in the noncommunist world (Mortimer 1974). The communists' ascent prompted a counter-mobilization by Muslim organizations and the armed forces, both fiercely anticommunist. Meanwhile, economic mismanagement and a deteriorating national scene ensured that by 1964–65 Indonesia was suffering hyperinflation, infrastructural collapse, and in some parts of the archipelago (including Dunham's own Kajar) famine.

It was in the context of this downward political spiral that junior army officers with communist sympathies staged a coup in Jakarta the night of 30 September 1965. The coup quickly fizzled, but not before taking the lives of several conservative generals in the senior army command. In the months that followed, the surviving army leadership struck back with a vengeance, mobilizing special forces and civilian militias (recruited most heavily from Muslim organizations) to hunt down and kill several hundred thousand alleged communists, whom they blamed for the coup attempt (Cribb ed. 1990; Crouch 1978). Indonesia's New Order government (1966 to May 1998) emerged in the aftermath of this trauma.

Notwithstanding the violence and authoritarianism that marked much of its rule, the New Order regime succeeded in setting in motion the momentous political and economic changes to which Dunham's research attests. The government courted foreign investment, eventually creating a booming manufacturing sector (Booth and McCawley eds. 1981). It repaired and extended the country's degraded transport and administrative infrastructure. It constructed schools and raised average years of schooling to the level of middle-income countries. The period also saw the growth of a small but open-minded Muslim middle class. At the same time the regime muzzled the press, persecuted opponents, and kept a watchful eye on Muslim and pro-democracy activists (Hefner 2000; Schwarz 2000).

It was this battened-down but fast-moving Indonesia to which Dunham turned her attention in the late 1970s and 1980s. Trained by Alice Dewey, the most celebrated economic anthropologist of postwar Indonesia (see Dewey 1962), Dunham intended for her research on rural metalworking to fill a gap in the anthropological literature on economy and society in rural Java. Since the early independence era, models of change in Java had focused on lowland wet-rice cultivation, on the assumption that most rural residents were paddy farmers, and paddy farming was more lucrative than nonagricultural activities. As Dunham explains in chapter 1, the first of these assumptions is misleading: half of Java's agricultural lands are dry-fields, not paddy (Hefner 1990), and much of the rural population engages in what the anthropologist Ben White (1976, 1977) has called "occupational multiplicity," engaging in a variety of nonfarm as well as agricultural pursuits. The second assumption is also empirically inaccurate. Some rural enterprises are more lucrative than paddy farming, and among the more profitable are blacksmithing and other types of metalworking.

Dunham's aim, however, was not just to correct broad-stroke characterizations of rural Java's economy. Dunham was also intent on refuting portrayals of Indonesian peasants as tradition-bound and irrational, prone to placing diffuse social needs above precise economic calculations. The man most responsible for this simplistic characterization, which was central to the Netherlands variety of Orientalism, was the Dutch economist J. H. Boeke (Boeke 1953). At the time of Dunham's research the dissertation that Boeke submitted in 1910 at Leiden University was still being widely quoted by economists and development consultants in Indonesia; I can personally attest that it is cited in some policy circles still today.

Elements of the Boekean legacy also made their way into the economic analyses of Clifford Geertz, the most celebrated cultural anthropologist of Indonesia in the postwar era (Geertz 1960; Geertz 1963a; Geertz 1963b; Geertz 1965; Geertz 1973). Geertz's *Agricultural Involution* (1963a; see also 1963b) had argued that agriculture in Java was stagnant, village industries were in decline, and the prospects for any kind of developmental breakout were limited, because mainstream Javanese values are antithetical to commerce. For Geertz, rural Java's delicately hewn but unproductive economic forms, which he termed "agricultural involution," were both cause and consequence of the island's stagnation. They also underlay what Geertz described as the "flaccid indeterminateness" of Java's "dispirited communities" (Geertz 1963a, 129). The last of Geertz's characterizations was perhaps the oddest. It overlooked the fact that since the early twentieth century Java had been swept by a series of mass-based social movements, as well as new forms of religious association; the action frames and social organization of both were anything but static (cf. Jay 1963; Shiraishi 1990). In the 1980s Indonesia was recognized as having the largest and most dynamic Islamic social welfare organizations in the world (Feillard 1995; Hefner 2000; Nakamura 1983).

Producers of inexpensive farm tools, the blacksmiths on whom Dunham trained her attention seem at first sight to be an unlikely candidates to provide an alternative understanding of Javanese economy and society. However, in the best anthropological manner Dunham used small facts to speak to larger truths. Although Boeke and Geertz had both predicted the continuing decline of rural industry, blacksmithing and metalworking generally boomed in the 1970s and 1980s. The number of workers employed in small enterprises tripled from 1975 to 1987. Already at least as high as their agricultural counterpart, wages in blacksmithing increased. The wage structure also remained relatively egalitarian, with the ratio between profit to the owners and wages to hired workers staying low. The fruit of New Order programs, electricity also arrived in the countryside in the 1980s, and soon blacksmiths were buying inexpensive electrical machinery. They also began to make abundant use of bank credit. Meanwhile, a better-endowed segment of the metalworking industry moved upmarket, producing gold and silver handicrafts for foreign and domestic consumers. In describing these developments Dunham demonstrates that native industries in general, and blacksmithing in particular, were anything but adrift in involutionary doldrums.

The biggest of the truths to which Dunham dedicated her research, however, had to do with changes in class structures and the economic organization of which the growth of rural industries was part. Indeed, Dunham's observations on the emerging political economy of rural Indonesia are among the book's most prescient. Her findings on this topic also provide the clearest vantage point from which to assess what Indonesia has become a generation on, and to understand Dunham as an anthropologist and human observer.

Like most rural researchers working in Indonesia in the 1970s and 1980s, Dunham rejected the claim of Boeke and Geertz that rural Javanese society is characterized by "shared poverty" and a general lack of class differentiation (cf. Alexander 1987; Alexander and Alexander 1982; Hart 1986; White 1983). She rightly observed that rural Java was marked by significant socioeconomic stratification well before the late colonial era (cf. Breman 1982; Elson 1978; Fasseur 1975; Kolff 1936). The growth of stratification tended to be cyclical, increasing during moments of prosperity and diminishing during political-economic instability. The New Order era, Dunham noted, was a time of growing prosperity and class stratification. Paddy production surged, rural industries blossomed, and new and more expensive consumer goods, like televisions and motorbikes, made their way even into remote hinterlands. "Capital is the engine of stratification," Dunham writes. But she also understood that the shift toward a more capital-intensive commercial economy was a political as well as an economic event. As she notes in chapter 1, the change was premised on the emergence of a "powerful rural élite," to which officials of the state looked for "political stability and dissemination of its message about development" (cf. Hart 1986; Husken 1979).

Both contemporary and subsequent studies have confirmed Dunham's findings; indeed, if anything, the trends she observed proved greater than most of us at the time ever imagined possible. To cite another example, in the 1980s Indonesia's vast agricultural uplands were undergoing the most capital-intensive commercial revolution that Indonesia's smallholder sector had ever seen (Hefner 1990; Roche 1985; Palte 1984). Upland farmers deserted the cultivation of traditional low-yield staples like maize and dry rice, and invested in capital-intensive cash crops, including fruits, vegetables, cloves, and premium varieties of Arabica coffee. The capitalization of upland agriculture transformed what had once been among the poorest of agricultural zones into one of the most dynamic. With the boom came the producer and consumer items about which Dunham speaks in her less prosperous village of Kajar: radios, televisions, motorcycles, small trucks, and new clothing fashions. The commercial boom also brought government programs, all of which depended on the state's cultivation of a rural élite (cf. Kahn 1980).

In her determination to represent the contours of the new rural economy we get the clearest glimpse of Dunham as a social observer and policy advocate. The picture that emerges is one of a scholar deeply committed to interdisciplinary research, reluctant to follow academic fashions, and determined *not* to substitute ideological shortcuts for empirical research. Even when talking about as thorny an issue as the emergence of a new rural élite (chapter 3), her description is finely wrought and careful. While agreeing with other researchers that the New Order was giving rise to greater class differentiation, Dunham felt the need to give the development a human face. She reported that wealthier villagers in Kajar dressed simply, behaved modestly, and interacted courteously with their fellows. Even speech styles — social indices pregnant with meaning in Javanese society (Smith-Hefner 1989) — tended toward an unpretentious informality. Dunham noted that members of the rural élite also participated in household and village rituals, famous for their emphasis on commonality-within-difference.

Dunham was aware of the human costs of social inequality, as well as the political consequences of New Order repression. But it is a testimony to her sense of fairness that in gazing across the period's horizons, she did not allow patches of darkness to obliterate all light. In chapter 2 she takes note of what is arguably one of the most significant but understudied New Order achievements: that even in modest Kajar, "school attendance rates have gone up" and the use of child labor in rural industry and agriculture has diminished "dramatically." Another example of Dunham's evenhandedness is visible in her descriptions of the merchants (*empu pedagang*) who market the blacksmiths' manufactures. Yes, Dunham insists, "capital is the engine of stratification," and in the world of blacksmithing these merchants are the cutting edge of new class formations. But Dunham goes on to point out that rural commerce is not the iron cage of immobility that some researchers have assumed. Village industry, she observes, provides "an alternative avenue to wealth and prestige for ambitious individuals," even those from poor smallholder families. Standing back and summarizing the rural scene, she writes, "The ethnographic data in this book indicate that entrepreneurship is in plentiful supply in rural Java."

The passage of time since the 1980s inevitably recommends some adjustments to Dunham's narrative, two of which bear special mention here. Dunham's conclusion that rural Indonesia in the 1970s and 1980s was in the throes of a great transformation in inequality and popular welfare was prescient. In retrospect, however, and perhaps ironically, it appears that Dunham—like everyone else writing at the time—underestimated the breadth and depth of the transformations taking place.

With the advantage of historical hindsight, we can appreciate that there were good reasons for Dunham's caution. She carried out the ethnographic portion of her research in a small village in the Gunung Kidul district of Yogyakarta, in south central Java. The author's choice of locale was ideally suited for the detailed ethnographic portrait that she hoped to make of blacksmithing. However, Kajar and Gunung Kidul were less intimately involved in the New Order's political and economic upheavals than were rural districts near the booming industrial cities of Java's north coast, the special manufacturing zones in south Sumatra and the Riau archipelago, or the mixed-industrial and estate-agricultural zones of Kalimantan and Sulawesi. By comparison with these regions, Gunung Kidul in the 1980s was a backwater. Nonetheless, if one travels to the region today, as I did to conduct interviews in 1999 and 2003 (having first visited the area in 1979), one is struck by how Dunham got the basic pulse of the place right. Twenty years ago, even this out-of-the-way corner of Java was experiencing enormous change. A generation on, road building, tourism, irrigation projects, commercial agriculture, and public education have transformed the region even further. Rural areas closer than Gunung Kidul to Indonesia's vast industrial and agricultural estates have experienced even more momentous changes.

A second observation follows from this first. It is that the specifically social and religious aspects of the changes Dunham witnessed in Kajar during the 1980s have also continued and deepened. Two changes stand out. The first concerns social class. In chapter 6 Dunham observes that despite growing inequality, the lived experience of social class in Kajar and rural Java is not particularly severe: "Obvious class markers such as differences in speech patterns, dress styles, etc. are generally absent or are relatively subdued. Wealthy villagers . . . take care to dress simply, behave modestly, and interact with everyone in the village in a friendly and courteous manner. . . . Speech patterns are uniform, and everyone participates in a common cycle of rituals and ceremonies." I encountered a similar pattern of a gentler, communitarian class culture in the upland villages in East Java where I carried out research in the late 1970s and mid-1980s (Hefner 1983; Hefner 1985; Hefner 1990; cf. Palte 1984; Schrauwers 2000; Smith-Hefner 1989).

Even in the 1980s, however, it was clear that class structures in Java were complex, and their complexity was increasing as Java's commercial transformation accelerated. Unlike Kajar or upland East Java, Java's agricultural lowlands had been colonized and commercialized for the better part of two centuries (Elson 1978; Fasseur 1975). Lowland villagers had long since grown accustomed to living with pronounced class inequalities (Hart 1986; Knight 1982; Kolff 1936). Ostentatious displays of wealth did not take the extreme forms seen in starkly stratified parts of the world like northern India or north-

east Brazil, but they had a notably harsher feel than in Kajar or upland Java. Moreover, the commercial pulse that surged through most
of rural Indonesia in the 1980s and 1990s eventually brought this
outward-looking and differentiated class culture into hinterland regions, even to quiet Gunung Kidul.

There was a second, specifically religious dimension to the quickened
pace of social change in the 1990s, also not yet fully apparent in the
Kajar of the 1980s. In her comments in chapter 3, Dunham offers
quick but perceptive observations on religion and society in the Gunung Kidul region. She comments, for example, that "Gunung Kidul
was and still is a strongly *abangan* cultural area, where Islam never
fully penetrated and where pre-Islamic beliefs and rituals prevail." Although most see themselves as Muslims, the abangan are Javanese
who adhere to a syncretic tradition which blends elements of nor-
mative Islam with ancestral and guardian-spirit veneration (complete
with food offerings; see Geertz 1960; Lyon 1970). A telltale index of an
abangan stronghold, at the time of Dunham's research Kajar did not
even have a mosque. Villagers celebrated religious holidays of a Javo-
Islamic rather than strictly Muslim nature.

In 2003 I collected oral histories on religious change in a village
just eight kilometers from Dunham's Kajar. Twenty years earlier, the
village had been an abangan stronghold like Dunham's community,
and most residents were uninterested in Islamic learning. By the mid-
1990s, however, even backwater villages in Gunung Kidul were feeling the effects of Indonesia's ongoing Islamic resurgence. My inter-
viewees recounted that just as in nearby Kajar, relations between
abangan and the observant Muslims known as *santri* had become
strained after the violence of 1965–66, which local villagers saw as the
work of santri Muslims (cf. Huizer 1974; Walkin 1969). Indeed, in the
early 1970s there was a small uptick in conversion to Christianity and
Hinduism in the region, as a few abangan shocked by the events of
1965–66 opted to exit Islam entirely (cf. Hefner 1993; Hefner 2004;
Lyon 1980).

The turn from Islam did not go deep, however; nor did it last long. In
the early 1980s formerly abangan villages in the Gunung Kidul region
began to do as their counterparts in many other parts of Java were
doing: build mosques, sponsor evening classes for Qur'anic recitation,
and dress in what most regarded as a more Islamic manner (Hefner

1987a; Hefner 1987b; Pranowo 1991). A decade later the trickle had turned into a flood, and the district was experiencing a full-blown Islamic resurgence. Some aspects of the resurgence showed the clear imprint of government programs, such as the two hours of weekly religious instruction required in all schools (Boland 1982). But the great religious reorientation was also the fruit of efforts by nongovernmental Islamic groups, including the "traditionalist" Nahdlatul Ulama (some forty million followers; Feillard 1995) and the "modernist" Muhammadiyah (some twenty-five million followers; Nakamura 1983). In the 1970s both of these organizations had identified Gunung Kidul as a target of proselytizing opportunity. They channeled resources into mosque building, madrasa education, and religious "appeal" (Ind. *dakwah*, Ar. *da'wa*). Today Gunung Kidul is not by any measure a bastion of strict-constructionist Islam. But it is no longer the "strongly *abangan* cultural area" it was a generation ago. This too is an important part of what Java has become.

An afterword is not the place for psychoanalytic speculation on the personality of a now deceased scholar, least of all one whom the afterword's author met only once. However, in reading Dunham's book, and in reflecting on it from the perspective of having conducted research in Java over the same period, I cannot help being struck by the independence and integrity of the author. Dunham was writing at a time when economic anthropology was a declining influence in Indonesian studies, and policy-oriented scholarship was disesteemed. A generation earlier, Clifford Geertz and Alice Dewey, members of the Harvard-based "Modjokuto" project of the early 1950s, had lain what appeared to be a solid foundation for the economic anthropology of Indonesia. In parts of the world like Latin America and sub-Saharan Africa, economic anthropology has evolved, but it has remained an important part of the academic scene to this day. In the wing of Indonesian studies based in the United States, however, economic anthropology in the 1980s lost ground to more strictly cultural approaches. The change took place despite the best efforts of economic anthropologists based outside the United States, including Jennifer Alexander, Sven Cederroth, Frans Husken, Tania Li, and Ben White.

The reasons for economic anthropology's loss of prominence in American Indonesian studies are too complex to outline here. But one influence merits mention: the ambiguous legacy of Clifford Geertz.

It is hard to exaggerate the scope of Geertz's influence in the Indonesian studies of the 1980s and 1990s. Reflecting his training in Weberian and Parsonian social theory, in the 1950s and early 1960s the young Geertz had grappled with the question of how to integrate culture into models of economic action. However, in later years he lost interest in this effort, and in formal methodologies in general. He shifted attention to an approach influenced by textual studies that he called "thick description" (Geertz 1973; cf. Geertz 1984). Whatever its achievements, which were impressive, in Indonesian studies in the United States Geertz's textualist turn had a damping effect on interest in the formal models of deliberation and "embedded" organization favored in economic anthropology, including that of Ann Dunham.

In the presentation I heard her give in Yogyakarta in 1985, Dunham signaled her awareness that cultural anthropologists of Indonesia were turning away from the type of economic anthropology to which she had dedicated herself. With her eclectic mix of economic analysis, ethnography, and policy recommendations, Dunham made it clear that she was determined to continue to swim against this tide. My sense that afternoon, and in reading her book two decades later, is that her reasons for this choice had less to do with academic fashion than with her deep affection for Indonesia and Indonesians. By the mid-1980s Dunham had begun to see the audience for her work as made up of not just academics but Indonesians, aid workers, and foreign analysts whose findings affect the lives of ordinary Indonesians. Rather than go with the academic flow, Dunham stayed true to a research program requiring varied and rigorous methodologies, all in an effort to speak truth to power and policy making.

This impression has remained with me over the years since that quiet afternoon in Yogyakarta more than twenty years ago. Like her book, her talk conveyed the sense of a scholar concerned about inequality and social justice. But her personality and writing style laced those commitments with other, no-less-interesting qualities: deep respect for the villagers with whom she had worked, an antipathy for ideological phrasings, and, not least, a reasoned hope for pathways toward a better future. In all these respects I hope that other readers might share my impression: that Ann Dunham's legacy remains relevant today for anthropology, Indonesian studies, and engaged scholarship.

References

Alexander, Jennifer. 1987. *Trade, Traders, and Trading in Rural Java*. Singapore: Oxford University Press.

Alexander, Jennifer, and Paul Alexander. 1982. "Shared Poverty as Ideology: Agrarian Relationships in Colonial Java." *Man*, n.s. 17, 597–619.

Boeke, J. H. 1953. *Economics and Economic Policy of Dual Societies, as Exemplified by Indonesia*. New York: Institute of Pacific Relations.

Boland, B. J. 1982. *The Struggle of Islam in Modern Indonesia*. The Hague: Martinus Nijhoff.

Booth, Anne, and Peter McCawley, eds. 1981. *The Indonesian Economy during the Soeharto Era*. Kuala Lumpur: Oxford University Press.

Breman, Jan. 1982. "The Village on Java and the Early-Colonial State." *Journal of Peasant Studies* 9, 189–240.

Cribb, Robert, ed. 1990. *The Indonesia Killings, 1965–1966: Studies from Java and Bali*. Clayton (Australia): Monash Papers on Southeast Asia no. 21, Centre of Southeast Asian Studies, Monash University.

Crouch, Harold. 1978. *The Army and Politics in Indonesia*. Ithaca: Cornell University Press.

Dewey, Alice G. 1962. *Peasant Marketing in Java*. Glencoe, Ill.: Free Press.

Elson, R. E. 1978. "The Cultivation System and 'Agricultural Involution.'" Research Paper no. 14. Monash University, Centre of Southeast Asian Studies.

Fasseur, C. 1975. *Kultuurstelsel en koloniale baten: De Nederlands exploitatie van Java, 1840–1860*. Leiden: Universitaire Pers.

Feillard, Andrée. 1995. *Islam et armée dans l'Indonésie contemporaine*. Cahiers d'Archipel 28. Paris: L'Harmattan.

Geertz, Clifford. 1960. *Religion of Java*. New York: Free Press.

———. 1963a. *Agricultural Involution: The Processes of Ecological Change in Indonesia*. Berkeley: University of California Press.

———. 1963b. *Peddlers and Princes: Social Change and Economic Modernization in Two Indonesian Towns*. Chicago: University of Chicago Press.

———. 1965. *The Social History of an Indonesian Town*. Cambridge: MIT Press.

———. 1973. "Thick Description: Toward an Interpretive Theory of Culture." *The Interpretation of Cultures*, 3–30. New York: Basic.

———. 1984. "Culture and Social Change: The Indonesian Case." *Man*, n.s. 19, 511–32.

Hart, Gillian. 1986. *Power, Labor, and Livelihood: Process of Change in Rural Java*. Berkeley: University of California Press.

Hefner, Robert W. 1983. "The Problem of Preference: Ritual and Economic Change in Highland Java." *Man*, n.s. 18, 669–89.

———. 1985. *Hindu Javanese: Tengger Tradition and Islam*. Princeton: Princeton University Press.

———. 1987a. "The Political Economy of Islamic Conversion in Modern East Java." *Islam and the Political Economy of Meaning: Comparative Studies in Muslim Discourse*, ed. William R. Roff, 53–78. London: Croom Helm.

———. 1987b. "Islamizing Java? Religion and Politics in Rural East Java." *Journal of Asian Studies* 46, 533–54.

———. 1990. *The Political Economy of Mountain Java: An Interpretive History*. Berkeley: University of California Press.

———. 1993. "Of Faith and Commitment: Christian Conversion in Muslim Java." *Conversion to Christianity: Historical and Anthropological Perspectives on a Great Transformation*, 99–125. Berkeley: University of California Press.

———. 2000. *Civil Islam: Muslims and Democratization in Indonesia*. Princeton: Princeton University Press.

———. 2004. "Hindu Reform in an Islamizing Java: Pluralism and Peril." *Hinduism in Modern Indonesia: A Minority Religion between Local, National, and Global Interests*, ed. Martin Ramstedt, 93–108. Leiden: KITLV.

Huizer, Gerrit. 1974. "Peasant Mobilisation and Land Reform in Indonesia." *Review of Indonesian and Malayan Affairs* 8, no. 1, 81–138.

Husken, F. 1979. "Landlords, Sharecroppers and Agricultural Labourers: Changing Labour Relations in Rural Java." *Journal of Contemporary Asia* 9, 140–51.

Jay, Robert R. 1963. *Religion and Politics in Rural Central Java*. Cultural Report Series no. 12. Yale University, Program in Southeast Asia Studies.

Kahn, Joel. 1980. *Minangkabau Social Formations: Indonesian Peasants and the World Economy*. Cambridge: Cambridge University Press.

Knight, G. R. 1982. "Capitalism and Commodity Production in Java." *Capitalism and Colonial Production*, ed. H. Alavi, P. L. Burns, G. R. Knight, P. B. Mayer, and Doug McEachern, 119–58. London: Croom Helm.

Kolff, G. van der. 1936. "The Historical Development of Labour Relationships in a Remote Corner of Java as They Apply to the Cultivation of Rice." Report C. Amsterdam: National Council for the Netherlands and the Netherlands Indies, Institute of Pacific Relations.

Lyon, M. L. 1970. *Bases of Conflict in Rural Java*. Research Monograph no. 3, University of California, Center for South and Southeast Asia Studies.

———. 1980. "The Hindu Revival in Java: Politics and Religious Identity." *Indonesia: The Making of a Culture*, ed. James J. Fox, 205–20. Canberra: Research School of Pacific Studies.

Mortimer, Rex. 1974. *Indonesian Communism under Sukarno: Ideology and Politics, 1959–1965*. Ithaca: Cornell University Press.

Nakamura, Mitsuo. 1983. *The Crescent Arises over the Banyan Tree: A Study of the Muhammadiyah Movement in a Central Javanese Town*. Yogyakarta: Gadjah Mada University Press.

Palte, Jan G. L. 1984. *The Development of Java's Rural Uplands in Response to Population Growth: An Introductory Essay in Historical Perspective*. Yogyakarta: Gadjah Mada University, Faculty of Geography.

Pranowo, Bambang. 1991. "Creating Islamic Tradition in Rural Java." Ph.D. thesis, Clayton, Victoria: Department of Anthropology, Monash University.

Roche, Frederick C. 1985. "East Java's Upland Agriculture: Historical Development, Recent Changes, and Implications for Research." Working paper. Malang, East Java: Brawijaya University, Agricultural Research Institute.

Schrauwers, Albert. 2000. *Colonial "Reformation" in the Highlands of Central Sulawesi, Indonesia, 1892–1995*. Toronto: University of Toronto Press.

Schwarz, Adam. 2000. *A Nation in Waiting: Indonesia's Search for Stability*. Boulder: Westview.

Shiraishi, Takashi. 1990. *An Age in Motion: Popular Radicalism in Java, 1912–1926*. Ithaca: Cornell University Press, 1990.

Smith-Hefner, Nancy J. 1989. "A Social History of Language Change in Mountain East Java." *Journal of Asian Studies* 48, 258–71.

Walkin, Jacob. 1969. "The Moslem-Communist Confrontation in East Java, 1964–65." *Orbis* 13, no. 3, 822–47.

White, Benjamin. 1976. "Population, Employment and Involution in a Javanese Village." *Development and Change* 7, 267–90.

———. 1977. "Rural Household Studies in Anthropological Perspective." Occasional paper. Bogor, Java: Agricultural Development Council.

———. 1983. "Agricultural Involution and Its Critics: Twenty Years after Clifford Geertz." Working Paper Series no. 6. The Hague: Institute of Social Studies.

BIBLIOGRAPHY

The naming system in Indonesia varies among its many cultures, but a large number do not use family names, and therefore many Indonesians, particularly Javanese, have only one name. Even when Indonesians have two or more names, the last name is not necessarily or even usually a family name. Indonesian bibliographies often alphabetize according to the first name rather than the last. I have nonetheless alphabetized according to the last name, feeling that this would be less confusing to non-Indonesian readers.

Alatas, Syed H. *Modernization and Social Change*. 1972. Sydney: Angus and Robertson.

———. 1977. *The Myth of the Lazy Native*. London: Frank Cass.

Alexander, Jennifer. 1987. *Trade, Traders, and Trading in Rural Java*. Singapore: Oxford University Press.

Alexander, Jennifer, and Paul Alexander. 1978. "Sugar, Rice and Irrigation in Colonial Java." *Ethnohistory* 25, 207–23.

———. 1979. "Labour Demands and the 'Involution' of Javanese Agriculture." *Social Analysis* 3, 22–44.

———. 1982. "Shared Poverty as Ideology: Agrarian Relationships in Colonial Java." *Man*, n.s. 17, 597–619.

Arief, Sritua, and Adi Sasono. 1980. *Indonesia: Dependency and Underdevelopment*. Kuala Lumpur: Meta.

Association for Advancement of Small Business. 1988. *The Struggle of Small Enterprises: The Case of Small Industries Ceramic, Plered, and Ironmongerey, Ciwidey*. Bandung: Association for the Advancement of Small Business.

Bellwood, Peter. 1985. *Prehistory of the Indo-Malaysian Archipelago*. Sydney: Academic.

Benda, Harry J. 1962. "The Structure of Southeast Asian History: Some Preliminary Observations." *Journal of Southeast Asian History* 3, no. 1, 106–38.

———. 1966. Review of Clifford Geertz, *The Social History of an Indonesian Town*. *American Anthropologist* 68, 1542–45.

Boediono. 1986. "Strategi Industrialisasi." *Prisma* 1 (January).

Boeke, J. H. 1953. *Economics and Economic Policy of Dual Societies, as Exemplified by Indonesia.* New York: Institute of Pacific Relations [contains *The Structure of the Netherlands Indian Economy* (1942) and *The Evolution of the Netherlands Indian Economy* (1946)].

———. 1954. "Western Influence on the Growth of the Eastern Population." *Economica Internazionale* 7, 358–69.

———. 1966. *Indonesian Economics.* The Hague: W. van Hoeve.

———. 1980. "Dualism in Colonial Societies." *Sociology of South-East Asia: Readings on Social Change and Development*, ed. Hans-Dieter Evers. Kuala Lumpur: Oxford University Press [repr. from *Indonesian Economics*, 167–92].

Booth, Anne. 1985. "Accommodating a Growing Population in Javanese Agriculture." *Bulletin of Indonesian Economic Studies* 21, 115–43.

———. 1988. *Agricultural Development in Indonesia.* Sydney: Allen and Unwin.

Booth, Anne, and Peter McCawley. 1981. "The Indonesian Economy since the Mid-Sixties." *The Indonesian Economy during the Soeharto Era*, ed. Anne Booth and Peter McCawley, 1–22.

Booth, Anne, and Peter McCawley, eds. 1981. *The Indonesian Economy during the Soeharto Era.* Kuala Lumpur: Oxford University Press.

Boserup, Ester. 1965. *The Conditions of Agricultural Growth: The Economics of Change under Popular Pressure.* London: George Allen and Unwin.

Breman, Jan. 1980. *The Village on Java and the Early Colonial State.* Erasmus University, Rotterdam, Comparative Asian Studies Program Series, no. 1.

Bronson, Bennet, and Pisit Charoenwongsa. 1986. *Eyewitness Accounts of the Early Mining and Smelting of Metals in Mainland South East Asia.* Bangkok: Thailand Academic Publishing.

Bruner, E. M. 1966. "Review: Peddlers and Princes; Social Change and Economic Modernization in Two Indonesian Towns: Clifford Geertz." *American Anthropologist* 68, 255–58.

Budi, R. P. 1981. "Pengembangan Kesempatan Kerja Nonpertanian di Pedesaan Indonesia" [The development of nonagricultural work opportunities in rural Indonesia]. *Analisa* 10, 220–33.

Burger, D. H. 1954. "Boeke's Dualisme." *Indonesie* 7, no. 3 (January), 177–98.

———. 1956. "Structural Changes in Javanese Society: The Supra-Village Sphere." Ithaca: Cornell University Modern Indonesia Project Translation Series.

Carey, P. 1981. "Waiting for the *ratu adil*: The Javanese Village Community on the Eve of the Java War (1825–1830)." Paper presented at the Anglo-Dutch Conference on Comparative Colonial History, Leiden.

Catley, Bob. 1976. "The Development of Underdevelopment in South-east Asia." *Journal of Contemporary Asia* 6, no. 1, 54–74 [repr. in *Sociology of*

South-East Asia: Readings on Social Change and Development, ed. Hans-Dieter Evers, 262–76 (Kuala Lumpur: Oxford University Press, 1980)].

Central Bureau of Statistics. 1973. *Laporan Industri Kecil / Kerajinan Rumah Tangga* [Report on small-scale manufacturing and handicraft]. *1972*. Jakarta: Central Bureau of Statistics [text in Indonesian only; tables in Indonesian and English].

———. 1974. *Laporan Industri Kecil / Kerajinan Rumah Tangga* [Report on small-scale manufacturing and handicraft]. *1973*. Jakarta: Central Bureau of Statistics [text in Indonesian only; tables in Indonesian and English].

———. 1977. *1974/1975 Industrial Census: Household and Cottage Industries*. Jakarta: Central Bureau of Statistics [Indonesian and English].

———. 1978. *1974/1975 Industrial Census: Small Manufacturing Establishments in Indonesia*. Jakarta: Central Bureau of Statistics [Indonesian and English].

———. 1985. *Susenas 1982: Report on Cottage Industry*. Jakarta: Central Bureau of Statistics [Indonesian and English].

———. 1987a. *Analisa Pendahuluan Hasil Sensus Ekonomi 1986* [Preliminary analysis of the results of the 1986 economic census]. Jakarta: Central Bureau of Statistics.

———. 1987b. *Analisa Perbandingan Industry Besar/Sedang, Kecil dan Rumahtangga* [Comparative analysis of large/medium, small and cottage industries]. Jakarta: Central Bureau of Statistics.

———. 1988. *Mining and Quarrying Statistics, Unincorporated Enterprises, 1986*. Jakarta: Central Bureau of Statistics [Indonesian and English].

———. 1989a. *Economic Census 1986: Home Industry Statistics, 1986*. Jakarta: Central Bureau of Statistics [Indonesian and English].

———. 1989b. *Economic Census 1986: Home Industry Statistics, 1987*. Jakarta: Central Bureau of Statistics [Indonesian and English].

———. 1989c. *Economic Census 1986: Small Scale Manufacturing Industry Statistics*. Jakarta: Central Bureau of Statistics [Indonesian and English].

———. 1990a. *Statistical Year Book of Indonesia*. Jakarta: Central Bureau of Statistics [Indonesian and English].

———. 1990b. *Labor Force Situation in Indonesia, 1989*. Jakarta: Central Bureau of Statistics [Indonesian and English].

———. 1990c. *Upah Buruh Menurut Jenis Pekerjaan* [Wages for hired workers by type of employment], *1989*. Jakarta: Central Bureau of Statistics [Indonesian only].

Chalmers, Ian. 1989. "How Relevant Is the Concept of Take-off?" Editor's introduction to dialogue section in *Prisma* 48 (December), 22–24.

Chen, Peter. 1980. "The Cultural Implications of Industrialization and Modernization in South-east Asia." *Sociology of South-east Asia: Readings on Social Change and Development*, ed. Hans-Dieter Evers. Kuala Lumpur: Oxford University Press.

Chuta, E., and S. V. Sethuraman. 1984. *Rural Small-Scale Industries and Employment in Africa and Asia: A Review of Programmes and Policies*. Geneva: International Labour Organisation.

Collier, William. 1981a. "Acceleration of Rural Development in Java." *Bulletin of Indonesian Economic Studies* 18, 84–101.

———. 1981b. "Agricultural Evolution in Java." *Agricultural and Rural Development in Indonesia*, ed. G Hansen, 147–73. Boulder: Westview.

———. 1981c. "Declining Labour Absorption (1878–1980) in Javanese Rice Production." *Kajian Ekonomi Malaysia*, 102–36.

Collier, William, et al. 1988. "Employment Trends in Lowland Javanese Villages." Paper prepared for U.S. Agency for International Development, April.

Cook, Scott. 1968. *Teitipac and Its Metateros: An Economic Anthropological Study of Production and Exchange in a 'Peasant-Artisan' Economy in the Valley of Oaxaca, Mexico*. Ph.D. diss., University of Pittsburgh.

———. 1970. "Price and Output Variability in a Peasant-Artisan Stoneworking Industry in Oaxaca, Mexico: An Analytical Essay in Economic Anthropology." *American Anthropologist* 72, no. 4, 776–801.

Dapice, David, and Donald Snodgrass. 1979. "Employment in Manufacturing, 1970–1977: Comment." *Bulletin of Indonesian Economic Studies*, 6 June [reply to McCawley and Tait].

Department of Industry, Republic of Indonesia. 1988. *Sekar Lati: Panduan Belanja Industri Kecil* [Melati flowers: Small industry shopping guide]. Jakarta: Department of Industry.

Dewey, Alice G. 1962. *Peasant Marketing in Java*. Glencoe, Ill.: Free Press.

Dobbin, Christine. 1983. *Islamic Revivalism in a Changing Peasant Economy: Central Sumatra, 1784–1847*. London: Curzon Press for the Scandinavian Institute of Asian Studies.

Donges, Juergen, et al. 1980. "Industrialization in Indonesia." *The Indonesian Economy*, ed. Gustav Papanek. New York: Praeger.

Donges, Juergen, Bernd Stecher, and Frank Wolter. 1974. *Industrial Development Policies for Indonesia*. Tübingen: J. C. B. Mohr.

Elson, R. E. 1978. "The Cultivation System and 'Agricultural Involution.'" Monash University, Centre of Southeast Asian Studies.

Evers, Hans-Dieter. 1980. "The Challenge of Diversity: Basic Concepts and Theories in the Study of South-East Asian Societies." *Sociology of South-East Asia: Readings on Social Change and Development*, 2–7. Kuala Lumpur: Oxford University Press.

———, ed. 1973. *Modernization in Southeast Asia*. Kuala Lumpur: Oxford University Press.

———, ed. 1980. *Sociology of South-east Asia: Readings on Social Change and Development*. Kuala Lumpur: Oxford University Press.

Firth, Raymond. 1966 [1946], 2nd edn. *Malay Fishermen: Their Peasant Economy*. London: Routledge and Kegan Paul.

Francis, Peter, Jr. 1991. "Beads and the Bead Trade in Southeast Asia." Paper distributed to accompany a lecture at the Ganesha Society, Jakarta, 19 March.

Frank, Andre Gunder. 1973. "Sociology of Development and Underdevelopment of Sociology." *Latin America: Underdevelopment or Revolution: Essays on the Development of Underdevelopment and the Immediate Enemy*, 21–94. New York: Monthly Review Press.

Furnivall, J. S. 1930. *Christianity and Buddhism: An Address to the Rangoon Diocesan Council, August 1929*. Rangoon: People's Literature Committee and House.

———. 1944. *Netherlands India: A Study of Plural Economy*. New York: Macmillan.

———. 1948. *Colonial Policy and Practice: A Comparative Study of Burma and Netherlands India*. Cambridge: Cambridge University Press.

Geertz, Clifford. 1956. *The Development of the Javanese Economy: A Sociocultural Approach*. Cambridge: MIT Press.

———. 1963a. *Agricultural Involution: The Processes of Ecological Change in Indonesia*. Berkeley: University of California Press.

———. 1963b. *Peddlers and Princes: Social Development and Economic Change in Two Indonesian Towns*. Chicago: University of Chicago Press.

———. 1973. Comments on Benjamin White's "Demand for Labor and Population Growth in Colonial Java." *Human Ecology* 1, 237–39.

Glassburner, Bruce, ed. 1971. *The Economy of Indonesia: Selected Readings*. Ithaca: Cornell University Press.

Gordon, A. 1978. "Some Problems of Analyzing Class Relations in Indonesia." *Journal of Contemporary Asia* 8, 210–18.

Hall, D. G. E. 1981. *A History of South-east Asia*, 4th edn. London: Macmillan.

Hall, Kenneth R. 1985. *Maritime Trade and State Development in Early Southeast Asia*. Honolulu: University of Hawaii Press.

Harris, M. 1970. *The Rise of Anthropological Theory: A History of Theories of Culture*. New York: Thomas Y. Crowell.

Hart, Gillian. 1978. "Labor Allocation Strategies in Rural Javanese Households." Ph.D. diss., Cornell University.

———. 1981. "Patterns of Household Labour Allocation in a Javanese Village." *Rural Household Studies in Asia*, ed. Hans P. Binswanger et al. Singapore: Singapore University Press.

———. 1986. *Power, Labor, and Livelihood: Processes of Change in Rural Java*. Berkeley: University of California Press.

Hart, Gillian, et al., eds. 1989. *Agrarian Transformations: Local Process and the State in Southeast Asia*. Berkeley: University of California Press.

Hartmann, Joerg. 1985. *Landlessness and Rural Employment in Indonesia.* Rome: Food and Agriculture Organization.

Heidjrachman, R. 1974. *Pengembangan Industri Kecil dan Kerajinan Rakyat di Daerah Istimewa Yogyakarta* [Development of small industries and people's handicrafts in Yogyakarta Special Region]. Lembaga Penelitian Ekonomi, Fakultas Ekonomi, Universitas Gadjah Mada, Yogyakarta.

Heinen, E., and Hermine Weijland. 1989. "Rural Industry in Progress and Decline." *About Fringes, Margins and Lucky Dips: The Informal Sector in Third World Countries*, ed. P. van Gelder and J. Bijlmer. Amsterdam: Free University Press.

Higgins, Benjamin H. 1955a. "The 'Dualistic Theory' of Underdeveloped Areas." *Ekonomi dan Keangan Indonesia* 7, 58–78 [repr. in *Economic Development and Cultural Change* 4 (1956), 99–115; also repr. in *Sociology of Southeast Asia: Readings on Social Change and Development*, ed. Hans-Dieter Evers, 46–56 (Kuala Lumpur: Oxford University Press, 1980)].

———. 1955b. "Economic Development of Underdeveloped Areas: Past and Present." *Land Economics* 31, no. 3, 179–95.

———. 1957. *Indonesia's Economic Stablization and Development.* New York: Institute of Pacific Relations.

———. 1968. *Economic Development, Principles, Problems and Policies*, rev. edn. New York: W. W. Norton.

Hoselitz, B. F. 1966. "Interaction between Industrial and Preindustrial Stratification System." *Social Structure and Mobility in Economic Development*, ed. N. J. Smelser and S. M. Lipset, 177–93. Chicago: Aldine.

Hughes, Helen. 1971. "The Manufacturing Industry Sector." *Southeast Asia's Economy in the 1970s*, by the Asian Development Bank, 186–251. New York: Praeger.

Husken, Frans, and Benjamin White. 1989. "Java: Social Differentiation, Food Production and Agrarian Control." *Agrarian Transformations: Local Process and the State in Southeast Asia*, ed. Gillian Hart et al., 235–65. Berkeley: University of California Press.

Itagaki, Yoichi. 1963. "Criticism of Rostow's Stage Approach: The Concepts of State, System and Type." *Developing Economies* 1, no. 1, 8–17.

———. 1968. "A Review of the Concept of the Dual Economy." *Developing Economies* 6, no. 2, 143–51 [repr. in *Sociology of South-east Asia: Readings on Social Change and Development*, ed. Hans-Dieter Evers, 66–75. Kuala Lumpur: Oxford University Press, 1980)].

Jacobson, Edward, and J. H. van Hasselt. 1975. "The Manufacture of Gongs in Semarang." *Indonesia* 19, 127–52, with 4 pages of key and 14 pages of plates [transl. by Andrew Toth of orig. Dutch edn published Leiden, 1907, by Rijksmuseum voor Volkenkunde].

Jaspan, M. A. 1961. *Social Stratification and Social Mobility in Indonesia: A Trend Report and Annotated Bibliography.* Jakarta: Gunung Agung.

————. 1965. "Review: Agricultural Involution: The Process of Ecological Change in Indonesia. Clifford Geertz." *Man* 65, 132–33.

————. 1975. "A Note on Palembang in 1832: Urban Manufacturing and the Work-Force." *Berita Kajian Sumatera* 4, no. 2, 5–8.

Jay, Robert R. 1963. *Religion and Politics in Rural Central Java*. Cultural Report Series no. 12. Yale University, Program in Southeast Asia Studies.

————. 1969. *Javanese Villagers: Social Relations in Rural Modjokuto*. Cambridge: MIT Press.

Kahn, Joel S. 1975. "Economic Scale and the Cycle of Petty Commodity Production in West Sumatra." *Marxist Analyses and Social Anthropology*, ed. Maurice Bloch, 137–58. New York: John Wiley and Sons.

————. 1980. *Minangkabau Social Formations: Indonesian Peasants and the World Economy*. Cambridge: Cambridge University Press.

————. 1982. "From Peasants to Petty Commodity Production in Southeast Asia." *Bulletin of Concerned Asian Scholars* 14, 3–15.

Kano, Hiroshi. 1980. "The Economic History of Javanese Rural Society: A Reinterpretation." *Developing Economies* 17, 3–22.

Kantor Statistik, Kabupaten Gunungkidul. 1990. *Gunung Kidul Dalam Angka* [Gunung Kidul in figures], *1989*. Wonosari: Kantor Statistik.

Kasryno, F., ed. 1984. *Prospek Pembangunan Ekonomi Pedesaan Indonesia* [Prospects for developing Indonesia's rural economy]. Jakarta: Yayasan Obor Indonesia.

Keyfitz, Nathan. 1985. "An East Javanese Village in 1953 and 1985: Observations on Development." *Population and Development Review* 11, no. 4, 695–719.

Koentjaraningrat. 1961. *Some Social-Anthropological Observations on Gotong Rojong Practices in Two Villages of Central Java*. Trans. Claire Holt. Cornell University, Modern Indonesia Project Monograph Series.

————. 1967. "Tjelepar: A Village in South Central Java." *Villages in Indonesia*, ed. Koentjaraningrat, 244–80. Ithaca: Cornell University Press.

————. 1975. *Anthropology in Indonesia: A Bibliographical Review*. The Hague: Martinus Nijhoff.

————. 1985. *Javanese Culture*. New York: Oxford University Press.

————, ed. 1967. *Villages in Indonesia*. Ithaca: Cornell University Press.

Kroeber, A. L. 1948. *Anthropology: Race, Language, Culture, Psychology, Pre-History*. New York: Harcourt, Brace.

Kuntowidjojo. 1977. "Economic and Religious Attitudes of Entrepreneurs in a Village Industry: Notes on the Community of Batur." Trans. M. Nakamura. *Indonesia* 12, 47–55.

Kuyvenhoven, Arie, and Huib Poot. 1989. "Between Inward- and Outward-Looking Development: Industry and Trade in Indonesia." *Indonesian Design of Industrialism: Emerging Norms for Increasing Life Chances in the Nineties*, ed. Selo Soemardjan, Kees Boender, and Pjotr Hesseling, part I,

Collected Papers for the Indonesian-Dutch Symposium at the Roosevelt Study Center, Middelburg, Netherlands, June 1989, 232–57.

LeClair, Edward E., and Harold K. Schneider, eds. 1968. *Economic Anthropology: Readings in Theory and Analysis*. New York: Holt, Rinehart and Winston.

Leiserson, M., et al. 1978. *Employment and Income Distribution in Indonesia*. Washington: World Bank.

Lempelius, Christian, and Gert Thoma. 1979. *Industri Kecil dan Kerajinan Rakyat: Pendekatan Kebutuhan Pokok* [Small Industry and People's Handicrafts: A Basic Needs Approach]. Jakarta: LP3ES.

Liedholm, C., and D. Mead. 1986. "Small-Scale Industries in Developing Countries: Empirical Evidence and Policy Implications." Unpublished MS.

Lluch, C., and D. Mazumdar. 1981. *Wages and Employment in Indonesia*. Washington: World Bank.

Lyon, Margo L. 1970. *Bases of Conflict in Rural Java*. Research Monograph no. 3, University of California, Center for South and Southeast Asia Studies.

Manning, Chris. 1988. "Rural Employment Creation in Java: Lessons from the Green Revolution and Oil Boom." *Population and Development Review* 14, no. 1, 47–80.

Maurer, Jean-Luc. 1984. "Agricultural Modernization and Social Change: The Case of Java over the Last Fifteen Years." *Masyarakat Indonesia* 2, 109–20.

McCawley, Peter. 1981. "The Growth of the Industrial Sector." *The Indonesian Economy during the Soeharto Era*, ed. Anne Booth and Peter McCawley. Kuala Lumpur: Oxford University Press.

———. 1983. "Survey of Recent Developments." *Bulletin of Indonesian Economic Studies* 19, 1–31.

McCawley, Peter, and Maree Tait. 1979. "New Data on Employment in Manufacturing, 1970–76." *Bulletin of Indonesian Economic Studies* 15, no. 1 (March).

Meier, G. M. 1964. *Leading Issues in Development Economics: Selected Materials and Commentary*. New York: Oxford University Press.

Mubyarto. 1978. "Involusi Pertanian dan Pemberantasan Kemiskinan: Kritik terhadap Clifford Geertz" [Agricultural involution and the eradication of poverty: a critique of Clifford Geertz], *Prisma* 7, no. 2, 55–63.

———. 1989. "Pancasila Economic Democracy for Industrialization." *Indonesian Design of Industrialism: Emerging Norms for Increasing Life Chances in the Nineties*, ed. Selo Soemardjan, Kees Boender, and Pjotr Hesseling, part I, *Collected Papers for the Indonesian-Dutch Symposium at the Roosevelt Study Center, Middelburg, Netherlands, June 1989*, 213–30.

Mukhopadhyay, Swapna dan Chee Peng Lim. 1985. *The Rural Non-farm Sector in Asia*. Kuala Lumpur: Asian and Pacific Development Centre.

Myint, H. 1964. *The Economics of the Developing Countries*. London: Hutchinson.

————. 1972. *Southeast Asia's Economy*. Harmondsworth: Penguin.

Nash, Manning. 1959. "Some Social and Cultural Aspects of Economic Development." *Economic Development and Cultural Change* 7 (1959), 137–49.

————. 1961. "The Social Context of Economic Choice in a Small Society." *Man* 219, 186–91 [repr. in *Economic Anthropology: Readings in Theory and Analysis*, ed. Edward E. LeClair and Harold K. Schneider, 311–22 (New York: Holt, Rinehart and Winston, 1968)].

————. 1964. "Southeast Asian Society: Dual or Multiple." *Journal of Asian Studies* 23 (1964), 417–23 [repr. in *Sociology of South-east Asia: Readings on Social Change and Development*, ed. Hans-Dieter Evers (Kuala Lumpur: Oxford University Press, 1980), 76–84, with comments by Benjamin Higgins and Lucian Pye].

Nibbering, J. W., and A. Schrevel. 1982. *The Role of Additional Activities in Rural Java: A Case Study of Two Villages in the Malang Regency*. Utrecht University, Department of Geography.

Nurmanaf, A., Rozany, and Soentoro. 1977. "Respons Masyarakat Desa Terhadap Kegagalan Panen: Kasus Batu Bata di Lanjan" [Reponse of villagers to harvest failure: case study of brickmaking in Lanjan]. Rural Dynamics Study, Agro-Economic Survey, Bogor.

Onghokham. 1975. "The Residency of Madiun: Priyayi and Peasant in the Nineteenth Century." Ph.D. diss., Yale University.

Paauw, Douglas. 1963. "From Colonial to Guided Economy." *Indonesia*, ed. Ruth T. McVey, 155–247. New Haven: HRAF.

Palmier, Leslie H. 1960. *Social Status and Power in Java*. London School of Economics, Monographs on Social Anthropology, no. 20. London: Athlone.

Papanek, Gustav, ed. 1980. *The Indonesian Economy*. New York: Praeger.

Penny, David, and Masri Singarimbun. 1973. "Population and Poverty in Rural Java: Some Economic Arithmetic from Srihardjo." Cornell University, International Development Monograph no. 41.

Poot, Huib. 1980. *Employment and Labour Force in Asia*. Bangkok: Asian Employment Programme, Asian Regional Team for Employment Promotion.

————. 1988. "The Industrial Sector of Indonesia: Performance and Policies." Working Paper, Ministry of Industry, Jakarta, and Netherlands Economic Institute, Rotterdam.

Poot, Huib, Arie Kuyvenhoven, and J. S. Jansen. 1990. *Industrialization and Trade in Indonesia*. Yogyakarta: Gadjah Mada University Press.

Raffles, Stamford. 1965 [1817]. *The History of Java*. Kuala Lumpur: Oxford University Press.

Raharjo, M. Dawam. 1987. "The Development of Small-Scale Industry in Indonesia." Institute of Social Studies, Policy Workshop on Small-Scale Industrialization, The Hague, May 1987.

Ramli, Rizal. 1982. "Industri Indonesia: Antara Tjuan dan Kenyataan" [Indonesian industry: between goals and reality]. *Prisma* 12, 25–37.

Rietveld, Piet. 1985. "Labour Supply for Additional Activities: A Microeconomic Approach." Fakultas Ekonomi, Universitas Kristen Satya Wacana, Salatiga.

———. 1986. "Nonagricultural Activities and Income Distribution in Rural Java." *Bulletin of Indonesian Economic Studies* 22, no. 3.

Rostow, W. W. 1960. *The Stages of Economic Growth*. Cambridge: Cambridge University Press.

Rucker, Robert L. 1985. *A Preliminary View of Indonesia's Employment Problem and Some Options for Solving It*. Jakarta: U.S. Agency for International Development.

Sadli, Moh. 1957. "Some Reflections on Prof. Boeke's Theory of Dualistic Economies." *Ekonomi dan Keuangan Indonesia* 10 (1957), 363–83.

Sajogyo. 1976. "Pertanian, Landasan Tolak Bagi Pembangunan Bangsa Indonesia" [Agriculture, the basis of Indonesian national development], introd. to *Involusi Pertanian* [Indonesian-language edition of *Agricultural Involution*], by Clifford Geertz, xxi–xxxi. Jakarta: Bhratara.

Saleh, Irsan Azhary. 1986. *Industri Kecil: Sebuah Tinjauan dan Perbandingan* [Small industry: a guide and comparison]. Jakarta: LP3ES.

Sandee, H., and Hermine Weijland. 1989. "Rural Cottage Industry in Transition: Roof Tiles Industry in the Regency Boyolali." *Bulletin of Indonesian Economic Studies* 25, no. 2, 79–98.

Sawit, M. Husein. 1977. "Kerajinan Traditional Tali: Arti Penting Bagi Keluarga Berpendapatan Rendah di Pedesaan, Kasus Malausma" [Traditional rope industry: importance for rural low-income families, case of Malausma]. Rural Dynamics Study, Agro-Economic Survey, Bogor.

Schrieke, B. J. O. 1955. *Indonesian Sociological Studies: Selected Writings of B. Schrieke*. The Hague: W. van Hoeve.

———, ed. 1929. *The Effect of Western Influence on Native Civilisations in the Malay Archipelago*. Batavia, Java: G. Kolff.

Schwaner, C. A. L. M. 1853. *Borneo: Beschruving van het Stroomgebied van den Barito*. Amsterdam.

Scott, J. 1976. *The Moral Economy of the Peasant: Rebellion and Subsistence in Southeast Asia*. New Haven: Yale University Press.

Selo Soemardjan. 1962. *Social Changes in Yogyakarta*. Ithaca: Cornell University Press.

———. 1989. "Cibaduyut and Cilegon: Industrialization from Within and Without." *Indonesian Design of Industrialism: Emerging Norms for Increasing Life Chances in the Nineties*, ed. Selo Soemardjan, Kees Boender, and Pjotr Hesseling, part I, collected papers for the Indonesian-Dutch Symposium at the Roosevelt Study Center, Middelburg, Netherlands, June 1989, 22–41.

Selo Soemardjan, Kees Boender, and Pjotr Hesseling, eds. 1989. *Indonesian Design of Industrialism: Emerging Norms for Increasing Life Chances in the Nineties*, part I, collected papers for the Indonesian-Dutch Symposium at the Roosevelt Study Center, Middelburg, Netherlands, June 1989.

Shand, R. T. 1986. *Off-farm Employment in the Development of Rural Asia*. Australian National University, Canberra.

Smail, J. 1965. "Review: Agricultural Involution: The Process of Ecological Change in Indonesia. Clifford Geertz." *Journal of Southeast Asian History* 6, no. 2, 158–61.

Soehoed, A. R. 1967. "Manufacturing in Indonesia." *Bulletin of Indonesian Economic Studies* 8 (October), 65–84.

———. 1988. "Reflections on Industrialization and Industrial Policy in Indonesia." *Bulletin of Indonesian Economic Studies* 24, no. 2, 43–57.

Soentoro. 1984. "Penyerapan Tenaga Kerja Luar Sektor Pertanian di Pedesaan" [The rural absorption of labor outside the agricultural sector]. *Prospek Pembangunan Ekonomi Pedesaan Indonesia* [Prospects for developing Indonesia's rural economy], ed. F. Kasryno, 202–62. Jakarta: Yayasan Obor Indonesia.

Solyom, Garrett. 1973. "Iron Smelting in Borneo: Another Possible Interpretation of Santubong 'Cylinders.'" Unpublished MS.

Solyom, Garrett, and Bronwen Solyom. 1978. *The World of the Javanese Keris*. Honolulu: East-West Center.

Staley, Eugene, and Richard Morse. 1965. *Modern Small Industry for Developing Countries*. New York: McGraw-Hill.

Steinberg, David Joel, ed. 1971. *In Search of Southeast Asia: A Modern History*. Honolulu: University of Hawaii Press.

Stoler, Ann. 1977a. "Rice Harvesting in Kali Loro." *American Ethnologist* 4, 678–98.

———. 1977b. "Class Structure and Female Autonomy in Rural Java." *Signs* 3, 74–89.

Sundrum, R. M. 1975. "Manufacturing Employment, 1961–1971." *Bulletin of Indonesian Economic Studies* 11, no. 1, 58–65.

Sutoro, S. Ann Dunham. 1982. "Women's Work in Village Industries in Java." Unpublished MS.

———. 1988. *Case Studies of KUPEDES Investment Loans*. Bank Rakyat Indonesia, Planning, Research and Development Department, November.

———. 1990. *Briefing Booklet: KUPEDES Development Impact Survey*. Bank Rakyat Indonesia, Planning, Research and Development Department, March.

———. 1991. *MARPOTSU Special Report No. 1: Village Financial Market Profiles*. Bank Rakyat Indonesia, Planning, Research and Development Department, August.

Swasono, Meutia F. 1975. "Beberapa Catatan Singkat Mengenai Entrepreneur di Indonesia" [A few short notes on entrepreneurs in Indonesia]. *Berita Antropologi* 7 (23 September).

Thorburn, Craig. 1982. *Teknologi Kampungan: A Collection of Indigenous Indonesian Technologies*. Stanford: Volunteers in Asia.

Timmer, Peter. 1973. "Choice of Technique in Rice Milling in Java." *Bulletin of Indonesian Economic Studies* 9, 57–76.

UNDP, DGIS, ILO, and UNIDO. 1988. *Development of Rural Small Industrial Enterprises*. Vienna: United Nations Industrial Development Organization.

UNIDO. 1978. *Industrialization and Rural Development*. New York: United Nations.

van der Kolff, G. 1936. "The Historical Development of Labour Relationships in a Remote Corner of Java as They Apply to the Cultivation of Rice." Institute of Pacific Relations, International Research Series, Report C.

van Gelder, P., and J. Bijlmer, eds. 1989. *About Fringes, Margins and Lucky Dips: The Informal Sector in Third World Countries*. Amsterdam: Free University Press.

van Geldern, J. 1929. "Western Enterprise and the Density of the Population in the Netherlands Indies." *The Effect of Western Influence on Native Civilisations in the Malay Archipelago*, ed. B. J. O. Schrieke. Batavia, Java: G. Kolff.

van Heekeren, H. R. 1958. *The Bronze Age of Indonesia*. The Hague: Nijhoff.

van Leur, J. C. 1955. *Indonesian Trade and Society: Essays in Asian Social and Economic History*. The Hague: W. van Hoeve.

van Niel, Robert. 1983. "Nineteenth Century Java: Variations on the Theme of Rural Change." Paper prepared for the South East Asia Summer Study Institute Conference.

Wallerstein, Immanuel. 1980. *The Modern World System II*. New York: Academic.

Weijland, Hermine. 1984. "Rural Industries: Sign of Poverty or Progress?" Collaborative Paper no. 6, Faculty of Economics, Satya Wacana Universitas Kristen, Salatiga.

———. 1989a. "Rural Industrialization: Fact or Fiction." *Indonesian Design of Industrialism: Emerging Norms for Increasing Life Chances in the Nineties*, ed. Selo Soemardjan, Kees Boender, and Pjotr Hesseling, part I, collected papers for the Indonesian-Dutch Symposium at the Roosevelt Study Center, Middelburg, Netherlands, June 1989, 279–300.

———. 1989b. "Rural Industry in Indonesia." Research Memorandum, Faculty of Economics, Free University, Amsterdam.

Wertheim, W. F. 1956. *Indonesian Society in Transition: A Study of Social Change*. The Hague: W. van Hoeve.

———. 1964. "Peasants, Peddlers and Princes in Indonesia: A Review Article." *Pacific Affairs* 37, 307–11.

————. 1973. "Do Not Overrate the Danger of Imperialist Software." *Journal of Contemporary Asia* 3, 471–72.

————. 1980. "Changing South-east Asian Societies: An Overview." *Sociology of South-east Asia: Readings on Social Change and Development*, ed. Hans-Dieter Evers, 8–23. Kuala Lumpur: Oxford University Press [repr. from *International Encyclopedia of the Social Sciences* I (1968), 423–38].

Wertheim, W. F., and T. S. Giap. 1962. "Social Change in Java, 1900–1930." *Social Change: The Colonial Situation*, ed. Immanuel Wallerstein, 363–80. New York: John Wiley and Sons.

Wertheim, W. F., et al., eds. 1961. *Indonesian Economics: The Concept of Dualism in Theory and Policy*. Selected Studies on Indonesia by Dutch Scholars, vol. 6. The Hague: W. van Hoeve.

White, Benjamin. 1973. "Demand for Labour and Population Growth in Colonial Java." *Human Ecology* 1, 217–36.

————. 1976a. *Production and Reproduction in a Javanese Village*. Ph.D. diss., Columbia University.

————. 1976b. "Population, Employment and Involution in a Javanese Village." *Development and Change* 7, 267–90.

————. 1979. "Political Aspects of Poverty, Income Distribution and Their Measurement: Some Examples from Rural Java." *Development and Change* 10, 91–114.

————. 1983. "Agricultural Involution and Its Critics: Twenty Years after Clifford Geertz." Working Paper Series no. 6. The Hague: Institute of Social Studies.

————. 1986. *Rural Non-farm Employment in Java: Recent Developments, Policy Issues and Research Needs*. The Hague: Institute of Social Studies.

————. 1989. "Java's Green Revolution in Long-term Perspective." *Prisma* 48, 66–81.

Wisseman, Jan, 1977. "Market and Trade in Pre-Majapahit Java." *Economic Exchange and Social Interaction in Southeast Asia*, ed. Karl Hutterer, 197–212. University of Michigan, Center for South and Southeast Asian Studies, Michigan Papers on South and Southeast Asia no. 13.

World Bank. 1979. *Indonesia: Cottage and Small Industry in the National Economy*. Washington: World Bank.

————. 1983. *Indonesia: Wages and Employment*. Washington: World Bank.

————. 1990. *Poverty: World Development Report 1990*. Oxford: Oxford University Press.

Yamada, Hideo. 1980. "Boeke's View of Eastern Society." *Sociology of Southeast Asia: Readings on Social Change and Development*, ed. Hans-Dieter Evers, 57–65 (Kuala Lumpur: Oxford University Press, 1980) [repr. from *Developing Economies* (Tokyo) 4, no. 3 (1966), 334–48].

Young, K. 1988. "Transformation or Temporary Respite? Agricultural Growth,

Industrialisation and the Modernisation of Java." *Review of Indonesian and Malayan Affairs* 22, 114–32.

Zerner, Charles. 1981. "Signs of the Spirits, Signature of the Smith: Iron Forging in Tana Toraja." *Indonesia* (Cornell South Asia Program) 31 (April), 88–112.

INDEX

Page numbers in *italics* refer to illustrations.

S. ANN DUNHAM (1942–95), mother of President Barack Obama and Maya Soetoro-Ng, earned her undergraduate, master's, and doctoral degrees, all in anthropology, from the University of Hawai'i at Manoa. Dunham spent years working on rural development, microfinance, and women's welfare through organizations including USAID, the World Bank, the Ford Foundation, the Indonesian Federation of Labor Unions, and Bank Rakyat Indonesia.

ALICE G. DEWEY, an Indonesianist, is Professor Emeritus of Anthropology at the University of Hawai'i.

NANCY I. COOPER is Adjunct Associate Professor of Anthropology at the University of Hawai'i.

MAYA SOETORO-NG, daughter of S. Ann Dunham and sister of President Barack Obama, has a doctorate in international comparative education from the University of Hawai'i.

ROBERT W. HEFNER is Professor of Anthropology and Associate Director of the Institute on Culture, Religion, and World Affairs at Boston University. He is President of the Association for Asian Studies.

Library of Congress Cataloging-in-Publication Data

Dunham, S. Ann (Stanley Ann)
Surviving against the odds : village industry in
Indonesia / S. Ann Dunham.
p. cm.
"A John Hope Franklin Center Book."
Revised version of the author's thesis (doctoral),
University of Hawaii, 1992.
Includes bibliographical references and index.
ISBN 978-0-8223-4687-6 (cloth : alk. paper)
1. Rural industries — Indonesia.
2. Blacksmithing — Indonesia.
3. Metal-work — Indonesia.
4. Indonesia — Rural conditions.
I. Dewey, Alice G. II. Cooper, Nancy I. III. Title.
HC447.D87 2009
338.4'768209598 — dc22   2009032835